Unceasing Fury

Texans at the Battle of Chickamauga

September 18–20, 1863

Scott L. Mingus Sr.
and Joseph L. Owen

SB
Savas Beatie
California

Library of Congress Cataloging-in-Publication Data

Names: Mingus, Scott L., Sr., author. | Owen, Joseph L., author.
Title: Unceasing Fury: Texans at the Battle of Chickamauga, September 18-20, 1863 / by Scott L. Mingus, Sr., and Joseph L. Owen.
Other titles: Texans at the Battle of Chickamauga, September 18-20, 1863
Description: El Dorado Hills, CA : Savas Beatie LLC, [2021] | Includes bibliographical references and index. | Summary: "Thousands of Confederate soldiers from Texas fought at the Civil War battle of Chickamauga in September 1863 in northern Georgia. Many left personal accounts, letters, diaries, and postwar reminiscences that authors Scott Mingus and Joe Owen have woven into the first detailed narrative of the significant role that Lone Star soldiers played in the war's second-bloodiest battle"— Provided by publisher.
Identifiers: LCCN 2021029924 | ISBN 9781611215557 (hardcover) | ISBN 9781611215564 (ebook)
Subjects: LCSH: Chickamauga, Battle of, Ga., 1863. | Texas—History—Civil War, 1861-1865—Regimental histories. | United States—History—Civil War, 1861-1865—Regimental histories. | United States—History—Civil War, 1861-1865—Campaigns. | Confederate States of America. Army. Granbury's Texas Brigade | Confederate States of America. Army. Gregg's Brigade | Confederate States of America. Army. Ector's Brigade | Confederate States of America. Army. Dreshler's Brigade
Classification: LCC E475.81 .M56 2021 | DDC 973.7/35—dc23
LC record available at https://lccn.loc.gov/2021029924

First Edition, First Printing

SB
Savas Beatie
989 Governor Drive, Suite 102
El Dorado Hills, CA 95762
916-941-6896 / sales@savasbeatie.com

Savas Beatie titles are available at special discounts for bulk purchases in the United States. Contact us for more details.

Proudly published, printed, and warehoused in the United States of America.

FSC www.fsc.org MIX Paper from responsible sources FSC® C011935

"When the sable shades of night draped the hills of Chickamauga with a mournful pall of earth-like silence, and the weeping stars lit the firmament over this weird-like, ghostly scene, where the demon ghouls of death were reveling in their gory feast and many a corpse lay ghastly pale in the arms of eternal sleep, the bugle notes of victory recalled from pursuit the shattered cohorts of the Southrons."

— Dr. John O. Scott, former Confederate surgeon,
in a speech before the Old Settlers Picnic at Sherman, Texas,
on Aug. 20, 1896. (Chattanooga Daily Times, Sept. 6, 1896)

Table of Contents

Foreword by David A. Powell
xi

Chapter 1: The Texans
1

Chapter 2: The Long Road to Chickamauga
21

Chapter 3: September 18—The Battle for the Bridges
48

Chapter 4: September 19, Morning—Ector's Brigade
70

Chapter 5: September 19, Early Afternoon—Gregg's Brigade
86

Chapter 6: September 19, Late Afternoon—Hood's Texas Brigade
99

Chapter 7: September 19, Evening—Deshler's Brigade
133

Chapter 8: September 20, Morning—Ector's and Deshler's Brigades
150

Chapter 9: September 20, Midday—Hood's Texans and Gregg's Brigade
174

Chapter 10: September 20, Late Afternoon and Evening
197

Chapter 11: Return to Chattanooga
211

Table of Contents (continued)

Chapter 12: The Gateway to the South Opens
240

Chapter 13: Legacy
253

Appendix A: Overall Casualties at Chickamauga in Texas Commands
259

Appendix B: Individual Texas Casualties at Chickamauga by Regiment
261

Bibliography
287

Acknowledgments
301

Index
305

About the Authors
320

List of Maps

Map 1: Tullahoma Campaign, June–July 1863 29

Map 2: Davis's Crossroads, September 11, 1863 35

Map 3: Chickamauga, September 18, 1863 55

Map 4: Chickamauga, Reed's Bridge, Afternoon, September 18, 1863 59

Map 5: Chickamauga, Ector's Attack, 10 A.M., September 19, 1863 80

Map 6: Chickamauga, Gregg's Attack, 3:45 P.M., September 19, 1863 93

Map 7: Chickamauga, Robertson's Attack, 4:30 P.M., September 19, 1863 109

Map 8: Chickamauga, Cleburne's Attack, 7:30 P.M., September 19, 1863 137

Map 9: Chickamauga, Cleburne's Attack 10–11 A.M., September 20, 1863 160

Map 10: Chickamauga, North Dyer Field, 12:15 P.M., September 20, 1863 183

Map 11: Chickamauga, Snodgrass Hill, 2–6 P.M., September 20, 1863 203

Map 12: Chattanooga, Tunnel Hill, November 25, 1863 223

List of Illustrations

Chapter 1

West Chickamauga Creek 3
Gen. Braxton Bragg, CSA 4
Brig. Gen. James Deshler, CSA 7
Col. Roger Q. Mills, 6th-10th-15th Texas Cavalry 9
Brig. Gen. Matthew D. Ector, CSA 11
Col. Julius A. Andrews, 32nd Texas Cavalry 12
Brig. Gen. John Gregg, CSA 13

List of Illustrations (continued)

Brig. Gen. Jerome B. Robertson, CSA 15
Col. Thomas Harrison, CSA 18
Lt. Col. Gustave Cook, 8th Texas Cavalry 19

Chapter 2

Battle of Murfreesboro 22
17th and 18th Texas Cavalry flag 23
Maj. Gen. Patrick R. Cleburne, CSA 25
Wartrace, TN 26
Cleburne marker, Wartrace, TN 27
Maj. Gen. William S. Rosecrans, USA 28
Sgt. William W. Heartsill, 10th Texas Cavalry 30
Lt. Gen. D. H. Hill, CSA 31
Pvt. Lawrence A. Daffan, 4th Texas 41
Stephen's Gap on Lookout Mountain 47

Chapter 3

Brig. Gen. Bushrod Johnson, CSA 49
Wartime image of Lee and Gordon's Mill 50
Modern image of Lee and Gordon's Mill 51
Crawfish Springs, Chickamauga, GA 52
Maj. Gen. George H. Thomas, USA 53
Maj. Gen. John Bell Hood, CSA 56
Minty's Union cavalry crossing Reed's Bridge 60
"Confederate Artillery," Alfred R. Waud 62
Modern view of the Alexander-Viniard Road 69

Chapter 4

John Ross House 71
Brig. Gen. Nathan B. Forrest, CSA 74
Capt. Judson W. Bishop, 2nd Minnesota 76
Capt. Ryland Todhunter, assistant adjutant general, Ector's brigade 78
Capt. Constantine Buckner "Buck" Kilgore, adjutant, Ector's brigade 79
"CSA Line Advancing," Alfred R. Waud 85

List of Illustrations (continued)

Chapter 5

Brig. Gen. Joseph Wheeler, CSA 87
Maj. Khleber Van Zandt, 7th Texas 89
Col. Hans C. Heg, USA 91
Kurtz and Allison print of a Confederate firing line in the woods at Chickamauga 92
Iron marker commemorating position of Bushrod Johnson's division on Sept. 18 95

Chapter 6

Brig. Gen. Evander M. Law, CSA 100
Postwar image of Quartermaster Sgt. J. B. Polley, 4th Texas 101
Postwar image of Color Sgt. George A. Branard, 1st Texas 103
Postwar image of Sgt. D. H. Hamilton, 1st Texas 105
Pvt. John C. West, 4th Texas 108
Capt. James T. Hunter, 4th Texas 110
Maj. Jefferson C. Rogers, 5th Texas 115
Capt. Tacitus C. Clay, 5th Texas 121
Postwar image of Sgt. Val C. Giles, 4th Texas 122
Maj. Gen. Alexander McCook, USA 125
La Fayette Road at the site of the former Viniard Farm 127

Chapter 7

Col. Franklin C. Wilkes, 17th-18th-24th-25th Texas Cavalry 136
Sgt. Benjamin F. Grady, 25th Texas Cavalry 139
Lt. Gen. James Longstreet, CSA 147

Chapter 8

2nd Lt. Oliver P. Bowser, 15th Texas 151
Maj. Gen. John C. Breckinridge, CSA 155
Mortuary monument where Brig. Gen. James Deshler was killed 169

Chapter 9

Col. Van H. Manning, 3rd Arkansas 175

List of Illustrations (continued)

Sgt. John C. Cox, 5th Texas 179
North Dyer Field looking north toward the knoll 180
"Kneeling Rifleman," Alfred R. Waud 185
Capt. George T. Todd, 1st Texas 187
"Hood Wounded at Chickamauga," *Illustrated London Times*, Dec. 26, 1863 191
Approximate location where General Hood was wounded 192
Pvt. J. K. P. Blackburn, 8th Texas Cavalry (Terry's Texas Rangers) 195
The George Brotherton house was located along the La Fayette Road 196

Chapter 10

Iron marker commemorating the position of
Deshler's brigade on Sept. 20 198

Chapter 11

Capt. George Littlefield, 8th Texas Cavalry (Terry's Texas Rangers) 214
"A dead soldier," Alfred R. Waud 215
Pvt. William Oliphant, 6th Texas 217
Pvt. Sam R. Burroughs, 1st Texas 227
Capt. Charles M. Winkler, 4th Texas 229
Confederate prisoners in Chattanooga awaiting
transportation to northern prisons 233
Lt. Jesse P. Bates, 9th Texas 234
Pvt. Henry W. Berryman, 1st Texas 238

Chapter 12

"The Rebels Firing on Our Supply Train," *Harper's Weekly*, Jan. 9, 1864 241
Chattanooga, circa 1864 243
Cleburne's Repulse of Sherman at Missionary Ridge, Nov. 25, 1863 245
"Rebel wounded coming in as prisoners on the field of battle," Alfred R. Waud 247
Statue of Maj. Gen. Patrick R. Cleburne at Ringgold 248
Gen. Joseph E. Johnston, CSA 250

Chapter 13

State of Texas Monument at Chickamauga 257

List of Abbreviations

CCNMP: Chickamauga and Chattanooga National Military Park
CSR: Compiled Service Records
CV: Confederate Veteran
ETHJ: East Texas Historical Journal
GPO: Government Printing Office, Washington, DC
LOC: Library of Congress
LSU: Louisiana State University
MOLLUS: Military Order of the Loyal Legion of the United States
NPS: National Park Service
NARA: National Archives and Records Administration
OR: Official Records of the War of the Rebellion
RG: Record Group
SHQ: Southwestern Historical Quarterly
SHSP: Southern Historical Society Papers
THM: Texas Heritage Museum, Hill College
TSHA: Texas State Historical Association
UNC: University of North Carolina
USAHEC: United States Army Heritage and Education Center
UTSA: University of Texas-San Antonio

Foreword

The battle of Chickamauga lasted three days, involved nearly 130,000 combatants, thousands more non-combatants, civilians and soldiers alike, and produced roughly 35,000 casualties. In terms of violence and human suffering, it was the second largest battle of the American Civil War, trailing only the bloodletting at Gettysburg. While several other battles saw larger total numbers of men involved, Chickamauga excels in another grim way: virtually all the troops on both sides that met on those blood-soaked fields participated fully in that combat. Both the Union commander, Maj. Gen. William Starke Rosecrans, and the Confederate leader, Gen. Braxton Bragg, threw all their men into this fight. Few reserves were husbanded, and only a handful of regiments were assigned duties that took them away from the contest—it was "do or die" for the men of both sides from September 18 to 20, 1863.

Chickamauga was one of the most important battles of the war. It was also a struggle that both sides would assert as a victory. How can that be?

First, to its importance. As the summer of 1863 closed, the cause of Southern independence was looking increasingly unlikely. Robert E. Lee's retreat from Gettysburg allowed the Federals to claim a decisive victory in Pennsylvania, no matter how close-run a thing the fighting had been. Though tactically Gettysburg might be deemed a draw, Lee's decision to return to Virginia confirmed the Army of Northern Virginia's operational defeat. Simultaneously, the loss of Vicksburg, Mississippi, could not be described as anything other than a wholesale Confederate disaster, with Lt. Gen. John C. Pemberton's entire Rebel army of 30,000 men surrendering to Union Maj. Gen. Ulysses S. Grant.

Rosecrans's Army of the Cumberland, by contrast, drove Bragg's Confederates out of Middle Tennessee via a campaign of brilliant maneuver. Because that campaign did not culminate in a major battle, however, it passed unnoticed nationally, overwhelmed in the newspaper headlines by news of Gettysburg and Vicksburg. Then, in September, Rosecrans launched a new effort aimed at Chattanooga. As if to answer the Union's earlier successes, Bragg, after abandoning Chattanooga to Union forces on September 9, suddenly won a seemingly decisive victory of his own against those invading Federals at Chickamauga.

To all outward appearances, Bragg and his Army of Tennessee delivered a drubbing to the Army of the Cumberland. A third of the Union army was routed off the field in the middle of the last day's fighting. The remaining forces under Maj. Gen. George Thomas held on stubbornly for a time but were finally forced to retreat—albeit in a more organized fashion—just before dark. Several thousand Union prisoners, dozens of Federal cannons, and vast quantities of other equipment fell into Rebel hands. Rosecrans's defeat triggered a crisis response in the Union high command and bolstered Southern morale at a critical moment in the war, after the earlier battering to public opinion of the summer. The euphoric reaction to Bragg's success across the South, though slightly tempered with some dismay at the scope of his losses, seemed to confirm that the Confederacy had considerable life in her yet. The only question remaining to be answered was, could Bragg go on to seize the larger strategic fruits of that victory?

Which begs the second question: How could both sides claim victory? The answer was Chattanooga.

While the Federals had clearly experienced a severe reverse along the banks of West Chickamauga Creek, they suffered what can be termed a tactical defeat. The city of Chattanooga was the operational objective of the campaign, along with the two bridges that carried the Nashville and Chattanooga Railroad over the Tennessee River and a tributary at Running Water Creek. Chattanooga offered the Federal army the only water-level passage through the Appalachian Mountains for hundreds of miles, and hence, the only avenue of advance into the region which by 1863 had become the heart of the Confederate war machine: the growing industrial base of Georgia, Lower Alabama, and the Carolinas. With Chattanooga as their base, Union troops had a secure supply line extending toward Atlanta and the Deep South.

Outflanked to his south, Bragg abandoned Chattanooga on September 8, and the city fell to Rosecrans's men the next day. Even though Bragg's army besieged the town for a time in October and November, it would never return to

Confederate control. By 1864, with its rail connections restored, Chattanooga swelled with new construction, including massive new Union warehouses full of supplies for the next campaign.

Because Chattanooga remained firmly in Federal hands, Army of the Cumberland veterans insisted that though they lost the battle of Chickamauga, they won the Chickamauga campaign, since they took control of that campaign's most important objective. This theme is evident in defiant soldier correspondence starting immediately after the battle and would become only more evident over time, until it dominated Union post-war reminiscences and memoirs.

The fact that Chattanooga was never recaptured also explains the growing Confederate frustration that, within a month of the battle, had soldiers and civilians alike questioning the result of the battle. That frustration boiled over once Ulysses S. Grant arrived to break the Rebel siege in late November, a reversal of fortune that led to Chickamauga being seen as—in Daniel Harvey Hill's words—a "barren victory," bereft of any real result. The post-war Confederate understanding of the battle came to be dominated by a harsh condemnation of the Confederate commander, Braxton Bragg, who supposedly threw away the fruits of the hard-fought victory by not pursuing the beaten Federals and retaking Chattanooga when the chance was there. This sentiment can be seen very strongly in this book, *"Unceasing Fury": Texans at the Battle of Chickamauga, September 18-20, 1863*, in which the soldiers' criticism of Bragg runs deep, especially in the treasure trove of postwar accounts unearthed by Scott Mingus and Joseph Owen. As articulated in these pages, those sources bring the battle vividly to life, and they also shine a clear light on what came to be the agreed-upon wisdom about what went wrong for the Confederates at Chickamauga.

Which brings me to the point of this foreword. Mingus's and Owen's work is a delight to read, rich as it is with personal accounts and the individual details of so many of those Texans. In my own multi-volume study of the battle of Chickamauga, I tried to gather as many sources as possible in order to tell the story of the battle on an individual level while also covering its tactical, operational, and strategic aspects. I collected thousands of accounts, but I knew that I was a long way from finding all of them. In *Unceasing Fury*, I recognize several old friends from my own writing, but Mingus and Owen have also unearthed a host of new primary sources, and have used them very effectively here to describe the battle. What a treat it is to stumble upon fresh accounts.

Prior to the 1990s, there was a paucity of information in print on Chickamauga. Only a couple of tomes had been written on the battle, and a few campaign overviews described Chickamauga in the most perfunctory terms. While those books were excellent for what they covered, they could not match the details and in-depth analysis lavished on other Civil War battles. Even in the 2000s, when I decided to write about Chickamauga, a quick survey of titles revealed almost nothing in print on the battle. With the writing this foreword in 2020, however, I am happy to state that there are in fact multiple titles exploring the subject, including works on specific facets of the battle—detailed tactical monographs on aspects of the engagement that make deep use of primary source material.

And that source material is rich indeed. Chickamauga was an intense experience for the nearly 130,000 men who fought there, and collectively, they left thousands of accounts recounting their individual experiences—far more material, in fact, than can be used in any single volume. Ergo, it is with great pleasure that I welcome focused works like *Unceasing Fury*, which can narrow the lens sufficiently to let more material see the light of day. I have no doubt that every state that sent troops to Chickamauga could produce a similar outpouring of source material, and the study of the battle could benefit from this approach. What follows are dozens of stories from average Texans, caught up in the great battle. In the future I hope to hear from Indianans, Ohioans, Tennesseans, Illinoisans, and more.

It is also fitting that so many of the rank and file are given voice, since for the veterans of Chickamauga, that fight was the quintessential "soldiers' battle," a nasty brawl in the woods, shrouded by smoke and dust; where nothing went according to plan and generals had little influence on the outcome. When Chickamauga and Chattanooga National Military Park was formed in 1890, the committee appointed to oversee its design agreed that, unlike Gettysburg, they wanted no individual statues to generals placed on the field. Instead, regimental monuments would dominate the park, and a detailed narrative of the battle was presented on the iron war department tablets erected for every brigade and battery engaged there. In *Unceasing Fury*, Mingus and Owen have given us a tremendous collection of those voices from the ranks, the soldier's-eye view of the action.

Additionally, one of the strongest aspects of this work is its comprehensive nature. Often in popular Civil War parlance, the term "Texans" has come to refer primarily to the famous Texas Brigade of the Army of Northern Virginia, long associated with John Bell Hood and James Longstreet's First Corps. Certainly those Texans have earned undying fame for their role on many battlefields, and I do not begrudge them their time in the sun here. But Mingus and Owen have also delved deeply into all the other Texans who fought at Chickamauga; the 7th Texas in Gregg's Brigade, the 9th Texas and 10th, 14th and 32nd dismounted cavalry in Ector's brigade, as well as the 6th & 10th Texas and 15th, 17th, 18th, 24th & 25th Texas dismounted cavalry in Deshler's brigade. Rounding out the list are the 8th and 11th Texas cavalry and Douglas's Texas battery. In all, there were another fourteen regiments and one battery of Texas troops whose service was at times overshadowed by the soaring fame of those Eastern Theater Texans. Here, the research into their legacy matches that invested in Hood's more famous command.

As you read the words of these Texans at Chickamauga, bear in mind that they present what is indeed a soldier's-eye view of the battle, often colored by decades of hindsight. Not every nuance of their recollections will be technically correct. Time has a way of blurring men's memories, and as I read through the manuscript, I recognized details in their versions of their experiences that were not particularly accurate. Perhaps time and memory blended their recollections with those of friends, or facts were gleaned from their own readings on the great battle. For instance, I was struck by Capt. George Todd's recollection of seeing so many of the senior generals of the army of Tennessee assembled in one place on the morning of September 21: "Bragg, Longstreet, Breckenridge, Buckner, Forrest and Wheeler were all there present with us."

In reality, we know from other sources that a single gathering of all these men at the same place and time on that specific day was very unlikely. Though there were individual meetings—well-documented accounts of Bragg and Longstreet conversing on September 21 somewhere near the Dyer Farm, and of Bragg and Breckinridge reconciling in a triumphal ride up the La Fayette Road near the Kelly cabin, to name two such events—Bragg never held a full-scale commander's call or council of war to discuss options on September 21. Further, Todd's failure to note the presence of other senior commanders who would very likely have been present at such a meeting is also noteworthy—Polk, Hill, and Walker, to name three. Was Todd mistaken, or was his account correct? I don't know, but I still like the story he tells, and I think it very likely that he saw combinations of these officers (and others) during the days following the battle. Of course, Todd published his account of the 1st Texas Infantry about 1909, and by then time likely distilled such memories into a single event.

The truth is that any narrative based on recollections will inevitably run up against such discrepancies, and the best thing any author can do is let the men who penned them speak for themselves. Mingus and Owen have done a superb job in allowing just that. The material is rich, vivid, and simultaneously tinged with humor and horror—the way any narrative of such a bloody, awful, and awe-inspiring event should be.

My hope is that each book published on Chickamauga helps to inspire the next author or researcher to bring more such projects to fruition, revealing as they do new facets about this amazingly complex event. Above all, I hope this work inspires more people to visit Chickamauga and Chattanooga National Military Park, where they can follow in the footsteps of the men who so movingly described their unforgettable experiences at that place and time. Chickamauga was our very first national military park, created to preserve the unique landscape of the battle so that future generations could both study and remember the struggle that raged there.

David A. Powell

Chapter 1

The Texans

Some Confederates who fought at Chickamauga, Georgia, in mid-September 1863 lived before the war on the sparse, windswept plains north of Austin or the oft-sweltering areas around Houston. Before joining the military, they lived in strange-sounding places such as Nacogdoches, Sulphur Springs, Quitman, Flo, and Ferris. Several came from San Antonio, home of the famed Alamo mission. More than a few men traced their ancestry to rebellious Tejanos and Texans who fought Santa Anna and his Mexicans to gain independence. Some were bold, loud-talking adventurers, skilled with knife and gun; others were weather-grizzled farmers and cowpunchers or humble store clerks unused to violence. Some men made their living quietly fishing along the Gulf Coast while their comrades-in-arms came from the region along the Rio Grande or the vast bluebell-bedecked prairies. Some had Hispanic surnames; the rest were a mix of European ethnicities, most notably English, Scots-Irish, and German.

Now, they engaged in a bitter struggle for their independence and rights, a foundational fight to protect their homeland and way of life. Many in the ranks called themselves patriots and proud sons of Texas; hundreds wore a symbolic metal "lone star" on their weathered hats. To most Northerners, these men were wayward rebels who needed to return to the Union. To ardent abolitionists, they were traitorous pawns of an elite plantation class intent on preserving their slave-based economy, no matter the cost. Anxious family members considered these Southern soldiers loved ones far away from home with no return in sight and their destiny unknown.

They were Confederates. They were Texans.

Few soldiers in the Confederate Army of Tennessee were born in Texas, which had been a state for less than 18 years. Most had migrated there before the Civil War from other Southern states in the now-fractured Union. By 1860, the Lone Star State boasted a population of 604,000; almost a third of them were enslaved black individuals. A statewide referendum on secession in February 1861 resulted in a fourth of the voters saying no to leaving the United States. Governor Sam Houston, who was so instrumental in defeating Santa Anna and securing Texan independence in 1836, lost his office after refusing to swear allegiance to the new Confederate government. Lieutenant Governor Edward Clark replaced the legendary Houston, whose eldest son and namesake later joined the Confederate army. The sharp division in loyalties across Texas had severe consequences. Hundreds of pro-Union residents fled the state; some died in their efforts to escape. Tens of thousands of pro-secession men and boys of military age flocked to recruiting offices to enlist in the Confederate army.[1]

By the summer of 1863, just two years after secession, the lack of consistent Confederate military success had cooled the early ardor and optimism. Diseases had killed or debilitated thousands of Texas soldiers; thousands more lay in unmarked battlefield graves. In July, news of the Union victory at Gettysburg, Pennsylvania, and of the surrender of the besieged Confederate army at Vicksburg, Mississippi, tempered hopes for independence. The oft-fluctuating morale on the home front declined. Drought threatened the corn crop upon which many wives relied for sustenance and income while their husbands were off soldiering. That summer's scant rainfall affected the once-luxurious pastures where cattle grazed, impacting ranchers and beef contractors for the Confederate Army. The persistent Union naval blockade created shortages of many imported goods and negatively affected shipments of cotton, a vital cash crop.

Governor Francis R. Lubbock emphasized the "absolute necessity" of allocating additional funds to support servicemen's families. The legislature gave

1 For a good general study, see Kenneth W. Howell, ed., *The Seventh Star of the Confederacy: Texas During the Civil War* (Denton, TX: 2009). Francis R. Lubbock narrowly defeated Clark in the gubernatorial election of 1861.

West Chickamauga Creek from the modern Reed's Bridge. (*Scott Mingus*)

$600,000 for relief, but that amount proved insufficient. Many wives sent letters to their soldier husbands complaining of difficult circumstances. Those dire messages dampened morale within the Army of Tennessee as it slowly retreated from Murfreesboro, Tennessee, through Chattanooga, and into north Georgia. Few Texans realized that the army commander, Gen. Braxton Bragg, had recently decided to reverse course and was now going after the Yankees.[2]

2 Howell, *The Seventh Star*, 136, 251, 289.

Confederate Gen. Braxton Bragg commanded the Army of Tennessee. (*Library of Congress*)

Thousands of soldiers from Texas headed toward West Chickamauga Creek, a sluggish, steep-banked watercourse just south of the Georgia-Tennessee border. "The impression is of almost unbroken forest," one Confederate chronicled, "of a rather flat, thinly peopled, poorly tilled, wooded region . . . here and there a field of Indian corn, then just ripe, and occasionally an opening of glade-like, treeless land not under any crop, and straggling along on the [Chattanooga–La Fayette] highway, at intervals of a mile or half a mile, small farmhouses with their stables and corncribs." Chickamauga would be a difficult place to maneuver tens of thousands of soldiers with accompanying artillery and ponderous supply wagons into position for a pitched battle.[3]

3 Archer Anderson, *The Campaign and Battle of Chickamauga* (Richmond, VA: 1881), 22. Some period accounts use the spelling "LaFayette" or "Lafayette." West Chickamauga Creek empties into South Chickamauga Creek, which in turn is a tributary of the Tennessee River.

Mystery shrouded the distant origins of the evocative name "Chickamauga." Some wartime observers claimed it to be a hard-to-pronounce Cherokee word meaning "River of Death," or perhaps "Bloody River." After the war, others said, no, Chickamauga meant the "dwelling place of the chiefs" in a Creek dialect. Several modern scholars and linguists disagree and cite other possible Native American etymology. In any case, the rolling woods and hardscrabble farms near West Chickamauga Creek soon would become a dwelling place of the dead, including scores of Texans.[4]

Texas Troops at Chickamauga

The Army of Tennessee, under the overall command of 46-year-old Braxton Bragg, consisted of four corps as the battle of Chickamauga opened on September 18, 1863. Lieutenant Generals Leonidas Polk and Daniel Harvey Hill and Maj. Gens. Simon B. Buckner and William H. T. Walker led the respective corps, each of which contained at least two divisions. In turn, the divisions had two or three brigades of individual state or national Confederate regiments. Artillery battalions and batteries rounded out the organizational structure, with two small corps of mounted soldiers under Brig. Gens. Nathan Bedford Forrest and Joseph Wheeler. As the battle progressed, Maj. Gen. John Bell Hood took command of the portions of Lt. Gen. James Longstreet's corps (transferred from the Army of Northern Virginia) and other troops that trickled in via rail to reinforce Bragg.

On paper, Braxton Bragg's army at Chickamauga included seven regiments of Texas-designated infantry, 10 of cavalry, and a single Texas battery. Several commands consisted of returning prisoners from more than a dozen different regiments who were rejoining the ranks after their paroles. Bragg scattered the Texas cavalry units among various brigades in the Army of Tennessee's organizational structure. All except the 8th and 11th Texas Cavalry had permanently dismounted, campaigning as standard rifle-wielding infantry. The collection of Texas soldiers had diverse backgrounds, experience levels, and

4 "From the Battle Field," *Georgia Journal and Messenger* (Macon, GA), Sept. 30, 1863; "Chickamauga, or River of Death," *Richmond Daily Dispatch*, Oct. 2, 1863; Randy Golden and Col. Samuel Taylor, "Chickamauga—An Introduction," *Our Georgia History*, accessed Nov. 1, 2019, www.ourgeorgiahistory.com/wars/Civil_War/Chickamauga/chickamauga_01.html. West Chickamauga Creek forms the southeast border of the Chickamauga section of the modern Chickamauga and Chattanooga National Military Park.

leadership qualities. All would see their fair share of action in the late summer and early autumn of 1863.[5]

Churchill's/Deshler's Brigade

Brigadier General James Deshler's brigade served in Irish-born Maj. Gen. Patrick R. Cleburne's division of Lt. Gen. D. H. Hill's corps. The 6th and 10th Texas Infantry had been consolidated into a single new regiment along with the dismounted 15th Texas Cavalry for a combined 700 men under Col. Roger Q. Mills. The consolidated 17th-18th-24th-25th Texas Cavalry, Dismounted (767 men initially under Col. Clayton C. Gillespie but serving under Col. Franklin C. Wilkes by the time of Chickamauga) and the combined 19th-24th Arkansas under Lt. Col. Augustus S. Hutchison rounded out the new brigade. In total, Deshler had 1,783 men in his ranks at Chickamauga. Recently paroled prisoners of war from Fort Hindman in Arkansas made up these consolidated regiments. They had surrendered en masse at Arkansas Post on January 11, 1863, after a three-day battle when an overwhelming Union force under Maj. Gen. William Tecumseh Sherman surrounded the fort. More than 30 percent of the Texas prisoners had perished of illness in the cold Northern winter. After their release in April and return to duty, the parolees returned to duty in late May 1863 in a brigade under Brig. Gen. Thomas J. Churchill. Many of the combat-tested veterans in Bragg's army openly resented the new additions and branded them as cowards because they had surrendered.[6]

Thirty-year-old Brig. Gen. James Deshler commanded the brigade at the opening of the battle of Chickamauga. Confederate artilleryman E. Porter Alexander, Deshler's classmate in West Point's class of 1854, described him as "a

5 Office of the Quartermaster General, *The Battle of Chickamauga, September 19–20, 1863: Organization of the Army of the Cumberland and of the Army of Tennessee* (Washington, DC: 1932), 20, 22, 28, 29, 31.

6 O. P. Bowser, "Notes on Granbury's Brigade," in *A Comprehensive History of Texas 1685 to 1897*, 2 vols. (Dallas, TX: 1898), 2:741. For a history of this brigade throughout the war, see Danny Sessums, *A Force to be Reckoned With: A History of Granbury's Texas Infantry Brigade 1861–1865*, 2 vols. (Cactus Rose Press: 2017 and 2019). Strength numbers and details are from David A. Powell, *The Chickamauga Campaign: Barren Victory: The Retreat into Chattanooga, the Confederate Pursuit, and the Aftermath of the Battle, September 21 to October 20, 1863* (El Dorado Hills, CA: 2016), 274. Being scorned for surrendering was not unique to Churchill's brigade. For example, other regiments branded Col. George Willard's New York brigade as the "Harpers Ferry Cowards" after its surrender to Stonewall Jackson in September 1862.

Brig. Gen. James Deshler commanded a brigade in the Army of Tennessee. (*Library of Congress*)

rather small but very well built, active, energetic, & fine looking fellow with very attractive manners & qualities." After graduation, Deshler served in Kansas, Nebraska, and Colorado, as well as in the Utah War. Like many other Southerners, he resigned from the U.S. Army after the bombardment of Fort Sumter and joined the Confederate service. A bullet penetrated the 30-year-old Alabamian's thighs during the December 1861 battle of Allegheny Mountain in northwestern Virginia. After recovering, Deshler rose to brigade command as a colonel before Fort Hindman's garrison surrendered at Arkansas Post. He was the last brigade officer to lay down his arms, preferring to fight to the death until General Churchill ordered him to surrender. General Sherman approached the crestfallen Deshler. "Wishing to soften the blow of defeat," the bewhiskered Buckeye recalled, "I spoke to him kindly, saying that I knew a family of Deshlers in Columbus, Ohio, and inquired if they were relations of his. He disclaimed any relation with people living north of the Ohio, in an offensive tone." Exchanged and then promoted to brigadier general in late July, Deshler replaced Churchill in command of the so-called "Arkansas Post Brigade" a month before Chickamauga.[7]

The 6th Texas had mustered into service in mid-November 1861 at Camp Henry C. McCullough near Victoria, some 30 miles inland from the Gulf Coast. Several German immigrants dotted the ranks, along with a few men from France, Norway, Scotland, and other European countries. These volunteers included Pvt.

7 John H. Eicher and David J. Eicher, *Civil War High Commands* (Stanford, CA: 2001), 594; Gary W. Gallagher, ed., *Fighting for the Confederacy: The Personal Recollections of General Edward Porter Alexander* (Chapel Hill, NC: 1989), 298. Though Deshler retorted that he did not know any Northern Deshlers, his father was a native of Lehigh County in eastern Pennsylvania, and he still had relatives in the Allentown area. On July 9, T. J. Churchill requested a transfer back to the Trans-Mississippi Department, where he was serving at the time of the surrender of Arkansas Post. In 1881, Churchill became the 13th governor of Arkansas.

James Ramsay. Born in Perth, Scotland, the staunch Presbyterian had emigrated to Charleston, South Carolina, in the 1830s. He moved to Gonzalez, Texas, in 1840 and fought against native Indians at Salado, Plum Creek, and other engagements. Ramsay enjoyed a reputation as a "brave and fearless old soldier." The original 58 men of Company D, the "Matagorda Coast Guards," had signed up to patrol the waters of Matagorda Bay, hence their unusual nickname. The ladies of the small South Texas town hand-sewed the volunteers' first Confederate uniforms.[8]

After serving in the Western and Trans-Mississippi theaters, the 6th Texas surrendered at Arkansas Post in January 1863 and was paroled that April. The regiment briefly served in the Richmond, Virginia, area before being shipped back to the Western Theater and consolidated with the 10th Texas Infantry and 15th Texas Cavalry.

The 10th Texas had formed in the winter of 1861-62 with recruits from Freestone, Grimes, Houston, San Augustine, Tyler, and Washington Counties. The infantrymen spent most of the latter part of 1862 at Arkansas Post before surrendering. Kentucky-born Col. Roger Q. Mills commanded the 10th Texas. Mills, a Democratic attorney from Corsicana, served in the Texas House of Representatives in 1859-60 before enlisting as a private in the Confederate Army.

The 15th Texas Cavalry had been organized in McKinney in the summer of 1862 with recruits from Fort Worth and several counties throughout the area. Because of a shortage of fodder for its horses, the regiment dismounted later in the year. It then transferred to Arkansas Post, surrendered, and received paroles in May 1863.[9]

Clayton C. Gillespie's consolidated regiment had a similar story. The 17th Texas Cavalry's companies primarily came from Cherokee, Nacogdoches, Red River, and Smith Counties. They had mustered into Confederate service in the spring of 1862 and then dismounted in July. After participating in the Corinth campaign in October, the regiment served in various departments before being assigned to Arkansas Post. The 18th Texas Cavalry had formed in the spring of 1862 with recruits from the vicinities of Dallas, Denton, and Belton. They soon dismounted and transferred to Arkansas, where they served in Deshler's original

8 *The Galveston News*, Jun. 15, 1861, and Aug. 16, 1893.

9 C. Alwyn Barr, "The Making of a Secessionist: The Antebellum Career of Roger Q. Mills," *The Southwestern History Quarterly*, no. 79, Oct. 1975, 129-144 (*SHQ*); Joseph M. Lance, III, *Patrick R. Cleburne and the Tactical Employment of His Division at the Battle of Chickamauga* (Auckland, New Zealand: 2015), 43.

Col. Roger Q. Mills commanded a consolidated regiment in Deshler's brigade. (*Library of Congress*)

brigade before surrendering to Sherman. The 24th and 25th Regiments, formed in April 1862 in Hempstead in southwestern Texas, were also known as the 2nd and 3rd Texas Lancers. Both dismounted regiments surrendered at Arkansas Post. Gillespie, an antebellum Methodist minister, had led the 25th Texas Cavalry since its inception. His counterpart in the 24th Texas, Colonel Wilkes, was also a Methodist preacher, and had once supervised the Waco Female College. Several members of the 24th, including recruiting officer Lt. Frederick W. "Fritz" Neuhaus, were natives of Germany. Neuhaus had graduated from a college along the Rhine River before emigrating in 1852 to Lavaca County, where he was a Texas Ranger and successful cattle rancher.[10]

Captain James P. Douglas's Texas battery supported Deshler's brigade at Chickamauga. The command traced its origins to June 1861, when recruits from Dallas County and Smith County each formed a half battery of some 50 men apiece to be attached to the 3rd Texas Cavalry. Known variously as the 1st Texas Battery, the Dallas Light Artillery, and the Good-Douglas Battery, the reorganized command took the name Douglas's Battery in July 1862 after the men elected Lt. James P. Douglas captain. The 27-year-old Tyler newspaperman, a South Carolina native, had raised the original Smith County contingent. His soldiers considered him to be an experienced, levelheaded officer. Although the command originally carried six field pieces, it had only two 6-pounder smoothbores and two

10 John C. Rigdon, *Historical Sketch and Rosters of the Texas 18th Cavalry Regiment* (Cartersville, GA: 2018), 1-10; Lance, *Patrick R. Cleburne*, 43-44; *Hallettsville* (TX) *Herald*, Oct. 17, 1907; "Wilkes, Franklin Collett," *Handbook of Texas*, Texas State Historical Association, accessed Nov. 3, 2019, www.tshaonline.org/handbook/online/articles/fwi13.

12-pounder howitzers after its reorganization. Captain Douglas nicknamed one of the guns "Sallie" in honor of his girlfriend, Sallie White, back home in Tyler.[11]

Ector's Brigade

Ector's brigade of Walker's Reserve Corps included the 9th Texas and 10th, 14th, and 32nd Texas Cavalry, all dismounted. The non-Texas units in 41-year-old Brig. Gen. Matthew D. Ector's 1,200-man brigade were the 29th North Carolina, Maj. Thomas O. Stone's so-called sharpshooter battalion from Alabama, and Capt. Merriman Pound's Mississippi sharpshooter battalion. Years later one of the Alabama officers recalled, "When we first joined the brigade the Texans made all manner of sport of us—called us 'yallow hammers,' and 'mud turtles,' etc., and never let an opportunity pass to tease and worry us—frequently asking if 'our mothers knew we were out.'" By the fall of 1863, the relationship was changing. "We had been with Ector's brigade for nearly seven months," Capt. Samuel H. Sprott said, "and with all their wild reckless ways had become very much attached to both officers and men—especially Gen. Ector and his staff."[12]

Born in Georgia and educated in Kentucky, Matthew Duncan Ector served the Georgia legislature for a single term before turning to farming. After his wife died in 1848, he traveled to California, but returned to Georgia to settle affairs. He moved to Texas in 1850, practiced law, and edited a newspaper in Henderson. In 1855, his neighbors elected him to the state house of representatives. His second wife died in 1859. When the war erupted, he enlisted in the 3rd Texas Cavalry and later became colonel of the 14th Texas Cavalry. He was promoted to brigadier general in mid-August 1862 and handled his brigade well at the battle of Murfreesboro (known to the Federals as Stones River after the battlefield's most prominent terrain feature) at the end of the year. "General Ector's wife is dead and, like most old widowers he is foolishly fond of women," one of his staff officers,

11 Lewis Newton Fitzhugh, ed., *Cannon Smoke: The Letters of Captain John J. Good, Good-Douglas Texas Battery, CSA* (Hillsboro, TX: 1971); Andrew F. Lang, "Lone Star Pride: The Good-Douglas Texas Battery, CSA, 1861–1865," *East Texas Historical Journal*, vol. 45, issue 2, article 8, Oct. 2007, 26-32.

12 Billy Kurtz West, Jr., *Ector's Brigade in the Civil War* (Lubbock, TX: 1987); W. C. Dodson, "Errors Concerning Ector's Brigade," *Confederate Veteran*, vol. 13, no. 10, Oct. 1905, 457 (*CV*); Samuel H. Sprott, *Our Southern Home*, June 8, 1899. Companies A, D, and I of the 40th Alabama made up Stone's battalion. Like Pound's battalion, the parent regiments were taken captive when Lt. Gen. John C. Pemberton's army surrendered at Vicksburg. They were not trained or equipped as sharpshooters, although they took the name.

Brig. Gen. Matthew D. Ector commanded a brigade in the Army of Tennessee. (*The State Preservation Board, Austin, Texas*)

Capt. William H. Smith, complained upon being invited to a large party a few weeks after Murfreesboro. "He drags me out, very much against my will, to a serenade every few nights." The forced entertainment notwithstanding, Ector remained popular with his men.[13]

Many veterans in Ector's 9th Texas had fought at Shiloh, Perryville, and Murfreesboro. In mid-1863, the regiment, under 25-year-old Col. William Hugh Young, participated in Gen. Joseph E. Johnston's unsuccessful attempt to relieve the beleaguered Confederate garrison at Vicksburg. Young was born in Missouri in 1838. Three years later, his family moved to Texas, where his father became a judge in Grayson County and a general in the state militia. William graduated from the University of Virginia in June 1861, returned home, and volunteered as an aide-de-camp to Governor Clark. After serving as a captain in the 9th Texas, he received an appointment as a colonel in April 1862. One admirer characterized him as "a very gallant and efficient officer."[14]

Ector's three dismounted cavalry regiments had experienced considerable combat over the past year. The 10th Texas Cavalry was organized in the late summer of 1861 with 900 volunteers from Quitman, Tyler, and several counties in East Texas. In April 1862, the regiment dismounted and served in the Army of the West and then the Department of East Tennessee. After the battle of Richmond,

13 Ezra J. Warner, *Generals in Gray: Lives of the Confederate Commanders* (Baton Rouge, LA: 1959), 133; David V. Stroud, "Odessa History," accessed Feb. 2, 2020, www.odessahistory.com/ectora1.htm; W. H. Smith to My Dear Cousin, Jan. 26, 1863, Shelbyville, TN, "Civil War Letters of William Harlan Smith," *East Texas Family Records*, vol. 6, no. 1 (Spring 1982), 4. After transferring from Ector's staff back to the 7th Texas in Gregg's brigade, Captain Smith was killed at the battle of Raymond in May 1863.

14 Warner, *Generals in Gray*, 80-81; "Ector's Brigade in the Chickamauga Campaign," *The Standard* (Clarksville, TX), Nov. 7, 1863.

Col. Julius A. Andrews commanded the 32nd Texas Cavalry, Dismounted. (*DeGolyer Library, Southern Methodist University, Lawrence T. Jones III, Texas Photographs*)

Kentucky, in August 1862, the 10th Texas joined Ector's brigade. Lingering effects of a wound suffered at Murfreesboro forced Col. Matthew F. Locke, commanding the regiment, to resign in March 1863. Lieutenant Colonel Cullen Redwine Earp, an Alabama native and Mexican War veteran, therefore led the regiment at Chickamauga. Before the Civil War, Earp had farmed a 600-acre estate in Upshur County in East Texas.[15]

The 14th Texas Cavalry dated from the fall of 1861, when wealthy Tarrant County planter Middleton T. Johnson organized a regiment of volunteers from the eastern and northern parts of the state. It first served in Arkansas, losing more than 100 men to illnesses before first experiencing combat. The 14th dismounted in March 1862 at Little Rock and then served as infantry in Mississippi. In May of that year, the unit reorganized with John L. Camp of Gilmer, Texas, as its colonel. Camp, a prosperous cotton planter, was also one of the most successful lawyers in East Texas.[16]

The 32nd Texas Cavalry had organized in May 1862 at Corinth, Mississippi, with former members of Maj. Richard P. Crump's early-war cavalry battalion. Many fresh recruits filled out the new regiment. Twenty-four-year-old Julius A. Andrews, a Georgia native who had resettled in Jefferson, Texas, became colonel. One of his men called Andrews "a gallant and chivalric officer," and many regarded

15 Matthew K. Hamilton, "Tenth Texas Cavalry," *Handbook of Texas*, accessed Nov. 24, 2019, www.tshaonline.org/handbook/online/articles/qkt13. For more on Earp and the rediscovery of his long-forgotten grave site, see the *Longview* (TX) *News-Journal*, Apr. 24, 2008.

16 Tim Bell, "Fourteenth Texas Cavalry," *Handbook of Texas*, accessed Nov. 24, 2019, www.tshaonline.org/handbook/online/articles/qkf14: Thomas W. Cutrer, "Camp, John La Fayette," *Handbook of Texas*, accessed Nov. 24, 2019, www.tshaonline.org/ handbook/ online/articles/fca29.

Brig. Gen. John Gregg commanded a brigade in the Army of Tennessee at Chickamauga. (*Library of Congress*)

him as a "thorough tactician" despite the fact that he was one of the youngest full colonels in the Confederate Army. Several of his soldiers were veterans of the late-1861 fighting at Chustenahlah in the Indian Territory (modern-day Oklahoma) and at Pea Ridge, Arkansas, in March 1862. He efficiently led the 32nd in the fights at Murfreesboro and Jackson.[17]

Gregg's Brigade

At Chickamauga, the 7th Texas was one of the regiments in Gregg's brigade, as were the 3rd, 10th, 30th, 41st, and 50th Tennessee Infantry; the 1st Tennessee Battalion; and Bledsoe's 1st Missouri Battery. After a long, tiring train ride from east-central Mississippi, the soldiers arrived in northern Georgia the day before the battle. Their commander, Brig. Gen. John Gregg, had been a mathematics professor and lawyer in Alabama before moving to Fairfield in Freestone County, Texas, in 1852. He was a district judge and newspaper editor before serving as a delegate to the state's secession convention in Austin in January 1861. A month later, he represented his district in the Provisional Confederate Congress. He returned to Fairfield and organized the 7th Texas, serving as its first colonel. After surrendering at Fort Donelson in February 1862, he spent six months incarcerated in gloomy, dank Fort Warren in Boston Harbor. After being exchanged, he received a promotion to brigadier general and command of a 3,000-man brigade in the Army of Mississippi. One of his soldiers deemed him a "magnificent soldier and a splendid man, whom we all loved dearly." Another characterized him as "a

17 Tim Bell, "Thirty-Second Texas Cavalry," *Handbook of Texas*, accessed Nov. 24, 2019, www.tshaonline.org/handbook/online/articles/qkt32; "Ector's Brigade," *The Standard*.

grand scholar, able lawyer, brave and skillful soldier, and a simple-mannered gentleman."[18]

After the fall of Fort Donelson, the Federals sent most of the men of the 7th Texas to prison camps in the North until their exchange in September, and Colonel Hiram Bronson Granbury took command of the 7th Texas after Gregg's promotion to brigadier general. Born in Mississippi in 1831 to a Baptist preacher and his wife, Granbury moved to Waco, Texas, in the early 1850s. After studying law at Baylor, he became an attorney and district judge in McLennan County. He married an Alabama woman and settled in Fairfield, where he was a judge and newspaper editor. He organized an infantry company at the start of the war and later became major of the 7th Texas. Granbury surrendered at Fort Donelson and was exchanged in October. In March 1863, his 25-year-old wife, Fannie, died at age 25 in Mobile, Alabama, of ovarian cancer. Granbury, unable to afford a headstone, buried her in an unmarked grave in Magnolia Cemetery.[19]

Military officials had reconstituted Granbury's 7th Texas with scores of fresh recruits in early 1863. The Texans, as part of Maj. Gen. William H. T. Walker's division of the Army of Mississippi, then fought well at Raymond and Jackson, Mississippi, in May. But at Raymond, Granbury lost half of his 300 men, including his lieutenant colonel and several experienced officers. To refill the depleted ranks, Confederate officials added more recruits, as well as returning convalescents, to the regiment.

Robertson's Brigade

The 1st, 4th, and 5th Texas and 3rd Arkansas Infantry, detached to Tennessee from Gen. Robert E. Lee's Army of Northern Virginia in early September 1863, made up Brig. Gen. Jerome B. Robertson's famed 1,300-man Texas Brigade. Sergeant David H. Hamilton of the 1st Texas bragged that the brigade was "a great fighting machine, always ready and willing to fight, from the day it was organized until the day when the ragged half-starved remnant of a few hundred men surrendered at Appomattox." Many observers agreed; Hood's Texans (named for the previous commander, John Bell Hood) had deservingly gained widespread renown. Most of the men were veterans of Gettysburg, the Civil War's bloodiest

18 Eicher and Eicher, *Civil War High Commands*, 267; John Berrien Lindsley, *The Military Annals of Tennessee. Confederate. First Series.* (Nashville, TN: 1886), 285; S. A. Jonas, "As to Gen. Gregg," *National Tribune*, Jun. 30, 1892.

19 Warner, *Generals in Gray*, 114, 118-119.

Brig. Gen. Jerome B. Robertson commanded a brigade of Texans and Arkansans temporarily transferred from the Army of Northern Virginia to the Army of Tennessee.
(*Texas Baptist Museum, Independence, Texas*)

battle. The bulk of the brigade arrived in northern Georgia via rail from Virginia the day before the battle of Chickamauga began.[20]

Jerome Bonaparte Robertson had volunteered for military service during the Texas Revolution in 1836, but arrived in the Lone Star State too late to see combat. He briefly returned home to Woodford County, Kentucky, where he married. He and his in-laws settled in Texas in 1837, where he gained a reputation as an adept physician and occasional Indian fighter. A long-time politician, he served in the state legislature and at the 1861 secession convention. When war erupted, he raised a company in what became the 5th Texas. He progressed through the ranks, culminating in November 1862 with a promotion to brigadier general in charge of the Texas Brigade. The 48-year-old replaced the popular John Bell Hood when Hood ascended to divisional command. Robertson's men affectionately nicknamed him "Aunt Polly" for his concern for their welfare.[21]

The 1st Texas (popularly known as the "Ragged Old First") contained companies from 12 different counties. It had suffered staggering losses at Sharpsburg (Antietam) and Gettysburg, but it was still a capable, veteran fighting force. Shortly before Chickamauga, its commander, Lt. Col. Philip A. Work, departed because of illness, and Capt. Richard J. Harding replaced him. Harding, a Richmond native, had attended the Virginia Military Institute for three years. While still a cadet, he witnessed the hanging of abolitionist John Brown, who had led the failed raid at Harpers Ferry in October 1859. Chickamauga was Harding's first battle in command of a regiment.[22]

The 4th Texas also marched to Chickamauga under a new leader, Lt. Col. John P. Bane. Like Harding, the 27-year-old Bane was a Virginian by birth. He had moved to Texas in 1860, and when the war began, he formed a company of volunteers as its captain. Rising to the rank of major, he took temporary command of the 4th Texas after Col. John C. G. Key and Lt. Col. Benjamin F. Carter suffered wounds at Gettysburg. Colonel Key briefly returned to duty after a short recovery

20 D. H. Hamilton and W. H. Morrison, eds., *History of Company M, First Texas Volunteer Infantry, Hood's Brigade* (Waco, TX: 1962), 31. For primary accounts of Hood's men at Gettysburg, see Joseph L. Owen and Randy S. Drais, *Texans at Gettysburg: Blood and Glory with Hood's Texas Brigade* (Stroud, UK: 2016).

21 "Robertson, Jerome Bonaparte," *Handbook of Texas*, accessed Nov. 1, 2019, www.tshaonline.org/handbook/online/articles/fro28.

22 *Clarion-Ledger* (Jackson, MS), Feb. 13, 1903. In his official report, Robertson credited Capt. David K. Rice as the initial commander at Chickamauga. After the war, Harding claimed he was in charge the entire time.

but still was unwell. Bane was promoted to lieutenant colonel and assumed command of the regiment. His ranks included Cpl. Robert H. Clements, a veteran of the navy of the former Republic of Texas.[23]

The soldiers of the 4th Texas came from a diverse mix of counties when the regiment formed in April 1861. After the forced resignation of its unpopular original colonel, John Bell Hood assumed command. Hood, a Kentuckian, served in Texas with the U.S. Army before the war. The 1853 West Point graduate was wounded while fighting Comanches in 1857. He enlisted in the Confederate army in April 1861 as a Texan because of Kentucky's official neutrality. Hood initially commanded cavalry before being named colonel of the 4th Texas in September. In February 1862, he took command of the newly formed Texas Brigade.[24]

The 5th Texas, the third of Robertson's Lone Star regiments, was recruited in October 1861 in 11 counties throughout the state. The original recruits included Pvt. Sion Record Bostick, one of three scouts who had captured Santa Anna after the battle of San Jacinto in April 1836. He was no longer in the ranks of the "Bloody Fifth" by Chickamauga, having received his discharge after Sharpsburg. Privates Albert and William Cooper also had ties to the Texas Revolution. Their father had survived the Goliad Massacre, in which Santa Anna's soldiers executed most of Col. James Fannin's unarmed Texian prisoners. Thirty-nine-year-old Maj. Jefferson C. Rogers, a Mexican War veteran originally from Tennessee, led the regiment. In 1852, he moved to Milam County, Texas, where he was the sheriff for several years. He followed that with stints as a district clerk and a Texas Ranger.[25]

Harrison's Cavalry Brigade

Joseph "Fighting Joe" Wheeler's cavalry corps included the 8th and 11th Texas Cavalry Regiments in the 2nd Brigade of Brig. Gen. John A. Wharton's division. The Tennessee-born Wharton had been a wealthy attorney and plantation owner in

23 "Bane, John Pierson," *Handbook of Texas*, accessed Nov. 1, 2019, www.tshaonline.org/handbook/online/articles/fba54: "The Old Tom Green Rifles," *Austin American-Statesman*, Jun. 6, 1897. For an excellent early, first-person history of the 4th Texas, written by its chaplain, see Rev. Nicholas A. Davis, *The Campaign from Texas to Maryland, with the Battle of Fredericksburg* (Richmond, VA: 1862).

24 For a detailed account of Hood's life, see Stephen M. Hood, *John Bell Hood: The Rise, Fall, and Resurrection of a Confederate General* (El Dorado Hills, CA: 2013).

25 Bill Stein, "Consider the Lily: The Ungilded History of Colorado County, Texas," *Nesbitt Memorial Library Journal*, vol. 7, no. 2, May 1997, 79; "Rogers, Jefferson Carroll," *Handbook of Texas*, accessed Nov. 1, 2019, www.tshaonline.org/handbook/online/articles/froao.

Col. Thomas Harrison commanded a cavalry brigade in Wharton's division. (*Library of Congress*)

Brazoria County, Texas, before the war. In 1861 he enlisted in the 8th Texas Cavalry as the captain of Company B. Colonel Benjamin F. Terry, a prosperous sugar planter and veteran of the battle of Manassas, Virginia, had organized the regiment in August 1861. He suffered a mortal wound in December 1861 in an engagement in Kentucky, but his men retained the name "Terry's Texas Rangers." Wharton succeeded Terry in command and led the 8th Texas until he was promoted to brigadier general. He commanded a division under Wheeler at Chickamauga. Colonel Thomas Harrison, a former Waco attorney, now led what had previously been Wharton's brigade. In turn, Lt. Col. Gustave Cook oversaw the 8th Texas Cavalry. The Alabama-born Cook was a prewar attorney and judge in Fort Bend County. He had enlisted as a private in the Rangers; now, he was its senior field officer.[26]

Mexican War veteran and former U.S. marshal William C. Young organized the 11th Texas Cavalry in early October 1861 with men from the former 3rd Texas Cavalry and fresh recruits from several counties in North Texas. Their unorthodox training regimen included frequent marksmanship contests, horse riding competitions, and other frontier exercises, all liberally spiced with whiskey, women, and music. The regiment, sent to the Indian Territory, fought at Chustenahlah on December 26, 1861, and was at the battle of Pea Ridge the following March. The regiment was reorganized in May 1862 after the conscription act brought in fresh manpower. After fighting dismounted in several battles, including Murfreesboro, the regiment remounted and transferred to the cavalry corps in January 1863. The 11th's commander at Chickamauga was Col. George R.

26 Warner, *Generals in Gray*, 331-332; Bryan S. Bush, *Terry's Texas Rangers: History of the 8th Texas Cavalry* (Nashville, TN: 2002), 2-10; William Wharton Groce, "Major General John A. Wharton," *SHQ*, vol. 19, no. 3, Jan. 1916, 271-278.

Lt. Col. Gustave Cook commanded the 8th Texas Cavalry (Terry's Texas Rangers) at Chickamauga. (*The State Preservation Board, Austin, Texas*)

Reeves, a wealthy landowner and former sheriff of Grayson County. At the start of the war, he had donated the land for Camp Reeves, the regiment's original training site.[27]

In addition to the designated Texas troops, scores of individual Texans served at Chickamauga in various regiments or batteries credited to other states. Marshall resident Dr. Nathaniel A. Morgan, for example, served in the 1st Georgia Volunteers because the Texas regiments had filled their quota of surgeons. Some recruits, like Pvt. Samuel Houston Hargis, were working or living outside the Lone Star State at the time of their enlistment. Born in 1842 in Nacogdoches County, Hargis enrolled in the 2nd Arkansas Mounted Rifles at Bentonville in July 1861. Other men traveled back to their birth states to sign up with family members and old friends. Douglas J. Cater, an Alabama-born violinist and pianist living in Rusk County, Texas, enlisted as a bugler in the 3rd Texas Cavalry at Dallas in 1861. He transferred to the 19th Louisiana on June 29, 1862, to be with two of his brothers. He was the 19th's chief musician at Chickamauga, where his sibling Lt. Rufus Cater was killed.[28]

A few soldiers with Texas ties enlisted because of the promise of bounty money or other inducements. Many left their wives and children, or elderly parents, to fend for themselves on the home front. The longer the war dragged on, the more these men missed their loved ones. Chickamauga offered a rare chance for a significant victory in the Western Theater, one that might bring the soldiers a step

27 Tim Bell, "Eleventh Texas Cavalry," *Handbook of Texas*, accessed Nov. 25, 2019, www.tshaonline.org/handbook/online/articles/qke11; *The War of the Rebellion: A Compilation of the Official Records of the Union and Confederate Armies*, 128 vols. (Washington, DC: 1880-1901), Series 1, vol. 4, page 95 (Hereafter cited as *OR*. All references are to Series 1 unless otherwise noted.); *Dallas Herald*, Sept. 25, 1861.

28 Samuel H. Hargis, *Anecdotes and Incidents of the Civil War* (Ardmore, Indian Territory: self-published, 1894), 1-123; Compiled Service Records (CSR) of D. J. Cater, National Archives and Records Administration (NARA) Record Group 109, M320 (Louisiana, roll 0302) and M323 (Texas, roll 0018); Charles David Grear, *Why Texans Fought in the Civil War* (College Station, TX: 2012), 52-53. Two other brothers died of disease; D. J. Cater survived the war.

closer to returning home. That prospect provided enough motivation for them to fight hard enough to whip the Yankees once and for all. "Statistics show that the Lone Star State, though sparsely settled during the War between the States, contributed between fifty and sixty thousand men for military service to the Confederacy," a Texas newspaperman noted, "and we all know that Texas soldiers fought on battlefields from Missouri to Kentucky to the Gulf of Mexico and from Pennsylvania to the Rio Grande." Now, many of them headed toward Chickamauga.[29]

29 *Marshall* (TX) *News Messenger*, Mar. 9, 1923. According to Stephen B. Oates in "Texas Under the Secessionists" (*SHQ*, vol. 67, no. 2, Oct. 1963, 187), Texas raised 58,000 cavalrymen and 30,000 infantry and artillerymen for Confederate service. Conversely, more than 2,100 Texans joined the Union Army.

Chapter 2

The Long Road to Chickamauga

Throughout 1863, the Texas commands in the Army of Tennessee followed convoluted paths to West Chickamauga Creek. After defeat at Murfreesboro in early January, Braxton Bragg withdrew his battered but still potent army 30 miles south to the Highland Rim of the Cumberland Mountains. His pioneers constructed strong defensive positions in several narrow mountain passes north of the Duck River. Rebels commanded the roads leading south to Chattanooga, a vital railroad hub along the Tennessee River in the shadow of Lookout Mountain. Bragg needed to protect this transportation network if Maj. Gen. William S. Rosecrans's Army of the Cumberland moved south. Bragg established his headquarters in Tullahoma, Tennessee, and began solidifying his position.[1]

Contrary to his expectations, Rosecrans chose not to test the Confederate lines. He settled into winter camp, significantly strengthening and reinforcing his

1 The 1860 U.S. Census listed Chattanooga as having 2,545 residents. Gettysburg was of comparable size, at 2,390 people. Four key railroads radiated from Chattanooga, going to Nashville, Memphis, Atlanta, and Knoxville. That network sparked the town's growth to almost 7,000 people by 1870.

Battle of Murfreesboro. Capturing a Confederate Flag. (*Missouri Historical Society*)

own lines in case Bragg chose to attack. He had lost 13,000 soldiers, including hundreds of experienced officers, at Murfreesboro. Despite what President Abraham Lincoln deemed a "hard-earned victory" in a congratulatory message to Rosecrans, Union losses had exceeded Confederate casualties by 1,200 men. Nevertheless, the outcome of the fighting boosted morale in the North and dampened it in the South.[2]

During the long winter, many of Bragg's soldiers reflected on the war's long-term prospects. In February, Capt. James P. Douglas predicted from his battery's rudimentary camp near Shelbyville, Tennessee, that the upcoming spring and summer campaigns would show the North that the war was no longer worth fighting. The Texan boasted, however, if the Yankees did want a fight, then "our veteran army is prepared." Some of Bragg's troops shared Douglas's optimism and

2 For useful background material, see Earl J. Hess, *Banners to the Breeze: The Kentucky Campaign, Corinth, and Stones River* (Lincoln, NE: 2000).

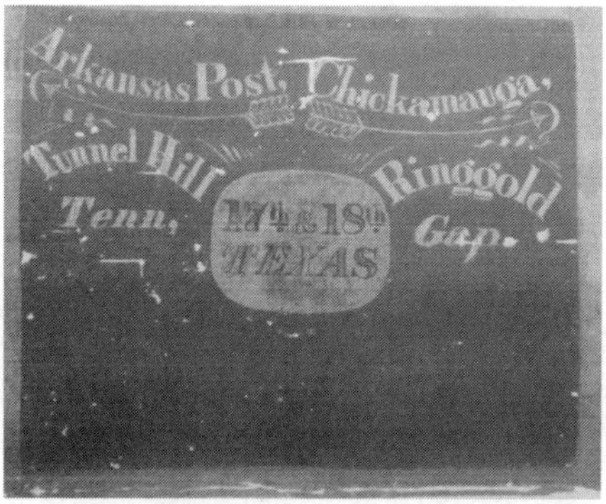

A battle flag of the consolidated 17th and 18th Texas Cavalry, Dismounted, with the names of prominent battles added. (*Texas State Archives*)

confidence despite the lingering sting of the loss at Murfreesboro and subsequent retreat. Other soldiers disagreed as persistent cloudy skies and periods of cold rain sapped their psyche.[3]

The grumbling continued into spring as morale further dropped and desertions increased. Private Dunbar Affleck of the 8th Texas Cavalry complained that he did not have a horse and would remain without one until he saved up enough money for a purchase. "A good horse will cost about five-hundred dollars if not more," he lamented in a letter home. Anticipating success, he asked his parents to forward his saddle and pistols. "I don't think the war will last much longer," he opined. "I expect to be home by the first of October next."[4]

More Texans soon joined Affleck in Bragg's army. Following their exchanges, over a thousand Arkansas Post parolees arrived in Tullahoma in May. They included most of Col. Clayton C. Gillespie's 25th Texas Cavalry. "We were captured at Arkansas Post," Sgt. Benjamin F. Grady recounted, "and spent some three months in Camp Butler, not far from Springfield, Illinois, and were sent after our exchange to Bragg's army at Tullahoma, Tennessee." Few men were in fighting condition after spending so much time in captivity.[5]

Dr. Adolphus A. Lawrence, the 24th Texas Cavalry's surgeon, groused, "At the surrender of Arkansas Post many were absent on furlough, and on detail; many made their escape, not wishing to be included in the surrender: and most all of these remained and served on this side of the [Mississippi] river, having connected themselves with other commands." Lawrence added, "Thus, in conjunction with

3 See Lang, "Lone Star Pride," 34, for more on Douglas's battery during this period. CSR documents for individuals in the various Texas regiments indicate that dozens of men departed without permission, and few returned to the ranks.

4 Robert W. Williams, Jr., and Ralph A. Wooster, eds., "With Terry's Texas Rangers: The Letters of Dunbar Affleck," *Civil War History*, vol. 9, no. 3, Sept. 1963, 318-319.

5 B. F. Grady, "Amid the Crash of Shells on the Field of Chickamauga. Scenes from That Mighty Drama Unrolled before the Eyes of One of the Actors Therein," *News and Observer* (Raleigh, NC), Jan. 17, 1904.

the heavy mortality, resulting from the cold and want of a winter's imprisonment, reduced the regimental muster rolls so that on their arrival at Tullahoma, it was deemed expedient to adopt a system of consolidation, much to the dissatisfaction of all concerned, with the exception, perhaps, of a few of the officers."[6]

The organizational consolidation created a command problem, with too many experienced officers vying to fill the few available positions in the combined regiments. Many of them transferred to the Trans-Mississippi Theater or resigned their commissions. Some of the remaining officers criticized the decision to consolidate their regiments. "I have now a very fine command, but it is not my old Tenth," Col. Roger Q. Mills griped to his wife. "I had rather command my old one, though small, than a half-dozen blended. . .. [I]t makes me sorrowful, every time I think of my old Rgmt. having lost its identity." Captain Bryan Marsh of the 17th Texas Cavalry mourned, "The old 17th regiment is no more. She was buried at Tullahoma on the 23rd of [May] by Parson C. C. Gillespie of the 25th." Brigadier General Thomas Churchill, who had led the defenders of Arkansas Post, took command of the consolidated brigade.[7]

Bragg assigned Churchill's brigade to a division under Maj. Gen. Patrick R. Cleburne, an Irish immigrant from County Cork. On June 3, the division rendezvoused near Wartrace, Tennessee, about 15 miles northwest of Tullahoma. Admirers deemed the charismatic Cleburne the "Stonewall of the West" because of perceived similarities in his performance to the famed General Jackson of the Army of Northern Virginia. Cleburne began drilling his men, including Churchill's revamped brigade, to improve their martial abilities. The 18th Texas Cavalry's Pvt. Alexander L. Orr commented that Colonel Gillespie's consolidated regiment exhibited the strictest discipline he had ever seen. The men drilled seven hours every day, often under Cleburne's watchful gaze. Morale improved as the brigade slowly gained an esprit de corps. Orr's brother James mentioned that Cleburne "drilles us very hard; we will soon be as well drilled as any troops in the servis." Captain Marsh of the 17th Texas Cavalry informed his wife, "It used to make me mad to hear the Trans Miss Army called the ragamuffin army but I am compell[ed]

6 A. A. Lawrence, "Medical Records of Granbury's Brigade," *Galveston Daily News*, Jul. 22, 1866. Lawrence was new to the Confederate service, having received his appointment from the secretary of war on May 14, 1863.

7 R. Q. Mills to his wife, Jun. 13, 1863, Roger Q. Mills Papers, University of Texas Archives, Austin; "The Confederate Letters of Bryan Marsh," *Chronicles of Smith County* (Tyler, TX), vol. 14, issue 2, Winter 1975, 9-30, 41-55; Bowser, "History of Granbury's Brigade," 742.

Maj. Gen. Patrick R. Cleburne led a division in Hill's Corps at Chickamauga. (*Library of Congress*)

now to acknowledge it to be so. We ner knew what soldiering ment until since we have bin hear."[8]

Another soldier recalled that "'Old Pat' was always sober, calm and alert, and moved rapidly on the line of strict obedience to orders, no matter who got hurt by obeying them. Cleburne demanded equally strict obedience upon the part of his brigade and regimental officers, and woe it was to the man who disobeyed, for he would feel the displeasure of his stern but just division commander." Cleburne's performance was "superb" in combat. The discipline he instilled in his men enabled them to follow him into action without wavering or falling aside. "He never sent, but led his men into the storm of battle," the unidentified soldier added.[9]

The time in Wartrace drilling the troops proved well spent. With warmer weather and better discipline in the ranks, Churchill's soldiers began to feel more optimistic. On June 15, Sgt. William Heartsill of the consolidated 6th-10th Texas–15th Texas Cavalry wrote that when the bands played "Dixie" or "The Bonnie Blue Flag" at night, "the boys make these Tennessee Beech groves ring with their Texas yells, all as happy and as merry as if on a picnic excursion." He added, somewhat solemnly, that the men did not seem to realize that they could be dead in a few days. "Tis well," Heartsill commented, "for it would make us all feel miserable to mope around and dread our future destiny but let us go at it like men

8 John R. Lundberg, *Granbury's Texas Brigade: Diehard Western Confederates* (Baton Rouge, LA: 2012), 124; Marsh, "The Confederate Letters of Bryan Marsh," 24-25; John Q. Anderson, ed., *Campaigning with Parsons' Texas Cavalry Brigade, CSA.: The War Journal and Letters of the Four Orr Brothers, 12th Texas Cavalry* (Hillsboro, TX: 1967), 108.

9 "Pat Cleburne," *Honey Grove* (TX) *Signal*, Jan. 21, 1910; Bowser, "History of Granbury's Brigade," 742.

Modern view of Wartrace, Tennessee (*Phil Spaugy*)

and 'stare fate in the face.'" Many Texans were anxious to redeem their reputations as soldiers.[10]

General Bragg did not have time to concern himself with the parolees' training or morale. He focused on the Federals, occasionally dispatching cavalry to harass Rosecrans's forward pickets and supply lines. Rosecrans believed he lacked sufficient trained horsemen to both counter the pesky Rebels and gather intelligence. He remained stationary inside his extensive earthworks, "Fortress Rosecrans," near Murfreesboro, much to senior officials' growing chagrin in Washington. Even the Confederates took notice. "It is very evident that Rosecrans wishes and intends to avoid our fortifications at Tullahoma," Chaplain Robert F. Bunting of Terry's Texas Rangers opined. "They are formidable, and he is not intending to risk his reputation and the ruin of his army by an attack upon them." The Pennsylvania-born Presbyterian preacher added, "Mystery seems to envelop his movements. A short time will doubtless develop his wily plans." Many Texans

10 W. W. Heartsill and Bell Wiley, eds., *Fourteen Hundred and 91 Days in the Confederate Army: A Journal Kept by W. W. Heartsill For Four Years* (Jackson, TN: 1953), 131. Captain Leroy M. Nutt of Louisiana commanded a makeshift infantry unit made up of various recently released Arkansas Post captives (mostly cavalrymen from his state and Texas). They were assigned to the 10th Texas Infantry as Company L.

Marker commemorating Cleburne's division in Wartrace, Tennessee (*Phil Spaugy*)

believed that Bragg was awaiting news from Vicksburg before acting. Union forces were closing in on the last remaining significant Confederate-held bastion on the Mississippi River.[11]

In Washington, President Lincoln and Secretary of War Edwin M. Stanton grew increasingly impatient with Rosecrans's prolonged inaction. The initial blush of the Stones River victory had worn off in the five months since the battle. Major General Ulysses S. Grant was enjoying early success as he moved his army toward Vicksburg. Because of Rosecrans's prolonged inertia in Middle Tennessee, Lincoln fretted that Bragg might send all or part of his army to reinforce the hard-pressed Confederate forces in Mississippi, a chess move that could retard Grant's progress or halt him altogether. Lincoln and Stanton wanted General-in-Chief Henry W. Halleck to prod Rosecrans into attacking Bragg. At the same time, Maj. Gen. Ambrose E. Burnside planned to invade East Tennessee, a mountainous region with significant pockets of strong pro-Union sentiment. Such an incursion would threaten the rail connections between Chattanooga and Richmond. Timely

11 Thomas W. Cutrer, ed., *Our Trust is in the God of Battles: The Civil War Letters of Robert Franklin Bunting, Chaplain, Terry's Texas Rangers* (Knoxville, TN: 2006), 141.

Maj. Gen. William S. Rosecrans commanded the Army of the Cumberland.
(*Library of Congress*)

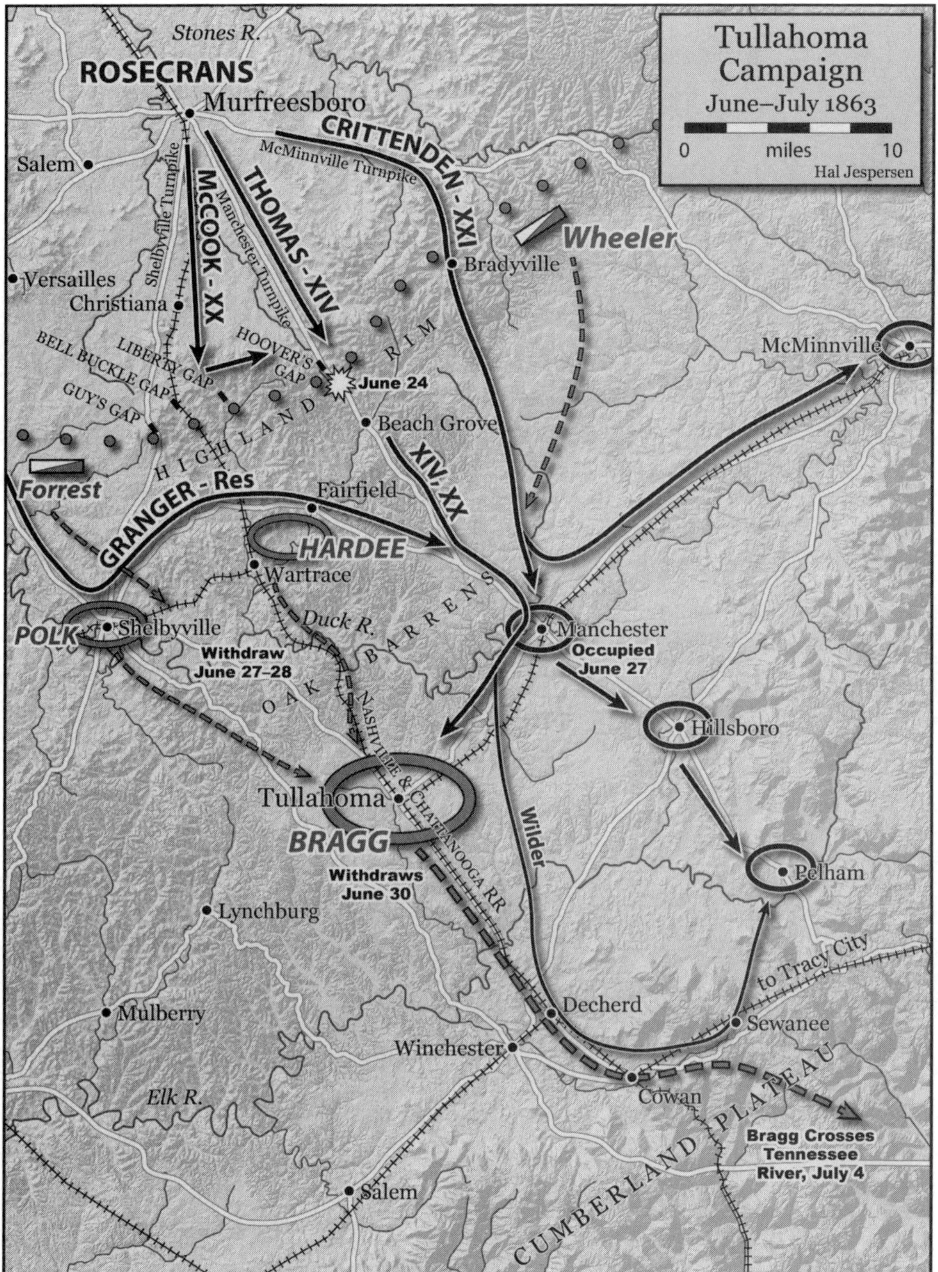
Tullahoma Campaign
June–July 1863
0 miles 10
Hal Jespersen
Stones R.
ROSECRANS
Murfreesboro
CRITTENDEN - XXI
McMinnville Turnpike
Salem
THOMAS - XIV
McCOOK - XX
Manchester Turnpike
Shelbyville Turnpike
Wheeler
Bradyville
Versailles
Christiana
LIBERTY GAP
HOOVER'S GAP
BELL BUCKLE GAP
GUY'S GAP
June 24
HIGHLAND RIM
Beach Grove
McMinnville
XIV, XX
Forrest
GRANGER - Res
Fairfield
HARDEE
Wartrace
OAK BARRENS
Duck R.
POLK
Shelbyville
Withdraw
June 27–28
Manchester
Occupied
June 27
Hillsboro
NASHVILLE & CHATTANOOGA RR
Tullahoma
BRAGG
Withdraws
June 30
Wilder
Pelham
Lynchburg
to Tracy City
Mulberry
Decherd
Sewanee
Winchester
Cowan
Elk R.
CUMBERLAND PLATEAU
Bragg Crosses
Tennessee
River, July 4
Salem

Sgt. William W. Heartsill, 10th Texas Infantry, Deshler's brigade. (*SCV #2042 Camp, Marshall, Texas*)

coordination between Burnside and Rosecrans might prove problematic for Confederate strategists.[12]

A frustrated General Halleck tersely wired Rosecrans on June 16. "Is it your intention to make an immediate movement forward?" he asked. "A definite answer, yes or no, is required." Rosecrans responded, "In reply to your inquiry, if immediate means tonight or tomorrow, no. If it means as soon as all things are ready, say five days, yes." He finally put his 60,000-man Army of the Cumberland in motion on June 23–24 after notifying Halleck that "[t]he army begins to move at three o'clock this morning." The Tullahoma campaign was finally underway.[13]

Tullahoma and the Retreat to Chattanooga

Rosecrans finally attacked Bragg's right flank at Hoover's Gap on June 24. Union Col. John T. Wilder's "Lightning Brigade," mounted Illinois and Indiana infantrymen wielding deadly seven-shot Spencer repeating rifles, pushed aside Confederate defenders and fortified the hills south of the gap. After being unable to retake the vital pass over the next two days, Bragg reluctantly began withdrawing on the 26th. Southbound trains steaming for Tullahoma carried some of his men, but most Confederates walked. Churchill's mixed brigade of Texans and Arkansans crossed the Duck River on the afternoon of June 27 and slogged through a driving rainstorm toward Tullahoma. The persistent downpour chilled the soldiers to their bones, and morale sagged again. "Hour after hour we marched through the mud, so tired we can scarcely put one foot before the other," Sgt. William W. Heartsill of the 10th Texas complained; "every few hundred yards may

12 James R. Sullivan, *Chickamauga and Chattanooga Battlefields: Chickamauga and Chattanooga National Military Park*, Georgia-Tennessee, National Park Service Historical Handbook Series, no. 25 (Washington, DC: 1956), 4-5.

13 *OR* 23, pt. 1, 10.

Lt. Gen. Daniel Harvey Hill commanded a corps in the Army of Tennessee. (*Library of Congress*)

be seen one, two or half a dozen men by the roadside sick or too tired to go further without rest."[14]

In the face of these successive flanking movements, most of Bragg's forces continued to retreat southeasterly toward Tullahoma, their progress slowed by persistent, heavy rains. Most Texans rarely saw any Yankees during the retrograde; Colonel Harrison's 8th and 11th Texas Cavalry were the exception. The two regiments crossed the Duck River on June 28 and moved in the direction of Tullahoma. Two days later, the 11th participated in a sharp firefight with Yankees along the rain-swollen Elk River. The 8th's chaplain, Robert F. Bunting, praised the troopers' calm presence under fire. "The 11th Texas sat on their horses in line of battle and fought most gallantly and desperately," Bunting recorded. "They lost several men and a large number of horses. There are no better fighters in the army than the gallant 11th."[15]

Bragg abandoned Tullahoma on July 1, and Churchill's brigade protected the rear as the army crossed the Elk River. The Texans skirmished that day with elements of Maj. Gen. Alexander M. McCook's XX Corps. Bragg finally paused at Chattanooga on July 4. The vanguard of the Army of Tennessee soon waded across the Tennessee River and encamped near Lookout Mountain to the southwest. Rosecrans received plaudits for his often-brilliant flanking maneuvers that opened the door to Chattanooga at the cost of only 570 men. To his dismay, the highly publicized twin victories at Gettysburg and Vicksburg overshadowed his actions.[16]

14 Heartsill, Fourteen Hundred and 91 Days, 134.

15 J. W. Stewart, "Proceedings of Granbury's Brigade," *Report of the Proceedings of the Various Associations of Ex-Confederates Held at Dallas County, Texas, August 6th, 7th, 8th and 9th, 1884* (Dallas, TX: 1884), 294; Cutrer, *Our Trust is in the God of Battles*, 169.

16 Heartsill, *Fourteen Hundred and 91 Days*, 136-137. For more on the tumultuous period from June 23 to July 4, see Christopher L. Kolakowski, *The Stones River and Tullahoma Campaigns: This Army Does Not Retreat* (Mount Pleasant, SC: 2011).

Some of Bragg's soldiers held strong opinions about Rosecrans's performance vis-à-vis that of their controversial commander. The 8th Texas Cavalry's Chaplain Bunting complained about the retreat. "I do know that the army has been greatly demoralized by it, and Gen. Bragg has been universally cursed," he wrote. "To say the truth, he was out-generaled in every sense of the word. The future will decide the wisdom or the folly of the movement. As yet I see it as a profound mystery." He groused that the Army of Tennessee "can out-retreat anything in the Confederacy."[17]

The long march through the mud took a physical and psychological toll on many of Bragg's men, especially the former prisoners still rebounding from the Arkansas Post surrender and months of forced inactivity in Northern prison camps. Many straggled on the march. After a 15-mile hike in a rainstorm on July 3, trying to overtake Churchill's brigade, the 10th Texas's William Heartsill was "completely worn out." He complained, "I cannot make anything out of this infantry business; it beats me decidedly. My feet are almost one solid blister and my shoulders are worn out." Many others shared his sentiments.[18]

Heartsill and his footsore companions continued to tramp south over the next few days. The 15th Texas Cavalry's Lt. Robert M. Collins, fighting illness, became separated from his regiment and was now well in front of the brigade. On July 6, he approached the Tennessee River at Kelly's Ford, five miles west of Chattanooga. There, he encountered a group of other soldiers, most of them fellow Texans. Several provost guards watching the crossing refused to allow the men to go over the pontoon bridge until their respective commands arrived. "Our Corps commander Gen. [William J.] Hardee was there," Collins related. "A long keen Texas soldier said he was going over anyhow; when he started, Gen. Hardee drew his sword and made a dive for him. The fellow jumped into the river and the General plunged in after him on horseback. This created some excitement and no little amusement for the boys." Collins, a dry-goods clerk in Decatur before the war, walked across the bridge while all eyes were on Hardee. Later, the balance of Churchill's brigade arrived. The Texans crossed the pontoons and camped on the slopes of Racoon Mountain for three days. Then they took trains to Tyner's Station, 12 miles east of Chattanooga, to rejoin Cleburne's division. By the end of

17 Cutrer, *Our Trust is in the God of Battles*, 173.

18 Heartsill, *Fourteen Hundred and 91 Days*, 136-137.

July, newly promoted Brig. Gen. James Deshler replaced Churchill, who had requested a transfer back to the Trans-Mississippi Theater.[19]

Bragg's other forces continued to arrive at Chattanooga throughout July. "The army remained at Shelbyville, Tennessee, for some time, then moved on south by way of Tullahoma to Chattanooga and encamped there," Pvt. James K. Polk Blackburn of the 8th Texas Cavalry recalled. "Our individual regiment acting as scouts and guards for the rear moved leisurely along after our army, delaying the enemy's movements as far as they might attempt to follow." Terry's Rangers followed the Nashville, Chattanooga, and St. Louis Railroad to reach Chattanooga. In mid-July, the Rangers went into camp along Silver Creek in rural Floyd County, Georgia, and enjoyed two weeks of rest.[20]

The respite boosted their morale and confidence. In August, Pvt. Robert E. Hill bragged to his sister: "I believe that our Regt. stands head and shoulders above any other in this department for gallantry on the Field, for our good behavior while in camp and for intelligence among the men—I am Proud of the Texas Rangers." He then cautioned, "And now My Dear Sister the hour of Trial is coming for the South. The time that is to try the Patriotism of every man. The Enemy are gathering their Hosts for a final crushing act, and we must meet them. You must not become discouraged at nothing which may happen. All shall work out right in the end. Charleston may be taken, Richmond may be evacuated, Mobile may fall into the hands of the enemy and still we are not conquered."[21]

Many of his soldiers thought Bragg should take the offensive. "The repulse of Lee at Gettysburg and the fall of Vicksburg occurred simultaneously," Quartermaster Sgt. Joseph B. Polley of the 4th Texas recalled. "Such disasters cast a pall of gloom over the South, and the timorous grew weak of faith. Meade's army was again within striking distance of Richmond and Rosecranz [sic] in the West was

19 Robert M. Collins, *Chapters from the Unwritten History of the War between the States: Or, the Incidents in the Life of a Confederate Soldier in Camp, on the March, in the Great Battles, and in Prison* (St. Louis, MO: 1893), 140. Churchill's brigade was the last Confederate infantry to cross the river, according to Sgt. W. W. Heartsill (page 137 of his memoirs). Heartsill was among the group of Texans waiting for the brigade to arrive.

20 J. K. P. Blackburn, "Reminiscences of the Terry Rangers," *SHQ*, vol. 22, July 1918, 143-144. The Rangers' campsite was a few miles outside of Rome, Georgia.

21 Pauline S. Goldmann and Michelle M. Haas, *Letters from the Carnival of Death: Correspondence from Three of Terry's Texas Rangers* (Corpus Christi, TX: 2014), 90.

driving the Confederates under Bragg out of Tennessee into Georgia. Some movement was necessary to restore the confidence of the Southern people."[22]

Bragg, meanwhile, faced internal command issues. General Hardee and several other senior officers openly questioned tactical decisions Bragg had made at Murfreesboro. Hardee, the author of a well-known tactical manual, soon departed the Army of Tennessee. Lieutenant General Daniel Harvey Hill, a North Carolinian who had served under Bragg in the Mexican War, arrived from the Eastern Theater to assume command of the reorganized Second Corps. The Confederate war department also merged the Department of East Tennessee, which included Maj. Gen. Simon Bolivar Buckner's 18,000 men, into Bragg's Department of Tennessee. Having thus bolstered his army, the department asked Bragg if he could take the offensive against Rosecrans. He hesitated, citing issues with unfavorable terrain and potential problems with logistics and supply. He preferred to stay on the defensive and wait for Rosecrans to attack him. He also worried about the threat that Burnside's Federals posed to Knoxville. He began consolidating his forces around Chattanooga and the Tennessee River, using his cavalry (including the 8th and 11th Texas) to protect his flanks and gather intelligence on Union movements. Meanwhile, on August 4, the war department ordered Rosecrans to move forward and cross the Tennessee River. "Old Rosey" demurred and cited several reasons, including waiting until mid-August for the corn crop in Eastern Tennessee and northern Alabama to ripen as a food supply.[23]

Rosecrans's delay allowed Bragg to obtain more troops. Brigadier General Matthew D. Ector's brigade (which included the 9th Texas and the 10th, 14th, and 32nd Texas Cavalry, dismounted) returned to the Army of Tennessee in August. Bragg had transferred Ector's and Brig. Gen. Evander McNair's brigades in early May 1863 to Gen. Joseph E. Johnston's Army of Mississippi, which unsuccessfully tried to relieve Vicksburg. Ector's 1,300 men moved by rail from Mississippi to Chattanooga between August 23 and 30 to rejoin Bragg. Assigned to Brig. Gen. W. H. T. Walker's Reserve Corps, their first assignment was picket duty along the Tennessee River, an often mundane and thankless task, but a necessary one. Ector's brigade marched to Rome, Georgia, on September 4 to help repel a rumored Union attack on Rome or Atlanta. Bragg decided to pull back into northern Georgia and await fresh troops. Private Jim Turner of the 6th Texas

22 "Reminiscences of a Private," *San Antonio Daily Express*, Apr. 22, 1906.

23 J. Littleton Rogers, *The Civil War Battles of Chickamauga and Chattanooga* (Chattanooga, TN: 1942), 8.

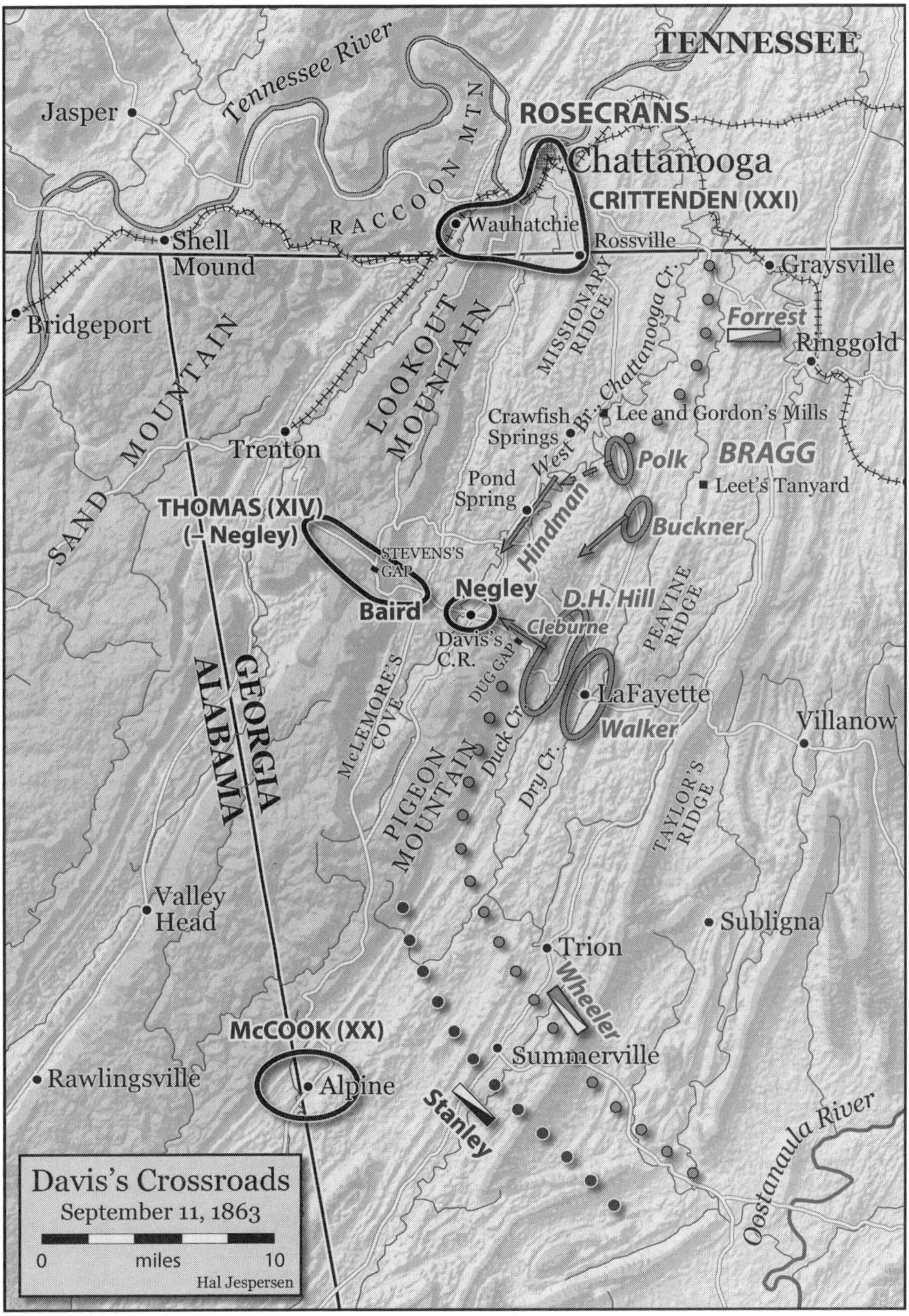
TENNESSEE
Tennessee River
Jasper
ROSECRANS
Chattanooga
RACCOON MTN
CRITTENDEN (XXI)
Wauhatchie
Shell Mound
Rossville
Graysville
Bridgeport
LOOKOUT MOUNTAIN
MISSIONARY RIDGE
Forrest
Ringgold
SAND MOUNTAIN
Crawfish Springs
Lee and Gordon's Mills
Trenton
Polk
BRAGG
Pond Spring
Leet's Tanyard
Hindman
Buckner
THOMAS (XIV) (– Negley)
STEVENS'S GAP
Baird
Negley
D.H. Hill
Cleburne
Davis's C.R.
PEAVINE RIDGE
DUG GAP
LaFayette
Walker
GEORGIA
ALABAMA
McLEMORE'S COVE
Duck Cr.
Dry Cr.
Villanow
PIGEON MOUNTAIN
TAYLOR'S RIDGE
Valley Head
Sublignа
Trion
Wheeler
McCOOK (XX)
Summerville
Rawlingsville
Alpine
Stanley
Oostanaula River
Davis's Crossroads
September 11, 1863
0 miles 10
Hal Jespersen

recalled, "In the early part of September we marched down to Chattanooga and through that city. We halted near the edge of the city and waited for hours for troops to file by and then we took up the line of march to cover the retreat from Chattanooga."[24]

After Rosecrans sent his troops across Lookout Mountain to threaten the vital railroad to Atlanta, Bragg abandoned his vulnerable lines along the Tennessee River on September 8 and withdrew from Chattanooga. Two days later, he established his new headquarters in La Fayette, Georgia, some 28 miles south of Chattanooga. Rosecrans soon occupied Chattanooga. A Marietta, Georgia, newspaper correspondent later conversed with two of Bragg's scouts, who claimed to have infiltrated Chattanooga in disguise that week. According to the spies, the Federals were present in significant force, but they were not molesting the citizens or personal property. More importantly, "the enemy was doing very little towards fortifying the place, save repairing the old works constructed by our engineers during the summer." The reporter reflected the prevailing opinion that Bragg would soon strike: "General Bragg was heard to remark a few evenings since, that he intended to go direct to Nashville. Everybody in the front is jubilant with hope and impatient for the forward move—officers and men alike."[25]

Residents began fleeing northern Georgia, many by rail, and crowding into Atlanta. "It is truly distressing to see, as we do here, women and little children accustomed to almost every comfort and luxury, escaping with a few articles which they can pack in their trunks, and leaving their commodious dwellings a prey to the enemy," a reporter lamented. "Every train for a week has been crowded with persons of this description." The state reserve troops had assembled in Atlanta, and thousands of other soldiers were on their way. Military hospitals overflowed with sick soldiers, and strangers and refugees filled the private houses and hotels. "The vast army of consumers gobble up everything in the way of edibles," the

24 West, *Ector's Brigade*, 27-34; "Ector's Brigade," *The Standard*; Heartsill, *Fourteen Hundred and 91 Days*, 136-137; Deanne Labenski, ed., "Jim Turner, Co. G, 6th Texas Infantry, C.S.A., from 1861 to 1865," *Texana*, vol. 12, no. 2, 1974, 162. Ector's ordnance report for September 3 is illustrative. The brigade had 144 .54-caliber Mississippi Rifles, 686 .57-caliber rifles, 278 .58-caliber rifles, and 277 .69-caliber smoothbore muskets. Each man carried 40 rounds in his cartridge box. Ector had seven ammunition wagons carrying a total of 6,000 .54-caliber cartridges, 40,000 .57-caliber cartridges, 17,000 .58-caliber cartridges, and 10,000 .69-caliber cartridges. (Source: CSR of Lt. L. W. H. Magruder, Ordnance Officer, Walker's Division.)

25 "Shadow," *Daily Clarion* (Meridian, MS), Sept. 27, 1863. Bragg established his headquarters at the Chattanooga Academy. In 1936, one hundred years after it was constructed, the two-story brick building was renamed John B. Gordon Hall after the former Confederate general and governor of Georgia.

reporter continued. "Beef has gone to $1.50 per pound. Chickens $2.50 to $3 apiece when you can find them. Bacon $2.25 a pound. Butter $2 a pound, and mean at that."[26]

While civilian refugees streamed southward, Bragg believed his best chance for victory was to defeat Rosecrans's four widely separated corps in detail. His first goal was an eastbound Federal column that had entered McLemore's Cove, a deep, "V"-shaped cul-de-sac in northwestern Georgia between Lookout Mountain and its eastern spur, Pigeon Mountain. On September 10, Bragg ordered Thomas Hindman's and D. H. Hill's troops to attack Maj. Gen. James S. Negley's isolated division at Davis's Crossroads. Major General Patrick Cleburne led one of Hill's two divisions, with brigades under Brig. Gens. James Deshler, Lucius E. Polk, and Sterling A. M. Wood (the other division served under John C. Breckinridge, former U.S. vice president and 1860 Democratic presidential nominee). Bragg's plans went awry, partially due to Hill's reluctance to attack and to an illness that had left Cleburne bedridden. The following day, miscommunication spoiled another chance for the Rebels to destroy Negley's force, which caused Bragg to reprimand Hindman.

An incensed Bragg had lost an opportunity to cripple the scattered Federals in McLemore's Cove before significant reinforcements arrived. The Union troops retreated in good order north toward Stephen's Gap on Lookout Mountain as Rosecrans began to consolidate his forces before moving toward La Fayette. "The Yankees left in such hot haste they left lots of good picking for us," the 15th Texas Cavalry's Lt. Robert Collins gloated. "After nightfall, footsore, weary and disappointed, we marched back to the highlands where we had left in the morning." Deshler's brigade and the rest of Cleburne's dust-covered soldiers returned to guarding the vital passages on Pigeon Mountain that blocked the most direct route to Bragg's main army at La Fayette.[27]

Many of the Arkansas Post parolees, tired of the constant disdain from their comrades in the Army of Tennessee, yearned for a chance for redemption. They blamed D. H. Hill for not moving promptly to the attack. One Texas soldier offered another possible explanation for the failure: "It is very certain there were Union sympathizers who aided them in getting out of a very closed place, as the

26 "From North Georgia," *Savannah Daily News*, Sept. 18, 1863.

27 Sullivan, *Chickamauga and Chattanooga Battlefields*, 14-15; Collins, *Chapters*, 148-149; Bowser, "History of Granbury's Brigade," 742. West Chickamauga Creek and Missionary Ridge both originate in McLemore's Cove, which is about 20 miles southwest of Chattanooga.

well-known passes were guarded and they couldn't have gotten out without help."[28]

Bragg soon received additional 2,500 reinforcements in the form of McNair's returning brigade and Brig. Gen. John Gregg's Tennessee brigade, which included Col. Hiram Granbury's 7th Texas. After the Vicksburg campaign, these forces had encamped along the Chickasawhay River near Enterprise, Mississippi. The commander of the Army of Mississippi, Gen. Joseph E. Johnston, dispatched McNair's and Gregg's brigades in response to Bragg's concerns that the Yankees might threaten Atlanta. Gregg's soldiers had boarded trains on September 7 for the lengthy roundabout journey through Mobile and Atlanta to the Ringgold area. On the night of September 14, a Western and Atlantic train containing part of the brigade ran off the tracks two miles north of Marietta. The train, though undamaged, resumed the trip, but the engineer needed to put on steam to make up the lost time. At a curve in a deep cut near what is now Emerson, Georgia, the highballing troop train collided about midnight with a southbound 15-car train carrying some of Bragg's sick and lightly wounded men. Thirteen soldiers of the 50th Tennessee and 1st Tennessee Battalions and a handful of other passengers died. The crash injured more than 60 soldiers, who were sent to Marietta for treatment. The shaken survivors did not arrive at Catoosa Platform until the evening of September 17, just in time to be ordered out to repel Union cavalry raiders.[29]

Bragg continued to worry about Federal movements on his flank from Wills Valley and McLemore's Cove. He kept Joe Wheeler's cavalry on the road, and alternated Brig. Gen. John Wharton's division between Summerville and Alpine in Chattooga County and La Fayette. Tom Harrison's troopers spent time picketing the Pigeon Mountain passes and felling trees as obstructions. The cavalrymen also protected the vital crossings of West Chickamauga Creek near La Fayette. "It was very dry and warm, and the dust was almost unendurable," Chaplain Robert F. Bunting of the 8th Texas Cavalry wrote. "But suffocating as it was, it seemed our

28 "Letter from Adolphus," *Corsicana* (TX) *Daily Sun*, Sept. 29, 1911.

29 "Gregg's Brigade at Chickamauga," *Galveston Weekly News*, Nov. 11, 1863; *OR* 24, pt. 3, 1031; *The Daily Sun* (Columbus, GA), Sept. 15, 1863; Lindsley, *Military Annals of Tennessee*, 287, 450, 561; *Richmond Daily Dispatch*, Sept. 21, 1863. The victims of the crash were interred near the site, but were reburied in Marietta across the street from the Georgia Military Institute nine days later. The location grew into the town's Confederate cemetery, the largest in Georgia. One of the widows, Nancy Martin, lost a postwar lawsuit against the W&A Railroad for the death of her husband, a captain in the 50th Tennessee.

luck to make one trip every twenty-four hours. But every day hastened the crisis." In a spirited skirmish on September 17, Federal troopers killed Col. William N. Estes of the 3rd Confederate Cavalry and captured several of his men. In a lively scuffle near Alpine, the Northerners drove back Terry's Texas Rangers and captured Pvt. Gus Hart of Company H, as well as wounding several much-needed horses.[30]

Chaplain Bunting was correct. Every passing day hastened the crisis for Bragg's Army of Tennessee as the Yankees consolidated their forces for a potential push into the heart of Georgia. Unknown to the 8th and 11th Texas Cavalry troopers, however, additional help was on the way.

Hood's Texans Ride the Rails to North Georgia

While Deshler's brigade helped Cleburne protect Catlett's Gap and Dug Gap on Pigeon Mountain, and Tom Harrison's cavalrymen kept a wary eye out for Yankees, significant reinforcements headed west from Virginia to join Bragg's army. Bragg, however, was not yet aware that they were coming. President Jefferson Davis, Secretary of War James Seddon, and their military strategists in Richmond decided to shift nine brigades and an artillery battalion of Lt. Gen. James Longstreet's First Corps of the Army of Northern Virginia to assist Bragg's operations. This necessitated the movement of more than 10,000 men of Maj. Gens. Lafayette McLaws's and John Bell Hood's divisions 800 to 900 miles to railheads in northern Georgia in just 11 days. With Knoxville and its important railroad in Burnside's hands, the best remaining option was to go through Atlanta, but that route was 260 to 360 miles longer than the optimal one through East Tennessee. The trip involved coordinating 16 different railroads, not all of which used the same track gauge, on multiple routes. Not all the railroads intersected, further complicating matters; as a result, periodic marches between depots and time-consuming reloading of the railcars were required. Quartermaster General Alexander R. Lawton and Maj. Frederick W. Sims of the railroad bureau and their

30 "Letter from the Rangers," *Houston Tri-Weekly Telegraph*, Sept. 30, 1863; Tam Brooks, "In and Out of Prison," *CV*, Nov.-Dec. 1921, vol. 29. nos. 11-12, 421-422. Guards escorted Harrison's prisoners to the Tennessee River near Chattanooga before taking them south to Union-held Bridgeport, Alabama. They were later taken by train to Camp Morton, on the fairgrounds in Indianapolis, for incarceration.

respective staffs planned and coordinated the complicated movement with local railroad officials.[31]

It was soon time to move the designated troops to the Virginia railheads. Since early August, Hood's Texans (Robertson's brigade of the 1st, 4th, and 5th Texas and the 3rd Arkansas) had been camped just south of Fredericksburg. The soldiers drew new uniforms from the Richmond Depot, including bluish, close-fitting shell jackets and light blue pants; from a distance, the clothes resembled Union garb. On September 3, the brigade moved 20 miles down the Rappahannock River to Port Royal in rural Caroline County, Virginia. Four days later, the Texans and Arkansans received orders to be ready to move at 4:00 the next morning. They broke camp before dawn on September 8 and marched 12 miles to Milford Station on the Richmond, Fredericksburg, and Potomac Railroad. The soldiers crammed into box cars and flat cars that night. Some climbed onto the roofs for more space and fresh air. They traveled south to Richmond, with most arriving in the Confederacy's capital city on the evening of September 8 or early the next morning. Several Texans visited the local saloons.[32]

On a warm and sunny September 9, the Texans began crowding into railcars on the Richmond sidings for the week-long trip to northern Georgia. It would take multiple trains to convey the entire brigade. All supply wagons, baggage wagons, and camp equipment stayed behind. Each man carried his rifle, cartridge box, haversack, and accouterments, plus his blanket roll and a few personal effects. In some cases, regiments split up on different trains.[33]

31 Lee White, "Trains to Georgia Changed Direction of Civil War," *Chattanooga Times Free Press*, Sept. 1, 2013; William Glenn Robertson, "Rails to the River of Death: Railroads in the Chickamauga Campaign," *Civil War*, vol. 9, no. 6, Nov.-Dec. 1991, 55. Major General George Pickett's division and the Washington Artillery remained near Petersburg, Virginia, and did not accompany the rest of Longstreet's Corps to Georgia. Brigadier General Micah Jenkins' brigade was added to Hood's division.

32 D. Augustus Dickert, *History of Kershaw's Brigade* (Newberry, SC: 1899), 268; George Skoch and Mark W. Perkins, *Lone Star Confederate: A Gallant and Good Soldier of the Fifth Texas Infantry* (College Station, TX: 2003), 96. See also Kyle J. Foley, *Hood's Texas Division in the Battle of Chickamauga: A Historical Analysis* (Master's thesis, U.S. Army Command and General Staff College, 2003), 4. Some officers, including Capt. J. J. McBride of the 5th Texas, brought along their personal slaves (Levi Miller account, *The Daily News-Record*, Harrisonburg, VA, Jun. 18, 1915).

33 For details, see John E. Clark, Jr., *Railroads in the Civil War: The Impact of Management on Victory and Defeat* (Baton Rouge, LA: 2001). Only five of Longstreet's nine brigades arrived in time to participate in the battle of Chickamauga. Longstreet's artillery, under Col. Edward Porter Alexander, did not arrive in Dalton, Georgia (about 12 miles from Chickamauga), until five days after the battle.

Postwar image of Pvt. Lawrence A. Daffan, 4th Texas Infantry. (*Courtesy of Andy Smith*)

Private Alfred C. Sims of the 1st Texas recalled that "General Hood met us at the depot and made us a short speech from the platform, but he did not tell us where we were going. About which there were many conjectures." The Texans profusely cheered Hood, whose left arm was still tightly bandaged in a sling from his severe Gettysburg wound. Several soldiers urged the injured general to join them for the trip; he agreed to do so and took a later train. The previous evening, in the camp of the 3rd Arkansas, those soldiers had similarly shouted, "Come on General Hood, go with us. No battle without General Hood!"[34]

The trains conveying Benning's Georgians south to Petersburg pulled out first, followed by Robertson's Texans and Arkansans. The last of Hood's trains to depart Richmond in the first wave carried Law's Alabama brigade. Behind them, the rest of Longstreet's forces were heading to Richmond. Men crowded on top of the cars, cheering "as if on a picnic" as they passed groups of bystanders. "We were simply loaded in and on trains of boxcars and sent flying to the west as fast as the worn-out rolling stock of the railroads could carry us over the rough and dangerous tracks," wrote Cpl. Miles V. "Pony" Smith of the 4th Texas. Longstreet's chief of staff, Lt. Col. G. Moxley Sorrel, complained, "Never before were such crazy cars—passenger, baggage, mail, coal, box, platform, all and every sort wobbling on the jumping strap-iron—used for hauling good soldiers." Many soldiers peered at the populace as they passed through Southern towns. According to the 1st Texas's Cpl. Orlando T. Hanks, the crowds lacked any men other than "an old grandsire or

34 George T. Todd and Harold B. Simpson, eds., *First Texas Regiment* (Waco, TX: 1963), 17; A. C. Sims, "1st Texas Infantry Regiment," circa 1909, Hood's Texas Brigade Files, Texas Heritage Museum–Historical Research Center, Hill College, Hillsboro; Calvin Collier, *"They'll Do to Tie To!" The Story of the Third Regiment, Arkansas Infantry, C.S.A.* (Little Rock, AR: 1961), 154.

wounded soldier, his arm in a sling, or hopping on his crutches, at home on a furlough."[35]

One young Texan learned that his regiment had left Virginia without him, so he hustled to catch up to avoid charges of desertion. Eighteen-year-old Pvt. Lawrence A. Daffan of the 4th Texas had been visiting cousins who lived 12 miles east of Fredericksburg. "One warm September evening," Daffan recalled, "we saw the dust rising down the main road, and we slipped around to see what it was. We went through the corn . . . to see what was coming. The army was moving." The lads went closer for a better look. "The first brigade was Benning's, of Georgia; the second was Law's, of Alabama; and the third was Hood's Texas Brigade, my brigade. I saw the Fifth Texas pass, then came the Fourth, my regiment, and I wondered where they were going." Daffan proceeded at once to Richmond, where he learned the brigade had left for Georgia. He reported to the provost marshal, who understood the circumstances and gave the young soldier transportation and rations to Resaca, Georgia.[36]

The deplorable condition of many of the railroads compounded the arduous task of transferring the bulk of Longstreet's Corps to Georgia. "In those days the Southern railroads were but lightly built & equipped, &c.," Lt. Col. E. Porter Alexander of Longstreet's artillery asserted after the war; "[N]ow, for two years they had been cut off from all sorts of supplies of railroad material but what their own small shops could produce. Naturally, therefore, the movement of our corps, considered in the light of modern railroading, was very slow." He added, "Preference was given to the infantry—or at least to Hood's & McLaws' divisions." Alexander's guns would not leave Petersburg until September 17.[37]

Intelligence reports on the Confederate movements began to arrive at the war department in Washington. Leading Northern newspapers picked up the story within days. There was "scarcely a doubt that Lee's Army is being depleted to reinforce Beauregard and Bragg," the New York Times mentioned on September 11. According to correspondent Lorenzo L. Crounsee, "Longstreet's corps has

35 M. V. Smith, "Historical Reminiscences Conducted by J. B. Polley, Floresville, Texas," *San Antonio Daily Express*, Dec. 5, 1909; G. Moxley Sorrel, *Reflections of a Confederate Staff Officer* (New York and Washington: 1905), 189; "O. T. Hanks Reminiscences, 1861-1865," 1918, Dolph Briscoe Center for American History, University of Texas at Austin. Kershaw's South Carolina brigade departed White Oak Station on Sept. 15.

36 *Waxahachie* (TX) *Daily Light*, Feb. 16, 1907. Daffan rejoined the regiment in time for the third day of fighting at Chickamauga on Sept. 20.

37 Gallagher, ed., *Fighting for the Confederacy*, 286.

been ordered west and south, the largest portion of it going to General Bragg, and the balance probably to Charleston. A division of this corps moved from their camp near Fredericksburg on Tuesday morning, 8th inst., at 3 o'clock, and it was generally understood among the private soldiers that it was going to Charleston."[38]

More than 200 miles south of Alexander's 26-gun battalion, Hood's Texas Brigade was now in North Carolina. While stopped at a railroad intersection in Weldon, the Corsicana Guards of the 4th Texas encountered a large group of Tar Heel soldiers on another train heading south. Almost a thousand barrels of sticky resin rested on the ground nearby. Some Texans began tossing handfuls of it at the North Carolinians, who angrily loaded their weapons in response. "It was all the officers could do to stop it," Pvt. James M. Polk observed; "if they hadn't intervened there would have been blood shed right there." From Weldon, the Texans passed through the verdant North Carolina countryside. "The train was heavily loaded and we traveled slow," Polk added. "Some were on top of the cars; one fellow playing a fiddle; and the fellow down in the car blowing a horn, all happy lords, yet knowing at the same time that we were going right into another big killing and many of us would go to our long homes." Some soldiers used their bayonets, knives, or swords to punch holes in the walls to ventilate the cramped boxcars. Eventually, they removed all the outer boards, leaving only the framework of the cars.[39]

The men of the 4th Texas subsisted on hardtack and uncooked bacon for most of the journey. It was a grueling trip for the regiment, including a lengthy stretch on the Wilmington and Weldon Railroad. In Sgt. J. B. Polley's words, "Save at Wilmington, N. C., where it stayed a day and night and made its only change of train, it had no relief between Richmond and Atlanta from the constant joltings of springless freight cars running over roadbeds made rough by constant usage, and

38 *New York Times*, Sept. 11, 1863. Crounsee, a daring front-line reporter, had lost the use of an arm in 1862 after being struck by a Confederate shell fragment. He also had two horses shot from under him during the war.

39 J. M. Polk, *Memories of the Lost Cause; and Ten Years in South America* (Austin, TX: 1907), 18-19. The Texans took the Petersburg Railroad from Virginia south to Weldon, where most transferred to the Wilmington and Weldon Railroad to journey south through Wilmington and Florence to Kingsville, South Carolina. Polk's train went west and then north, indicating that his group likely used the alternative route through Raleigh, Charlotte, and Columbia to Kingsville. From Kingsville, all the troop trains used the single track through Augusta to Atlanta before heading north to Catoosa Platform near Ringgold.

seldom repaired." Polley lamented the loss of his knapsack and number 3 cloth gaiters that another soldier stole from him during an unguarded moment.[40]

After arriving in Wilmington on September 11, eleven Texans visited a seedy waterfront area known as "Paddy's Hollow." They soon became drunk and unruly. After three municipal guardsmen arrived to regain control, Robertson's boys staggered forward in a ragged charge. A rather one-sided melee ensued. One Texan clubbed a guardsman on the side of the head and savagely beat another, while a third local received two non-lethal stab wounds to his ribcage. The trio of North Carolinians prudently withdrew, and the victorious Texans resumed their partying.[41]

A handful of unfortunate Texans never made it to their intended destination. Praised for bravery at the battle of Sharpsburg, Dr. Andrew C. Crombie, the assistant surgeon of the 1st Texas, suffered life-threatening injuries in a train wreck while on his way to Georgia. The 4th Texas's Dr. A. J. Scott died after falling off a moving railcar. Far less tragic but of tactical importance on the battlefield, Capts. Clinton M. Winkler and William H. "Howdy" Martin of the 4th Texas did not arrive until after Chickamauga. The absence of these experienced line officers meant that their respective first lieutenants would command Companies I and K during the fighting.[42]

The lengthy rail journey to Georgia was far more mundane for most other Texans. "Nothing of interest occurred on the trip except at every depot crowds of ladies were to be seen with flowers, refreshments, etc.," recalled an enthused Pvt. Robert Campbell of the 5th Texas. "At night bonfires were built along the railroad. Everybody appeared to be overflowing with patriotism." At times, the crowded troop train steamed past passenger trains at rail sidings. Citizens in fine clothes poked their heads from the windows to converse with the passing soldiers. "We would employ ourselves by obtaining their fine important hats off their heads as

40 Polley, *Hood's Texas Brigade*, 198-199; J. B. Polley, *A Soldier's Letters to Charming Nellie* (New York and Washington, DC: 1908), 140.

41 "Assault on the Guard," *Wilmington Daily Express*, Sept. 17, 1863, citing the *Daily Journal*, Sept. 11, 1863. Located north of today's Red Cross Street, Paddy's Hollow contained more than three dozen saloons.

42 *Augusta Constitutionalist*, Sept. 16, 1863; Harold B. Simpson, *Hood's Texas Brigade: A Compendium* (Hillsboro, TX: 1977), 557; Harold B. Simpson, ed., *Touched with Valor: Civil War Papers and Casualty Reports of Hood's Texas Brigade* (Hillsboro, TX: 1964), 77; R. H. Bassett to John H. Reagan, Sept. 26, 1863, Chickamauga-Chattanooga National Military Park (CCNMP). A. C. Crumbie was killed in March 1864 after returning to duty with the regiment, according to his CSR documents in the National Archives.

they put these out the windows to see and question us," Campbell continued. "They would find their hats gone for when they looked around—behold! Their hats were fully on the heads of the 'dirty soldiers' (as they called us), who was flying away at [the] Rail Road spur."[43]

A train carrying the 4th Texas paused at Sumter, South Carolina, where local ladies and some refugees from Charleston served a sumptuous feast to the soldiers. Despite having only 15 minutes for the stop, the Texans enjoyed the repast. One latecomer had no such fortune. "By the time I got to the table it was crowded to overflowing and I found myself completely cut off from a plate," he moaned as he watched his comrades "act the hog." A lady with a pretty smile offered him a cold sweet potato, which he ate even though he did not like them. He was more grateful when a nearby gentleman handed him a cigar.[44]

Private John C. West and some of his companions in the 4th Texas's "Lone Star Guards" had permission to leave their train in Columbia, South Carolina. They spent two days in the capital city before boarding another train to catch up to their regiment. West used the opportunity to have his clothing washed to rid it of the vermin that "skirmish at will over the soldier's body," and soon "fell in love with South Carolina's hospitality." He continued, "At every depot and station throughout the state the ladies, old and young, flocked in loaded with baskets of provisions, fruits and delicacies of every character which these scant times afford, which were offered amid smiles and tears and expressions of congratulations and encouragement to every soldier. Rags and dirt seemed to be a recommendation where gilt and brass failed to excite attention."[45]

According to South Carolina diarist Mary Chesnut, whose husband was an aide to Jefferson Davis, "At Kingsville, I caught a glimpse of our army. Longstreet's Corps was going west. . .. It was a strange sight—one part of it. There were miles, apparently, of platform cars, soldiers rolled in their blankets, lying in rows, heads all covered, fast asleep. In their grey blankets, packed in regular order, they looked like

43 Skoch and Perkins, *Lone Star Confederate*, 96; Joe Joskins (penname of Robert Campbell), *A Sketch of Hood's Texas Brigade of the Virginia Army* (1865), Rare Books Collection, University of Texas–San Antonio, 139.

44 See Clark, *Railroads in the Civil War*, for details.

45 John C. West, *A Texan in Search of a Fight: Civil War Diary and Letters of a Soldier in Hood's Texas Brigade* (Waco, TX: 1901), 110-111.

swathed mummies." An awful feeling of depression came over Chesnut. "All these fine fellows were going to kill or be killed," she thought.[46]

A Branchville and Columbia Railroad train carrying members of the 5th Texas paused in Orangeburg, South Carolina. Private Rufus K. Felder of Company E, the "Dixie Blues," had a pass to visit family and friends who lived there. "I was proud to see the reception given us by the ladies as the cars stopped," the youthful Felder later informed his mother in Chappell Hill, Texas. "They had gathered at the depot in numbers & showered the potatoes and bread in the cars which was very acceptable to our hungry boys. They all say if they ever get wounded, they will go to Orangeburg." The train slowly steamed out of town for Atlanta, leaving Felder to enjoy his prolonged visit with his paternal kin. He would miss the fighting at Chickamauga, as would dozens of other furloughed soldiers.[47]

On September 13, the first of Robertson's men arrived in Atlanta, where they found Benning's Georgians camped along the tracks. Benning had to wait for Gregg's and McNair's brigades to pass through town, and the resultant traffic jam delayed his departure on the single line to Ringgold by a full day. General Bragg began hearing reports that the vanguard of the Army of Northern Virginia troops was now in Atlanta, but he remained uncertain as to when the rest of Longstreet's men would get there. The Texans and Arkansans drew several days' rations of hardtack and salted pork, and they rested until recalled to the trains for the 115-mile final leg of the journey on the Western and Atlantic Railroad. On the evening of September 17, the lead elements of the 1st Texas detrained at a burnt bridge over South Chickamauga Creek near Catoosa Platform. They were about three miles southeast of Ringgold, the home of several military hospitals established earlier in the year. Other trainloads of Hood's fragmented division reached Catoosa over the next several hours, and General Hood himself was due the following day at noontime. Few men knew of his impending arrival. Their corps commander, Lt. Gen. James Longstreet, would get there until the next day. A handful of men, including Pvt. R. W. Blalock of the 1st Texas, were ill and needed hospitalization.

46 Mary Boykin Chesnut, *A Diary from Dixie*, edited by Isabella D. Martin and Myrta Lockett Avary (New York and London: 1914), 241.

47 Stephen Chicoine, ed., "'Willing Never to Go in Another Fight': The Civil War Correspondence of Rufus King Felder of Chappell Hill," *SHQ*, vol. 106, Jul. 2002–Apr. 2003, 587-589. Felder had moved to Texas with his widowed mother and siblings in 1855 when he was 15 years old. His brother-in-law, Thomas Elliott of the 24th Texas Cavalry, Deshler's brigade, died at Chickamauga.

Stephen's Gap on Lookout Mountain as seen from McLemore's Cove. (*Scott Mingus*)

Private Robert Campbell and the other early arrivals rested and prepared three days' rations, realizing that a battle loomed.[48]

The prospect of a significant fight weighed heavily that night on many of Braxton Bragg's Confederates that night. They knew they would soon meet Rosecrans's Army of the Cumberland on the battlefield once again. Reports circulated that the Yankees had crossed the Tennessee River and were pouring through the passes on Raccoon and Lookout Mountains. Despite the intervening months, several Texans still had vivid memories of the horrors of Murfreesboro. "It is true that when I reflect that this may possibly be the last day's entry in my journal," Sgt. William Heartsill of Deshler's 10th Texas fretted, "I feel a strange and inexpressible dread of the morrow." He was not alone in that unsettling sentiment.[49]

48 Collier, *They'll Do to Tie To!*, 154; Skoch and Perkins, *Lone Star Confederate*, 96; *Atlanta Daily Intelligencer*, Oct. 1, 1863; CSR for R. W. Blalock, 1st Texas, RG109, M323 (Texas, roll 0246), NARA. Catoosa Platform was nothing more than a wooden platform along the track serving the nearby Catoosa Springs resort. The Confederates had turned the area into a large supply depot and the resort into a hospital.

49 Heartsill, *Fourteen Hundred and 91 Days*, 150.

Chapter 3

September 18— The Battle for the Bridges

With the recent welcome reinforcements to his army, Braxton Bragg now fielded approximately 60,000 soldiers. Lieutenant General James Longstreet was still en route on the railroads, along with additional men who over the next day or two would bring the army's total to 65,000. Bragg formed a provisional division under Brig. Gen. Bushrod R. Johnson from the recent arrivals at Ringgold. That new command consisted of Johnson's own Tennessee brigade (temporarily under Col. John S. Fulton), Brig. Gen. Evander McNair's brigade from Arkansas and North Carolina, and Brig. Gen. John Gregg's Tennessee brigade, which included the 177 men of the veteran 7th Texas. All told, Johnson commanded 3,755 men, most of whom had considerable combat experience.[1]

Bragg gathered his chief subordinates on the morning of September 15 at his headquarters in La Fayette and informed them that he planned to attack Rosecrans's scattered forces. He wanted to push across West Chickamauga Creek north of the Union positions at Lee and Gordon's Mills (a grist mill and attached

1 "Gregg's Brigade at Chickamauga." Strength numbers are from David A. Powell, *The Chickamauga Campaign: A Mad Irregular Battle: From the Crossing of Tennessee River through the Second Day, August 22–September 19, 1863* (El Dorado Hills, CA: 2014), 227; K. M. Van Zandt to My Dear Wife, Sept. 28, 1863, Van Zandt Family Papers, Marshall, TX.

A native of Ohio, Brig. Gen. Bushrod Johnson commanded an improvised "provisional brigade" in the Army of Tennessee. (*Library of Congress*)

general store and nearby sawmill along West Chickamauga Creek about 15 miles north of La Fayette). Seizing the Chattanooga–La Fayette Road would cut the Federals off from Chattanooga and force them to attack Bragg after his army entrenched. The next day, he distributed Special Orders No. 245 to his corps commanders, exhorting his soldiers to march against the enemy and crush him.

For various reasons, that plan failed to come to fruition until the 18th, giving Rosecrans time to concentrate his army by the night of September 17. Rosecrans's left, comprised of Maj. Gen. Thomas L. Crittenden's XXI Corps, rested near Lee and Gordon's Mills. Two other corps stretched to the west and south through McLemore's Cove and along the base of Lookout Mountain, with his reserve corps just south of Chattanooga at Rossville. "Old Rosey" and his trusted chief of staff, future President James A. Garfield, established army headquarters in the hilltop Gordon-Lee Mansion overlooking Crawfish Springs. A lengthy telegraph line back to Chattanooga provided communication with the war department in Washington. Assistant Secretary of War Charles A. Dana, who had recently arrived to accompany the Army of the Cumberland as an "observer," periodically wired dispatches to his superior, Edwin Stanton.[2]

About 1:00 a.m. on September 18, Bragg, from his new headquarters at Leet's Tanyard, sent orders for Walker's and Buckner's corps to cross Chickamauga Creek by 6:30 a.m., while his other forces also advanced against Crittenden. He wanted to crush the XXI Corps and control the La Fayette and Dry Valley Roads leading to Missionary Ridge and beyond to Chattanooga. That success would force

2 *OR* 30, pt. 2, 37-38, 76. James Gordon owned much of the land around the mill complex until his death earlier in 1863. His son-in-law, James Lee, was the miller. The restored mill is about 12 miles south of Chattanooga and 12 miles west of Catoosa Platform.

Wartime image of Lee and Gordon's Mill. (*Library of Congress*)

Rosecrans's remnants to retreat southwest into the mountains, and Bragg could retake the city at his leisure. He wanted Leonidas Polk's corps to divert the Federal left flank near Lee and Gordon's Mills while D. H. Hill's Corps anchored the army's left. Joe Wheeler's cavalry, including the 8th and 11th Texas, would screen Polk and Hill. Forrest's cavalry was to perform the same function on the far right. From north to south, Bragg planned to have Bushrod Johnson's provisional division cross the creek at Reed's Bridge; Walker's Reserve Corps (including Ector's brigade with the 9th Texas and the dismounted 10th, 14th, and 32nd Texas Cavalry) at Alexander's Bridge; Buckner's Corps at Thedford's Ford; and Polk's Corps at Dalton's Ford. Deep and swift-flowing, the steep-banked, meandering West Chickamauga Creek was largely impassable except for the scattered fords and bridges.[3]

3 Sullivan, *Chickamauga and Chattanooga Battlefields*, 14-15. Arthur Leet, an Irish-born Methodist minister, owned the large tanyard and mill about eight miles southwest of Ringgold. On the morning of Sept. 18, Bragg moved his headquarters there.

Modern view of the restored Lee and Gordon's Mill. (*Scott Mingus*)

Unknown to Bragg, his adversary was not idle. Rosecrans had recently moved Maj. Gen. George H. "Pap" Thomas's XIV Corps northeasterly to the defensible ground behind and to the left of Crittenden. The Virginia-born Thomas's four divisions guarded the La Fayette Road to the west of Reed's Bridge. Major General Alexander McCook's XX Corps moved through McLemore's Cove, with Maj. Gen. Gordon Granger's reserves in position to support Thomas and Crittenden in case of a Rebel attack. Part of Col. Robert H. G. Minty's brigade of veteran cavalrymen guarded Reed's Bridge. The mounted infantrymen of Col. John T. Wilder's "Lightning Brigade" and their feared seven-shot Spencer repeating rifles screened the crossings between Alexander's Bridge and Lee and Gordon's Mills.[4]

4 Ibid.

Modern view of Crawfish Springs at Chickamauga, Georgia. (*Scott Mingus*)

The Attack on Pea Vine Bridge
September 18

Dawn came at 6:03 on a chilly Saturday, September 18, in northern Georgia. By then, Bushrod Johnson's provisional division, along with three artillery batteries recently assigned to him, had been on the road for an hour. Bragg had previously instructed Johnson to march south via Pleasant Grove Church to Leet's Tanyard and then turn north toward Alexander's Bridge. Johnson, the Quaker-educated son of an ardent Ohio abolitionist, had marched at 5:00 a.m. toward Bragg's headquarters. After tramping some three miles, one of Bragg's staff officers intercepted the column and informed Johnson of the change in plans. He now was to cross Reed's Bridge, about six miles due west of Ringgold, and then turn to the south and sweep up West Chickamauga Creek to Lee and Gordon's Mills. Johnson dutifully countermarched to Ringgold and turned his long column, with Fulton's

Maj. Gen. George H. Thomas commanded the XIV Corps of the Army of the Cumberland. (*Library of Congress*)

brigade in the lead, onto Reed's Bridge Road. Great clouds of thick, choking dust soon blanketed the procession, which was now well behind schedule because of the unplanned, extra six-mile round trip. Bragg's assistant artillery officer overtook the column with a message to push on vigorously and engage the enemy force regardless of its strength.[5]

A few miles behind Johnson, at Catoosa Platform, John Bell Hood's division of Longstreet's Corps was preparing to march. General Hood was not present; his train was due to arrive about noon. Brigadier General Evander M. Law now temporarily led the division, with Col. James Sheffield assuming command of Law's brigade. The transplants from the Army of Northern Virginia, beginning with Brig. Gen. Jerome B. Robertson's 1,300-man brigade, were to follow Johnson to Reed's Bridge. Most of the 3rd Arkansas had arrived early that morning, joining the three Texas regiments. Brigadier General Henry L. "Rock" Benning's 1,200 Georgians had orders to stay behind and guard the stores at Catoosa Platform. Sheffield's 2,000 Alabamians, unable to prepare rations before they left Virginia, finally did so. Robertson's Texans and Arkansans, each carrying only their rifle-muskets and 40 rounds of ammunition, filed into a column and began marching to Ringgold.[6]

Several of Robertson's men were still on incoming trains and would not arrive until the next day or later. John C. West, the 4th Texas private who had taken a furlough at Columbia during the train ride from Virginia, overtook his regiment at dawn at the burnt bridge just past Catoosa Platform. He found his comrades "all astir and making ready to move. I had no time to rest; but marched off immediately, passing Ringgold between eight and nine o'clock in the morning." Some of Brig. Gen. Nathan Bedford Forrest's cavalrymen joined Robertson's column at Ringgold.[7]

5 *OR* 30, pt. 2, 3; Powell, *A Mad Irregular Battle*, 231; "Report of Brig. Gen. B. R. Johnson," *Southern Historical Society Papers* (*SHSP*) (Richmond, VA: 1895), vol. 13, 393-394. Everett's (9th Georgia), Bledsoe's (1st Missouri), and Culpeper's (South Carolina) batteries were assigned to Johnson. For a good biography of Johnson, see LeRoy H. Fischer, *Yankee Quaker, Confederate General: The Curious Case of Bushrod Rust Johnson* (Kent, OH: 1971).

6 Skoch and Perkins, *Lone Star Confederate*, 96; *Reminiscences of Rev. N. C. Denson—Co. H., 3rd Arkansas*, unpublished manuscript, Hood's Texas Brigade Files, CCNMP. Per Bragg's instructions, Forrest was supposed to screen Johnson's advance, but instead was still in the rear.

7 West, *A Texan in Search of a Fight*, 111.

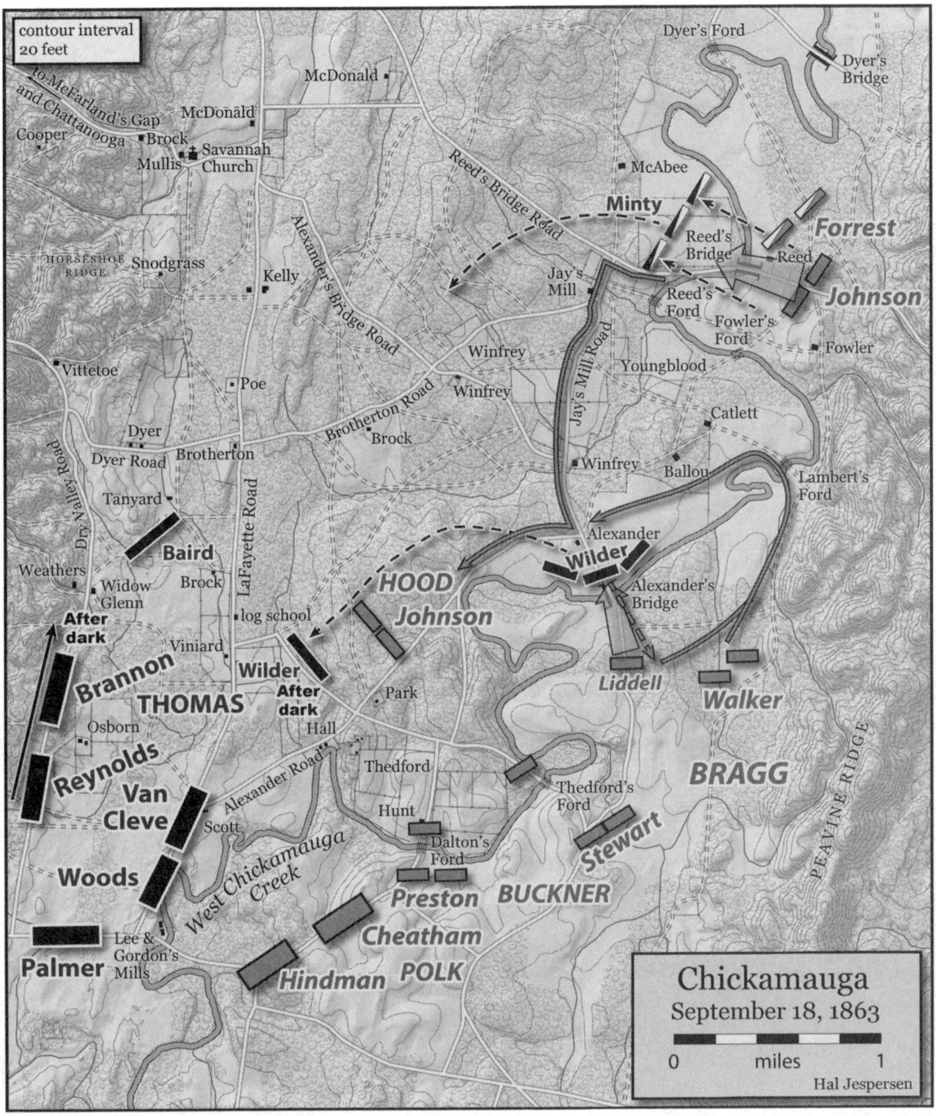

"Here we first heard of Yanks ahead, and putting out flankers moved on cautiously and slowly," Private West recorded. Just outside Ringgold, Pvt. Alfred C. Sims of the 1st Texas received an unusual order that may have saved his life. "We had gone about three miles when General Robertson sent word to Col. [Philip A.] Work to send him a bare-footed man," he later explained. "I being bare-footed and convalescent, Col. Work ordered me to report to Gen. Robertson at the head of the brigade, which I did." Robertson ordered Sims to go back to divisional headquarters at Tunnel Hill and tell the commissary officer to have three days'

Maj. Gen. John Bell Hood led a division that was transferred from the Army of Northern Virginia to the Army of Tennessee. (*Library of Congress*)

rations cooked and forwarded to the brigade. Sims could rest and then return with the slow-moving wagons. He later reflected, "And then it was that I escaped one of the most bloody conflicts that Company F ever had to encounter." Colonel Work also did not accompany his regiment to the front. Exhausted from exposure and stress, he was suffering from what was termed "fatigue." Turning over command of the regiment to his senior captain, R. J. Harding, Work was evacuated to a hospital in the rear before heading to Selma, Alabama, to recuperate.[8]

The veterans of the Army of Northern Virginia got their first look at the challenging terrain in the Chickamauga region. The unimproved, red-dirt road to the creek passed through a relatively unbroken forest of scrub oak, pine, and cedar trees, intermixed with mature hardwood stands of oak and hickory. Vines, briar patches, thickets, and dense underbrush choked the thick woods. Occasionally, the Confederates tramped past modest farmsteads, a far cry from the spacious cultivated areas over which they had fought in Virginia, Maryland, and Pennsylvania thus far in the war. Fresh water was not plentiful other than a few small watercourses. A drought in northern Georgia had drained many of the available springs and wells. Clouds of dust hovered around the marching column, caking the soldiers and adding to their travail.

The 4th Texas's Sgt. J. B. Polley claimed that Robertson's men passed a column of Lt. Col. Gustave Cook's 8th Texas Cavalry. Hood's Texans and Terry's Texas Rangers warmly greeted one another along the roadside. Some of them had not seen their acquaintances and friends since their enlistments in 1861. "It was the

8 Ibid.; A. C. Sims, "1st Texas Infantry Regiment," Texas History Museum, Austin, TX (THM). Some accounts suggest that Work assigned Capt. David Rice, not Captain Harding, to command the 1st Texas. Work resigned from the army on Nov. 12, 1863.

first Texas command we had met since the beginning of the war," Polley recalled, "and as many of them were personally known to us, salutations were exchanged by the lifting of hats and the waving of handkerchiefs." He added, "Its victories many, its defeats few, we Texans of the Virginia army watched its career with an interest not felt in any other troops from our State. In sober truth, it was the only body of Texas cavalry which, emulating the bravery and heroism of Bonham, Travis, Crockett, and their compatriots in the Alamo, had won distinction, and for that reason the members of the First, Fourth and Fifth Texas recognized and hailed its members as kindred spirits."[9]

Shortly before 11:00 a.m., ahead of Robertson, Bushrod Johnson's vanguard approached Peeler's Mill on Pea Vine Creek, an insignificant stream two miles east of Reed's Bridge. A local "goober" on an old mule rode up and mentioned that the Yankees were "down thar on the creek and you'uns will be in to it mighty quick if you go down thar." The Georgia countryman was right. Captain Heber S. Thompson and a Union cavalry patrol were indeed near the creek. Spotting the oncoming Rebels, Thompson sent a messenger galloping back to Colonel Minty to inform him that the enemy was "coming in bunches." As Thompson skirmished with the 23rd Tennessee, the Irish-born Minty arranged about 600 of his men in a battle line on a wooded ridge 180-200 yards west of Pea Vine Creek. His force consisted of the 4th Michigan Cavalry, the 7th Pennsylvania Cavalry, three battalions of the 4th U.S. Cavalry, and a two-gun section of the Chicago Board of Trade Battery.

Uncertain of what lay ahead, Johnson halted his column near Rock Spring and deployed Col. John S. Fulton's Tennessee brigade into line. He sent Bledsoe's 1st Missouri Battery to duel with Minty's brace of guns. In all, Johnson had roughly 5,000 men available. Nathan Bedford Forrest soon arrived with the remnants of Brig. Gen. John Hunt Morgan's force that had raided southern Indiana and Ohio in the summer before surrendering. Few in number, the Kentucky and Tennessee troopers dismounted and joined Johnson's forward skirmish line. Forrest assumed overall command. He and Johnson did not realize they already outnumbered the Union cavalrymen, and additional help was on the way.[10]

9 Polley, Hood's Texas Brigade, 199-200. Despite Polley's remembrance, the 8th Texas Cavalry is not known to have been near Ringgold that day.

10 Johnson, *SHSP*, 394-395; *Pulaski* (TN) *Citizen*, Sept. 8, 1887. This was Johnson's former brigade, now under the command of Col. John S. Fulton. For an excellent account of the preliminary fighting on Sept. 18, see Powell, *A Mad Irregular Battle*, 225-268. Pea Vine Creek is

Earlier that morning, General Bragg had dispatched some of Maj. Felix H. Robertson's reserve artillery to support Hood's division. The Texas-born Robertson now led two batteries totaling eight guns from the vicinity of La Fayette toward Reed's Bridge. Approaching Pea Vine Bridge, Robertson's scouts discovered a large unidentified force in their front. Robertson accordingly halted the column and ordered his ranking subordinate, Capt. Charles L. Lumsden, "a fine officer," to come forward. Upon Lumsden's arrival, Major Robertson explained the reason for the halt and asked him to take command while he went out alone to investigate. Robertson assured Lumsden that he would not surrender without a fight. The 24-year-old Robertson walked alone toward the unknown force. He soon reached a point where he could see several distant men darting back and forth across the road. As he cautiously advanced, he heard a man cry out, "It is Felix." The voice belonged to his father, Jerome, the commander of Hood's Texans. After exchanging greetings, Felix took his guns to the front as the infantrymen stepped aside.[11]

Meanwhile, ahead of the two Robertsons, Bushrod Johnson sent Fulton's brigade across Pea Vine Creek. It took considerable time to cross the foliage-lined, waist-deep watercourse. Briar thickets in some of the surrounding fields slowed several barefooted Tennesseans. Fulton's Confederates toiled uphill on "very rough and uneven" ground toward Minty while their forward skirmishers repulsed a brief Union advance. Forrest's men methodically flanked the southern part of the Federal line on Pea Vine Ridge. Minty spotted a telltale dust cloud in the distance and believed that another enemy force was moving toward Dyer's Ford and/or Red House Bridge, the next two crossings of West Chickamauga Creek to the north. Minty had only a small detachment on picket duty at Dyer's Ford, so he appealed to Colonel Wilder to send reinforcements. Wilder accordingly dispatched the 72nd Indiana, 123rd Illinois, and two field pieces.[12]

While Colonel Minty prepared for the Rebels, Jerome Robertson's Texans were still off to the east trudging along Reed's Bridge Road. About noon, as the 4th

---

spelled Peavine Creek in some accounts. The name came from the many wild pea vines that grew along its banks.

11 "Felix Robertson Tells [of] Seeing Hood Wounded in the Thigh at the Battle of Chickamauga," *The Eagle* (Bryan, TX), Jun. 27, 1925; Foley, *Hood's Texas Division*, 39. Felix Robertson later became the only Texas-born soldier to attain the rank of general in the Confederate army.

12 *OR* 30, pt. 2, 488; Johnson, *SHSP*, 395. As it turned out, the threat was a phantom one; no Confederates were marching to either Dyer's Ford or the nearby Dyer's Bridge.

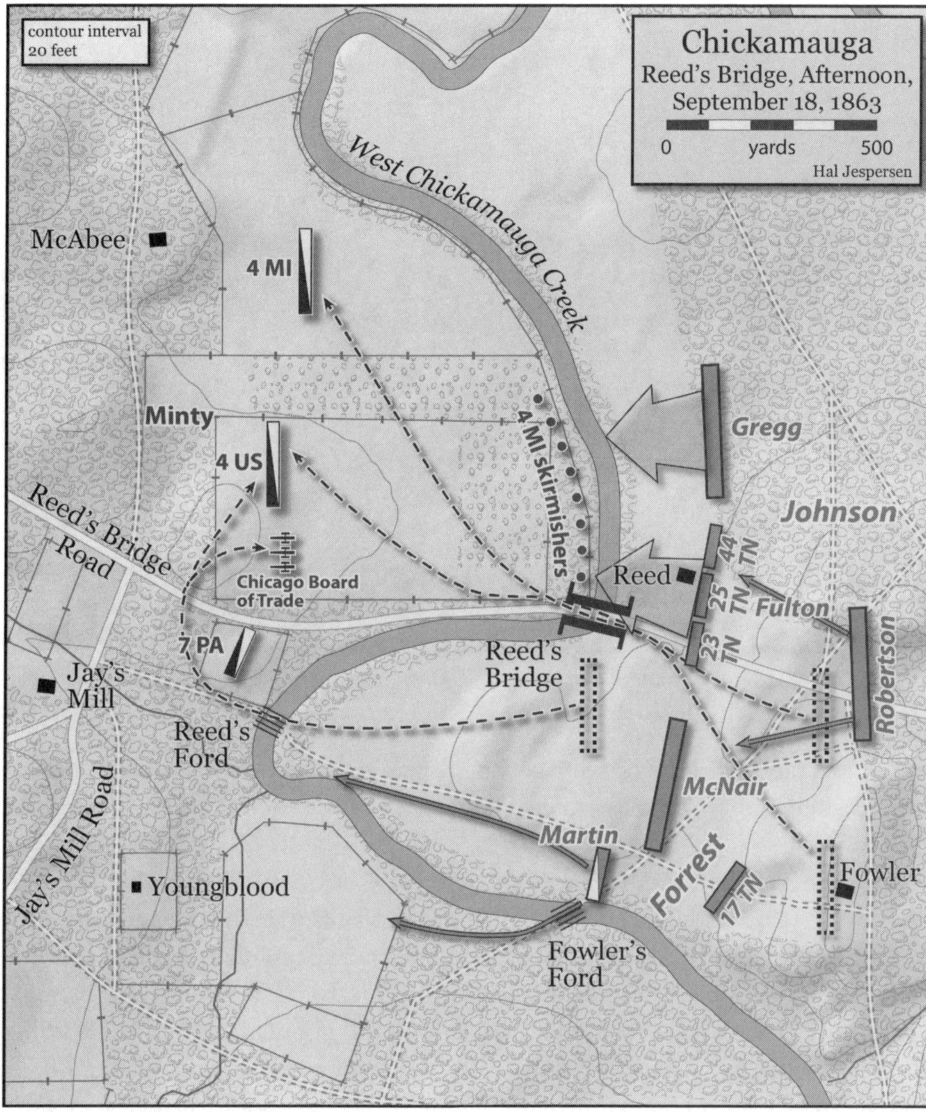

Texas passed through "quite a narrow defile," the 4th Texas's Pvt. John C. West recalled, "we heard considerable firing in front; here we were ordered to load and await orders. While here I saw citizens, men, women and children, hurrying to the rear. I saw one poor creature overloaded with coverlids, tin pans, cups, &c., with a child on each side and two or three bawling behind. She fell down three times, but still scrambled on for life, while the sputtering fire of the muskets in the surrounding hills was sounding in her ears." He added, "We soon moved off the road by the left flank and were drawn up and advanced in line of battle for about

Minty's Union cavalry crossing Reed's Bridge. (*National Park Service*)

half a mile and halted. We remained there awaiting developments while cavalry were dashing hither and thither, feeling the pulse of the enemy and discovering his positions."[13]

John Bell Hood, meanwhile, had arrived at Catoosa Platform and was on his way to locate Bushrod Johnson. After stepping off his train, he had ordered some nearby soldiers of the 2nd Georgia of Benning's brigade to dig entrenchments and rifle pits on the east side of the railroad to protect it from Union raiders. His sturdy roan, "Jeff Davis," leapt from the train, and Hood mounted and headed north to Ringgold, where he received an order from Bragg to proceed on the road to Reed's Bridge and assume command of the column. He was soon on his way. Felix Robertson's artillerymen first spotted the oncoming Hood. They refrained from giving him the customary shout of welcome, lest the noise alert the enemy. Every

13 John C. West, "Fourth Texas Infantry at Chattanooga," *Houston Weekly Telegraph*, Nov. 17, 1863; West, *A Texan in Search of a Fight*, 111-112. The newspaper published a letter from West to his brother, the details of which differ slightly from his later book.

man, however, lifted his hat in acknowledgment of Hood's surprise presence as he passed through the line to overtake Johnson.[14]

The Attack on Reed's Bridge

About noon, as Confederate pressure increased on his flanks, Colonel Minty slowly withdrew his force from Pea Vine Ridge and headed down the declivity west toward Reed's Bridge. He concealed the Chicago Board of Trade Battery's guns in some thick brush near the narrow wooden span and formed his cavalry to resist the Rebel advance. Johnson, meanwhile, reached the crest of Pea Vine Ridge, where he discovered three dead Yankees and another that was mortally wounded. He learned the opposition was only "three or four regiments of mounted men." Forrest swung to the south with his cavalry and the 17th Tennessee in order to flank the position and pillage what he believed was the Federal camp. While heading down the western slope of Pea Vine Ridge, Johnson saw Minty off in the distance and realized he could flank the smaller force. He ordered General Gregg to form his brigade into a battle line to Fulton's right. Rolling terrain and brush-choked stands of pine and oak slowed the Confederate advance.[15]

The hidden section of the Chicago Board of Trade Battery opened fire as Fulton's line of Tennesseans emerged from a gap at the foot of Pea Vine Ridge. Minty sent squadrons of the 4th Michigan and 7th Pennsylvania forward to engage the Rebels. Johnson reacted by deploying McNair's brigade into line to Fulton's left. Minty's two guns helped retard the slow but steady Confederate advance. Several miles away, the men of Deshler's brigade heard firing in the distance. "Occasionally, the terrible bursts of shells were heard," the 24th Texas Cavalry's Capt. Samuel T. Foster penned in his diary. "The cannon fire kept giving the ground a fair shake."[16]

14 Ibid.; John Bell Hood, *Advance and Retreat: Personal Experiences in the United States and Confederate States Armies* (New Orleans, LA: 1880), 61; J. C. Allen, "An Empty Sleeve," *Knoxville Daily Journal*, Jan. 24, 1890.

15 For an excellent account, see Eric J. Wittenberg, *Holding the Line on the River of Death: Union Mounted Forces at Chickamauga, September 18, 1863* (El Dorado Hills, CA: 2018).

16 Nick Barron, Jr., ed., "The Diary of Captain Samuel F. [sic] Foster, CSA," pg. 49, *Civil War Times Illustrated* Collection, USAHEC, Carlisle, PA. Samuel Thompson Foster, a 33-year-old South Carolina native, was an attorney and the chief justice of Live Oak County, Texas, before the war.

Alfred R. Waud sketch of Confederate artillery opening fire upon Minty's cavalrymen, who are dismantling Reed's Bridge. (*Library of Congress*)

Johnson's infantrymen slowly turned both Federal flanks. Colonel Minty withdrew his troopers across the creek using Reed's Bridge and Dyer's Ford to the north. Though the last of Minty's men to cross the bridge removed its floor planks and railings and tossed them into the creek, they did not have time to destroy the structure. Confederates from Fulton's 23rd Tennessee hastily repaired it using boards from the nearby Reed house and barn, ignoring pesky Yankee sharpshooters. After forming a new line about 700 yards west of the creek, Minty positioned his skirmishers out in front and awaited the Confederates.

General Hood arrived at Reed's Bridge about this time. "A small body of Federal cavalry was posted upon an eminence a short distance beyond," he recalled. "On my arrival upon the field I met for the first time after the charge at Gettysburg a portion of my old troops, who received me with a touching welcome." After exchanging pleasantries with General Johnson, Hood learned of his subordinate's plans and added a few touches of his own. The battle line was "to be broken by filing onto the road," and "a few picked men" would head to the front to support the skirmishers. He held Robertson's brigade in reserve southeast of McNair to protect the left flank.[17]

17 Hood, *Advance and Retreat*, 61; Johnson, *SHSP*, 395.

Major Felix Robertson soon unlimbered two guns to augment a section of Everett's battery of the 8th Georgia Artillery that was already in position to exchange fire with the two Chicago rifled guns. "We were answered promptly by the rebels with four pieces—I could see them when they loaded," one of Minty's Michigan cavalrymen recalled. During the ensuing exchange, a shell fragment killed an unidentified woman staying at Jacob and Sallie Reed's house. A mother of two, she was standing on the porch cheering on the 23rd Tennessee when she was hit. Johnson sent the rest of Fulton's Brigade forward to attack the forward Union skirmish line east of Reed's Bridge.[18]

Fulton's van crossed the creek shortly after 3:00 p.m. and drove off Minty's rearguard. Johnson brought up the rest of his division and crossed at the bridge and nearby ford. Forrest's troopers continued to the southwest to flank the Federals at Fowler's Ford. A soldier in the 7th Texas later stated that when the Yankees made their final stand, "we charged at a double quick." It was not Confederate pressure alone, however, that led to Minty's subsequent withdrawal.[19]

The colonel had learned that Wilder had been outflanked at Alexander's Bridge and had removed the planks from the decking before withdrawing toward Lee and Gordon's Mills. Minty followed suit shortly before 5:00 p.m., leaving the west bank uncontested. With their way clear, Johnson's men paused and reformed. Some of Robertson's Texans later took more credit than was due for the hard-earned victory. "We were hurried from the trains into line of battle," Capt. George Todd of the 1st Texas recalled. "We advanced some miles that evening, crossed Chickamauga creek, and routed the enemy in our front." A few men were more pragmatic. "We ran into some Federal cavalry and knocked some of them off their horses," the 5th Texas's Pvt. James M. Polk wrote; "some of our men secured new cavalry hats."[20]

18 *Pulaski* (TN) *Citizen*, Sept. 8, 1887; *The Eagle* (Bryan, TX), June 27, 1925. Robertson later stated that Forrest gave him the order to fire; Hood claimed he had done so. The Reed family later said the first cannon to fire at Chickamauga was in their yard. See Randall Franks, "Battle of Chickamauga: Civil War: Catoosa's Bloodiest Days," accessed Dec. 19, 2019, www.cityofringgoldga.gov/BattleofChickamauga.aspx.

19 D. H. Haines, "Records of the 4th Michigan Cavalry," Bentley Historical Library, University of Michigan; "Gregg's Brigade at Chickamauga," *Galveston Weekly News*, Nov. 11, 1863; *Pulaski Citizen*, Sept. 8, 1887. Several soldiers in the 10th Alabama suffered severe stings from yellow jackets while wading the creek.

20 Todd, *First Texas Regiment*, 17-18; Polk, *The Confederate Soldier*, 23. Elements of Walker's Reserve Corps pushed Wilder back, despite the Union troopers' use of their Spencer repeating

The Evening March to Alexander's Bridge Road

With Minty finally out of the way, Johnson's division and Robertson's Texas Brigade advanced a quarter of a mile south to William Jay's steam-powered sawmill. Just past the wood-frame building, Johnson planned to turn southwest (right) on Brotherton Road and head for the La Fayette Road to connect with Walker's reserve division. This was the shortest route from the mill to that key road. Instead, General Hood ordered the column to use the narrow Jay's Mill Road to connect farther south with Alexander's Bridge Road. One of Gregg's regiments took the lead in a wide battle line with the rest of the command trailing in a dusty column of companies. Some of Forrest's available cavalrymen screened the T-shaped formation's vulnerable right flank and the trailing wagon train.[21]

Minty's withdrawing troopers offered only token resistance. "We moved on about two miles," the 4th Texas's Pvt. John C. West wrote, "and were again formed in the line of battle and advanced about half a mile across some very pretty little fields, with hills on the opposite side, suggesting the idea of sharpshooters, &c.; indeed we all expected a volley every moment and went through all the fears and motions incident to a charge. We were much relieved at finding only some cavalry who discharged a few shots too high to hit anybody and disappeared without a shot from our side."[22]

At the smoldering ruins of the Alexander house, Hood turned to the southwest on Alexander-Viniard Road and moved through the forested bottomland west of the creek. Private Robert Campbell of the 5th Texas noted, "As we marched along, we would come to a burning house; nearby could be seen a mother with her little children clustered around her—tears streaming from their eyes. Their all was swept in flames." Confederate artillery fire had set their home ablaze during Walker's earlier advance against Wilder.[23]

---

rifles. Ector's Brigade was in reserve in the third line of the attack. Buckner's pioneers later replaced the planks on Alexander's Bridge.

21 Foley, *Hood's Texas Division*, 39; Johnson, *SHSP*, 396; Golden and Taylor, "Chickamauga—An Introduction," accessed Dec. 18, 2019, www.ourgeorgiahistory.com/wars/Civil_War/Chickamauga/chickamauga_01.html.

22 West, *A Texan in Search of a Fight*, 112.

23 Skoch and Perkins, *Lone Star Confederate*, 96; *Pulaski Citizen*, Sept. 8, 1887. Note that according to Dave Powell, "The Alexander cabin was unoccupied at the time, and no one had lived there for nearly a year, since the owner fled to avoid a murder charge. James Gordon's

Trouble awaited John Bell Hood at dusk. Scouts from Wilder's Lightning Brigade spotted the Rebel column coming down the road two-and-a-half miles south of Jay's Mill. Colonel Wilder halted his mounted infantrymen and hastily formed a battle line facing to the northeast and stretching perpendicular to the Confederates from Tabler and Ann Viniard's property to Thedford's Ford. An hour passed as Hood formed his plan of attack and deployed most of Gregg's Brigade into a line parallel to Wilder just west of the Park house. Gregg's 44th Tennessee protected the wagon train as a rear guard. Bushrod Johnson positioned Fulton's Brigade to Gregg's right, with McNair in a second line behind them. Robertson's men were to McNair's right rear, facing northwest. Additional Union troops from Col. George Dick's brigade of Wood's division soon arrived to join Wilder and Minty. It was almost 9:00 p.m. before the Confederates stepped off through the timber. The Buckeyes of the 59th Ohio waited until Col. Hiram Granbury's 7th Texas came within 50 yards, and then fired a sudden volley that sent the Southerners scattering for cover. Three Texans fell wounded; Sgt. William P. Sanders suffered mortal injuries. "The whole Yankee army was in our front—mainly at Lee and Gordon's mill—on our right flank and rear," Bushrod Johnson believed, "while our army was still on the east side of the Chickamauga."[24]

Hood decided against risking a general engagement in the darkness. "We bivouacked in line, near a beautiful residence which had been fired by the enemy, and then almost burned to the ground," he wrote. Robertson's Brigade, still in battle line, rested in the woods and fields along the Alexander-Viniard Road, some 800 yards east of the Viniard house and the La Fayette Road. Hood required a third of his men to stay awake while the remainder slept on their arms. The Confederates could hear the distant sound of the Yankees cutting down trees to construct breastworks. The 4th Texas's Private West related, "Judging by moving of troops and rumbling of artillery during the night. I felt pretty sure that 'the wool-tearing' would come off in the morning." To prepare for that eventuality, the Confederates hastily constructed obstructions in their front to slow down any enemy cavalry.

---

slaves were farming the land." The identities of the sobbing woman and her children remain unknown.

24 Peter Cozzens, *This Terrible Sound: The Battle of Chickamauga* (Urbana, IL: 1992), 113-114; K. M. Van Zandt to My Dear Wife, Sept. 28, 1863, Van Zandt Family Papers, Marshall, TX. Sergeant Sanders died the next morning. Another soldier in the 7th Texas suffered a severe head wound but lived.

Johnson sent skirmishers into an open field east of the Viniard house and dispatched scouts as close to the La Fayette Road as prudent.[25]

During the night, part of the 69th Ohio, from Col. Daniel McCook's brigade of the Reserve Corps, unexpectedly captured 22 Confederates, including the entire eight-member brass band of Hood's division. McCook's men had arrived earlier in the day after Minty had called for reinforcements. Now, in the darkness, the unsuspecting Confederate musicians walked into the Buckeyes' camp a hundred yards from the intersection of Reed's Bridge and Jay's Mill Roads. "Well, I'll be d—n! Where did you fellows come from?" a startled Confederate uttered before surrendering. A handful of surgeons of McNair's brigade made the same mistake, as did other stragglers and rear-echelon troops. The sullen prisoners included a major, whose fine horse was presented to "Colonel Dan." McCook, after interrogating the captives, believed that McNair's brigade was isolated on the west side of the creek.[26]

Meanwhile, Brig. Gen. Matthew Ector's brigade, part of Walker's reserve division, crossed West Chickamauga Creek at Byram's Ford after discovering that Wilder's Union cavalrymen had partially dismantled Alexander's Bridge. "[The Yankees] succeeded in their work, not however until they were severely chastised," Cpl. Robert C. Graves of the 32nd Texas Cavalry recalled. "They left on the opposite bank some 20 or 30 dead soldiers. It was one of those waspy, ten-minute fights in lightning order. It is one of the kind that gets a soldier in about the same condition that a cub wolf would be with a pack of hounds in close pursuit—SKEART [scared]." According to Graves, the brigade marched along the creek in a four- or five-mile round trip before returning to where the dead Federals lay. The Texans then made their evening camp near the ruins of the Alexander house.[27]

September 18 had been mild during the daylight hours, but the temperature unexpectantly plunged below freezing overnight. "At 10 P. M. we lay down to rest, having thrown out our pickets," the 5th Texas's Private Campbell reported. Several

25 Susannah J. Ural, *Hood's Texas Brigade: The Soldiers and Families of the Confederacy's Most Celebrated Unit* (Baton Rouge, LA: 2017), 187; Hood, *Advance and Retreat*, 61; Johnson, *SHSP*, 396; West, *A Texan in Search of a Fight*, 112.

26 Henry J. Aten, *History of the Eighty-fifth Regiment Illinois Volunteer Infantry* (Hiawatha, KS: 1901), 103; Larry J. Daniel, "Jay's Mill: The Opening Action of the Chickamauga Campaign," *North & South*, vol. 9, no. 3, June 2006, 51.

27 "A Premonition," The *Clarksville* (TX) *News*, Jun. 1, 1899. Byram's Ford (also called Lambert's Ford) was about a mile northeast of Alexander's Bridge.

fellow Texans took the opportunity to visit nearby camps, including that of Ector's brigade. Captain George Todd of the 1st Texas "saw that night, as we lay in camp on a road, for the first time since the war began, my younger brother Jim, who was a Lieutenant in Co. K [32nd Texas Cavalry], Ector's Brigade. I hunted him up and soon found him on line camped on [the] same road near our Brigade." The siblings from Jefferson, Texas, enjoyed a pleasant, unexpected reunion.[28]

One of Bragg's veteran artillerymen later wrote about Longstreet's fresh transplants from the Army of Northern Virginia, including the Texans in their new bluish clothing: "Our first impression was partly caused by the color of their uniform, but more by its uniformity, and the superior style of their equipments, in haversacks, canteens, and knapsacks. The contrast between them and Gen'l Bragg's motley, ragged troops was striking in the extreme. If this command was a specimen of Lee's troops, they are certainly superior to the troops of the Army of Tennessee, in dress," he stressed.[29]

Private Thomas J. Beall of the 7th Texas summed up the long day for John Gregg's brigade: "Leaving Ringold [sic] on Friday morning we skirmished all day with the enemy and late in the evening we came up with Gen. Forrest and escort, who under cover of our arms, crossed the Chickamauga, and slept on the battlefield Friday night." Law's and Benning's brigades, which had marched from Ringgold to reinforce Hood and Johnson, camped on the east side of the creek near Reed's Bridge.[30]

By midnight, Braxton Bragg had about 9,000 troops on the west side of West Chickamauga Creek in seven brigades, not just one brigade as Colonel McCook mistakenly believed. For some of Bragg's soldiers, the disquieting darkness accentuated the gnawing fear that they might be killed or maimed the next day. Some did not have to wait until dawn to become casualties; several opposing regiments exchanged sporadic fire well after dark. A few of Robertson's men, including one of the Perry brothers of the 1st Texas, suffered serious wounds. A round whizzed through Pvt. Eugene Osceola Perry's cap box and lodged in his hip,

28 Todd, *First Texas Regiment*, 18. Jim Todd was shot through his thigh on the following day and then severely wounded at Kennesaw Mountain in 1864. At six feet three inches tall, George Todd was one of the tallest men in the regiment. He resigned his commission a month after Chickamauga to go home to Jefferson, Texas, to care for his ailing father. He later returned to the army as adjutant of the 3rd Texas Cavalry.

29 W. A. Brown, quoted in Larry J. Daniel, *Soldiering in the Army of Tennessee* (Chapel Hill, NC: 1991).

30 *Dallas Daily Herald*, Aug. 7, 1884.

carrying some caps with it. The injury proved to be incredibly painful but was not lethal.[31]

James Deshler's brigade camped four miles southwest of Lee and Gordon's Mills in order to protect the approach from the south. It had been a long, tiring day on the road for the Texans and Arkansans. They and the rest of Cleburne's division had started the day in wind-chilled Catlett's and Dug Gaps on Pigeon Mountain fronting McLemore's Cove. About 10:00 a.m., Deshler's soldiers began to hear distant cannonading to the north, and they could only guess as to its origin. "[E]very man strained his ears to catch the welcome sound," teenaged Pvt. William J. Oliphant of the 6th Texas recalled. "It was the firing at Crawfish Springs, twenty-five miles away, and was the opening of the great battle." Buglers quickly sounded attention and the men sprang into place in the ranks. "Away we went at a rapid pace over rugged hills and dusty lanes," the youthful Indiana native added. The Confederates were soon on the march toward Bragg's headquarters on the east side of West Chickamauga Creek. Private Benjamin Seaton of the 10th Texas noted in his diary, "On a forced march to [Lee &] Gordon Mill—15 miles—heavy cannonading and small arms fire vary hard on both sides." According to Lt. Robert Collins, "We were moving north, there was quite a high wind blowing, the dust in the road was deep, making it very disagreeable." Collins and his fellow Arkansas Post parolees were anxious to show their mettle in combat after all those hard hours of drilling at Wartrace under Pat Cleburne.[32]

About 4:00 p.m., Deshler's weary men arrived at the Henderson farm near Glass's Mill, a multistory frame structure on the southeastern bank of West Chickamauga Creek about two miles south of Crawfish Springs. After making camp near the 8th and 11th Texas Cavalry, they tried to rest despite the intense cold and strong winds that had whipped up the dust along the road. The soldiers huddled under what blankets they carried or could scrounge up. Many fretted about what the morning's light might bring. "If I am not greatly mistaken," Sgt. William Heartsill of the 6th-10th Texas-15th Texas Cavalry predicted, "this time

31 Ural, *Hood's Texas Brigade*, 187. Four of the Perry clan—Clinton, Eugene, Howard, and Edward—served in the 1st Texas. Howard was killed at Antietam in September 1862 and Eugene died at the Wilderness on May 6, 1864.

32 James M. McCaffrey, ed., *Only a Private: A Texan Remembers the Civil War: The Memoirs of William J. Oliphant* (Houston, TX: 2004), 44; Harold B. Simpson, ed., *The Bugle Softly Blows: The Confederate Diary of Benjamin M. Seaton*, 40; Collins, *Chapters*, 150. Crawfish Springs, named for a Cherokee chieftain, was the centerpiece of James Gordon's 2,500-acre plantation in Walker County. Oliphant's father, a jeweler, had moved his family to Texas in 1853 when William was seven years old.

Modern view of the area where Wilder's brigade defended the Alexander-Viniard Road. (*Scott Mingus*)

tomorrow will see many a lifeless form strewed over these valleys, whose hearts now pulsate with life and great expectations for the future. We know not our future and would not if possible, but leave all to the great I AM; who governs the life of one man as carefully as he rules the destinies of a World. It is true that when I reflect that this may possibly be the last day's entry in my journal; I feel a strange and inexpressible dread of the morrow."[33]

Heartsill was not alone in his concerns. Sleep came uneasily that night to many soldiers of the Army of Tennessee and their new colleagues from the Army of Northern Virginia.

33 Harold B. Simpson, *The Bugle Softly Blows: The Confederate Diary of Benjamin M. Seaton* (Waco, TX: 1965), 40-41; Heartsill, *Fourteen Hundred and 91 Days*, 150.

Chapter 4

September 19, Morning—Ector's Brigade

Before the frosty dawn of September 19, Maj. Gen. William S. Rosecrans positioned Maj. Gen. George Thomas's XIV Corps on his left, interposing his three divisions between the Confederates and Chattanooga. Thomas's line connected on the right (south) with Maj. Gen. Alexander McCook's XX Corps. Major General Thomas Crittenden's XXI Corps remained concentrated near Lee and Gordon's Mills, slightly in front of the other two corps. Rosecrans ordered Maj. Gen. Gordon Granger's Reserve Corps to return to Rossville, a village on the Chattanooga–La Fayette Road near the Tennessee border about 10 miles north of Lee and Gordon's Mills. That position would allow Granger to contest any enemy flanking movements in that direction. A brigade under Col. Daniel McCook, Jr., one of Alexander McCook's many brothers in the Federal service, was encamped near the La Fayette Road–Reed's Bridge Road intersection about a mile west of Reed's Bridge. McCook's men, along with Col. John G. Mitchell's brigade, had arrived late on September 18 in response to Col. Robert Minty's calls for assistance.[1]

1 Sullivan, *Chickamauga and Chattanooga Battlefields*, 15. Alexander and Daniel were part of the famous "Fighting McCooks" from northeastern Ohio. Two brothers and 13 of their sons

Postwar image of the home of Cherokee chief John Ross, for whom the village of Rossville took its name. President Andrew Jackson had ordered the Cherokee of northern Georgia removed to the Indian Territory (modern Oklahoma). White settlers had since claimed the land. (*Library of Congress*)

Braxton Bragg's jagged line of battle roughly paralleled West Chickamauga Creek. The left of Maj. Gen. Simon Buckner's Corps was near Dalton's Ford about a mile south of Lee and Gordon's Mills. Next in line, Law's and Bushrod Johnson's divisions manned the left-center. Major General W. H. T. Walker's Reserve Corps rested farther north near Alexander's Bridge. Brigadier General Frank Cheatham's division of Polk's Corps formed the reserve, with Lt. Gen. D. H. Hill's Corps and the rest of the Army of Tennessee within supporting distance. Brigadier General Joe Wheeler had concentrated his cavalry corps, including the 8th and 11th Texas, near Glass's Mill, two miles south of Crawfish Springs, not far from Hill's divisions.

served in the Union Army; six of them became generals. Another brother had died in 1842 near Brazil while in the U.S. Navy.

After guarding the fords south of Lee and Gordon's Mills, the troopers saddled up early in the day and moved north toward the front, but stayed in reserve.[2]

"Old Pete" Longstreet and his remaining infantry brigades were still on trains heading for northern Georgia and would not arrive in time for the fighting. Bragg established his field headquarters just east of Thedford's Ford. He was unaware of Thomas's and McCook's repositioning during the night, and still believed that Rosecrans's left was somewhere near Lee and Gordon's Mills. That misconception influenced his tactical decisions early on September 19. Compounding the issue, Nathan Bedford Forrest, instead of screening Hood's right flank, had taken his mounted men east of Chickamauga Creek the previous evening. He left a single detachment to guard Reed's Bridge after he withdrew.[3]

The soldiers of the Army of Tennessee had an old saying that army mules knew when a battle was imminent, braying and squealing before the shooting started. An Irishman in one of Brig. Gen. John Gregg's Tennessee regiments at Chickamauga reinforced this belief: "Be this as it may, the mules made the woods ring with their unmusical voices." Several men took the racket as an omen. In the Confederate camps, some soldiers committed their thoughts to paper. A Texan in Deshler's brigade recorded, "This morning is still cool but the day promises to be pleasant." The ambient weather in Catoosa and Walker Counties notwithstanding, "pleasant" was not a word that most soldiers in the Army of Tennessee or their foes would associate with September 19, 1863, by sundown.[4]

Shortly after daylight, General Forrest took Brig. Gen. Henry B. Davidson's 1,900-man mounted brigade on a reconnaissance from Alexander's Bridge north toward Reed's Bridge to develop any Yankee presence; reports of suspected enemy activity in the area had filtered into Bragg's headquarters. Just after 7:00 a.m., an advance squadron of the 1st Georgia Cavalry tangled with Lt. William Faulkner's detail of the 86th Illinois, which was taking empty canteens to a small spring near Jay's Mill. McCook, meanwhile, dispatched the 69th Ohio to destroy Reed's Bridge

2 Edward Betts and C. E. Park, *Map of the Battlefield of Chickamauga* (1896), Plate 3, Alabama Department of History and Archives, Montgomery, AL; "Letter from the Rangers," *Tri-Weekly Telegraph*, Sept. 30, 1863.

3 Deborah Thedford, whose family owned the farm on which Bragg made his headquarters, ministered to so many wounded men in her house after the battle that she became known as the "Mother of Chickamauga."

4 *Pulaski Citizen*, Sept. 8, 1887; Heartsill, *Fourteen Hundred and 91 Days*, 151. An article from one of Gregg's 10th Tennessee soldiers in the *Pulaski Citizen*, Sept. 8, 1887, mentioned that a heavy frost covered the ground on Saturday morning.

in order to isolate McNair's brigade. After a brief skirmish, McCook withdrew to report the Rebel presence near the bridge.[5]

Once back at the La Fayette Road, Colonel McCook encountered George Thomas, whose Union XIV Corps had just finished a night march from Crawfish Springs as part of Rosecrans's shifting of troops northward. Thomas, determined to attack what McCook believed to be a single Confederate brigade, dispatched Brig. Gen. John M. Brannan's division. Shortly before 7:30 a.m., Brannan deployed Col. John T. Croxton's 2,000-man brigade. The 250 men of Davidson's 10th Confederate Cavalry soon charged Croxton's battle line in the open, old-growth woods north of Brotherton Road and west of Jay's Mill. After a brief volley that emptied several saddles, the 10th fled in disorder through Davidson's primary line, disorganizing it.[6]

Forrest formed a new, dismounted line along Jay's Mill Road anchored around Capt. Gustave A. Huwald's Tennessee battery. Realizing the Yankees would eventually overpower his badly outnumbered men, Forrest sent his couriers and orderlies, including Pvt. Junius "June" Peak of the 7th Kentucky Cavalry, galloping south. They carried instructions for Lt. Gen. Leonidas Polk and other commanders to bring up infantry and artillery support. With all his available messengers gone and no reinforcements in sight, Forrest soon went looking for help himself. He rode south to Brig. Gen. Claudius Wilson's brigade of Walker's Reserve Corps near Alexander's Bridge. After Wilson initially refused to help without orders from his superior, General Walker, Forrest had General Bragg approve the request. Once Wilson's Georgians and Louisianans marched north to Jay's Mill and deployed, the charismatic Forrest ordered the brigade to advance. After scrapping briefly with Croxton's Yankees, Wilson and Davidson withdrew to regroup. General Thomas dispatched Brig. Gen. Absalom Baird's division to augment Brannan on the Federal left. This action began a long day that saw Rosecrans, Bragg, and their respective corps commanders feed their available forces into action piecemeal instead of concentrating them for a decisive blow.[7]

5 A general overview of the battle of Chickamauga is beyond the scope of this work. There are many good books on the oft-confusing fighting. The authors suggest works by Robert Carter, Peter Cozzens, David Powell, and William Glenn Robertson. See the bibliography for a list of titles. Powell includes a useful map of the opening action at Jay's Mill in *The Maps of Chickamauga*, page 49.

6 Powell, *The Maps of Chickamauga*, 50-51.

7 "Those Texans," *San Antonio Light*, Oct. 20, 1945; "Forrest at Chickamauga," *The Southern Mercury* (Dallas), March 30, 1905; Albert Disbrow, *Glimpses of Chickamauga: A Complete Guide to*

Brig. Gen. Nathan Bedford Forrest commanded two divisions of Confederate cavalry at Chickamauga. (*Library of Congress*)

Ector's Brigade Goes In

At dawn on Saturday morning, Brig. Gen. Matthew D. Ector's soldiers cooked breakfast in their camp near the burned Alexander house and nearby blacksmith shop. Shortly after 8:00a.m., the 1,200-man brigade, known in some quarters as

All Points of Interest on This Historic Battle-Field. (Chicago, IL: 1895), 80-81; A. P. Adamson, *Brief History of the Thirtieth Georgia Regiment* (Griffin, GA: 1912), 35-36. Although born in Kentucky, June Peak grew up in Texas. When the war began, he returned to his native state to enlist and served under John Hunt Morgan. He suffered two wounds at Chickamauga.

"the Chubs," followed Claudius Wilson's troops. In the excitement, Ector failed to notify General Walker, his corps commander. "The order came ringing down the line to [go] forward in quick step," the 32nd Texas Cavalry's Pvt. Robert C. Graves remembered. The brigade hastily marched north on Jay's Mill Road. "The momentary booming of the heavy artillery and the occasional rattle of the musketry warned us of the dreadful conflict fast approaching," Graves added; "[T]his awful storm of death and destruction seemed to widen and stretch to the right and left as far as our ears would let us hear. This is the moment, and the trying ordeal of a soldier's grit, the dark gloom of death itself is written upon every leaf and he has less time to think and realize his perilous situation."[8]

Ector's brigade arrived at Jay's Mill about 9:00 a.m. "On, on, our columns rushed, first by the right and then by the left flank, until our line passed nearby an old saw mill," Graves continued. "For a brief space of time suspense and anxiety filled every heart, while hope and despair came and went like the ebb and flow of the ocean's tide. The woods in every direction seemed to be alive with the searching and hissing missiles of death and destruction itself."[9]

The Texans encountered some of Forrest's wounded men heading for the rear. "Some were hobbling along supported by some friend," a soldier recalled; "others were holding shattered arms." The refugees included "a fine-looking officer sitting on his horse pressing his hand to his chest while the blood was trickling down his body." It was a grim reminder of what potentially lay before Ector's troops. Private William E. Whitsett of the 9th Texas later bragged that Forrest's cavalry "came near being swamped but for our timely arrival." Ector soon formed a line of battle in the mature, widely spaced timber straddling Reed's Bridge Road, with Wilson's brigade deployed off to his left. According to Whitsett, the 9th Texas was "the extreme right Regiment and Co. H was the extreme right Co. of Infantry in Genl. Bragg's Army." Forrest was in overall command of the lengthy battle line. Ector dispatched his adjutant, Capt. Constantine Buckley "Buck" Kilgore, to make sure that Forrest would cover his flanks. Forrest gruffly replied, "I'll take care of it." Davidson's

8 "A Premonition," *The Clarksville* (TX) *News*, June 1, 1899. Ector was in nominal command of Walker's old division, as the assigned officer, Brig. Gen. States Rights Gist, was still in Rome, Georgia, as the battle began. McNair's Arkansans good-naturedly called Ector's men "Chubs," while the Texans called the Arkansans "Joshies." See J. G. McCown, "About Ector's and McNair's Brigades," CV, vol. 9, no. 3, Mar. 1901, 113.

9 "Battle of Chickamauga," *Des Moines Register*, Jun. 1, 1902; "A Premonition." Ector's assistant adjutant general, Capt. Ryland Todhunter, said the brigade crossed Byram's Ford about 8:00 a.m. He mistakenly called it Bryan's Ford.

Capt. Judson W. Bishop, 2nd Minnesota Infantry. (*Library of Congress*)

dismounted cavalrymen near Jay's Mill, whose horses were in the rear, had the assignment.[10]

Ector, Kilgore, and Forrest did not know that fresh Union troops were on their way. General Brannan had dispatched Col. Ferdinand Van Derveer's brigade east on Reed's Bridge Road to attack the Confederates, with Col. John M. Connell's Ohio and Indiana infantrymen in support. Despite having made a night march, Van Derveer's soldiers were eager for a scrap. "Our way lay aside a ridge of low elevation, with easy slopes to either side," the 2nd Minnesota's Capt. Judson W. Bishop reported; "the land, so far as we could see, being covered with trees mostly of small size, and without underbrush, giving an open view of perhaps forty rods or more in every direction." They headed east a mile and a half toward the creek before brushing back the 1st Georgia Cavalry. The 2nd Minnesota deployed on the left (north) of the road, with the 35th Ohio to the right. Half of Lt. Frank Smith's Battery I, 4th U.S. Light Artillery, stayed in the road while the other half moved to the Buckeyes' right flank. The 87th Indiana formed a second line behind the Minnesotans.[11]

Matt Ector had arrayed his brigade in a long line of battle astride Reed's Bridge Road, several hundred yards east of Van Derveer's oncoming line. Dressed in a new gray uniform and a linen duster, General Forrest rode up to the Chubs and "told us very soon he would show us the Yanks," Cpl. J. G. McCown of the 32nd Texas Cavalry remembered. As Forrest passed the regiment, William B. Gholston

10 Powell, *A Mad Irregular Battle*, 311; "William E. Whitsett, Private, Company H," *Lamar County Texas Genealogy Research*, accessed Dec. 18, 2019, www.lamarcountytx.org/civilwar/whitsett.shtm. The city of Kilgore, Texas, is named for Buck Kilgore. The 28-year-old Georgia native enlisted in 1861 with his anti-secessionist father and grown brothers. His father died at the 1861 battle of Wilson's Creek in Missouri.

11 J. W. Bishop, "Van Derveer's Brigade at Chickamauga," *Glimpses of the Nation's Struggle*, Minnesota Commandery, MOLLUS, Sixth Series (Minneapolis, MN: 1909), 58.

stepped out of the ranks. The diminutive private cried out, "General, you can't show us the Yanks any too soon, for I am barefooted." Lack of footwear notwithstanding, Bill Gholston and Ector's Confederates readied themselves to go in.[12]

According to Capt. Samuel H. Sprott of Stone's Alabama battalion, "Presently, a staff officer dashed up, saluted Gen. Ector, and directed him to lead his brigade forward at once to the support of Gen. Wilson." The line stepped off about 9:15. Ector's understrength five infantry regiments and the Alabama and Mississippi battalions surged northwesterly, while to the south Wilson's brigade again engaged Croxton. Indiana-born Sgt. Festus O. Conner carried the colors of the 9th Texas, a task he had proudly performed since Shiloh. Soon, Ector's forward skirmishers engaged their blue-clad counterparts. "A spluttering skirmish fire broke out away to our right and front," the 2nd Minnesota's Captain Bishop reported, "and changing direction to face it the regiments moved off the road to the right about a hundred yards, where we halted as the enemy came into view."[13]

Lieutenant Stephen J. Tanner of the 9th Texas remembered, "We continued to advance and fire, driving in the Union picket line until we came in sight of the Union line of battle some 150 or 200 yards away. . . I saw the Union line lie down and knew the heavy firing would commence at once." Spotting the Confederates coming over a small rise, a Minnesotan noticed "the heads of a solid line of men in gray coming toward us in something like a rush." The Northerners unleashed a telling volley. "The battle was promptly opened by both opposing lines," Captain Bishop recalled, "our battery remaining in the road and firing over our heads and through the interval between our regiments. In a few minutes the enemy's fire began to weaken, and presently their line broke and went to the rear out of our sight." The Federals soon began firing at will.[14]

"We soon met the first line of the enemy," Ector's assistant adjutant general, Capt. Ryland Todhunter, reported, and "the contending forces [fought] at close

12 *Austin American-Statesman*, Dec. 24, 1899. Gholston was wounded at Chickamauga but would survive.

13 "Sumter in the Civil War," *Our Southern Home* (Livingston, AL), May 18, 1899; Bishop, "Van Derveer's Brigade at Chickamauga," 58; Powell, *A Mad Irregular Fight*, 312; Maj. Raymond Scott Eresman, *Union and Confederate Infantry Doctrine in the Battle of Chickamauga* (Fort Leavenworth, KS: 1991), 24-25.

14 *OR* 30, pt. 2, 249; Stephen J. Tanner and E. Russell Tanner, compiler, *The Stephen Jennings Tanner Autobiography and Tanner Family Genealogy* (Boulder, CO: 1970), 42-43; Powell, *The Maps of Chickamauga*, 54; Bishop, "Van Derveer's Brigade at Chickamauga." The Yankees captured Tanner's entire picket line, other than himself.

Capt. Ryland Todhunter, assistant adjutant general, Ector's brigade. (*Confederate Veteran*)

range, almost within the smoke of their rifles and the flames of their batteries." Rifle-muskets and revolvers crackled as the lines exchanged fire under the smoke-shrouded tree canopy. One of Stone's Alabamans recalled, "We were fighting Thomas' Corps, and that meant hard licks." He added, "Our loss in this brief struggle was terrific. Gen. Ector had his horse killed under him, and was himself wounded, but he did not leave the field." Ector soon withdrew his brigade to regroup.[15]

Injured and dying men languished between the lines. "Other wounded soldiers had fallen close to me," an unidentified Confederate recalled, "and I could hear their low moans between the hissing shot. Bullets hurdled above us and raked the earth about us on all sides. Branches cut from the trees by shot and shell fell like hail-stones." As the Federals charged, the helpless men "lay in the path of the bullets and one by one died slowly."[16]

About this time, the anonymous Rebel's corps commander, General Walker, arrived at the front. Earlier that morning, as the Georgia-born general conversed with General Hood and other officers, he had heard the outbreak of heavy firing off to the right front. "By God!" Walker cried out. "They are attacking my division!" He hurried to Bragg, who authorized him to attack with all the force he had. Walker and an aide quickly mounted and headed toward the sound of the guns. He soon learned that Forrest, without authorization, had commandeered Ector's brigade, that the Federals were present in great numbers, and that Wilson

15 "Battle of Chickamauga," *Des Moines Register*; "Sumter in the Civil War."

16 "Horrible War Memories," *Indiana* (PA) *Weekly Messenger*, Jul. 31, 1889.

Capt. Constantine Buckner "Buck" Kilgore, adjutant, Ector's brigade. (*The Texas State Preservation Board*)

and Ector had both fallen back in disarray. He rode south a mile to bring up Brig. Gen. St. John Liddell's 4,000-man division to resume the offensive.

Matt Ector remained uneasy about his left flank, where Forrest's dismounted cavalrymen remained in line near Jay's sawmill. He again sent Buck Kilgore to locate Forrest, who was near Huggins' Tennessee battery. When Kilgore relayed Ector's concerns, Forrest became irate. "He turned around on me and shouted," Captain Kilgore recalled in 1908, "loud enough to be heard above the terrible din, 'Tell General Ector that, by God, I am here, and will take care of his left flank as well as his right.'"[17]

Ector Goes in Again

Ector's line again moved forward at about 10:00 a.m. "I shall never forget that moment," S. H. Sprott, the Alabama sharpshooter captain, remembered. "Gen. Ector though wounded rode out in front of his brigade, and gave the commands: 'Attention battalions. Shoulder arms. Right shoulder shift arms. Forward—Guide center—March!' These commands were given and executed just as if we had been on review." The 2nd Minnesota's Captain Bishop recalled, "They soon came back with a fresh attack more energetic and persistent than the first, intending apparently to sweep us out of the way, without spending too much more valuable time on the job." Assistant adjutant general Ryland Todhunter described this second charge: "Together with Gen. Liddell's division, viz: Walthall's and Govan's infantry brigades, on the left of our former position, we fought over nearly the same thick woods and brush as before. We met them with such a clash and deadly aim that the

17 Powell, *A Mad Irregular Battle*, 316.

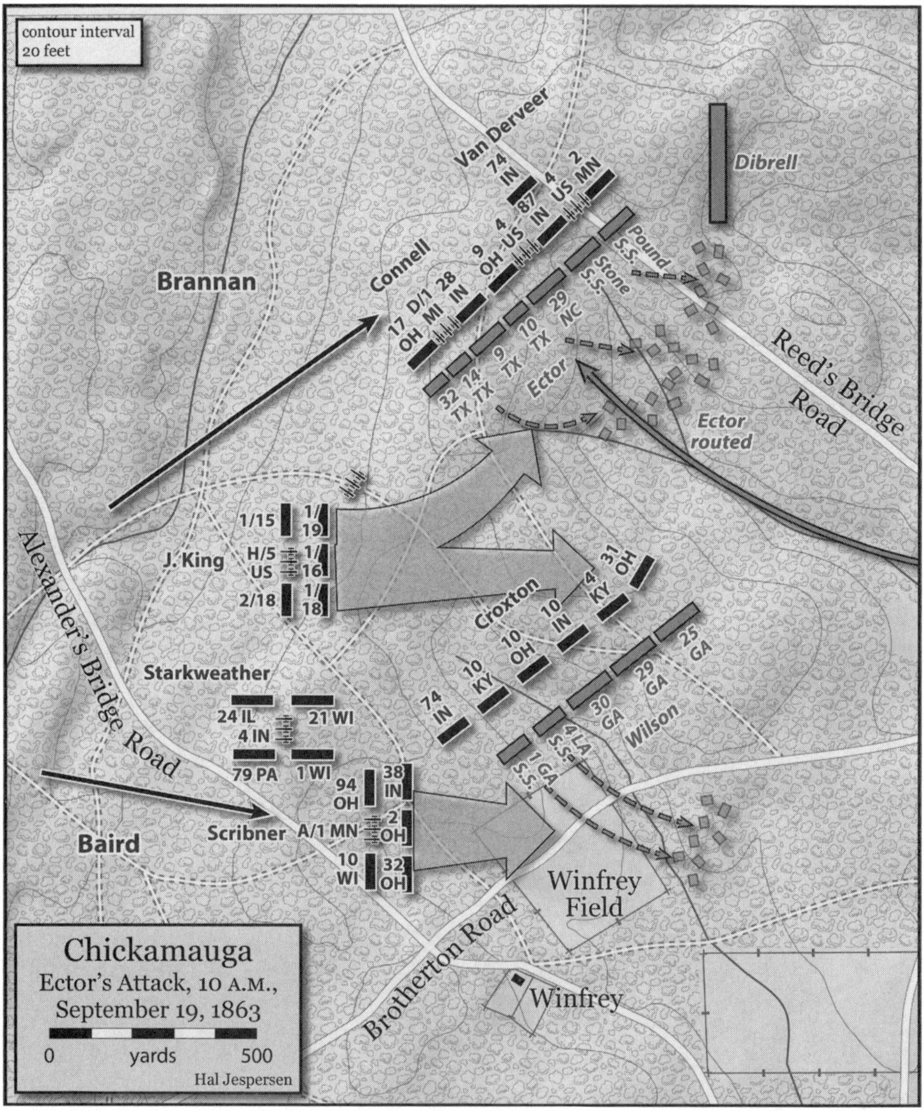

Chickamauga
Ector's Attack, 10 A.M.,
September 19, 1863

first line was again driven back upon their second line, fighting stubbornly for every foot of ground yielded."[18]

Across the way, Lt. Col. Henry V. Boynton of the 35th Ohio admired his opponents' courage. "Ector and Wilson of Walker's division, and Walthall and Govan of Liddell's, all marching to the assistance of those contending in the hell of

18 "Sumter in the Civil War"; "Battle of Chickamauga," *Des Moines Register.*

battle, became, in turn, as hotly engaged themselves in front of Baird," he wrote. "Nothing could exceed the valor of these troops. There was nothing in the way of desperate fighting, either of infantry or artillery, which they were not called to face. And they did face it with a courage seldom equaled, and which it was impossible to surpass."[19]

"Our boys again dashed into the smoke of union musketry," the 32nd Texas Cavalry's Pvt. Robert C. Graves recalled, "and the very flame of the batteries, with their deadly fire and the undaunted courage with which they charged, and the war yell that none but Texans gave, moved the Federal line with great loss until quickly reinforced and relieved by new lines." A minié ball crashed through Graves's elbow, requiring amputation. "Suffice to say that the piece of arm from the elbow down, including hand and all," Graves proudly wrote, "I dedicated at Chickamauga to the cause of the south."[20]

General Ector enjoyed some initial success. "From this time the fighting was severe and continuous," Private Graves claimed, "our column slowly but steadily forcing the Federals back towards Chattanooga, every inch of ground being won by hard fighting and unprecedented courage." This determined charge also freed a few Confederates taken prisoner in the last attack, including Pvt. James H. Wade of the 10th Texas Cavalry. Though wounded, Wade rejoined Company G and resumed fighting.[21]

Another line of Federals (two regiments of Connell's brigade and Battery D, 1st Michigan Artillery) soon appeared in support, despite General Forrest's bold promise to protect Ector's flanks. "Our Texas brigade, in pursuit of the enemy, obliqued too much to the right, which again left us without flank support," Captain Todhunter recalled. "Both sides were badly used up, our brigade loss having been one-third of the men in action. The Federals, in sending fresh troops into action, moved a command parallel to our Texas brigade in very close range, possibly not exceeding seventy-five yards. As soon as we discovered their colors and dress through the bush our Texans gave them a close volley and rushed upon them,

19 H. V. Boynton, "Splendid Fighting," *Galveston Daily News*, Aug. 11, 1889.

20 "A Premonition."

21 Ibid.; "William E. Whitsett, Private, Company H"; "Ector's Brigade in the Battle of Chickamauga," *The Standard* (Clarksville, TX), Nov. 7, 1863; *Graham* (TX) *Leader*, Nov. 16, 1911.

which completely frustrated and drove them back in great confusion. The ground at this point seemed to be covered with dead and wounded."[22]

The youthful Col. Julius A. Andrews of the 32nd Texas Cavalry, carrying the regimental flag after several previous color-bearers had fallen, himself went down with a severe thigh wound. A nearby private, John D. Neal of the 10th Texas Cavalry, grasped the banner and waved it aloft to rally the men. Andrews's loyal adjutant, Lt. George M. Lindsay, took a bullet to the hip and was out of action. Captain James S. Dixon and Lt. Luther A. Williams of the 32nd died while attacking Lt. Frank Smith's Battery I, 4th U.S. Artillery. Privates J. M. Spinks, Stoke Hutchins, P. B. Barber, and four other men of the 10th Texas Cavalry came within 50 yards of the enemy guns before halting and taking cover. They fired several times while Ector's brigade fell back a short distance.[23]

Both sides went prone 50 to 60 yards apart. Lieutenant Smith's crews fired canister rounds and explosive shells into Ector's ranks. One gunner observed that the blasts were "literally lifting the prostrate foes at the point of impact high in the air and hurling them back." According to the 10th Texas Cavalry's James M. Watson, several of Ector's combatants sheltered behind nearby rocks, lying down to load their weapons and then rising to their knees to fire at the outstretched Federals. "I saw their officers several times trying to get their men to charge us," Watson noted, "but the Yankees stayed put."[24]

Undaunted, the Confederates rose and fought on until Brig. Gen. John H. King's Regular Army brigade of Baird's division arrived to relieve Croxton's exhausted Federals. As the Regulars entered a field covered with fine underbrush, they heard the shrill yells of the advancing Rebels above the roar of battle. Just before Ector's infantrymen reached King's line, Wilson's brigade, a few hundred yards to the south, and Forrest's hard-pressed men on the right began to fall back as additional Federal flanking columns threatened them. Ector withdrew a second

22 "Battle of Chickamauga," *Des Moines Register.*

23 "Ector's Brigade in the Battle of Chickamauga"; J. M. Spinks, "Thrilling and Varied War Experiences," CV, vol. 15, no. 4, Apr. 1907, 168; Oscar P. Heath, "The Battle of Chickamauga as I Saw It," Battery I, 4th U.S. Artillery File, CCNMP. Colonel Andrews recovered and reassumed command in the months after Chickamauga. He was wounded again in 1864 during Hood's Tennessee campaign but returned to duty before the war ended.

24 Heath, "The Battle of Chickamauga as I Saw It"; "Battle of Chickamauga," *Des Moines Register*; Judy Watson McClure, ed., *Confederate from East Texas: The Civil War Letters of James Monroe Watson* (Quanah, TX: 1976), 26.

time. In response, King wheeled his brigade to the left in a double line, intending to strike the enemy in the flank and roll him up "like a curtain."[25]

The Regulars' appearance stunned the Confederates. "When we first discovered them, they were in the act of firing," Captain Sprott mentioned, "and we were soon met with a blinding sheet of flame and leaden hail. Our brigade, already fearfully cut up by the morning's work, was unable to cope with this new and formidable force and there was nothing to do but fall back. I looked back over the ground we had traversed, covered with our dead and wounded, and it looked like a long, long distance to the point from which we had started but there was no other alternative so back we went, bleeding, broken—almost annihilated."[26]

According to Pvt. C. B. Carlton of the 10th Texas Cavalry, Ector's brigade was "flanked on the left & commenced falling back in confusion." General Ector, fearing his command might get cut off and surrounded, dispatched the dutiful Buck Kilgore to reconnoiter. The adjutant had not proceeded far when he encountered enemy skirmishers, who ordered him to halt. At the risk of his life, Kilgore wheeled his horse and galloped back to Ector. He began piloting the brigade toward the rear under severe fire from King's leftmost battalions.[27]

The Confederates were "fighting more like bulldogs than human beings," according to adjutant general Todhunter. "With soldiers falling almost at every point," they worked their way eastward under Kilgore's guidance. The 9th Texas's Col. William H. Young dropped with a severe chest wound, and Lt. Samuel C. Fitch died at his side. Ector's regiments moved by the right flank, a maneuver they initially achieved without confusion. The brigade became scattered as the retrograde progressed, however, and it again passed in front of King's firing line. Scores of Ector's men, including Sgt. J. Allen Templeton and Pvt. Moses Walters of the 10th Texas Cavalry, were cut off and taken prisoner. Ammunition was low;

25 "A Premonition"; "William E. Whitsett, Private, Company H"; "Battle of Chickamauga," *Des Moines* (IA) *Register*, Jun. 1, 1902; "At the Battle of Chickamauga," Henry B. Freeman Papers, Wyoming Historical Society, Cheyenne, as quoted in Powell, *A Mad Irregular Battle*, 318; John C. King, "A Boy in Battle," *Farmland* (IN) *Enterprise*, Oct. 23, 1903. The teenaged King was in the 16th U.S. Infantry.

26 "Sumter in the Civil War."

27 Francis F. McKinney, *Education in Violence: The Life of George H. Thomas and the History of the Army of the Cumberland* (Chicago, IL: 1991), 232; Dr. John O. Scott, "Chickamauga," *Galveston Daily News*, Aug. 18, 1896.

most of Ector's soldiers had expended the 40 rounds they had carried into the battle.[28]

One of Ector's men later recalled, "[The brigade] was again forced to retire, for a short distance, finding itself greatly outnumbered, and the supporting brigades . . . having given way after making a most gallant fight." The 9th Texas's Private Whitsett complained, "We charged twice and were driven back." Forrest ordered Col. George G. Dibrell's newly arrived Tennessee brigade to form on Ector's right. The cavalrymen arrived about 10:30 a.m., while Ector's men were withdrawing after being flanked on their left. "Our first impression was that they [Ector's survivors] were retreating in confusion, but they soon satisfied us of our mistake," a Confederate trooper mentioned. Ector's soldiers were not whipped (at least in their opinions), but the brigade was in shambles after two hours of hard fighting.[29]

Across the woods, King's Regulars halted their pursuit of the retreating Rebels. "Never shall I forget that day of shot and shell," Pvt. John C. White of the 16th U.S. recalled. Reportedly only 13 years old, White may have been the youngest combatant at Chickamauga. "I have been schooled in the horrors of war and its terrible earnestness," he added, "but the long-continued fighting, running into the night, with its scene of death and suffering, made me feel woefully desolate. A sickening sensation all but mastered me."[30]

While the Regulars regrouped, adjutant Buck Kilgore brought Ector's survivors back to Jay's Mill at about 11:00 a.m., capturing some wayward Federals along the way. It had been a harrowing journey. The 32nd Texas Cavalry had taken the most losses, including 40 men now in Union hands. The Federals had seized a total of 138 of Ector's men, including Pvt. William Donahue of the 14th Texas Cavalry. Donahue, from Denton County, told his captors that he was a loyal citizen and had enlisted through false misrepresentations. He wanted to take the oath of allegiance to the United States. Another captive, Pvt. William S. Fuller, also took the oath and enlisted in the 6th U.S.[31]

28 "Battle of Chickamauga," *Des Moines Register*; "A Premonition"; C. B. Carlton to David G. Templeton, Oct. 13, 1863, John A. Templeton Papers, Dolph Briscoe Center for American History, University of Texas.

29 "Forrest's Old Brigade at Chickamauga," *Memphis Appeal*, Oct. 21, 1863; "Ector's Brigade in the Battle of Chickamauga"; "William E. Whitsett, Private, Company H."

30 *The Inter-Ocean* (Chicago, IL), Sept. 20, 1903.

31 "Ector's Brigade in the Battle of Chickamauga"; CSR of Pvt. William Donoho/Donahue, William S. Fuller, and John Hale, 14th Texas Cavalry, NARA Record Group 109, M323, Texas,

Confederate line advancing through the forest toward Union troops, by Alfred R. Waud. (*Library of Congress*)

Ector's Texans and the two attached sharpshooter battalions recuperated the rest of the day in reserve. They occasionally had to endure heavy artillery fire but suffered few additional casualties. Plenty of other Texans in the Army of Tennessee, however, were destined to fall that day.

roll 0081. Private John Hale, captured on Sept. 20, later joined the U.S. Navy. Several other men, mostly conscripts, also took the oath.

Chapter 5

September 19, Early Afternoon—Gregg's Brigade

With Walker's Reserve Corps out of the fight, Braxton Bragg turned to Brig. Gen. Benjamin F. "Frank" Cheatham's large five-brigade division of Polk's Corps about noon. Massed in the dense woods south of farmer John Brock's cleared field, Cheatham's 7,000 soldiers steadily advanced west toward La Fayette Road. Fresh Federal reinforcements from the XXI Corps finally checked them and overran an isolated Confederate battery. Brigadier General Alexander P. Stewart's division of Buckner's Corps charged and recovered the guns after pushing back the Union line near the farm of George and Mary Brotherton. Additional reinforcements arrived for both armies and deployed into position. By early afternoon, other flashpoints loomed along the jagged Confederate line that now stretched from Brig. Gen. William Preston's division at Hall's Ford north to Jay's Mill and the McAbee farm, where Walker's Reserve Corps and Nathan Bedford Forrest's men rested after their morning fight.[1]

Gregg's, Deshler's, and Robertson's brigades had thus far remained unengaged. Many Texans wrote in their diaries, ate a quick meal, or rechecked their

1 Betts and Park, *Map of the Battlefield of Chickamauga*, Plate 3. For a detailed analysis of the overall fighting on Sept. 19, see Powell, *A Mad and Irregular Battle*. The 65-year-old Brock had two sons in the Confederate Army at Chickamauga.

Brig. Gen. Joseph Wheeler commanded two divisions of Confederate cavalry at Chickamauga. (*Library of Congress*)

weapons and equipment. Some managed to catnap despite the roar of the ongoing battle to the north. Ominously, the thunder of artillery and crackle of musketry kept drawing closer to the center of the Army of Tennessee. In reserve to the south, the men of Breckinridge's and Cleburne's divisions awaited orders to march to the battlefield. After being held in reserve for several hours, Wheeler's cavalry, including the 8th and 11th Texas Cavalry Regiments, moved briskly down the creek to intercept a Federal wagon train reportedly passing through McLemore's Cove. Enemy cavalry drove them off, and the Southern horsemen retired to the vicinity of Glass's Mill. Chaplain Robert F. Bunting of the Texas Rangers blamed Wheeler for the failure, complaining, "It is evident we have too many commanders and not enough of system."[2]

Similar command issues plagued Bragg's infantry at Chickamauga. Another Ranger later opined, "Imagine Stonewall Jackson in Bragg's place!" Much of Bragg's army sat idle while fighting raged on the northern part of the battlefield. Brigadier General John Gregg's 1,400-man brigade of Bushrod Johnson's provisional division manned the Confederate left-center. They were aligned along a low ridge in the woods bordering the Alexander-Viniard Road about 800 to 1,000 yards east of La Fayette Road. The 7th Texas and 50th Tennessee were on the left near the Park farm, the 30th and 10th Tennessee rested in the middle, and the 3rd Tennessee and 41st Tennessee were on the far right. The entire line faced to the southwest. Gregg threw out a heavy picket line into a shallow hollow to his front. Colonel John S. Fulton's 870 Tennesseans were off to their right (facing west) with Brig. Gen. Evander McNair's 1,200 Alabamians and North Carolinians in reserve behind Gregg. Johnson posted Bledsoe's 1st Missouri Battery to Gregg's right with Everett's Georgia guns on the right of Fulton. He kept Captain Culpeper's South Carolinians in reserve behind McNair. Law's division had deployed to Johnson's right, and Brig. Gen. William Preston's men were to his left rear. Preston, however, did not connect with Gregg, leaving the left of the 50th Tennessee vulnerable.[3]

At one point, General Gregg rode his "fiery mare" along his battle line. As he reached the center of his brigade, the Texan halted and addressed his soldiers: "All I have to say to you, my brave comrades, is to maintain the character which you

2 "Letters from the Rangers," *Houston Tri-Weekly Telegraph*, Sept. 30, 1863.

3 Leonidis B. Giles, *Terry's Texas Rangers: The 8th Texas Cavalry in the Civil War* (Austin, TX: 1911), 43; Johnson, *SHSP*, 396; Lindsley, *Military Annals of Tennessee*, 450-451.

Maj. Khleber Van Zandt, 7th Texas, Gregg's brigade. (*University of Texas at Arlington*)

have already won at Raymond." Thus inspired, Gregg's veteran soldiers readied themselves for the fight they knew was coming.[4]

At midday, the Confederates lay prone in the woods behind fallen logs and other cover, including a low ledge of rocks. According to Sgt. John T. Goodrich of the 3rd Tennessee, "The shells from the enemy's batteries and the 'Zip, zip!' of Minie balls became more frequent and effective. A considerable number of the brigade were wounded while lying in line of battle." The early casualties included a staff officer assigned to the brigade. Major Khleber M. Van Zandt was holding onto a tree limb while watching the distant Federals. A little to his rear, General Gregg was calmly observing the action from a low hill. A captain came up to Van Zandt and asked, "Why doesn't General Gregg order us to advance?" Before the captain had finished speaking, an incoming artillery shell killed him.[5]

Little did Gregg or his officers know that trouble, in the form of Brig. Gen. Jefferson C. Davis's division of the XX Corps, was on its way. Davis's men left Crawfish Springs at noon and marched north to Rosecrans's headquarters at the hilltop home of 23-year-old widow Eliza Glenn. Davis then sent Brig. Gen. William P. Carlin's 2nd Brigade and Norwegian-born Col. Hans Christian Heg's 3rd Brigade eastward into action. The latter consisted of the 25th and 35th Illinois, 8th Kansas, and 15th Wisconsin, a regiment recruited among the Badger State's

4 Robert W. Ikard, "Lieutenant Thompson Reports on Chickamauga: A Comparison of Immediate and Historical Perspectives of the Battle," *Tennessee Historical Quarterly*, vol. 44, no. 4, Winter 1985, 421.

5 John T. Goodrich, "Gregg's Brigade in the Battle of Chickamauga," *CV*, vol. 22, no. 6, June 1914, 264; Sandra L. Myres, ed., *Force Without Fanfare: The Autobiography of K. M. Van Zandt* (Fort Worth, TX: 1995), 100. The captain is identified as "Thompson"; his full identity and regiment are uncertain.

large Scandinavian population. Lieutenant John McLean's 8th Wisconsin Light Artillery unlimbered in an open field by the Glenn house to support the advancing line. Carlin's brigade aligned off Heg's right flank, with the 1st Brigade in reserve. The blue-clad soldiers slowly moved toward Gregg's position. Heg's line crossed La Fayette Road, passing the rude "Lost Corner School." This single-room log structure sat just inside the woods on the eastern side of the La Fayette Road and north of the Viniard-Alexander Road. The soldiers could hear firing off to their left as they traversed the vine-covered scrub oak and pine woods. "But in our front," Col. John A. Martin of the 8th Kansas recalled, "the silence was death-like. We still moved on."[6]

Shortly before 2:00 p.m., Heg's 1,200 troops, without any forward pickets, surged through the timber into the hollow where Gregg had placed his picket line. The 15th Wisconsin, with the 8th Kansas on its right, led the way, with the two Illinois regiments following in a second line. The Kansans followed their mascot, a barking black dog named "Old Soldier." The Federals opened fire at close range on Gregg's unsuspecting picket line, which disintegrated. The Texas general quickly dispatched Lt. Col. James J. Turner of the 30th Tennessee to investigate the sudden gunfire. Just then, the surviving pickets raced out of the ravine and started running toward Gregg's main line. Turner rode forward to inquire as to the reason for their sudden flight. Not getting an answer and failing to rally them, he stopped and peered through the thick young pines. Fifty yards away, two dark lines of Yankees headed straight at him. A minié ball slammed into his right breast as he turned to ride away. He staggered back to the main line and collapsed. The first wave of Yankees poured over the rise and opened fire "with an earnestness and deadly furor that I have never seen equaled," Turner remembered. The sudden volley dropped scores of Confederates.[7]

"This attack was fierce," an unidentified 7th Texan related. "The bullets flew so thickly that their wind fanned the hair of the men." The 50th Tennessee's Lt. Col. Thomas W. Beaumont was killed early in the action, and Maj. Christopher W. Robertson took command of the regiment. The musketry "swept on in steady vollies [sic] to the left," the Texan explained. Firing from behind trees, fallen logs,

6 Office of the Quartermaster General War Department, *The Battle of Chickamauga*, 6-7; "Letter from Col. Martin," *Weekly Atchison* (KS) *Champion*, Oct. 8, 1863. Davis had shot and killed fellow Union Gen. William "Bull" Nelson the previous year after an argument in Louisville, Kentucky, but was released. Ironically, he now led some of Nelson's former troops.

7 Cozzens, *This Terrible Sound*, 199; Theodore C. Blegen, ed., *The Civil War Letters of Hans Heg* (Northfield, MN: 1936), 39-40; Lindsley, *Military Annals of Tennessee*, 450-451.

Col. Hans C. Heg commanded a brigade in Davis's division, Twentieth Corps, Army of the Cumberland. (*The Wisconsin Historical Society*)

and the rocky ledge, the Confederates unleashed a devastating volley at Heg's front line.[8]

"The timber was very heavy as was also the underbrush, so we could but imperfectly see the enemy," Col. Ole Johnson of the 15th Wisconsin reported. Colonel Martin of the 8th Kansas wrote that a "volley was poured into our ranks, rapidly succeeded by another, and another. . . . Our men replied with promptness and effect. . . . The roar of musketry at this time was deafening." Both sides engaged in a stand-up firefight, with the combatants firing at will. "For [a] quarter of an hour the war was terrible," Martin added. "Still the brigade held its ground, cheered on by the gallant . . . Colonel Heg, who was everywhere present, careless of danger." After his men fired six or seven volleys, Heg pulled the 8th Kansas and 15th Wisconsin back 10 to 15 yards to avoid a crossfire from artillery on his left. After they had fired another dozen rounds, Heg ordered his men to fix bayonets and charge the Rebels.[9]

Nearly half of Gregg's officers were down by then. Lieutenant Colonel Samuel Thompson of the predominantly Irish 10th Tennessee lost a leg. Wounded soldiers streamed to the rear for treatment. With casualties mounting, Gregg boldly decided to try to break the Yankee line. "The rebels then advanced with a shout, pouring into our ranks the most deadly volleys," Colonel Martin wrote. He and Ole Johnson struggled to maintain their lines as Gregg's Confederates sustained their fire. "They came up in column four lines deep, passing their front line, which had been concealed behind a stone barricade [the rocky ledge]," Martin added. "Our flank was exposed, and another fire was opened in our rear and left, by a body who

8 "Gregg's Brigade at Chickamauga," *Galveston Weekly News.*

9 "The Fifteenth Wisconsin in the Battle of Chickamauga—Letter from the Commanding Officer," *Wisconsin State Journal* (Madison, WI), Dec. 23, 1863; "Letter from Col. Martin"; *OR* 30, pt. 1, 529, 533.

Kurtz and Allison print of a Confederate firing line in the woods at Chickamauga. (*Library of Congress*)

had moved rapidly around our left and to the rear. The ground was piled with the dead and wounded."[10]

Martin's Kansans eventually pulled back under intense enemy fire, leaving their beloved mascot dead in the woods. The dog had plenty of company. "Six Captains and two Lieutenants, and over a hundred men of the Eighth, lay dead or wounded, and the loss in the other regiments of the brigade was equally as great," Martin reported. "My own horse had been shot under me. Col. Heg, commanding [the] brigade, gave the order to fall back, and the men retreated, stubbornly contesting every inch of ground." The 8th Kansas fell back some 30 yards, leaving the Norwegians and Swedes of the 15th Wisconsin on their own. "I halted the 15th and held the ground waiting for orders," Colonel Johnson recalled, "but as the other regiment was falling back, and the enemy advancing on our right flank, which was exposed, I ordered a retreat, which was conducted, firing as [we] fell back."

10 "Gregg's Brigade at Chickamauga"; Lindsley, *Military Annals of Tennessee*, 561; Johnson, *SHSP*, 396; "Letter from Col. Martin."

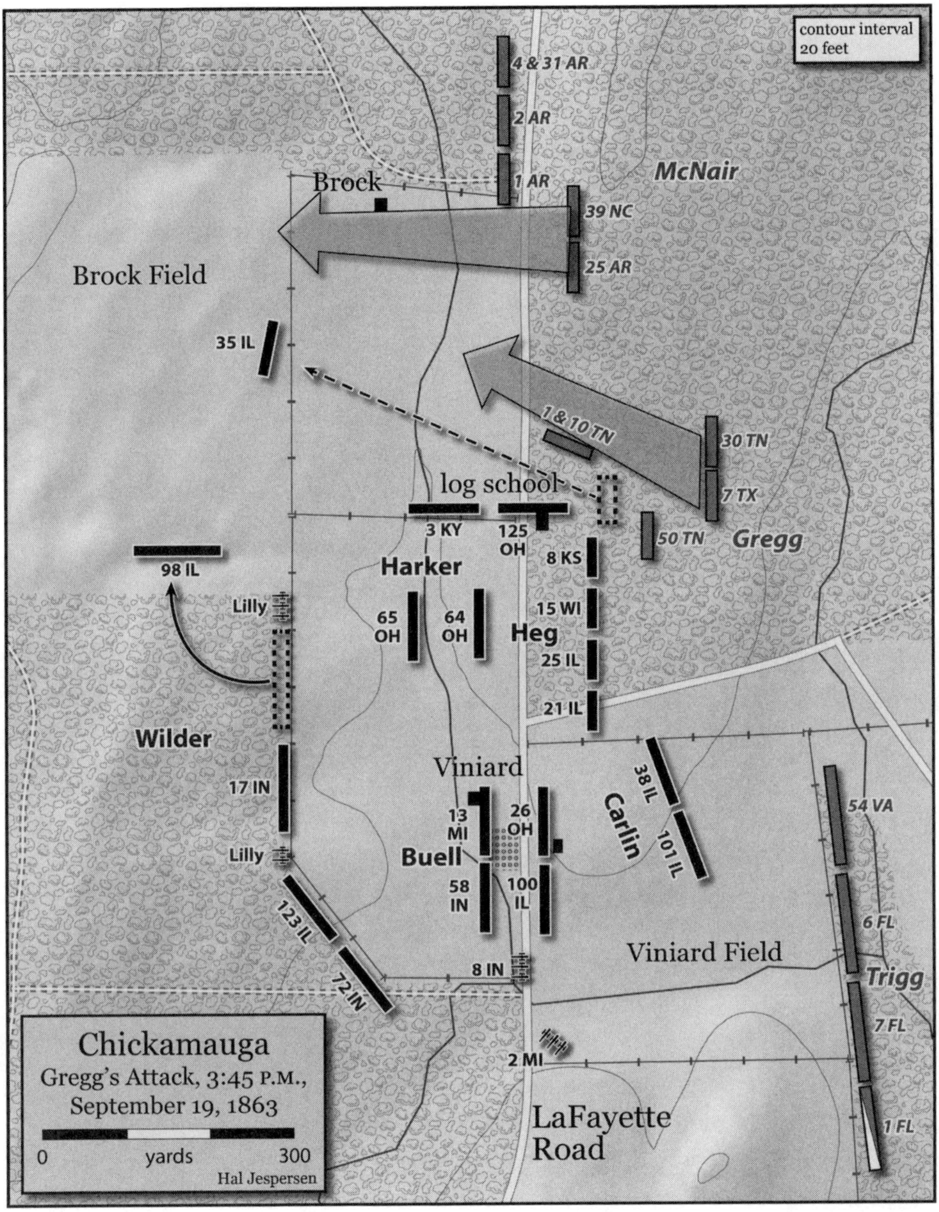

Chickamauga
Gregg's Attack, 3:45 P.M.,
September 19, 1863

Gregg's oncoming men shot down the Badgers' color-bearer; another soldier picked up the fallen flag and carried it off before the Confederates could seize it.[11]

11 "The Fifteenth Wisconsin in the Battle of Chickamauga"; "Letter from Col. Martin."

Colonel Heg brought up the 25th Illinois, which passed through the now-prone ranks of the 15th Wisconsin on a little knoll, and counterattacked. The Kansans and Badgers rose and joined them, despite taking scattered friendly fire from their rear. Gregg's Confederates wavered, fell back 200 yards, and steadied themselves. The Tennesseans and Texans halted the Federal advance with a blistering series of volleys, then resumed the offensive. "Again the fire opened, more severe than before," Colonel Martin wrote of Gregg's defenders and their nearby supports. "The rebels were massed in overpowering numbers before us. They advanced steadily, our men mowing them down by their destructive fire, but being themselves in turn decimated again. We were beaten back, and again rallied, again advanced." Martin added, "The ground was now one heap of mangled bodies. Men fell like the leaves of autumn, but the Eighth fought with a fury and courage unsurpassed. Again the enemy opened, this time accompanied by artillery."[12]

Everett's Battery (Company E, 9th Georgia Artillery) fired from the left of Fulton's brigade and behind Gregg's 17th Tennessee, which enfiladed Heg's reserve 35th Illinois. Bledsoe's Missouri battery, supporting Gregg, hit the Federals from the front. Bushrod Johnson soon brought up Culpeper's South Carolina battery to fill the void beyond the left of Gregg's 50th Tennessee. Hans Heg finally withdrew about 2:15 p.m. after his remaining men fired a few final rounds. His survivors reformed around Carlin's brigade behind a fence some 30 yards west of La Fayette Road. Badger Colonel Johnson noted, "We were all driven across a field [West Viniard] on the other side of which we again formed and the enemy did not deem it prudent to follow."[13]

The situation soon changed.

Gregg Goes in Again

Heg's shattered brigade and most of the other nearby Northerners retreated before Johnson's division. About 2:30 p.m., John Bell Hood ordered a general attack to relieve the pressure on Cheatham's division. Bushrod Johnson cautioned his command to "preserve its connections, to wheel slowly, and to touch to the right." He limbered his three batteries and ordered their respective leaders to accompany the infantry and go into action "whenever opportunity permitted."

12 "Letter from Col. Martin."

13 Cozzens, *This Terrible Sound*, 199; "The Fifteenth Wisconsin in the Battle of Chickamauga."

Iron marker commemorating the position of Bushrod Johnson's division on September 18.
(*Scott Mingus*)

Hood's division, now under Brig. Gen. Evander Law, would support Johnson's left.[14]

Cheatham dispatched a courier to advise John Gregg to be cautious and not mistake his men, who were also advancing at the enemy, for Yankees. McNair's brigade, advancing from its position in reserve, lost cohesion as it moved through the underbrush-choked timber. Johnson's guns fired by section and moved with the infantry. Fulton's brigade drifted off to the right (northwesterly) some 600 yards in the woods and attacked Edward King's brigade of Brig. Gen. Joseph J. Reynolds's division of the XIV Corps. As Fulton struck their flank, King's soldiers were battling A. P. Stewart's Confederates southeast of the Brotherton farm. The pressure from Fulton's and Stewart's combined attacks sent the Federals tumbling back through the field.[15]

Meanwhile, confusion reigned as the rest of Law's Confederates pushed onward. Gregg's and Fulton's brigades crisscrossed with Robertson's Texas Brigade, which was headed in a southwesterly direction. Gregg's brigade soon fragmented. On the right, the 3rd and 41st Tennessee, as Johnson had instructed, preserved their connection with the left of Fulton's 17th Tennessee and accordingly wheeled when Fulton headed to the northeast. Sergeant John T. Goodrich of the 3rd Tennessee noted, "We reached an opening and found that the right wing of Gregg's brigade was far in advance of any other troops." That was because the two center regiments, the 1st and 10th Tennessee, advancing less obliquely, had moved straight ahead. Farther left, the 7th Texas and 30th Tennessee were still stationary and engaged with the enemy. The 50th Tennessee moved well to the south, extending its line until it advanced in open order as skirmishers. Gregg's brigade now was in the general shape of an inverted "V" (or, as some soldiers described it, a wedge) from north to south.[16]

Johnson ordered the 39th North Carolina and 25th Arkansas from McNair's reserve to angle to the south to fill the widening gap between the 50th Tennessee and 7th Texas. The two fresh regiments advanced at a quickstep past the left of the 7th Texas, which was still enduring "a terrific fire." Screaming the Rebel yell, they charged about 200 yards. Determined not to be outdone, Colonel Granbury shouted for the 7th Texas to charge. Mixing their own war cries with those of the

14 Johnson, *SHSP*, 397.

15 "Casualties of the Battle," *The Weekly Advertiser* (Montgomery, AL), Sept. 30, 1863.

16 Goodrich, "Gregg's Brigade in the Battle of Chickamauga," 264; Johnson, *SHSP*, 398.

Arkansans, Granbury's men joined the "wild race to win the field." According to the unidentified 7th Texan, "Down the slope, across the fields, through hedges went the now excited men, and regardless of the rain of death that was poured into them from left, right and front, rolled against the Federal line like an avalanche." The 30th Tennessee followed suit. Heg's and Carlin's lines wavered and fell back 500 yards with some of Gregg's men in pursuit.[17]

The charging 39th North Carolina and 25th Arkansas roared past Heg's far left flank (the 35th Illinois) into West Brock Field, with Gregg's left wing several hundred yards distant in the woods. McNair's two regiments poured across the La Fayette Road, past Benjamin Brock's small house 100 yards away, and into a field of Indian corn. Colonel David Coleman of the 39 North Carolina believed they had traveled almost three-quarters of a mile from their starting position. Lieutenant Colonel Eli Hufstedler of the 25th Arkansas, pierced by five balls, fell in the mad dash.[18]

Yankees soon began firing on either side of Gregg's advancing wedge, threatening "their utter annihilation." Gregg prudently withdrew his left and center regiments about halfway to his original starting point. There, he and the remaining officers rallied the men before continuing the assault. Early in this renewed advance, a spent ball struck Colonel Granbury in the abdomen. Though it did not penetrate his skin, the violent impact left extensive bruising and soreness. In significant pain, the former district judge and recent widower turned over command of the 7th Texas to Major Van Zandt. Gregg, finding himself in danger of being flanked, withdrew east into the woods across the La Fayette Road.[19]

Meanwhile, Col. Charles G. Harker's fresh brigade from Brig. Gen. Thomas J. Wood's division of Crittenden's XXI Corps was warily advancing northward on the La Fayette Road. The nearby woods seemingly were alive with Rebels in short order. Harker, at one point facing Confederates on three sides, dispatched Col. Emerson Opdycke and two Ohio regiments to take on Gregg's exhausted men east of the road. The 98th Illinois of Col. John T. Wilder's Lightning Brigade and a

17 "Gregg's Brigade at Chickamauga"; Powell, *A Mad Irregular Battle,* 461.

18 Dr. William Glenn Robertson, Lt. Col. Edward P. Shanahan, Lt. Col. John I. Boxberger, and Maj. George E. Knapp, *Staff Ride Handbook for the Battle of Chickamauga, 18–20 September, 1863* (Fort Leavenworth, KS: 1992), 35, 85-87; "Gregg's Brigade at Chickamauga"; *OR* 30, pt. 2, 499-500.

19 Lundberg, *Granbury's Texas Brigade,* 102; *Dallas Daily Herald,* Aug. 7, 1884; K. M. Van Zandt to My Dear Wife, Sept. 28, 1863, Van Zandt Family Papers.

section of Capt. Eli Lilly's 18th Indiana Battery on the edge of West Viniard Field opened on McNair's two isolated regiments.[20]

Part of Robertson's brigade had advanced to the right of the 50th Tennessee, which contracted its line to connect with the 3rd Arkansas and 1st Texas. Together, they began pressuring the Federal line. During a lull, John Gregg reformed his brigade in the timber east of the Benjamin Brock farm and La Fayette Road. In the late afternoon, he and his staff rode forward to reconnoiter. He encountered unknown troops, 50 or 60 yards away, partially concealed in the underbrush across the ravine. When Gregg rode over and asked their identity, they replied, "64th Ohio." Wheeling his mare, he galloped away as several shots whistled past him. A Minié ball struck Gregg in the back of the neck and exited through his lower face. He played dead as several enemy skirmishers walked up to him. They removed his sword, brace of pistols, and spurs as trophies before returning to their ranks. When they were out of sight, he rolled into some underbrush.[21]

John Gregg did not have to hide very long. Several Confederate skirmisherssoon emerged from the shadows. They located him and recovered his horse, which was standing nearby. His rescuers proved to be fellow Lone Star soldiers—Hood's Texans.[22]

20 Cozzens, *This Terrible Sound*, 259-260; Goodrich, "Gregg's Brigade in the Battle of Chickamauga," 264.

21 "Gregg's Brigade at Chickamauga"; *Galveston Weekly News*, Nov. 11, 1863; "Casualties of the Battle"; *National Tribune*, Nov. 11, 1886.

22 Johnson, *SHSP*, 399.

Chapter 6

September 19, Late Afternoon—Hood's Texas Brigade

Shortly after dawn, Brig. Gen. Jerome Robertson's weary Texans and Arkansans rose in their northwest-facing line near the Alexander house. During the long night, General Hood had established a rotation of keeping a third of the men awake in case the Yankees suddenly attacked. The soldiers nibbled the hardtack and rancid bacon issued to them during their train stop in Atlanta. The question "What next?" dominated their breakfast conversation. The men began hearing the distant reports of light musketry, indicating that the opposing skirmishers were already at work, as well as occasional heavy firing well off to the right as the morning progressed. After forming in a column about 10:00 a.m., the four regiments headed southwest on the heavily wooded Alexander-Viniard Road toward the left-center of Bragg's line. They halted several hundred yards northeast of the Viniard farm and filed to the right along a low ridge into the forest.[1]

The Texans formed a roughly 300-yard-wide reserve battle line to the left rear of Bushrod Johnson's division. Colonel Van H. Manning's 3rd Arkansas deployed to the left, with the 1st, 4th, and 5th Texas arrayed successively to the right. Hood

1 Polley, *Lone Star Confederate*, 206. Several Texans mentioned arriving on Sept. 19, having missed the fight for Reed's Bridge.

Brig. Gen. Evander M. Law led Hood's division after Hood was wounded. (*Texas Heritage Museum-Historical Research Center*)

had turned over his division to Brig. Gen. Evander Law and now was a nominal corps commander. He placed Law's Alabama brigade (now under Col. James Sheffield) to Robertson's right, with Brig. Gen. Henry L. Benning's Georgia brigade behind it. Off to Hood's left were the divisions of Maj. Gen. Thomas Hindman (from Polk's Corps) and Brig. Gen. William Preston (Buckner's Corps). Hood lacked adequate sightlines and the ability to deploy field guns in the thickets. Complicating the matter was Colonel Sheffield's lack of staff officers—Hood kept his division staff with him as he ascended to corps command. Law did the same with his aides when he assumed command of the division.[2]

As Sheffield's and Benning's men formed their respective battle lines, John Bell Hood rode by on his spirited roan, "Jeff Davis." His appearance surprised the soldiers, who had not yet heard that Hood was on the field. They believed their beloved leader was still convalescing in Richmond. Yet here he was in the Georgia woods, with his injured left arm in a tight sling, now directing their deployment. Men cheered and waved their hats as the charismatic Hood rode past, reaching the line of the Texans. Hood removed his hat and intoned, "Boys, I am glad to see you. You must whip this battle here." One Rebel believed there was something "awfully beautiful and solemnly prophetic" about Hood's remarks. "We'll do it, general," came the reply. With that affirmation, the infantrymen settled into position to await further orders, which came an hour later when Hood instructed the Texas Brigade to move forward almost a mile. The line finally halted behind Johnson's division

2 Skoch and Perkins, *Lone Star Confederate*, 96; Jim Ogden, "Texans at Viniard Field, Chickamauga," National Park Service battle walk, Sept. 2017, posted to YouTube on Oct. 2, 2017. Benning and Law/Sheffield had marched from Reed's Bridge that morning to rejoin the division.

Postwar image of quartermaster Sgt. Joseph B. "J. B." Polley, 4th Texas Infantry. (*Texas Heritage Museum-Historical Research Center*)

half a mile from the La Fayette Road. Again, the men lay down amid the trees to wait.[3]

With time on their hands, many soldiers fretted about what awaited, perhaps even the end of their lives. "Now you can imagine without experiencing [it] how awful and terrible this feeling of suspense is," the 5th Texas's Pvt. Robert Campbell recalled. He almost welcomed the order to advance for no other reason than to relieve the uncertainty. "I lay there, dreaming of home & of friends and the associations of my life before the way." He believed he would be shot in the upcoming fight and prayed it might be through his left arm.[4]

As the Texans and Arkansans waited, they did not have much of a view. "The larger part of the fighting done at Chickamauga was in the somber shadows of thick growths of large pine timber," Quartermaster Sgt. J. B. Polley of the 4th Texas related. "The soil sterile, it was only now and then that a clearing gave the combatants access to uninterrupted sunlight. Under the trees there was much undergrowth of various kinds. It was difficult for an officer on horseback to get an extended view in any direction, and to footmen it was simply impossible. Short as was the line occupied by the Texas Brigade, neither flank of it could be seen from the other."[5]

In the dense timber, the soldiers could not see the distant combat, but they could hear it. "About half past ten or eleven o'clock a most tremendous fire of musketry was opened on our right," the 4th Texas's Pvt. John C. West; what he heard was the main action shifting south with Frank Cheatham's five brigades

3 *Huntsville* (AL) *Daily Confederate*, Oct. 17, 1863; Polley, *Hood's Texas Brigade*, 208; *Houston Tri-Weekly Telegraph*, Nov. 16, 1863.

4 Joskins, *A Sketch of Hood's Texas Brigade*, 144.

5 Polley, *Hood's Texas Brigade*, 205.

attack on the Federals. Bragg soon sent Brig. Gen. A. P. Stewart's division to support Cheatham. According to West, the roar of battle continued for two hours without more than two minutes' intermission. "It reminded me," he mused, "of rain on a tin roof, where at intervals the storm rages with tremendous fury, then lulls but still continues as sounds grow faint or distant according to the changes of the varying wind." Lieutenant Benjamin I. Franklin of the 5th Texas recalled that the "volleys of Musketry exceeded anything I have ever heard. Our men driving the enemy slowly but steadily; they resisting stubbornly."[6]

The artillery barrage reminded some Texans of the roar of a tornado or a herd of runaway cattle. Others thought of an earthquake. "The earth beneath us seemed to tremble with its concussions, the trees above us to rock back and forth," Joe Polley observed. "Judging alone from the sound, it appeared to me that every man of both armies must soon be killed or wounded." He and his comrades wondered why the din of the fighting seemed to neither to recede nor increase. They heard little of the yelling so typical of battles in Virginia, and eventually learned that the opposing lines at Chickamauga often stood 200 to 300 yards apart and blazed away at each other as fast as the men could reload. They realized that this "slugfest" fighting method would not work in Virginia's farmland, where troops could usually charge the enemy on sight. Private Bill Calhoun voiced the general sentiment. "Boys," he declared, "if we've got to stand in a straight line and become stationary targets for the Yankees to shoot at from a rest, this old Texas brigade of our'n is a goin' to run like hell."[7]

Robertson's men indeed were stationary targets, much to their chagrin. "We were deployed in line of battle on a ridge on which was some timber," wrote Sgt. David H. Hamilton of the 1st Texas. "We remained there under a heavy shelling until two o'clock in the afternoon; by this time the Yankee batteries had about topped all the timber around us. The shells had kept every man as busy as a cranberry merchant dodging their flying fragments." The Confederates could hear the "singing noise" of the artillery rounds whizzing overhead before crashing into the trees.[8]

Wesley and Ed Francis of the 4th Texas were among six brothers from Guadalupe County who served in the Confederate army. Their father, a wealthy

6 West, *A Texan in Search of a Fight*, 113; B. I. Franklin to Mary Franklin, Oct. 2, 1863, CCNMP.

7 Polley, *Hood's Texas Brigade*, 207; "Reminiscences of a Private," *San Antonio Daily Express*, Apr. 22, 1906.

8 Hamilton, History of Company M, 31.

Postwar image of Color Sgt. George A. Branard, 1st Texas Infantry. His left eye was permanently blinded from a shell fragment at the battle of Gettysburg. (*Courtesy of Patty Branard-Gambino*)

plantation owner, had been a cavalryman under the famed Juan Seguin during the 1836 Texas Revolution. Wesley now huddled in the woods at Chickamauga with his comrades in Company A, listening to the battle. Color Sergeant Edward M. Francis was in the center of the regiment with the color guard. "I felt like I wanted to talk to him," Wesley later admitted, "but, I did not and I shall ever regret that I did not." He added, "I believe I felt more anxiety here than at any other previous battle."[9]

Wounded soldiers from Cheatham's division began streaming through the Texans' line. Private James M. Polk of the 5th Texas noticed an artilleryman heading for the rear, shouldering his swab. He thought the man must have lost his battery in the confusion. A black servant was heading to the front to take dinner to his captain. Near Polk's position, he passed another slave walking to the rear. They briefly conversed, with the second man mentioning that the captain was dead. The two noncombatants marveled that the white people were shooting each other. After a shell knocked down a treetop and another whizzed by, the two slaves fled to safety.[10]

The constant roar indicated that Hood would soon need the Texans' services. The veterans understood this imminent danger but knew how to cope with the stress. After first giving their undivided nervous attention to the firing, the men began to relax. Some took time to scribble a quick letter home or record their thoughts in their diaries. Others exchanged gossip and pleasantries with old friends along the battle line. Sergeant Polley encountered two former college classmates, who recalled events from their student days. At the time, some of Robertson's late

9 "Francis Fought for Texas Independence," *Seguin* (TX) *Gazette-Enterprise*, Mar. 5, 1986. Three of the Francis boys died during the war.

10 Polk, *A Confederate Soldier*, 23-25.

arrivals were marching to rejoin the brigade. "We pulled up to a platform [Catoosa] in the vicinity of Ringgold," Color Sgt. George A. Branard of the 1st Texas recalled. "On stopping at this platform we were hustled out at a lively rate, and don't you forget it. We formed in marching order at once." The Texans could hear the popping of musketry as they marched.[11]

Sergeant William A. Fletcher of the 5th Texas's Company F was another late arrival. "When we left the train, we were marched a few miles and thrown into line of battle," he recalled. A few bullets from the fight to their front came uncomfortably close. Under the nervous strain, the prewar carpenter from Beaumont fell asleep, as he had at previous battles. "Sleep always has a quieting effect, if only for a few minutes, and I have often remarked that if a fellow wanted a fight out of me, I would advise him not to wake me up to get it, for I would be cocked and primed for the fray."[12]

Branard, Fletcher, and their comrades likely reached the scene at 2:00 p.m., during a brief lull on Robertson's front. The weather had warmed considerably by then, making the afternoon rather pleasant after the chilly morning frost. Like Bill Fletcher, several men dozed off. During the respite, the 4th Texas's Sergeant Polley and his friend Pvt. Jack Sutherland smoked and chatted. They were happily puffing away when they heard the sharp command "Attention!" Sutherland immediately removed his pipe from his lips to get ready to go into action, but Polley admonished, "Go on with your smoking, man. It'll be an hour before we get under fire." Sutherland replied, "No, I'll not smoke anymore, just now." He knocked the ashes and embers from the pipe and stuck it in his pocket. Polley kept smoking. It was the last pipeful of Zarvona tobacco he had brought with him on the train ride from Virginia, and he wanted to finish it. He did not get that indulgence; just three minutes later, a fierce battle erupted directly in their front when Gregg's brigade resumed its fight. Robertson's Texans and Arkansans formed into a battle line while bullets, shell fragments, and round shot flew around them. Still drawing on his pipe, Polley stood next to Sutherland. Farther along the line, someone shook the dozing Bill Fletcher awake.[13]

11 Polley, *Hood's Texas Brigade*, 207; "How a Presentiment Came True," *Galveston Daily News*, May 20, 1900.

12 William A. Fletcher, *Rebel Private: Front and Rear: Memoirs of a Confederate Soldier*, (Beaumont, TX: 1908), 97.

13 That sudden fighting was Johnson's division returning to action at 2:30 p.m., per Hood's orders.

Postwar image of Sgt. D. H. Hamilton, 1st Texas Infantry. (*Courtesy of Kenny Dee*)

Polley and Sutherland soon spotted John Bell Hood returning from reconnoitering the front, and the Texans shouted in admiration as the general passed his old brigade on his way to the division's rear. Hood had not traveled more than 20 yards when a solid shot or unexploded shell struck the ground about 30 feet in front of Polley and Sutherland. The ball ricocheted and passed over their heads so close that they could feel the wind as it whistled past. "It scared me," Polley admitted, "and, I am confident, my face turned white as a sheet." He pulled his hat down over his face to hide his pallid countenance. Glancing at Sutherland, he found to his relief that he was not alone in his abject terror at the close call: Jack's face was as white as his own. "It is hardly necessary to add," Polley mentioned, "that I ceased smoking, and so lost the benefit of half a pipeful of precious Zarvona."[14]

After viewing the terrain and assessing the tactical situation on the firing line, General Hood sent word between 2:45 and 3:00 for his former division to support Bushrod Johnson's division, which was then fighting Heg's and Carlin's brigades. Hood wanted General Law to wheel his entire division to the southwest and follow Johnson toward the La Fayette Road a half mile away. Sheffield, Robertson, and Benning prepared their respective brigades to move forward. As the 1st Texas formed, a Federal artillery shell knocked the top from a tree. It toppled onto Pvt. John "Muly" Stewart, striking him on the head. A field surgeon ran over and called for litter-bearers to carry the disoriented soldier off the field. Muly presently began to regain his senses. Frightened, he raced for the rear as the physician cursed him. "He ran like a deer, except that he made as much noise as a yoke of oxen," the 1st Texas's Sgt. D. H. Hamilton remembered. Standing nearby, Pvt. Willoughby Tullos

14 Polley, *Hood's Texas Brigade*, 208-209.

called out, "Whoa, Muly!" but the terrified soldier continued to sprint toward the field hospital.[15]

The Initial Attack on the Viniard Farm

Robertson had orders to maintain contact with Sheffield's Alabamians on his right flank. About 3:30 p.m., his long line of Confederates began walking southwest through the woods, with skirmishers 200 yards in front. "We were ordered forward," the 5th Texas's Pvt. Robert Campbell remembered with a touch of Texas swagger, "and with audacity we obeyed the order." Incoming Federal shells were bothersome, but the canopy of treetops offered some protection. The Texans and Arkansans had not gone far when they started encountering a steady stream of wounded soldiers, shirkers, and played-out stragglers heading to the rear. "You fellers'll catch hell in thar," one man shouted as he approached the line of the 4th Texas on Robertson's right-center. "Them fellers out thar you ar goin' up agin, ain't none of the blue-bellied, white-livered Yanks an' sassidge-eatin' forrin hirelins you have in Virginny that'll run at the snap of a cap—they are Western fellers, an' they'll mighty quick give you a bellyful o' fightin'." A few of these refugees fell in with the Texans.[16]

The 3rd Arkansas and 1st Texas remained on the left, with the 4th and 5th Texas on the right. The left two regiments soon entered an area in which grazing cattle had reduced the foliage over the years. The going was much more challenging for 4th and 5th Texas, which were still navigating an overgrown section of the woods. Dense smoke and the forest canopy limited visibility to the point where many men on Robertson's right could not see their file leaders. "The underbrush and mescaline vines were so thick and interwoven that it was almost impossible to get through, and of course our lines were broken and irregular," Sgt. Valerius C. Giles of the 4th Texas observed. "Those who were not so badly embarrassed by brush and vines naturally got ahead, causing companies and even regiments to lap over each other, which created any amount of confusion. Our advance through the

15 Hamilton, *History of Company M*, 32-33. Stewart remained at the field hospital for three days while receiving treatment for his head and facial injuries.

16 *OR* 30 pt. 2, 427; Joskins, *History of Company M*, 144; Polley, *Hood's Texas Brigade*, 209.

deep-tangled jungle was slow. . . . We could see nothing as we groped our way through the wilderness." The skirmishers kept a sharp eye for the enemy.[17]

"After advancing about half a mile through scrub oak, dogwood, and vines," Giles continued, "we came to a little glade with a dry branch meandering through it." As the regiment emerged from the cedar glade's east side, a Union major on a splendid bay galloped into view. He waved his arm and appeared to be warning the Rebels to fall back. A Texan cried out, "Don't shoot him!" but two or three men fired individually, followed by a full volley that dropped the officer and his steed into the ravine. The Texans continued to move forward with the dead Federal sprawled on his back, "perfectly still with his arms stretched out on each side of his body." The first Confederate to arrive reached down and started to unfasten the man's belt, hoping to take it and a holstered pistol. Another Texan, however, darted over and grabbed the gun from the holster, then rushed off with it. "Soldiers who saw the performance laughed," Giles added, "but the fellow holding the belt swore like a pirate and called the other rogue and thief." No one could quite figure out the Yankee's motives for the strange behavior that led to his death. Some men thought he may have been trying to surrender.[18]

On the left, the 3rd Arkansas and 1st Texas approached Virginia-born Tabler Christian Viniard's hardscrabble farm. Some 75 yards west of the road, a dry gully cut through the northern section of what later became known as "West Viniard Field." This seasonal drainage ditch was between 1.5 and 3.5 feet wide and 6 to 8 feet deep. It angled toward the sloping field's southeastern corner just before the intersection of the Glenn-Viniard and Alexander-Viniard Roads. The ditch, lined with bushes and occasional willows, then ran eastward parallel to the latter lane for several hundred yards at the southern edge of "East Viniard Field." The southwestern corner of the field featured a small, wooded hill that ran north to the farmhouse and went west across the road into West Viniard Field. Several fence lines divided East Viniard Field and this hill into sections. Woods bordered the uneven field on three sides.[19]

17 *Ural, Hood's Texas Brigade*,187; "In Storm of Battle," *New Orleans Times-Democrat*, May 25, 1903.

18 "In Storm of Battle"; Laswell, *Rags and Hope*, 201-202. Giles's article differs slightly in dates and details from his wartime journal, as quoted in Laswell. In the paper, Giles says that this description is for the Sept. 19 advance, but some contemporary authors place it on the 20th in North Dyer Field.

19 *OR* 30, pt. 1, 669; Edward Ruger, "Map of the Battlefield of Chickamauga, September 19th and 20th, 1863," sheet no. 2, Julius Bien and Company, 1892; Sartain, History of Walker

Pvt. John C. West, 4th Texas Infantry. (*Texas Heritage Museum-Historical Research Center*)

The 1st Texas advanced behind Lt. John H. Wooters's Company I, which deployed out front as skirmishers. After going about 200 yards through the open timber northeast of the Viniard house, Wooters sent word back to Capt. R. J. Harding that the enemy was advancing on his left flank. According to Color Sgt. George A. Branard, "While my regiment was moving through the wood, which was somewhat cleared of timber on our right, when crack, crack went a gun. Our flanking skirmishers had run into a squad of Yankee pickets. My regiment was moved to the left and to the front, climbing over a rail fence, thence into a briar patch, but met no Yankees. After moving around in different positions expecting an attack, we moved back and into the road again." The line continued its slow advance.[20]

The left of the 3rd Arkansas came under enemy fire after advancing another 300 yards. Robertson authorized Col. Van Manning to shift two companies by the left flank to counter the threat. The general thought the enemy was merely a small force sent as a diversion to threaten his flank; there were far more Yankees in East Viniard Field, however, than he realized. The 38th Illinois and 101st Ohio of Carlin's brigade had aligned on the south side of East Viniard Field behind a brush-lined rail fence bordering the dry ditch. Manning, quickly realizing what he faced, asked Robertson if he could realign his entire regiment to the southwest to deal with them. Learning of this development, Robertson halted his three Texas

County, 108. Viniard's kinsman James, a Confederate soldier, died of smallpox in a Union prison camp. Tabler joined the Union Army in 1864 and died on Aug. 21 from acute diarrhea in a field hospital in Bridgeport, Alabama. In some accounts, including the one on Tabler's headstone, the surname is spelled "Vineyard."

20 Ural, *Hood's Texas Brigade*, 187; "How a Presentiment Came True."

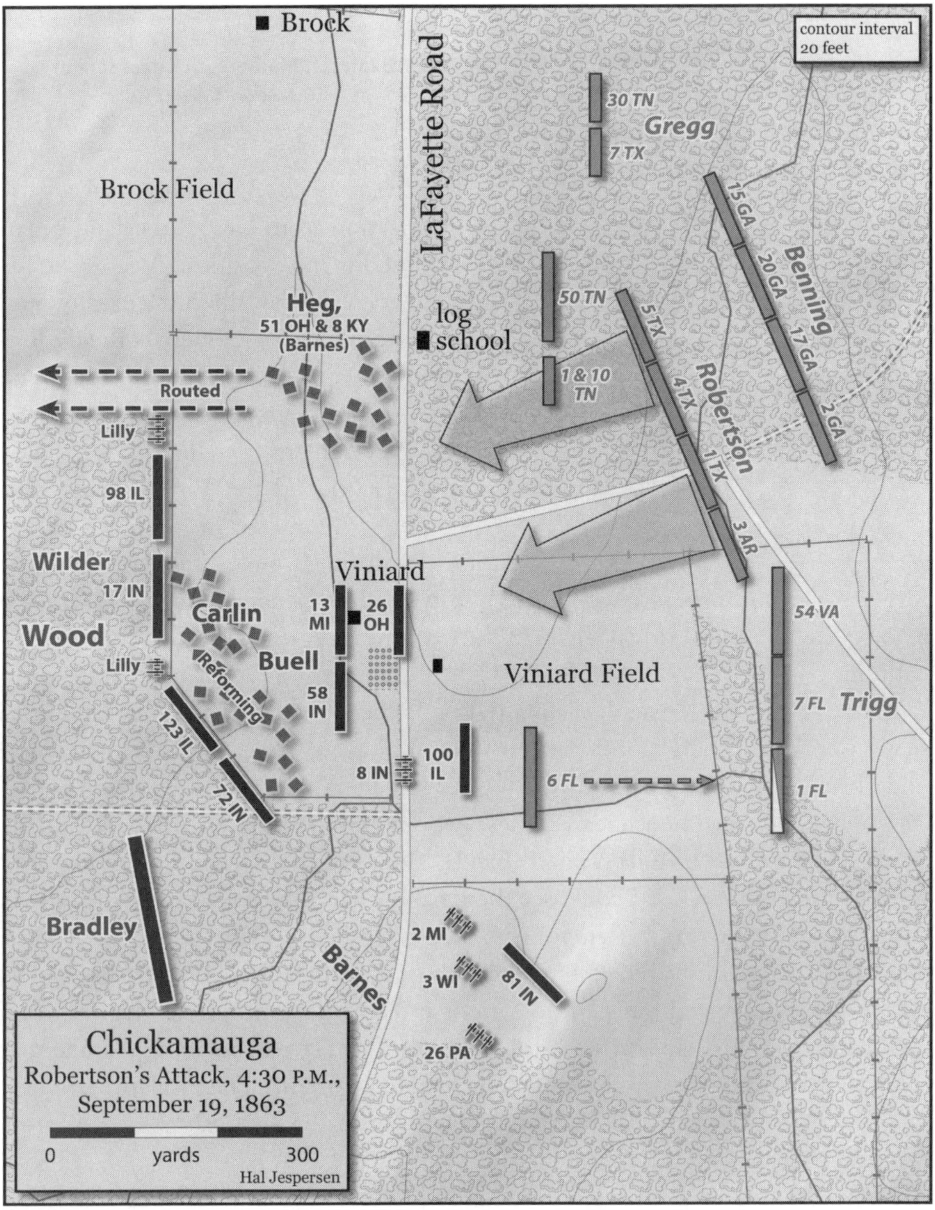

regiments and sent a courier galloping back to General Law to request permission to change his brigade front to counter this unexpected threat.[21]

21 *OR* 30, pt. 2, 513.

Capt. James T. Hunter, 4th Texas Infantry. (*Confederate Veteran*)

After securing the necessary authorization from Law, Robertson began maneuvering into position. As a result, his rightmost regiment, the 5th Texas, would no longer guide on Colonel Sheffield's left, creating a gap between the brigades. The three Texas regiments, straddling the Alexander-Viniard Road, angled southwest toward the Viniard farm with Benning's Georgians in support. It was likely during this movement that Robertson's skirmishers encountered the wounded General Gregg lying in the woods. Robertson's arrival enabled Col. Cyrus A. Sugg's 50th Tennessee to withdraw.[22]

After crossing Alexander-Viniard Road, the 4th and 5th Texas entered a section of thin, open woods, where the trees were larger and the vines and underbrush much less thick. Visibility and maneuverability thus were much better. As soon as the regiment cleared these woods, the Texans encountered enemy skirmishers arrayed in East Viniard Field. "We advanced to within one hundred yards of the Yanks, when I could see them plainly lying and squatting in the bushes and scant undergrowth," Pvt. John C. West recalled. "There was a small field beyond them and a little hill on the other side of it, from which a battery annoyed us a little as we advanced but had no serious effect on our progress." Just as West spotted the skirmishers and was about to shoot, "a cry passed along the line that these were our own men, but very few seemed to regard it." The similarity between the new clothing from the Richmond Depot and the Federals' blue uniforms proved confusing.[23]

22 "Casualties of the Battle"; *OR* 30, pt. 2, 454-455; Simpson, *The History of Hood's Texas Brigade*, 341; Foley, *Hood's Texas Brigade*, 50. Gregg was evacuated on Sunday via train to Atlanta, per the Rome, *Tri-Weekly Courier*, Sept. 22, 1863.

23 West, *A Texan in Search of a Fight*, 114; "In Storm of Battle."

Private James M. Polk remembered how he learned the distant men's identity: "As soon as the Federals discovered our approach, they gave us a salute by waving the Stars and Stripes at us, in order to ridicule the idea of us coming at them." A concealed double line of Yankees suddenly fired a single rolling volley. "A sharp fire commenced on our left of the brigade and extended down the line to the right," Capt. James T. Hunter reported. "Up to the time we met this line our progress had not been impeded except by a line of skirmishers and a heavy fire of grape and canister." The volley surprised the Confederates, Sergeant Polley remembered, with "many of our bravest and best falling, dead or wounded, before they pulled a trigger." Private Lawrence Daffan said the "Texans received a terrible volley of musketry there, the most terrible during the war." He added, "Had the Federals shot low, they all would probably have been killed; from six to thirty feet on the trees showed the terrible volley of musketry. The men who fell were shot in the breast or head, which indicated excited and high shooting by the Federals." According to Private Polk, "It seemed that every third or fourth man in our line was cut down. Billie Carroll and Tobe Riggs both fell not over five or six feet from me. We lost Dock Childers [Childress] and Chisum Walker. . . . I suppose if we had stopped there and given the Federals time to reload their guns they would have killed the rest of us, but we moved on them with loaded guns."[24]

Private Stephen M. "Tobe" Riggs of Company I of the 4th Texas had been ill that morning. Polk, his cousin, had suggested he not go into battle. When the order came, Riggs went forward anyway. Now, the soldier from Corsicana fell with a mortal wound at the first volley. Desperately, he called to his captain, James R. Loughridge, "Oh, Lord! What shall I do?" Recalling a promise to Tobe's parents to take care of their son, Loughridge stooped down and placed his hand on the dying man's head. "My friend!" he instructed. "Place your trust in the Lord Jesus Christ."[25]

A few frightened 4th Texans immediately bolted for the rear before the Yankees could reload, including an unidentified soldier in Company D who had a reputation as an "all-around good fellow" in camp and on the march. He shirked

24 Polk, *A Confederate Soldier*, 25, 27; *OR* 30, pt. 2, 514; Polley, *Hood's Texas Brigade*, 209; *Waxahachie Daily Light*, Feb. 16, 1907. Hunter was a career lawman before the war, serving as a Texas Ranger, deputy sheriff, and the constable of Huntsville, Texas.

25 Stewart, *Report of the Proceedings of the Various Associations of Ex-Confederates*, 23; Mrs. A. V. Winkler, *The Confederate Capital and Hood's Texas Brigade*, (Austin, TX, 1894), 144-145. Mrs. Winkler was the wife of the 4th Texas's Capt. Charles M. Winkler, who was not present at the battle.

combat, however. Intensely afraid of Yankee bullets, he had managed to avoid every previous battle in Maryland and Virginia. Before the assault began, his file leader, Jack Smith, promised the company he would escort this "weak brother" through the fight. Ignoring Smith in the confusion of the Yankee volley, the coward took to his heels. No one saw him again until after the battle.[26]

Stunned soldiers looked around for the source of the sudden fusillade. "For almost a minute we failed to locate their line," Sergeant Polley recalled. "Then we discovered they were lying down, and shooting from behind trees, fallen logs and other cover." According to Cpl. Miles V. "Pony" Smith of Company D, someone yelled, "There they are, boys! Give it to them!" The Confederate skirmishers dropped down and awaited the arrival of the main line before springing up and rejoining the ranks. The 4th Texas fired a volley in reply and then surged forward. "Before the Yanks could reload," Corporal Smith remembered, "we were right in among them, our guns also empty, and such a mix-up as we had! Most of our antagonists took advantage of our empty guns to make for the rear as fast as their legs could carry them, but a large number had the grit to seek to hold their ground, and with this we had, for a brief time, a hand-to-hand conflict."[27]

"Their main body gave way before our impetuous rush, but with a reluctance that was not encouraging, and formed another line a hundred yards in rear of the first," Sergeant Polley claimed. "Such of them, though, as had shelter, stood their ground behind it and fought gamely until disabled, or surrounded and forced to surrender. The need to capture such squads compelled our folks to make the battle somewhat personal and individual, and while as a command the brigade moved steadily on, its units fought on their own hook."[28]

"The regiment moved up in fine style, and met and charged the enemy gallantly, driving them from their position," Captain Hunter reported. "They then took refuge behind a house, some fencing, &c." As the men of the 4th Texas closed in on the Federals, they received heavy fire from artillery, as well as renewed musketry. They halted in the northwestern corner of East Viniard Field and exchanged shots with the foe. Sergeant Polley soon became and hastened from the firing line to the rear. A bullet struck Lieutenant Colonel Bane in the arm. Before leaving the field to seek medical attention, he called out to Captain Hunter and told

26 *San Antonio Daily Express*, Dec. 5, 1909.

27 Ibid.; M. V. Smith Reminiscences, Texas Heritage Museum, Hill College (THM).

28 Polley, *Hood's Texas Brigade*, 209.

him to take command. Hunter protested that Captain Bassett outranked him. But Bob Bassett's Company G was on the right side of the regiment, so Bane instructed Hunter, "There is no time to see Bassett; take command."[29]

Off to the left of the 4th Texas, the 1st Texas moved into East Viniard Field to support the 3rd Arkansas. It found Yankees "posted in large numbers in a ravine covered by thick undergrowth," according to Capt. Richard J. Harding. "The Yankees in front of us occupied an old farm," Sergeant Hamilton recalled; "[T]hey had torn down the rail fences and made breastworks of them for about a mile in length and were lying behind this barricade when we charged them. When we got within about one hundred yards of them, they arose, fired one volley and ran like turkeys. That one volley, however, was very destructive. All who were not killed or wounded raised the Rebel Yell and took up the chase."[30]

Private James M. Leach of the 1st Texas went down with a wound that severed a muscle in his lower right leg. It would be three months before he could limp around and almost a year before he could rejoin the regiment, and even then it was against doctors' orders. Caught and returned to the hospital, he would take off again. "I joined the army to fight, so I ran away," he explained. After multiple escapes and a five-week stint in the guardhouse with nothing but cornmeal and water, Leach would compromise and become a hospital ward master for the rest of the war.[31]

Despite harassing fire from Robertson's skirmishers, the 2nd Minnesota Artillery and 3rd Wisconsin Artillery, 200 yards away on the rise in the southwestern part of East Viniard Field, continued to hurl deadly canister rounds at the advancing Rebels. The Union field pieces, with support from Carlin's 81st Indiana, soon forced the 1st Texas and 3rk Arkansas to withdraw into the woods. On the way, some of the Confederates found temporary relief behind scattered trees or swells in the ground. As Robertson rallied north of the Alexander-Viniard Road, Col Robert C. Trigg's brigade of Floridians and Virginians advanced into East Viniard Field and checked Col. Sidney M. Barnes's oncoming Federal brigade of Van Cleve's division.

29 J. T. Hunter, "Hard Fighting Fourth Texas," *CV*, vol. 14, no. 1, Jan. 1906, 22; Polley, *Hood's Texas Brigade*, 210.

30 *OR* 30, pt. 2, 513; Hamilton, *History of Company M*, 34.

31 "Veteran James Leach tells of his experience in Civil War," *Bryan* (TX) *Daily Eagle*, July 4, 1925. Although the article gives his name as James M. Leach, his CSR says "William Leach." The facts in that record, including his being detailed as a ward master, match, so this is likely the same man.

After Robertson's officers reformed their men, the 3rd Arkansas and 1st Texas surged forward a second time, but both regiments again stalled under intense musketry and artillery fire. "My line steadily advanced, the enemy contesting every inch of ground," General Robertson reported, "until I reached the fence that divides the two fields on the crest of the hill." The Minnesota and Wisconsin batteries, which had been waiting for the Rebels to reappear, opened with grape and canister, raking the hill. Robertson quickly pulled his men behind the crest for protection from the barrage.[32]

While the fighting raged, Pvt. Alfred C. Sims of the 1st Texas was still back in Tunnel Hill with the commissary supply. He could hear the roar of cannon and the rattle of small arms. Anxious to know the fate of his friends in Company F, he started walking toward the battlefield. On the way, he encountered Pvt. Ben Bradham, who was heading to the rear after being shot in the big toe. Bradham advised, "I'll tell you there is hell there ahead, and you have the general's permission to stay out it and you had better do it."[33]

"Hell" indeed lay ahead at the Viniard farm. General Robertson would soon face fresh enemy troops. Major General Thomas J. Wood, commanding the 1st Division of Crittenden's XXI Corps, had dispatched Col. George P. Buell's brigade to support Carlin and Heg. Buell positioned his regiments—the 100th Illinois, 58th Indiana, 13th Michigan, and 26th Ohio—in a double line generally parallel to the La Fayette Road in the open terrain southwest of the Viniard buildings. A spur of intervening woods jutted into the field near the orchard off to Robertson's right. Thus, he had only limited knowledge of the 4th's activities and could tell nothing of what was happening with the 5th Texas beyond the trees. The 4th and 5th Texas now fought independent of brigade command and control.[34]

The 4th and 5th Texas Attack the La Fayette Road Line

When the 4th Texas made its initial advance into East Viniard Field, Maj. Jefferson C. Rogers's 5th Texas approached Heg's and Carlin's Federal line along the La Fayette Road. The "Bloody Fifth," on the far right of the brigade, negotiated a hill in the overgrown woods east of the roadway. Union shells crashed through

32 Yeary, *Reminiscences,*151; East Texas Historical Society, *East Texas Family Records*, vol. 2, no. 2, Summer 1978, 4; 30, *OR* pt. 2, 511.

33 Sims, "1st Texas Infantry Regiment," THM.

34 *OR* 30, pt. 1, 503.

Maj. Jefferson C. Rogers, 5th Texas Infantry. (*Confederate Veteran*)

the timber as the soldiers descended the rise, and Rogers kept the long line moving despite losing a few men. At the edge of the woods, he encountered the enemy in force. His regiment, with its rightmost companies crossing the road, pressed Heg's and Carlin's Federals.

At that point, the woods extended much farther out toward the Federal line than to the left or right. Therefore, the 5th advanced under cover of the trees almost 200 yards farther than the 4th Texas to its left. With the 5th's strength concealed from most of the Federals, some of Carlin's and Heg's soldiers believed the Rebels were flanking them. After delivering a single volley, they fled across West Viniard Field to the cover of woods. Some Yankees sheltered inside the small log schoolhouse along the La Fayette Road and fought stubbornly while their comrades retreated. "I was very much surprised and a little scared for I had never run any before," admitted a bandsman in the 58th Indiana. According to the Bloody Fifth's Capt. Tacitus T. Clay, "it was with the greatest difficulty that our men could be held back from their pursuit." Private Robert Campbell recalled that "the ardor of the boys could not be restrained, so with a Texas yell we went at them and drove them—run them like dogs—until our regiment, the Fifth, got so far ahead of the brigade, we had to fall back to prevent being flanked on both sides."[35]

Fire from the 1st Texas, 3rd Arkansas, and the 4th Texas's left also drove back Carlin's brigade to Heg's right. The men fled across West Viniard Field and through the ranks of Wilder's Lightning Brigade. According to a soldier in the 72nd Indiana, Carlin's men "gave way and came back in dreadful confusion. They were

35 W. K. Brown to Mrs. Sarah Johnson, "Letter Tells How Rebs Whip Union," *The Crosbyton* (TX) *Review*, Sept. 7, 1961; *OR* 30, pt. 2, 515-516; Skoch and Perkins, *Lone Star Confederate* 96.

generally throwing away their knapsacks, in some instances their weapons. They ran over us like sheep."[36]

Heg's Federals rallied and moved forward shortly after 4:00 p.m., but the Texans countered with another emotional charge. For half an hour, short-range fighting raged around the La Fayette Road and at the log schoolhouse. "We came to close quarters," Lt. Benjamin I. Franklin reported, "punishing them severely and driving them in confusion." The 33-year-old Colonel Heg fell wounded, and died the next day. Colonel John Martin of the 8th Kansas succeeded him. Carlin and Martin withdrew their shattered brigades west behind Wilder's Lightning Brigade and Eli Lilly's 18th Indiana Battery, leaving the schoolhouse and roadway in Confederate hands.[37]

The Confederates were in hot pursuit. "We were ordered to charge," Sgt. William Fletcher recalled, "so we plunged forward with a yell, firing as fast as we went. When near, the enemy broke, and with but little effort at returning fire, so things were going our way fast." He noticed a high, well-built worm fence about 50 yards to his left-front behind the fleeing Federals, and supposed they had not thought the Rebels would repulse them or they would have torn it down in order to clear their rear. About 60 yards from the corner of this fencing sat the Viniard house, with a dirt chimney on its south side. "A great number of the enemy who were running down the fence and turning the corner attracted my attention from my immediate front," Fletcher continued. "Between the house and fence, there was a block that extended nearly back to the corner of the fence—a great majority of them were in a pushing motion and jammed and at close range. I got two shots and thought—oh, for a shotgun loaded with buckshot!" He realized he could not reload in time to get a third shot off before the mob escaped, so he headed forward at a "long trot." Just as he passed the house, some 20 feet to his left, he felt something strike his left foot. He fell backward into a large hole Tabler Viniard had made to excavate dirt for his chimney. "I saw I was well protected, and from the sounds, I supposed a piece of flying shell hit hard enough to trip me. There had been no pain up to this time, so the idea struck me that I was not wounded and had a coward's position, and I was liable to be seen in it."

36 Powell, *The Maps of Chickamauga,* 102, citing the William H. Records Diary at the Indiana State Library.

37 B. I. Franklin to Mary Franklin, Oct. 2, 1863, CCNMP. Heg was the highest-ranking soldier from Wisconsin to die during the Civil War.

Sergeant Fletcher glanced down and noticed holes on both sides of his left shoe. He pulled it off to discover that a bullet had passed through his foot. He was tempted to stay in the protective hole but feared being captured if the regiment fell back, so he limped about 75 yards toward the woods. He spotted a wounded Yankee sheltering behind a 20-inch-diameter oak. "Pain here struck me and I felt faint," Fletcher recalled, "so with a hop or two I was at the Yank's side, and as there was no room enough for two, I gave him a shove, saying: 'The day is ours.'" The Northerner fell over on his side, motionless but groaning. Fletcher took his spot behind the large tree, leaned against it, and rested.

A sudden volley sent several bullets whistling past him. He heard the distinctive Texas yell and knew the boys were again charging. He peered around the oak to see the action. The Texans were "charging in scattered battle line and the enemy firing from solid column," Fletcher recalled. "I knew the enemy were doing but little harm as though discretion was the better part of valor and that I would hop on." He got up and headed toward the rear. Every hundred feet or so, the pain would become so blinding that he stumbled and fell. Determined to get aid, he rose and repeated the process several times. Spotting a dead Yankee, he paused to rummage through his pockets. Finding little of value in the "poor haul," he removed the corpse's knapsack and slung it over his shoulders. He picked up a gun to use as a crutch but soon discarded it, learning he could make better time by hopping. Fletcher soon encountered a Confederate crouching in the woods. He chastised the coward for not being at the front and said, "You can help me then, and that way be doing something for your country." The man agreed. Resting his hand on the soldier's shoulder, Fletcher resumed his quest to get to the aid station. They were not making fast enough time, however, and Fletcher fell again with blinding pain. His new companion asked him if he had been shot again, to which Fletcher replied, "No, and I will not need your services."

They spotted the Confederate reserve in the woods just ahead. When one of the reserves asked the coward how the fighting was going, he claimed the Yankees were "killing lots of our men." When Fletcher hopped into their ranks, he received the same question and answered, "We are giving them hell, boys!" They responded, "He had been there, you bet." A few hundred yards behind the reserves, Fletcher spotted an ambulance and climbed inside. He examined his captured knapsack, finding letters from the dead Yankee's girlfriend. He read that she looked forward to reuniting with her love when the Rebs were whipped and the war was over. The "[l]etters did not arouse any sympathy in me," Fletcher later admitted, and he felt not "one pang of regret for being a party to breaking up that match. She wanted me whipped—she got that; I wanted dead Yankees—I got that. So both at least got a part of their wants satisfied." It was dark by the time Fletcher arrived at the field hospital. He reclined on some straw for bedding about 50 feet from an operating table on which surgeons desperately worked to save the lives of his fellow Confederates.[38]

While Bill Fletcher hobbled to the rear, the 4th Texas struggled in the northwest corner of East Viniard Field. As the soldiers advanced toward the Viniard house, they were caught in a maelstrom of Union fire. At one point, Sgt. Val Giles saw a terrified soldier shooting straight up in the air and praying as heartily as one of Oliver Cromwell's Roundheads ever did during the English Civil War. "The Presbyterians of 1646 prayed loud and sang hymns in battle," Giles recalled, "but they shot straight at the Cavaliers every time." This soldier paid no attention at all to Lt. Allen G. Killingsworth's remonstrations and kept reloading and blazing away at the sky, all the while fervently praying. He was wasting ammunition, and Captain Joe Billingsley threatened to cut him down with his sword if he did not shoot at the enemy that filled the woods in front. The man retorted, "You can kill me if you want to, but I am not going to appear before my God with the blood of my fellow man on my soul." He never flinched but stood erect, exposed to every enemy volley.[39]

Captain George Estep's 8th Indiana Battery had accompanied Buell's brigade to the Viniard farm. Estep unlimbered his four six-pounder smoothbores and two 12-pounder howitzers east of the La Fayette Road, with the left half of the battery in the woods and the right in East Viniard Field just in front of the house. The Hoosier officer soon learned that Rebels were driving the Federal troops in his front. Fearing that he might fire on his men, Estep rode over to the battery commander to his right, Capt. George R. Swallow of the 7th Indiana, to learn the locations of the enemy and friendly troops. Swallow told Estep that his battery had been firing at a range of 800 yards, but the distance to the Confederates was closing fast. Estep galloped back to the 8th Indiana and ordered the right section to fire explosive shells at a range of 700 yards, believing this would not impact his men. In moments, however, "the battery was filled with men falling back through it in great confusion." Estep immediately ceased firing until everyone had passed through his line. Before he could open, heavy fire from 4th Texas's left wing chased his crews away from their guns. The Southerners killed five horses hitched to a limber just

38 Fletcher, *Rebel Private*, 100.

39 "In Storm of Battle"; Laswell, *Rags and Hopes*, 208.

outside of the Viniard house. Crewmen and volunteers from Buell's 26th Ohio managed to drag the isolated cannon to safety.[40]

Meanwhile, to the north, Major Rogers, with Capt. John S. Cleveland's capable assistance, finally rallied the disorganized, overly enthusiastic 5th Texas. The soldiers reformed into a battle line in front of the dry ditch behind the Viniard house. The men of the Bloody Fifth remained at the ditch for at least an hour, with the Federals occasionally advancing and firing volleys of musketry and hurling grapeshot and canister. Rogers sent several messengers to the 4th Texas, which was well off to the 5th's left rear, to inform it of his current position. "We held them in check, preventing any forward movement in our immediate front or flanks," Capt. T. T. Clay reported, "and we thus remained until ordered to fall back." After retiring some 250 yards across the La Fayette Road, Major Rogers halted the regiment in the woods, where the men fought "Indian style," using whatever cover they could find. He sent two or three messengers to General Robertson to call for support, but none of the couriers got through. The 4th and 5th Texas regiments were on their own.[41]

While Rogers futilely waited for Robertson's instructions, Federals from Carlin's depleted brigade advanced from a line of brush several hundred yards from the 5th Texas. "We had the great disadvantage of being distinctly seen by the enemy, while they were seldom visible to us," General Carlin later wrote. "Our line was in very open woods, or in the cleared land." He spotted the Rebels to the east: "Their scouts and skirmishers in butternut clothes could be seen clinging to the trees on the far side."[42]

Private Campbell of the 5th Texas recalled that, with "a whoop, that only a Yank can give," the Northerners charged. Major Rogers cried, "Keep cool, boys. Save your position and aim at the whites of their eyes. Allow them to approach as near as possible." The Texans held their fire until the Yankees came within 100 yards, then fired a telling volley. "No sooner had our balls left on their mission of death than the voice of Rogers was heard 'Charge them, boys!'" Campbell added, "and with a Texas yell we ran at them, bayonets fixed, and as they knew it, we were right on them, and soon had them running for dear life." Riding into their midst,

40 *OR* 30, pt. 1, 676-677; *Indiana at Chickamauga* (Indianapolis, IN: 1901), 291.

41 *OR* 30, pt. 2, 516; Joskins, *A Sketch of Hood's Texas Brigade*, 146.

42 William P. Carlin, "Military Memoirs," *National Tribune*, Apr. 16, 1885. Carlin had previously dispatched the 21st Illinois to support Heg's brigade, leaving him with the 38th Illinois, 81st Indiana, and 101st Ohio.

Carlin pleaded with them and begged them to return, and then began to ridicule them. Nothing worked. The panicked soldiers refused to listen, whereupon Carlin, seething with anger, began using language "more forcible than polite." The runners disappeared into the bushes and trees.[43]

About 4:30 p.m., Buell's fresh Union brigade suddenly emerged from the brush and headed straight for the 5th Texas, now exposed in the open field and again subjected to enemy artillery fire. "Half the regiment stopped to shoot at them," Campbell noted, "while about 100 of us took after the running Yanks, and also made for a battery that was pouring a heavy fire upon us." He added, "We were fighting awful odds." Campbell had made it about halfway to the battery when a canister ball struck him in the left arm, deadening it down to his fingers. "I started for the rear with enough minnie balls and 'burst shells' singing about me as to make me increase my speed and dodge every second." A minié ball slammed into Cpl. L. B. Dortch's temple. Permanently blinded in both eyes, he awkwardly slumped to the ground. Lieutenant Joe Turner rushed over and stooped down to place Dortch in a more comfortable position in which to die. A bullet shattered Turner's humerus, and he had to endure lengthy surgery later that day to remove bone shards from the wound.[44]

According to Captain Clay, "The men followed the fleeing enemy to a ravine in the field, the brave Rogers all the time urging them forward, until he saw that our friends had failed to come up upon our right and left, when the order was reluctantly given to fall back. We were here exposed, in going in and returning, to an incessant shower of grape and canister from a battery on the opposite side of the field. It was in falling back from this field to our original position that the gallant Rogers fell from a severe wound, and the regiment is thus deprived for a time of the services of one of its best officers. In this last charge, the regiment sustained its greatest loss in men and officers." The casualties included Color Sgt. Nathan Oats, killed while carrying the flag. "On falling back under cover of the woods," Captain Clay reported, "[Captain John] Cleveland reformed the regiment and ordered

43 *OR* 30, pt. 2, 516; Skoch and Perkins, *Lone Star Confederate*, 96-97; Joskins, *A Sketch of Hood's Texas Brigade*, 146-147; Carlin, "Military Memoirs."

44 Skoch and Perkins, *Lone Star Confederate*, 97; Joskins, *A Sketch of Hood's Texas Brigade*, 148-149; "An Incident of Chickamauga," *The Countryman*, (Turnwold, GA), Dec. 5, 1863.

Capt. Tacitus C. Clay, 5th Texas Infantry. (*Texas Heritage Museum-Historical Research Center*)

Lieutenant [B. Pugh] Fuller forward with some 12 or 15 men, who held the ground until our wounded were removed."[45]

George Estep's 8th Indiana Light Artillery opened on the 5th Texans as they tried to cross West Viniard Field. Estep received a painful injury to his left arm but stayed in command. When Buell advanced back across the field to the La Fayette Road, he ordered Estep to accompany him with his remaining guns. After getting into position again near the house, the Hoosiers opened fire at a range of 90 to 100 yards at the enemy line then lying down in the woods. "I am positive that while in this position I did the enemy serious injury, his musket fire became so heavy, terrible and galling that to remain there longer was only to insure me that I would not have a horse left. I gave the order to limber to the rear. The execution of the order had scarcely begun when the infantry began to fall back, being charged by the enemy, who came yelling like devils. Three of my pieces were left on the field."[46]

Estep's abandoned guns sat some 150 to 200 yards obliquely to the left front of the 4th Texas. Captain Hunter, quickly deciding to seize them, ordered, "Left wing, left oblique, forward, charge!" Sergeant Giles recalled someone yelling, "Get out of this hell-hole; charge the battery!" He never learned who first uttered the cry, but a hundred voices echoed it. Color Sergeant Ed Francis waved the flag and screamed, "Come on boys!" An old, "worm-eaten" stake-and-rider fence bordered the opposite side of the road. A strong line of Union infantry posted behind it had not yet fired because of intervening friendly troops facing the 5th Texas. Hunter led the regiment across the field toward the guns. At the halfway point, the Federals loosed

45 *OR* 30, pt. 2, 516; Simpson, *Compendium*, 170. Oats had been a schoolteacher in Alabama before moving to Texas. Fuller commanded Company A, the "Bayou City Guards."

46 *OR* 30, pt. 1, *Indiana at Chickamauga*, 292-293. Later that day, a Federal charge recovered the abandoned guns, including the one left when the Confederates gunned down the five limber horses. Estep's crewmen and volunteers from Buell's 26th Ohio hand-pulled it to the rear, leaving the wrecked limber. Estep lost 21 horses on this day.

Postwar image of Sgt. Val C. Giles, 4th Texas Infantry. (*Dolph Briscoe Center for American History-University of Texas at Austin*)

a volley and then began firing at will. Private Wesley C. Francis looked for his brother Ed. "The last I saw of him he was bearing the banner he had borne through every battle without falter," Wesley wrote. "But soon I had to turn back. I never saw him more."[47]

According to Sergeant Giles, "We were now under a heavy fire, and our men were falling everywhere." Clouds of thick, stifling black smoke hugged the ground on this breezeless day. A lieutenant in the 4th Texas had a beautiful sweetheart back home with whom he regularly corresponded. He cherished her letters above all else, tying them in a bundle with a blue ribbon and tucking them in a black morocco notebook that he kept in a coat pocket. Now, the lieutenant urged his company forward. "He was a proud fellow, full of courage," Giles said admiringly, "and such men make the finest soldiers in the world." A minié ball struck the officer and knocked him to the ground. Though his comrades believed him to be dead, he was just stunned and sore. The ball had hit the notebook and had come to a stop embedded in the thick wad of letters.[48]

Because the Union line was much longer than that of the 4th Texas, the Confederates began receiving both frontal and enfilade fire, and their attack bogged down 50 to 60 yards from the fence. Some Federal batteries had unlimbered in a position to enfilade the line with grapeshot and canister. To avoid destruction, Captain Hunter ordered a retreat to the timber from which the

47 *OR* 30, pt. 1, 633; Hunter, "Hard Fighting Fourth Texas," 22; "In Storm of Battle"; "Francis Fought for Texas Independence."

48 "In Storm of Battle"; Laswell, *Rags and Hope*, 207-208. Just prior to Appomattox, the lieutenant's girlfriend jilted him and married a discharged soldier.

regiment had started its advance. He screamed, "Fall back to the road!" The men fled across the Alexander-Viniard Road into the thin timber.[49]

"I had never seen Company D as badly scattered as it was then," Cpl. Miles Smith later told a reporter. "When we halted out of range of the batteries, there were only eight or ten of us in the ranks together." Most of the officers had yet to arrive. Ans Jones sidled up to Smith and said, "Pony, you will have to take command of the company as you outrank the balance of us." Soon, the commissioned officers arrived and relieved Smith.[50]

Once in the open woods, the Confederates "took obstacle," a skirmish tactic where every man sought whatever shelter he could find. "The old road was more of a gully than road, and afforded protection for many of the men, but not for all," Sergeant Giles recalled. "Every tree, sapling and stump was occupied that was big enough to afford any protection. The Federal batteries beyond the old field were making our position a veritable hell on earth. Shells, grapeshot, canister, shrapnel and Minie balls were tearing through the air, while dirt, leaves limbs, and bark were falling and flying all over and around us."

Giles ducked behind a pine tree as the 4th Texans scrambled to seek shelter. Nearby, a group of frightened Union prisoners huddled in the road. Lieutenant Walsh Masterson yelled for them to go to the rear quickly. The Federals began running, with two of them grabbing each other's hands for support as they dashed toward Giles's tree. Just then, a distant Union cannon fired a round of grapeshot that struck one of the runners in the shoulder. He fell to his knees, cried out, "Oh Lord! I am done with the wicked world" and slowly sank to the ground. His partner kept on running. Giles believed this "was the meanest, most unsatisfactory place I struck during the whole war." "With my messmate, brave George W. Nichols, dead in the old road ten feet in front of me, J. K. P. Jones, a gallant boy of my company, dead twenty feet behind me, and that poor Yankee dead at my feet, men staggering and stumbling to the rear covered with blood, some swearing and some calling on God to protect them in their blind endeavor to find shelter from the storm of iron hail, made me feel like the world was coming to an end then and there."[51]

Captain Hunter called out, "Form on the colors!" To his dismay, however, he learned that Color Sgt. Ed Francis was dead, and no one had picked up the flag

49 Hunter, "Hard Fighting Fourth Texas," 22.

50 *San Antonio Daily Express*, Dec. 5, 1909; M. V. Smith Reminiscences, THM.

51 "In Storm of Battle"; Laswell, *Rags and Hope*, 202-204. Nichols and Jones, like many Texans who fell at Chickamauga, are buried in the Confederate cemetery at Marietta, Georgia.

during the retreat. Hunter dashed forward into East Viniard Field to retrieve the banner. He recalled that "the line of battle behind the fence opened on me and, though they shot my blanket and haversack full of holes and several in the flag, I was not touched. I don't think anyone during the war had more shots fired at him individually than I had on this occasion. I have always felt that the prayers of some good Southern woman must have been heard on my behalf." Before Francis died, he had advanced close enough to use his pistol, and fell with the flagpole underneath him. Hunter rolled the body over, grasped the staff, and carried the colors back to the regiment. He asked for a volunteer to carry the flag, and a Waco man, Fred Makeig of Company E, threw down his musket, bounded over, and bore the colors for the rest of the day.[52]

Hood's Final Push at the Viniard Farm

General Robertson rallied most of his disorganized men in a ravine in the woods. Once they reformed, he decided to try another assault to crack the Union line along the La Fayette Road. The 4th Texas's Pvt. John C. West advanced some 30 steps, pausing to load and fire five or six times. Private W. M. Hicks dropped dead near West, and Pvts. Billy Burton and Sam Chambers suffered wounds. According to West, the entire enemy line seemed broken and confused, other than two or three companies at the Viniard house off to his left. "I rushed on, waving my hat, until I was pretty well mixed up with them," he claimed. West took his bayonet off his musket because he had hurt his hand on it during his haste to reload so rapidly.

Just after West put the bayonet back into its scabbard, a Yankee bullet knocked off its entire handle. The ball slammed into him with such great force that it blinded and sickened him. Spitting blood, West fell to the ground, supposing his wound mortal. He had almost fallen on a severely injured Union soldier lying nearby. The Yankee asked West to unbuckle his belt, which he did with difficulty, but the soldier died before he could express his thanks. As West lay there, "It seem[ed] to me that a thousand bullets and grapeshot tore up the ground about me." As soon as

52 Hunter, "Hard Fighting Fourth Texas," 22; "In Storm of Battle.". Giles, by contrast, stated that Makeig picked up the fallen colors right after Francis fell and went forward before being hit. A third soldier then carried the colors.

Maj. Gen. Alexander McCook commanded the Twentieth Corps of the Army of the Cumberland. (*Library of Congress*)

he was able, he crawled to a nearby tree for shelter. When it was safe to do so, he headed back to a temporary field hospital in a barn.[53]

Robertson's line again closed on the Federals at the Viniard house, and bitter hand-to-hand fighting ensued. "The men fought around the house with the bayonet," the 4th Texas's Captain Hunter recorded, "and a number of the enemy were killed inside. No prisoners were taken." The close-order combat was intense as men fired at one another at point-blank range. Right in front of the cabin, a ball struck teenaged Pvt. Lawrence Daffan's gun between the ramrod and the barrel, shivering the stock. The impact knocked him down; it was the only time in the entire war that he suffered any kind of injury. Daffan was the young soldier who, while on leave at his cousin's house in Virginia, had watched his regiment march off to the train station. Now temporarily stunned, he soon rose to his feet and returned to the fight.[54]

Several Texans began sparring with about 20 of Heg's Yankees nestled in the Lost Corner Schoolhouse, a "dilapidated log house built for a blacksmith's shop," in Sergeant Polley's words. "The house stood at the far edge of the wood through which the brigade was making its way, and on account of intervening timber and undergrowth, could be seen from only a few points along our line. The fire from it was rapid and damaging, but for quite a while our folks failed to discover whence it came." A boyish-faced young German, Pvt. Julius H. Glazer of Company D, finally spotted the source. Shouting, he ran toward the building, followed by 10 to 15 men from all four of Robertson's regiments. The defenders, focused on other Texans to

53 Hunter, "Hard Fighting Fourth Texas," 22; West, *A Texan in Search of a Fight*, 114; Harold B. Simpson, *Gaines Mill to Appomattox: Waco & McLennan County in Hood's Texas Brigade* (Waco, TX: 1963), 160.

54 Hunter, "Hard Fighting Fourth Texas," 22; *Waxahachie Daily Light*, Feb. 16, 1907.

their left, were unaware of Glazer's approach until, when within 20 feet of the house, he called on them to surrender.[55]

The Yankees replied by firing at Glazer half a dozen times, causing two minor flesh wounds. He shot down one of the Federals, but two more ran out from behind the house. Spotting them, he tried to take refuge behind a nearby tree, but both Yankees bayonetted him. Unfazed, the young Texan reached for a cartridge. The enemy soldiers again rushed at him with leveled bayonets, and all three danced around the tree until Glazer fired his musket and killed one of them. Two more Yankees soon reinforced the remaining antagonist. Glazer held the trio at bay until his fellow Texans came up and shot down two of them.

The remaining assailant ran back into the schoolhouse. The Confederates cried, "Surrender!" to which the defiant Yankees retorted, "Take us if you can." A brief firefight ensued before the defenders, with half their number down, finally acknowledged that further resistance was futile. At this point, Julius Glazer remembered his injuries and headed toward the rear for treatment. When questioned as to why the Federals had not shot Glazer instead of attacking him with bayonets, their lieutenant replied, "Because he was a mere boy and after he fired his one shot, we thought it would be cowardly to shoot him. But if the fighting he did against two of our best men at first, and then against three, and that too, after he was four times wounded, is a sample of what you Texans are in the habit of doing, I am going to throw up my commission and return to peaceful pursuits."[56]

By now, it was after 5:00 p.m. A "very gallant" and authoritative-appearing Union officer dropped dead in front of Company E of the 4th Texas. An unidentified Texan grabbed the fallen man's sword but was himself shot minutes later. When comrades took him to the temporary field hospital a mile in the rear, he kept the trophy sword with him. Examining his prize, the soldier noticed an inscription on the blade: "Captain Haup, Co. I, 15th Wisconsin Volunteers." Robertson's beleaguered brigade fended off several attacks by Heg's/Martin's and Carlin's remaining men, Buell's brigade, Wilder's Lightning Brigade, and eventually Col. Luther Bradley's fresh brigade from Maj. Gen. Philip Sheridan's division of McCook's XX Corps. "Seeing that we were about to be flanked right and left," Capt. R. J. Harding of the 1st Texas wrote, "we fell back to the ravine under cover of a hill in the rear of the road occupied by the regiment." Outnumbered and facing superior firepower, Robertson slowly withdrew across East Viniard Field. The 3rd

55 Polley, *Waxahachie Daily Light*, 211.

56 *San Antonio Daily Express*, Dec. 5, 1909; Polley, *Hood's Texas Brigade*, 212-213.

La Fayette Road at the site of the former Viniard Farm. (*Library of Congress*)

Arkansas's Maj. John W. Reedy, "a good drill officer but very wicked," fell dead after uttering, "Oh Lord." A nearby Confederate picked up his sword.[57]

Robertson maintained order throughout the withdrawal. He fell back to the highest part of East Viniard Field near the intersection of the Alexander-Viniard and La Fayette Roads and sent for reinforcements and artillery support. The latter was not forthcoming, but Benning's infantry changed direction and moved into position. When Benning was ready, he ordered his men forward. "Just here, Gen. Robinson [Robertson], Polly we called him, commanding Hood's Texas brigade, rode past out front and said something to the men, which I did not understand," Pvt. William R. Houghton of the 2nd Georgia recalled, "but a shout was raised and

57 "Another Scrap of War History," *Waco Daily News*, Sept. 26, 1884; 30, *OR* pt. 2, 511, 513; *East Texas Family Records*, vol. 2, no. 2. The wounded soldier returned to action, leaving the sword in the hands of another patient, Private Colvin of Company A. Colvin, in turn, passed it to a sergeant who supposedly forwarded it through the ranks. No "Captain Haup" is on the roster of the 15th Wisconsin.

we broke into the double quickstep." The brigade moved at the right oblique but Houghton, on the extreme left of the line, did not hear the command and soon became separated from his comrades.[58]

The fighting intensified as the Georgians crossed the body-strewn field. Eli Lilly's 18th Indiana Battery moved into position to attack. A nearby shell burst gave General Benning a flesh wound to his chest and killed his horse. "Old Rock" remained on the field, urging his men to "give them hell!" Under intense fire from Wilder's men in the wood line at the far side of West Viniard Field, Benning's troops fell back to the dry ditch, where some of Robertson's soldiers still holed up. Finally, they withdrew into the woods, leaving perhaps a third of their number in the ditch.

Robertson's remnants, meanwhile, had advanced from the woods back into the Viniard fields. "This field, it seems had been occupied by a battery of artillery," the 1st Texas's Color Sgt. George Branard observed; "to judge by appearances there had been some hard fighting done before we came up." The "Ragged Old First" stopped next to some of Benning's brigade on the edge of the field. According to Branard, the Texans formed "behind what once could be called a rail fence, then only three rails high. It did not take us long to lie down behind these rails and commence to fire over to the opposite woods, where the Yanks were in full force."[59]

During this exchange of musketry, one of Benning's Georgians, a mere boy, came up to Branard and said, "Texas, I have a mother and sister at home, and this is my first fight with the Yanks." He gave his name, which Branard soon forgot, and then rambled about his home and past life and everything dear to him. The sergeant listened patiently and finally asked why the boy was so concerned. The youth replied, "I have been thinking all day that I would be killed in the first fight and here I am shooting over yonder at those Yankees and I expect to be killed almost any moment." Branard called over a lieutenant from the Georgia regiment and asked him to cheer up the lad. The officer replied that the boy was in his company, and he knew his mother. "I will watch him," he told Branard. The lad had moved some 10 feet to Branard's right and now crouched behind a few carelessly piled fence rails. From his knees, he loaded his gun, took deliberate aim, and fired. Just then, a minié ball slammed into his forehead, and he pitched lifeless among the rails. Branard turned and said to one of the color guards, "The Georgia boy is killed, as he

58 "Thrilling War Sketch," *Columbus* (GA) *Enquirer-Sun*, July 6, 1890.

59 "How a Presentiment Came True."

thought he would be." About five minutes later, the regiment received orders "to move down to the right and into the woods," Branard recalled. "The Yanks had brought artillery up and commenced to shell us, in our moving to the right, myself and some others used dead horses as breastworks, dodging first behind one, then another, what a man will do for safety when the pinch comes. Dead horses stopped many a bullet."[60]

Sergeant Branard recalled that he and some of his comrades sheltered behind "a complete line of dead Yankees," who "looked as though they all had been killed in that position, so straight the line and so many of them." One soldier was thinking about stealing a dead Federal's cap box because it was better than his, so he and Branard discussed the idea. While chatting, Branard heard his name called. He looked up and, to his sorrow, noticed two soldiers carrying Zeke Crawford, a youthful member of his color guard, on a litter. Crawford said, "George, I lost my hat. Get me one from a dead Yank and bring it to the hospital tonight." Branard asked whether he was hurt badly. Zeke replied, "A piece of shell hit me in the groin and tore half away." Despite the gruesome injury, Crawford remained cheerful. As the litter-bearers carried him to the rear, he called back, "George, don't forget to get me a hat." Branard later recalled, "Poor boy, he died soon afterward. I got the hat but he never wore it."[61]

After three futile calls for artillery support, a frustrated General Hood ordered Law's division to retire from the field around 6:00 p.m. The Texans, Arkansans, Alabamians, and Georgians had been in action for more than three hours. The sun was setting as they collected their wounded and withdrew into the woods some 150 yards east of the La Fayette Road. Hood's men formed a new defensive line with Trigg's Floridians and the Virginians of Brig. Gen. William Preston's division off to their left. The Texans and Arkansans bivouacked in the timber a half mile northeast of the Viniard house and began constructing breastworks, something they had not often had to do in the Eastern Theater.

The Aftermath

As Hood's Texans called roll and reflected on the afternoon's fighting, several men were missing. Most of them were dead or wounded on the Viniard Farm. Some of Robertson's best line officers and bravest soldiers had been killed or

60 Ibid.

61 Crawford died in a field hospital on Sept. 24.

seriously wounded. The dead included the 4th Texas's Lt. J. M. "Bob" Bookman, Lt. Samuel S. Streetman of the 5th Texas's "Milam Greys," and Lt. Warren W. Worthington of the 3rd Arkansas. Color-bearer Pvt. William H. Clark of the 5th Texas had fallen with a severe wound to his leg; his counterpart Ed Francis of the 4th Texas was dead. Private Wesley Francis recalled receiving his brother's personal effects: "His knapsack and all of his things were brought to me. The ball that killed him went through his breast and lodged in his knapsack."[62]

Other officers, including the wounded Capt. David K. Rice of the 1st Texas, were taken prisoner. Rosecrans wanted to interrogate Rice, so the guards took Rice some 250 yards behind Federal lines to army headquarters near the Widow Glenn house. "Rosecrans appeared dressed in plain black breeches, white vest and plain blouse and was surrounded by a gorgeous staff," Rice recalled. "The general is short and thick set, with a smooth face, rosy cheeks and lips, brilliant black eyes, and is very handsome. He is exceedingly affable and pleasant in conversation." Rosecrans dismounted, tapped him on the shoulder, and said, "Let's step aside and talk a little." He walked over to a fallen tree some 30 yards from his staff and sat down. He picked up a stick and began to whittle, all the while peppering Rice with questions about the locations of the Confederate lines, his brigade and division, whether Longstreet had arrived, and so forth. Disappointed with his vague and unhelpful answers, Rosecrans ordered that Rice be taken to the prisoner-holding area.[63]

The missing included the 5th Texas's Cpl. L. B. Dortch. Blinded in both eyes, the Livingston soldier remained on the Viniard farm in an area that Federal pickets controlled. They told the stricken Rebel they would take care of him and carry him to their field hospital, but they could not leave their posts. Dortch feared that the battle lines might trample him to death when the fighting resumed the next day. Bleeding profusely, he somehow clung to life throughout the chilly evening. After

62 *OR* 30, pt. 2, 512; "Francis Fought for Texas Independence." Clark recovered only to fall again, in 1864, while carrying the flag at the Wilderness. Wesley Francis would lose two other brothers by war's end.

63 CSR of J. M. Bookman, 4th Texas, NARA RG109, M323, Texas, roll 0284; "Interview Between Rosecrans and a Confederate Captain," *Houston Tri-Weekly Telegraph*, Nov. 3, 1863 After Rosecrans retreated to Chattanooga, Rice escaped, forded the Tennessee River, and eventually returned to the 1st Texas. He wore the "fine morocco boots" of Union Brig. Gen. Elon Farnsworth, who had been killed at Gettysburg. Rice bought them from a Texan who had taken them from the body.

the Federal pickets withdrew well after midnight, he lay alone until fellow Confederates found him in the morning.[64]

The survivors of Hood's Texas Brigade settled down for the night as best as they could. Several took out their journals or diaries and began to record their thoughts. Others reflected on the recent fighting, mourning lost comrades and discussing the Yankees' fighting ability. "The Kansas, Illinois, and Indiana men were in front of us, and they could stand killing better than any men I ever saw," Private Polk of the 4th Texas claimed. He discovered a bundle of 40 or 50 letters, mostly from women in Indiana, inside a knapsack he had taken off a dead Yankee. As he started to read the letters, he heard a horse approaching behind him. Polk turned around to see his old regimental colonel, John Bell Hood, looking at him from the saddle. "Well," the major general exclaimed, "you didn't get hurt!" Polk replied, "No, sir." Hood asked, "How did your regiment come out?" The private from Corsicana responded that quite a few had been lost, but he did not know how many. Hood said he was sorry to hear it and then rode off. "He knew us all by sight, but could not call our names," Polk claimed. "He was a social, kind-hearted man, but a little impulsive at times. He would often walk up to me and shake hands with me and talk to me, but never knew my name. . . . General Hood could get order out of confusion on a battlefield in less time and apparently with less trouble than any man I ever saw." Hood was not on his roan Jeff Davis; his favorite war horse was out of commission with a severe wound. He was now riding a valuable mare.[65]

Some soldiers in the Texas Brigade prowled East Viniard Field seeking fallen companions, making sure not to expose themselves unnecessarily to enemy pickets. The 3rd Arkansas's Sgt. Maj. Benjamin Hyatt informed Cpl. N. C. Denson that his messmate and bedmate, Sgt. James V. Williams, was down with a severe head wound. Denson and Cpl. John Hill left the ranks of Company K and went looking for Williams. They found their friend and bore him to a place of safety in the rear.[66]

At the field hospital, Sgt. William Fletcher of the 5th Texas was still lying on the straw bedding near the operating table. Since his wounded foot did not require immediate treatment, he had time to observe his surroundings. Near the table was a stout young man with a head wound that allowed brain matter to seep out. The man

64 "An Incident of Chickamauga."

65 Polk, *Memories of the Lost Cause*, 21; Polley, *Hood's Texas Brigade*, 203-204.

66 Denson Reminiscences, CCNMP; CSR of N. C. Denson, 3rd Arkansas, NARA RG109, M317, Arkansas, roll 0065.

would occasionally rise and then fall back down. Fletcher began contemplating the moral ethics of euthanasia for men so critically injured: "[W]hy it was that doctor or friend could not end one's misery, even if done with the best method at hand and that was only a rock or club." Mercy killings were okay for animals but not for soldiers. The workload for the surgeons piled up as more wounded men arrived. "The doctors looked worn. You would often hear at such times that they drank too much, but it must take a good nerve to stand it, and [alcohol was] the best remedy to prevent breaking down to go through, as I have seen it, the long hours that their duty calls."[67]

A few Texans shared disturbing premonitions that they too would need the surgeons' services. Color Sergeant George Branard, the 1st Texas's veteran flag-bearer, called his comrades around him and intoned, "Now, boys, you remember when I got this clip aside my head at Sharpsburg that put my left ear out of commission. I told you all about it in advance, but you would not believe me. The same thing happened at Gains [sic] Mill when I told you about it in advance about this game leg I got there. You have all laughed at me for saying that I knew in advance when I was going to catch it, and I want to go on record now before you all, and I want you as witnesses, I am going to catch it right here tomorrow." As he said this, he placed his hand on his left arm just about the elbow joint.[68]

While Robertson's men rested in the evening, they could hear the sound of a pitched battle off to the north. That rare night fighting produced some of Chickamauga's most confusing combat.

67 Fletcher, *Rebel Private*, 99-101.

68 *San Antonio Daily Express*, Apr. 4, 1909.

Chapter 7

September 19, Evening— Deshler's Brigade

Their lengthy march on Friday, September 18, across Pigeon Mountain to a campsite four miles southeast of Thedford's Ford had exhausted the men of Brig. Gen. James Deshler's brigade. The cold night made it hard to sleep, and there was little to eat in the morning. "Sunrise greeted us with a slight small arms fire," Capt. Samuel Foster of the 24th Texas Cavalry recalled. At 7:00 a.m., in the words of Sgt. William Heartsill of the 10th Texas, "The artillerists open the battle and now they are thundering away some three miles on our right (north) in the direction of Chattanooga." An hour later everything was quiet except for couriers and aides dashing to and fro, "all in perfect clockwork motion." The 10th was on the extreme left of Deshler's line, which formed the left of Cleburne's division of D. H. Hill's corps. "The battle is evidently going to be fought on our right but it may swing around our way," Heartsill wrote. A member of the 15th Texas Cavalry recalled many years after the war, "I filled my canteen with water, replenished my stock of ammunition, and was soon ready for the word, 'Forward.'"[1]

1 Barron "The Diary of Captain Samuel F. Foster, CSA," USAHEC, 49; Heartsill, *Fourteen Hundred and 91 Days*, 151-152; Anonymous, "The Gray and the Blue," *CV*, vol. 1, no. 3, Mar.

The roar of artillery again erupted off to the right about 10:00 a.m. "The cannonading is terrific," Sergeant Heartsill observed; "we cannot hear the small arms, on account o | f the distance and range of hills on our right." That was about the time their fellow Texans in Matt Ector's brigade resumed their fighting. Because of their isolated position, the soldiers could only speculate about the course of the battle. Rumors spread that Breckinridge and Longstreet had driven the Federals across the Chickamauga. Half an hour later, Deshler, in his first battle as a general, sent orders for the men to form and prepare to move out. They began marching by the right flank at 11:45 a.m. as other Confederate troops poured down the valley off to their left. Soon, the Texans could tell the fighting was intensifying. "Our boys are confident," Heartsill noted with pride as he walked. They did not know that Hill had received orders to take Cleburne's 5,100-man division to General Bragg at Thedford's Ford on West Chickamauga Creek.[2]

The four-mile march was accomplished in stages. One of Cleburne's staff officers galloped up to Deshler in mid-afternoon, hurriedly spoke a few words, and dashed away. Lieutenant Robert Collins of the 15th Texas Cavalry knew what that meant: They would soon be entering combat. "The boys all looked serious, and few were the jokes cracked," he admitted. "All realized that blood was going to be shed." A bugler sounded attention, and shouted commands followed: "Right face, forward, double quick march!" Cleburne's division arrived at Bragg's headquarters 90 minutes later and halted. Bragg sent the new arrivals to Lt. Gen. Leonidas Polk, the commander of the right-center of the Confederate line, for further instructions.[3]

About 4:00 p.m., Cleburne's infantry, with the brigade of youthful Brig. Gen. Lucius E. Polk in the lead, began wading West Chickamauga Creek at Thedford's Ford. Deshler's brigade was the third one to cross, trailing Brig. Gen. Sterling A. M. Wood's soldiers. The water level was as high as their waists; some men said it came up to their armpits. Fed by mountain springs, the creek was swift and cold. "Such was Cleburne's haste he did not give the men time to pick their way across, but marched them through in a solid column," reported Col. Roger Q. Mills of the consolidated 6th–10th Texas–15th Texas Cavalry. When the soldiers tried to pause to take off their brogans, Cleburne insisted, "Boys, go through that river; we can't

---

1893, 75. The unknown author, possibly William Taylor, served in Company A of the 15th Texas Cavalry.

2 Heartsill, *Fourteen Hundred and 91 Days*, 152.

3 *OR* 30, pt. 2, 187; McCaffrey, *Only a Private*, 45; Collins, *Chapters*, 151.

wait." Thoroughly soaked, his Confederates headed toward the rear of the right-center of the line, some two miles past the ford.[4]

Cleburne's men heard the roar of battle as they marched northward. "The firing on our left (west) is very heavy," Sergeant Heartsill scribbled in his journal; "for the past three hours the battle has raged with unceasing fury, our men are the masters of the field; having driven the enemy over two miles." Battleground refugees, shirkers, supply wagons, rear-echelon troops, reserve artillery, and ambulances all clogged the narrow roads parallel to the creek, significantly slowing the division's progress. At one point, Deshler's column passed a group of about 150 Union prisoners. Not long after came another batch of "blue coats," as well as swarms of stragglers and wounded men from both sides. The Arkansas Post parolees received catcalls and jeers when they passed veteran troops who realized their identity. They also encountered their old friends in Gregg's brigade, who were resting from their bitter fight near the Viniard Farm. "The 7th Texas is here," Heartsill noted; "some of our boys saw Capt. Charlie Talley as we were going into the fight; he is here braving dangers for a noble cause, his Company was badly cut up this evening."[5]

As the division headed toward the fighting, the soldiers passed General Forrest calmly reading a novel during a lull. Doctor James H. Wilkes, near Forrest, asked him, "General, is the fighting over for today?" Forrest pointed at the distant oncoming troops and reportedly remarked, "Do you see that large body of infantry marching this way in columns of fours? That is General Pat Cleburne's division; hell will break loose in Georgia in about fifteen minutes."[6]

About 5:30 p.m., Cleburne's vanguard reached Jay's Mill "just as the blood-red sun seemed to rest on top of Mission[ary] Ridge," in Lieutenant Collins's words. To Collins the sun looked like it was "taking a last look for the day at the two great armies of one blood and one nation, as they were in battle array against each other." Cleburne formed a line of battle behind Brig. Gen. St. John Liddell's played-out division. Cleburne's line extended along Jay's Mill Road from the steam sawmill almost due south for nearly a mile to the intersection with Alexander's Bridge

4 "Texas Abroad," *Galveston Daily News*, Dec. 26, 1893; "What Mills Saw," *Galveston Daily News*, Dec. 15, 1890; Lance, *Patrick R. Cleburne*, 75.

5 Heartsill, *Fourteen Hundred and 91 Days*, 152. Captain Charles E. Talley commanded Company D of the 7th Texas. He was captured in Nov. 1864 at the battle of Franklin and sat out the rest of the war in the Johnson's Island prison camp on Lake Erie in northern Ohio.

6 "Historical Society," *The Herald and Mail* (Columbia, TN), Mar. 15, 1907.

Col. Franklin C. Wilkes commanded the 17th-18th-24th-25th Texas Cavalry, Dismounted, in Deshler's brigade. (*The Texas State Preservation Board*)

Road. Lucius Polk's brigade was on the right of Cleburne's west-facing line. Wood's brigade was in the center on the Youngblood farm and Deshler's brigade was on the far left. Cleburne was to attack the Yankees in conjunction with Frank Cheatham's large division, which, though battered earlier that day, was still serviceable.[7]

Cleburne ordered his capable chief of artillery, Maj. Thomas R. Hotchkiss, to consolidate Capt. Henry C. Semple's Alabama battery and Calvert's Arkansas battery (under Lt. Thomas J. Key) behind Wood as a reserve. Hotchkiss's third battery, Texans under Capt. James P. Douglas, was to support Deshler. "General Deshler informed me that the Division was going to advance on the enemy," Douglas reported, "but, owing to the lateness of the hour and the roughness of the country, he did not think my battery could be made effective with safety, and in the absence of other orders, I should follow in the rear of the brigade and if he desired the battery, he would send for it."[8]

Deshler's brigade was about 300 yards to the right rear of A. P. Stewart's division. Deshler placed Col. Roger Q. Mills's consolidated 6th-10th Texas–15th Texas Cavalry on the left of his line, with Lt. Col. A. S. Hutchison's 19th-24th Arkansas in the center. Colonel Franklin C. Wilkes's 17th-18th-24th-25th Texas Cavalry formed on the right near the mill with orders to guide on Wood's left most units, the 18th Alabama Battalion and 33rd Alabama. Some of Cleburne's men started campfires to dry their soggy clothing, but a distant Union battery spotted

7 "Maj. Gen. Patrick R. Cleburne, Official Report, Battle of Chickamauga," *Daily American* (Nashville, TN), Feb. 20, 1890; *OR* 30, pt. 2, 155; Betts and Park, "Map of the Battlefield of Chickamauga," Plate 5. Polk commanded Cleburne's former brigade.

8 OR 30, pt. 2, 196; James P. Douglas and Lucia Thompson Rutherford, eds., *Douglas's Texas Battery, CSA* (Tyler, TX: 1966), 72; Lang, "Lone Star Pride," 34-35.

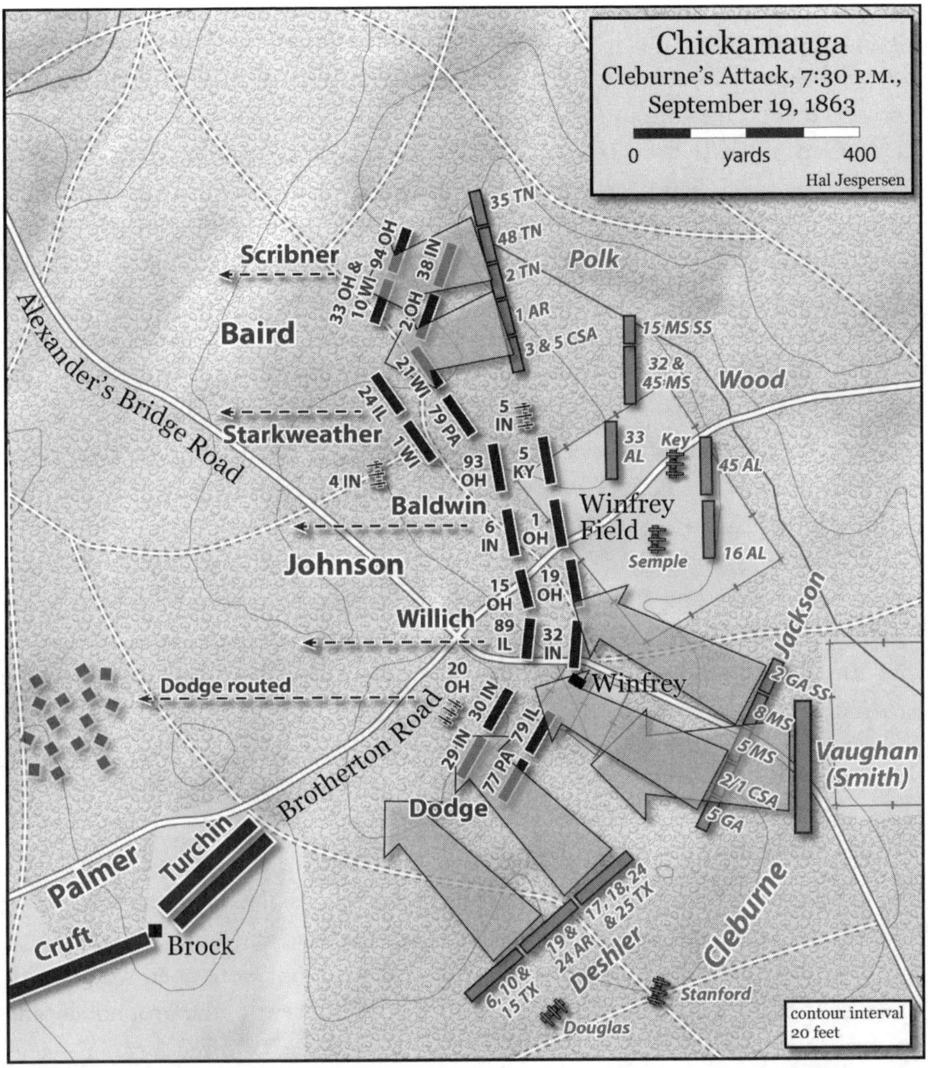

the smoke and sent a few rounds their way. The Confederates quickly extinguished the flames.[9]

St. John Liddell, frustrated that it had taken Cleburne so long to arrive, urged him to attack immediately. Cleburne deferred, deciding to wait until his commander, General Hill, was on the scene. It proved to be a short wait, as Hill

9 Edwin L. Drake, *Annals of the Army of Tennessee and Early Western History* (Nashville, TN: 1878), 53.

arrived shortly after Liddell's exhortations. Liddell commented, "General, I hope you will be quick, for a minute now will be worth an hour tomorrow." Pat Cleburne likely seethed at his former subordinate's subtle jab. "I now received orders from Lieut.-Gen. D. H. Hill to advance," Cleburne reported, "passing over [Liddell's prone] line, which had been repulsed, and drive back the enemy's left wing." He relayed Hill's instructions to his three brigade commanders, telling them to direct their movements on Wood as the center of the assault wave. Wood and Deshler deployed skirmishers 250 to 300 yards in front of their respective lines.

About 6:00 p.m., Cleburne's Confederates stepped off in a line almost a mile long, with most of his men passing through Liddell's line. Part of Deshler's brigade also had to pass through Preston Smith's stationary men, who would then rise and follow in a second line. Colonel Mills hurried among the ranks of the consolidated 6th-10th Texas–15th Texas Cavalry, offering words of encouragement to the men and giving instructions to his officers. Mills sent Company A of the 15th Texas Cavalry forward a couple of hundred yards as a skirmish line. "We were soon engaged in a rambling fire," one of the skirmishers, known only as "J. W. T." (possibly Pvt. William Taylor), recalled. Their Federal counterparts soon melted into the woods, leaving a few dead or dying comrades. J. W. T. encountered a prostrated Yankee trying to rise. The injured Illinois soldier flashed the Masonic sign of distress and asked for water. J. W. T. hastily tucked the Federal's knapsack under his head as a pillow and gave him a canteen, then ran forward to rejoin his company.[10]

Private Oliphant of the 6th Texas recalled that the "Texas yell was raised, and into the smoke of battle we dashed, passing through lines of Confederates who had been driven back by the enemy, and passing over the dead and wounded lying thick on the ground." General Cleburne reported, "In my front were open woods with the exception of a clearing (fenced in) in front of my centre, the ground sloping upward as we advanced." That field was on the George Winfrey farm. Yankees held the far western end near the intersection of Alexander's Bridge Road and Reed's Bridge Road, some 200 to 300 yards from Jay's Mill Road, with pickets out front.[11]

10 "The Gray and the Blue." The wounded Union soldier was likely Pvt. John Randolph of the 79th Illinois of Dodge's brigade. Captain Rhodes Fisher of Company G commanded the entire skirmish line on September 19 (*OR* 30, pt. 2, 193).

11 McCaffrey, *Only a Private*, 46; Craig L. Symonds, *Stonewall of the West: Patrick Cleburne and the Civil War* (Lawrence, KS: 1997), 144-145; "Maj. Gen. Patrick R. Cleburne, Official Report"; *OR* 30, pt. 2, 107.

Sgt. Benjamin F. Grady, 25th Texas Cavalry. After the Civil War, he represented North Carolina in the U. S. House of Representatives. (*Collection of U. S. House of Representatives*)

Cleburne faced Brig. Gen. Richard W. Johnson's brigade of Thomas's XIV Corps as he began his broad assault on Rosecrans's left. To the north (the Confederates' right) was Col. Philemon P. Baldwin's brigade, in line with Brig. Gen. John Starkweather's brigade of Baird's division to its left. The brigade of Prussian-born Brig. Gen. August Willich was south of Baldwin, with Col. Joseph B. Dodge's brigade arrayed in a double line off to Willich's right. Captain Peter Simonson's 5th Indiana Battery supported the left (1st Ohio and 6th Indiana) of Baldwin's line, while the 20th Ohio Battery and Battery A, 1st Ohio, were within supporting distance of Willich and Dodge.[12]

Deshler's oncoming line entered the scrubby timber west of the dirt road and slowed down considerably, while Wood's brigade moved into the eastern side of Winfrey Field but stopped several times. Colonel Wilkes almost immediately lost connection with the 18th Alabama Battalion and 33rd Alabama. "After going a short distance we were halted and a line of battle formed with Wood's Mississippi [and Alabama] brigade on our right," Sgt. Benjamin F. Grady of the 25th Texas Cavalry recalled, "but unfortunately the brigades formed an angle, the wings being in front of the point of junction, and as we advanced much confusion resulted." Colonel Alfred J. Vaughan, Jr., of the 13th Tennessee of Smith's brigade reported that a portion of Deshler's brigade "fell back on our line." General Smith ordered them to move forward, which they did.[13]

Deshler soon halted again in an attempt to consolidate and straighten his disjointed battle line. "The delays caused by efforts to rectify the line prevented us from coming in view of the enemy before dark," the 25th Texas's Sgt. Benjamin

12 Betts and Park, "Map of the Battlefield of Chickamauga," Plate 5.

13 "Amid the Crash of Shells at Chickamauga," *News and Observer* (Raleigh, NC), Jan. 17, 1904; *OR* 30, pt. 2, 188.

Grady explained, "and another unfortunate result was that two companies of us, K and B (which was next to K), became separated from the regiment, and were partially lost in the forest." A frustrated General Smith again rode up and urged the Texans to get moving. Guided by Wilkes, Deshler's brigade somehow veered more than 200 yards off course to the west. Hutchison's Arkansans and Mills's Texans followed suit to their left, opening a wide gap in Cleburne's line. Smith and Brig. Gen. John K. Jackson, both of Cheatham's division, did not realize that Deshler was gone, so they marched their brigades into the void. Neither Smith nor Jackson realized they were now in the middle of Cleburne's assault wave; they believed they were still in the second line, screened from the enemy. That erroneous assumption would prove to be tragic for Preston Smith.[14]

Meanwhile, Wood's and Polk's brigades to the north advanced well into Winfrey Field and made contact with Johnson's Federals, who were posted behind hastily constructed breastworks. The defenders included Willich's brigade, with Baldwin's 5th Kentucky and 93rd Ohio to its left and the two Ohio batteries in support. The Yankees opened a heavy fire of small arms and artillery. "For half an hour the firing was the heaviest I had ever heard," Cleburne reported. "It was dark, however, and accurate shooting was impossible. Each party was aiming at the flashes of the other's guns, and few of the shots from either side took effect." Union General Johnson later reported that an "overwhelming force" attacked his front, flank, and rear as the night progressed. "Here, the assault was terrific, but darkness soon prevented us from telling friend from foe." At times, the fighting was hand-to-hand. After his men repulsed several attacks and pushed back some of Wood's regiments, Johnson believed he was the "master of the field."[15]

Wood's beleaguered infantrymen needed artillery support, and soon received it. When Cleburne's division commenced its movement earlier in the evening, Major Hotchkiss sent word for his three batteries to move to the right of Wood's brigade. Captain Douglas moved his Texas battery in that direction, but before he could reach the designated point, Wood's infantry was fighting in Winfrey Field. Douglas wheeled his four guns to front west and unlimbered. He wanted "to present my front to the fire and also to be in an offensive position in the event our infantry were forced to retire." Douglas remained in this position for several minutes, during which time "a large number of infantrymen (200 or 300)

14 Brown, *One of Cleburne's Command*, 50-51; *OR* 30, pt. 2, 188.

15 "Maj. Gen. Patrick R. Cleburne, Official Report"; *OR* 30, pt. 2, 155, 535.

apparently a disorganized, routed or panic-stricken regiment [16th Alabama] of Wood's brigade ran through my battery."

Failing to rally the runners, Douglas limbered his guns and moved 200 yards to the left to a good position somewhat in the rear of where he supposed Deshler's brigade to be. After unlimbering the guns, he turned the battery over to Lt. John H. Bingham and rode northward to where Semple's Alabama battery was firing double rounds of deadly canister shells that sprayed out like shotgun blasts. Douglas wanted to talk to Major Hotchkiss but failed to find him. In the gathering darkness, Douglas returned to his battery, limbered the guns, and moved back to the right, where he reported to Captain Semple. There, he learned that Hotchkiss had been wounded and removed from the field. The Texans were about 80 yards from the Union line, so Douglas opened fire with two of his pieces.[16]

Deshler's brigade was left (south) of the chaos in Winfrey Field. The general ordered his men to lie down. Johnson's distant Union soldiers, many crouching behind felled trees in John Brock's field, began peppering the prone line with minié balls. Deshler told his troops to hold their fire. "We had to lie flat on the ground so as not to show ourselves," Capt. Sam Foster of the 24th Texas Cavalry recalled. "The Yanks then began firing at us. We were ordered not to fire back." He and his comrades privately questioned why they were being shot up without responding. "The Yanks kept blasting away at us with a terrible fury," Foster added, but only a handful of bullets found their mark in the gloom.[17]

"We were not more than 100 yards from the enemy's right flank, where he had a battery firing at the troops to our right," Colonel Mills commented. "We remained here some minutes." Deshler could not tell whether the battery was Union or Confederate, so he decided not to attack it. A pale moon struggled to shed its dim light through the treetops. Visibility was low and it was impossible to distinguish friend from foe. Willich fell back some 250 yards to a more advantageous position.[18]

16 *OR* 30, pt. 2, 196; Douglas, *Douglas's Texas Battery*, 72-73.

17 Barron, "The Diary of Captain Samuel F. Foster," 49-50; Brown, *One of Cleburne's Command*, 50-51.

18 "What Mills Saw"; *OR* 30, pt. 1, 538, 544. The battery likely was Capt. John Grosskopf's 20th Ohio, which fielded four three-inch rifles and two Napoleons. According to his commander, Captain Simonson Grosskopf "did not do too much" on Saturday night. He fired a few rounds "which endangered our own troops, and he was stopped." Colonel Dodge ordered the battery to retire to form a new line around which his infantry could rally if forced to withdraw.

Deshler soon resumed his advance through the thick woods. When a member of the 25th Texas Cavalry rose to join the ranks, he realized the man next to him had been dead for some time, shot in the head. Trying to move under fire in the dimly lit forest was a "bad piece of business," Captain Foster believed. "There was some heavy pine timber all around. Bullets flew through the trees like the wind. You could hear the bullets, zip - zip - zip, but you could not see them. You knew that they were passing very close."[19]

According to Private Oliphant of the 6th Texas, "After reforming our lines and resting a short time, we were again ordered forward, the enemy giving way as we advanced." As he and his comrades pushed toward the Brock Field, they noticed a bright light. "A field was burning and we were ordered to charge through it," Oliphant wrote. "A battery had been stationed in the field and it was still there." The guns had changed hands a couple of times and now had been abandoned. Earlier, fire from an opposing battery had ignited the high sage grass. A nearby fence also was in flames and "tall dead trees were blazing high in the air." It was a surreal scene. The wounded men lying in the field were in danger of being consumed.

The fire was not the only immediate danger. "The Federals on the opposite side of the field were pouring a deadly shower of shot and shell through the smoke and flames," Oliphant continued. "Bowing our heads and grasping our guns firmly we plunged into that vortex of hell. On emerging from the fire and smoke yelling like demons, we dashed at the Federals." For the Texans, "It was a fearful place. The heart-rending appeals of the wounded, some of whom were scorching, the hissing bullets and the screeching shells, made it an experience never to be forgotten." Clouds of smoke enveloped the timber. "We are in the midst of burning woods, dead and dying men, while shells, grape shot and minie balls are landing around profusely," Sergeant Heartsill stated. By then, Deshler's men had advanced 500 or 600 yards from their starting position before they let loose their first volley.[20]

Colonel Franklin Wilkes of the 17th-18th-24th-25th Texas Cavalry suffered a painful shoulder wound and turned over command to Lt. Col. John T. Coit. Sergeant B. F. Grady, in his first major battle, believed the firing was louder than anything about which he had read. The boys in his company said the rapidity of the

19 Barron, "The Diary of Captain Samuel F. Foster," 50; Brown, *One of Cleburne's Command*, 50-51.

20 McCaffrey, *Only a Private*, 46; Heartsill, *Fourteen Hundred and 91 Days*, 152.

musketry exceeded "pouring peas on a rawhide." A few soldiers, either through disorientation or cowardice, disappeared into the night. Sergeant J. H. Griffin took command of Company I when no one could locate its only commissioned officer. Griffin performed with such competence that Wilkes later recommended him for promotion to lieutenant.[21]

To the far right of Cleburne's line, Lucius Polk's brigade increased the pressure on both Starkweather's right and the 1st Ohio on Baldwin's left flank. The Confederates soon drove the Buckeyes and the 6th Indiana from the field and killed Colonel Baldwin. Captain Simonson had to spike and abandon a gun in his 5th Indiana Light Artillery when it became entangled in a fallen treetop. It was soon captured by the Confederates, becoming the last artillery piece to change hands on September 19. Baldwin's other two regiments also retired in short order. To the south, Willich eventually followed Baldwin's men to the rear. "You ought to have been here to of seen them run," Pvt. Alexander L. Orr of the 18th Texas Cavalry later claimed; "they threw hats, blankets, knapsacks, guns, and everything else." Union accounts suggest the withdrawal was far more orderly. Colonel Willich said he "fell slowly back in two lines" after some Confederates worked their way to the rear of the 32nd Indiana and fired a volley before disappearing. Dodge's men also soon began withdrawing slowly.[22]

"The firing slackened gradually when darkness grew near," Captain Foster noted. "When it got dark in the woods, it really got dark." The skirmishers of Col. Franklin Wilkes's 17th-18th-24th-25th Texas Cavalry slowly moved forward while probing for the Federals' new position. Unable to see very far, they "suddenly and unexpectedly" encountered a line of Yankees, the 77th Pennsylvania of Colonel Dodge's brigade, which captured them. Meanwhile, the soldiers of Wilkes's Companies B and K, still lost and seeking the rest of their regiment, also advanced cautiously. Though exposed to heavy fire during their sojourn, they had yet to lose a man. The occasional discharge of a gun in the distance indicated that Yankees still

21 Stephen Chicoine, *The Confederates of Chappell Hill, Texas: Prosperity, Civil War, and Decline* (Jefferson, NC: 2011), 111; B. F. Grady to his uncle, *Wilmington* (NC) *Daily Journal*, Oct. 25, 1863; Lance, *Maj. Gen. Patrick R. Cleburne*, 84-85. Griffin did not receive the promotion. Coit was a lawyer from South Carolina who had raised troops in Dallas at the start of the war.

22 McCaffrey, *Only a Private*, 46; Anderson, *Campaigning with Parsons' Texas Cavalry Regiment*, 122; *OR* 30, pt. 1, 535, 539-540, 564. Orr's brother Jim sustained a minor neck wound fighting against Johnson's Federals. According to Dave Powell, "This area had been heavily contested in earlier actions, and as a result, it was littered with the detritus of several different combats, which Orr doubtless mistook for signs of rout. Five or six different brigades crossed this ground over the course of the day."

lurked in the woods. Shortly before 7:30 p.m., the companies encountered several dozen men but could not tell whether they were friend or foe.[23]

As the wayward Texans stopped to assess the situation, a group of riders passed their right flank. General Smith, along with a staff officer, again was trying to figure out the reason for the unexpected delay. He did not realize that Deshler had obliqued to the left, so he assumed the riders were Confederates. According to Sergeant Grady, Smith expressed impatience at the mysterious party for being "in the way." When he asked their identity, he heard an alarming reply: "The 77th Pennsylvania." Those were the last words Smith ever heard. A sudden volley rang out, and he and the staff officer toppled lifeless from their mounts. Colonel Vaughan of the 13th Tennessee and his aide made the same mistake; the aide died but Vaughan was uninjured. Confederates immediately killed the Federal who had shot the aide. The Pennsylvanians now knew that they were facing Rebels, but not how many. "The entire squad, about sixty in number, frightened out of their wits, fired their guns into the treetops and surrendered, Company B escorting them to our rear guard," Grady claimed.[24]

At the sound of the shooting, Wilkes's main line charged through the woods and engaged the balance of the 77th Pennsylvania and the 79th Illinois to its left. The Texans loosed a "terrific enfilading fire" that killed or wounded several Yankees. Seventy-three survivors, including all three of the 77th's field officers, soon surrendered. The Confederates seized the colors of both regiments and freed the captured skirmishers. The 10th Texas's Sgt. William Heartsill wrote, "We also got their flag which is a beautiful one." Colonel Vaughan of Smith's brigade reported that his men, not the Texans, accepted the surrender of the 77th and its colors. Sergeant Grady tallied the prisoners at 197 men; Wilkes said he took a total of 250.[25]

Colonel Dodge's second line, the Hoosiers of the 29th and 30th Indiana, returned Wilkes's fire and held their ground. Dodge, unaware of the disaster that

23 Barron, "The Diary of Captain Samuel F. Foster," 50; Brown, *One of Cleburne's Command*, 50-51; "The Battle of Chickamauga," *Memphis Daily Appeal*, Sept. 22, 1863.

24 Brown, *One of Cleburne's Command*, 50-51; "Amid the Crash of Shells at Chickamauga," *News and Observer* (Raleigh, NC), Jan. 17, 1904; *OR* 30, pt. 2, 107-108.

25 John Obreiter, *The Seventy-seventh Pennsylvania at Shiloh: History of the Regiment* (Harrisburg, PA: 1905), 129; "What Mills Saw"; Heartsill, *Fourteen Hundred and 91 Days*, 152; "Amid the Crash of Shells at Chickamauga"; *OR* 30, pt. 2, 107-108; Grady to his uncle, *Wilmington Daily Journal*. In his official report, Colonel Wilkes credited Pvt. Lewis Montgomery of Company B and Sgt. C. C. Martin and Pvt. Benjamin G. Pippen of Company K for capturing the colors.

had swallowed up nearly all his 77th Pennsylvania and half of the 79th Illinois, tried to move his left two regiments more to the front. Like Preston Smith, he wandered into enemy lines in the darkness. Some of Wilkes's oncoming men took Dodge prisoner, but he soon escaped. Upon returning to his lines, he found that his superiors were withdrawing the remnants of his brigade after almost being surrounded.[26]

This was the last action of Saturday evening for Deshler's brigade. About 9:00 p.m. the Texans and Arkansans retired 200 to 300 yards and reformed their lines. As Roger Mills's regiment pulled back, "J. W. T.," the skirmisher who had given his canteen to the wounded Illinois soldier, again encountered the man. The Texan stooped over the fallen Mason to hear what he might say. "Brother," the Yankee gasped, "something tells me that we will live through this battle, and that we will someday meet again." The Texan clasped his hand and hastily joined his command. Little did he know that he would be summoned to meet the Yankee, John Randolph, decades later in a hotel room in New Orleans. The invalided Randolph was near death then, but he wanted to return the canteen and express his gratitude.[27]

Several of Deshler's wounded groped their way through the darkness to locate their brigade. Most needed medical attention and were sent to the rear. They included Boone Daugherty of the 18th Texas Cavalry, who had taken a shot in the face that tore off part of his lip and knocked out several teeth. Nearby soldiers who saw him fall reported him as dead. As Daugherty passed through his regiment, his friends were surprised to see him and, given his wretched condition, believed he was dying. A physician escorted him to a field hospital and dressed his wounds. Daugherty soon recovered and returned to the ranks.[28]

Cleburne's night attack had accomplished little, other than to haul in 300 prisoners, several caissons, two pieces of artillery, considerable ammunition, and two Union flags. That said, his losses had been relatively light. In the confusion and darkness, friendly troops had inflicted some of the casualties. For the men of Wilkes's and Mills's regiments, however, the night fight had brought redemption and satisfaction. Often ridiculed for surrendering at Arkansas Post, the men now had their first taste of victory. Private William H. Graham of the 18th Texas

26 *OR* 30, pt. 1, 556.

27 Anonymous, "The Gray and the Blue," 75-76.

28 "Wounded at Chickamauga," *Denton* (TX) *Record Chronicle*, Jan. 30, 1911.

Cavalry related, "After several skirmishes, our first regular battle was Chickamauga, where we held our ground, but lost many of as good men as ever went into any army." Mills's 6th-10th Texas–15th Texas Cavalry on the left of Deshler's line had scarcely been engaged but shared in the overall satisfaction.[29]

As the opposing armies established their final lines for the evening, someone shot an errant Union officer near Mills's regiment. The man was suffering and moaning loudly. After listening awhile, two or three Texans sought Mills's permission to bring him into Confederate lines. Mills objected, fearing they would make too much noise stepping through the bushes and would arouse the nearby Yankees. The would-be Good Samaritans quieted down for a short time, but their pangs of sympathy were too strong and the officer's pitiful moans were worse to endure than the roar of cannon. They persisted until Mills relented. Removing their shoes and taking a blanket with them, they crept out to the stricken Yankee. They quietly loaded him onto the blanket and brought him into their lines. He was weak and thoroughly chilled from the night air and loss of blood. Both sides had strict orders preventing campfires that night. Cleburne's men were especially chilled, given that their clothing had not yet dried from wading across the creek that afternoon. Nevertheless, Colonel Mills ordered some nearby soldiers to carry the prisoner to an old log cabin behind his lines, where a few Confederates kindled a concealed fire to keep him comfortable.[30]

While Roger Mills and his remaining men settled in for the night, Lt. Gen. James Longstreet was finally riding toward the battlefield; his journey had taken all day. The rickety Western and Atlantic Railroad train bearing Longstreet had pulled into Catoosa Platform with a series of jerks and bangs at about 2:00 that afternoon. As soon as Longstreet and two staff officers received their horses, they set off about four o'clock to locate Bragg's headquarters. Displeased that Bragg had not left a staff officer to greet and guide them, it took seven hours to find headquarters after several wrong turns and a close call with Union pickets. Bragg was asleep in an ambulance when they arrived but aides awakened him. After briefing Longstreet on the day's activities, Bragg gave him a map and described the various troop positions. He outlined his plans to renew the assault on Sunday morning, assigning Longstreet command of the army's left wing: Longstreet's Corps under Hood

29 Mamie Yeary, compiler, *Reminiscences of the Boys in Gray 1861–1865* (Dallas, TX: 1912), 275-276; *OR* 30, pt. 2, 191, 194. Wilkes lost four men killed and seven wounded. Hutchison's skirmishers captured three Federals.

30 "Texas Abroad," *Galveston Daily News*, Aug. 10 and Dec. 28, 1893.

Lt. Gen. James Longstreet commanded the left wing of the Army of Tennessee at Chickamauga. (*Library of Congress*)

(Robertson's, Law/Sheffield/Perry's, and Johnson's brigades, augmented with newly arrived Brig. Gens. Joseph Kershaw's and Benjamin Humphreys's brigades), Thomas Hindman's division, and Simon Bolivar Buckner's corps (Stewart's and Preston's divisions), as well as several battalions of artillery. The meeting soon ended. "An hour was quite enough to settle the plan and details," Col. G. Moxley Sorrel, Longstreet's aide, recalled, "since nothing could be simpler than the operation proposed for Rosecrans's destruction." Exhausted from the long trip, Longstreet and his staff "took to the leafy ground under the tall oaks and hickories for some sleep."[31]

Reinforcements from the Army of Northern Virginia continued to arrive. Two brigades of Maj. Gen. Lafayette McLaws's division detrained at Catoosa Platform that evening and followed guides to the battlefield. They reached the field about 1:00 a.m. and slept on their arms. About the same time, Deshler's brigade moved to the right and stopped at a former Union campsite near the Brock Field. "The dead and wounded were all about us all night," Lt. Robert Collins of the 15th Texas Cavalry remembered; "we could hear the wounded between ours and the Federal lines calling some of their comrades by name and begging for water. The night was cold and crisp, and the dense woodland was dark and gloomy; the bright stars above us and flickering light from some old dead pine trees that were burning in an old field on our left and in front, giving everything a weird, ghastly appearance."[32]

Sergeant William Heartsill later wrote, "There is still considerable confusion about our lines and some doubt as to the position of the enemy; as the fight was carried on so long in the night, our commanders are at a loss where to establish our lines." At 3:00 a.m., with the officers finally satisfied the new lines were safely away from the Federals, orders came that the men could finally light fires and get some rest. "We have literally walked on dead men all night," Heartsill added, "and now while campfires are casting their flickering rays over the battlefield, the scene looks horrible; hundreds of ghastly corpses mangled and torn are scattered around us. I can sit here by my little glimmering light and count a score of Federals; dead, and dying, for at this place the enemy had a battery planted during the first part of the

31 *OR* 30, pt. 2, 288; G. Moxley Sorrel, *Recollections of a Confederate Staff Officer* (New York and Washington: The Neale Publishing Co., 1905), 192-193. Colonel Sheffield had injured his back during the afternoon when his horse bolted at the explosion of a nearby artillery shell. Colonel William C. Oates of Little Round Top fame at Gettysburg temporarily assumed command until Col. William F. Perry could be located. Perry, the ranking colonel, took over Law's brigade while Oates returned to the 15th Alabama.

32 *Fayetteville* (AR) *Daily*, Sept. 20, 1904; Collins, *Chapters*, 151-152.

day and after a bloody resistance it was captured by the Confederates." He continued, "Nearly all the Texans east of the river are concentrated here and they will give a good account of the Lone Star State."[33]

Many soldiers mourned the loss of comrades and relatives or questioned the whereabouts of missing men. Officers scurried about making sure the pickets and other troops close to the enemy stayed alert. Some men scrounged for Union equipment and arms among the nearby casualties. "All night long we remained on the battlefield strung out on the skirmish line among the dead and wounded," the 6th Texas's Private Oliphant remembered, "and we began to realize some of the horrors of war." Thousands of wounded men still lay in the fields and woods, unable to make it to aid stations.[34]

Surgeons worked feverishly through the night to save as many men as possible. Dr. Nathaniel A. Morgan of Marshall, Texas, serving as a surgeon with the 1st Georgia Volunteers, believed that field hospitals exhibited "the dark side of 'glorious war.' There is no romance there. Thousands of wounded and dying lying stretched out on bits of straw or stretched on blankets, pale and haggard, calling for water! water! help! help! Then the operating table is a rude affair on forks covered with a blanket. The chloroform, sponges, knives and a pile of arms and legs under it. And blood everywhere and on everything." Several thousand more casualties in blue, gray, and butternut would join them on the morrow.[35]

33 Heartsill, *Fourteen Hundred and 91 Days*, 152-153.

34 McCaffrey, *Only a Private*, 46.

35 John Alan Logue, "A Texan Views the Civil War," *The Junior Historian*, vol. 22, no. 3, Dec. 1961, 17-18.

Chapter 8

September 20, Morning—Ector's and Deshler's Brigades

Sunday dawned bright with the temperature initially cool and bracing before warming significantly. "The autumn leaves were taking on their colors of amber and gold," 2nd Lt. Oliver P. Bowser of Deshler's brigade remembered years later. "The day was perfect, as if nature was smiling on the deadly faces, and pleased in contemplation of the terrible carnage and blood that were to make that day to be remembered in the history of men and warfare; Blue Ridge, Lookout Mountain and Missionary Ridge were to be silent witnesses of the awful struggle. There was no maneuvering, no strategy. The rank and file did the fighting. The officers simply put them in line and awaited results. The men of both armies seemed to be imbued with the fact that whoever gained the victory would gain it at a terrible price, and that ere the sun went down many of them would bivouac on Eternity's camping-ground; but it made them none the less determined."[1]

Bowser's comrades nervously awaited the resumption of hostilities. "It is now nearly daylight and I have not had a particle of sleep," Sgt. William W. Heartsill of the 10th Texas stated, "nor do I want any while this bloody work is going on." The sun rose on "a gloomy picture," in the words of Albert W. Gaines, an early student

1 Bowser, "History of Granbury's Brigade," 742-743.

2nd Lt. Oliver P. Bowser, 15th Texas Infantry. (*The State Preservation Board, Austin, Texas*)

of the battle. "The woods were enveloped in a dense fog, the air was filled with dust and smoke, and the atmosphere was laden with the odor of powder." Dead men lay everywhere, intermingled with soldiers too severely injured to reach field hospitals. "The sun, like a red ball, seen through the smoke and fog, had an angry look, presaging the awful red carnage of the day to come."[2]

"The result of the first day's fight was not a success for either army," Capt. Ryland Todhunter of Ector's brigade declared. "Both were completely used up and the losses were frightful." Ector was down to some 500 men. During the long night, the opposing army commanders committed to staying put and fighting it out. Their subordinates made slight adjustments to their respective organizational structures. For example, Captain James P. Douglas received orders to report with his Texas battery to General Deshler.

The opposing soldiers replenished their ammunition, reformed their lines, tended to their wounded, and constructed breastworks. The ringing sound of axes and heavy crashes of falling timber echoed through the woods and cedar glades. "We built a log breastwork, expecting to be attacked; but no such good fortune," Sgt. Ben Grady of the 25th Texas Cavalry bemoaned. The Confederates would be on the offensive this day.[3]

According to a member of the 7th Texas, "Our line corresponding to that of the enemy was in the form of a crescent, with the convexity towards the Federals,

2 Heartsill, *Fourteen Hundred and 91 Days*, 153; "Complete, Authentic Story of the Battle of Chickamauga," *Chattanooga Daily Times*, May 29, 1913. Gaines was a prominent postwar attorney in Chattanooga.

3 "Battle of Chickamauga," *Des Moines Register*, *OR* 30, pt. 2, 195; *Wilmington Daily Journal*, Oct. 15, 1863.

Polk commanding the right wing and Longstreet the left." The two divisions of D. H. Hill's corps, under Lt. Gen. Leonidas Polk's overall command, formed a long battle line. Cleburne's division (including Deshler's Texans and Arkansans) was south (left) of Breckinridge's division. Walker's Reserve Corps (including Ector's brigade) manned a second line behind Cleburne's center. To Cleburne's left, at the Confederates' convex angle, were four brigades of Cheatham's division, with Brig. Gen. John K. Jackson's brigade behind them fronting sharply to the northeast. Hood/Law and Stewart were in front of Cheatham in the left-center. Hindman's and Preston's divisions held the far left of the 2-mile-long line.[4]

During the night, Maj. Gen. William Rosecrans had pulled several divisions farther west to defensive positions closer to the La Fayette Road. Soldiers felled trees using artillery axes and piled brush and fence rails into knee-high breastworks. Major General George Thomas's XIV Corps remained on the left with Maj. Gen. Alexander McCook's XX Corps on the right. One division of Maj. Gen. Thomas Crittenden's XXI Corps supported Thomas, with his other two divisions in reserve. Most of Maj. Gen. Gordon Granger's Reserve Corps was two miles to the north along the Chattanooga–La Fayette Road at McAfee's Church.[5]

General Bragg planned for Polk's wing to assail the enemy on the extreme right (north) at dawn. Each Confederate division in line to the south would successively join in the attack. Longstreet's left wing was to await Polk's assault and then "take it up promptly." The whole line was then to push forward "vigorously and persistently against the enemy." On paper, the strategy looked promising to Bragg, but it would be difficult to execute cleanly because of the wooded terrain, the confusion of battle, and varying degrees of commitment from the officers involved. Most notably, Polk delayed commencing his attack, the linchpin of Bragg's ambitious plan, for several hours. "With increasing anxiety and disappointment," Bragg complained, "I waited until after sunrise without hearing a gun." He dispatched a mounted staff officer, Maj. Pollock B. Lee, to find the reason for Polk's tardiness. Getting nowhere, Bragg then summoned Polk to headquarters to restate his orders in person. All this took time. The guns stayed silent, other than sporadic skirmishing.[6]

4 "Gregg's Brigade at Chickamauga"; *OR* 30, pt. 2, 48.

5 Ruger, *Map of Chickamauga*, Plate 5; Powell, *The Maps of Chickamauga*, 139-143.

6 *OR* 30, pt. 2, 33. Leonidas Polk, the prewar bishop of the Episcopal Diocese of Louisiana, was a second cousin of President James K. Polk.

"At 8 o'clk skirmishing commences on our right," the 10th Texas's Sergeant Heartsill scribed in his ever-present journal; "in half an hour our Brigade takes up the music and it passes on to Longstreet's men on the left; who carry it on and on until the rugged cliffs of Lookout mountain catches the sound and echoes back the strain." On the north end of Deshler's line, the 15th Texas's Lt. Robert M. Collins noted that "[t]he boys all looked serious and determined, doubtless appreciating the fact, that before the sun went out of sight on the other side of Missionary Ridge and Lookout Mountain, that many of them will have crossed the river, and their spirits gone up amidst the din and smoke of battle, to the home of good soldiers and patriots beyond the stars."[7]

As skirmishers dueled and the opposing lines nervously awaited the resumption of hostilities, a few soldiers prowled the battlefield to rob the dead and wounded. Private Miles P. Cook of the 20th Ohio Artillery suffered arm and leg injuries during the previous day's fighting around the Winfrey farm. He lay on the field all night, at one point dressing the wounds of an Alabamian he remembered as "A. R. Carter," who returned the favor. Now, on Sunday morning, "the ghouls began to" make their rounds. A Texan approached him and ordered him to pull off his fancy new boots. Cook replied that he was wounded and could not do it. The Rebel retorted that he would have them off in a jiffy. As he grabbed the foot on his good leg and pulled off the boot, Cook screamed in pain. When the nearby Alabamian chided his fellow Confederate for his lack of feelings, the Texan picked up a musket with a bayonet attached. "I believe he meant to kill me," Cook recalled, "but as he thrust at me the bayonet passed through my right hip and entered the earth, pinning me fast." The Confederate then roughly braced a foot against Cook's body and pulled the other boot from his wounded leg. "Everything turned dark to me," Cook remembered, "although I did not lose consciousness." The Texan began to walk away with the prized boots. Carter, the injured Alabama soldier, quickly pulled a revolver from a nearby cavalryman's holster and killed the thief with a single shot in the back. "I expected we would both be murdered for this," Cook added, "but the fellow's own comrades came up and agreed that it served him right. They raised me up, cleaned the bayonet of all dirt, and then pulled it out as carefully as possible."[8]

7 Heartsill, *Fourteen Hundred and 91 Days*, 153; Collins, *Chapters*, 154.

8 "At Chickamauga," *Detroit Free Press*, Dec. 11, 1887. No "A. R. Carter" appears on the rolls of Alabama troops, so Cook apparently confused the man's name and regiment (he said Carter was in the 9th Alabama).

While a handful of Texans proved to be common thieves, the majority remained in their battle lines eating breakfast and awaiting the order to advance. The morning repast for the 15th Texas Cavalry's Lieutenant Collins consisted of blue Florida beef and cornbread washed down with cold water. He and several other line officers carried rifle-muskets, like their enlisted men. Soon, "someone who seemed to have the right kind of authority" came along the line and disarmed the captain and lieutenants. That left a dismayed Collins with a "little straight Confederate sword, so dull that it wouldn't cut cheese and too blunt to stick into a stack of hay." It was an inauspicious start to the day.[9]

Many men believed they would shortly hear the order to form up and march into combat. They began to grumble when no such instructions came by 9:00 a.m. "Somebody's mistakes caused us to remain in a state of expectancy," Sergeant Grady complained. Most of Deshler's Arkansas Post parolees chafed for a chance to redeem themselves. "Why all this delay?" Lieutenant Collins wondered. Soon, he spotted Bragg and Longstreet riding through the line of Nutt's company of the 10th Texas on their way to view the front. Believing that their marching orders were finally about to arrive, Deshler's men tightened their belts, pulled their hats well down on their heads, and prepared to meet the enemy.[10]

From his headquarters east of Alexander's Bridge, two miles from his main line, Polk finally got the ball rolling about 9:30. Major General John Breckinridge, the former vice president of the United States, ordered his three brigades forward to engage the left of Thomas's XIV Corps near the John McDonald farm. To Bragg's further disappointment, "The troops were moved to the assault in detail and by detachments, unsupported." It would be a long day for Bragg, one that, like the previous day, saw a myriad of lost opportunities. Polk later tried to deflect the blame to Bragg's staff and his own subordinates, most notably D. H. Hill, but he eventually faced charges of disobeying orders. Hill, in turn, denied receiving orders from Polk to advance early in the morning. The longstanding dysfunction in the Army of Tennessee's senior leadership had reared its ugly head again at the most inopportune time.[11]

Despite the delay in launching the assault, Breckinridge had some initial success in turning the Union left flank, and then moved south parallel to the La

9 Collins, *Chapters*, 154-155.

10 "Amid the Crash of Shells at Chickamauga," *News and Observer* (Raleigh, NC), Jan. 17, 1904; Collins, *Chapters*, 155; Heartsill, *Fourteen Hundred and 91 Days*, 153.

11 *OR* 30, pt. 2, 33, 48, 55-56.

Maj. Gen. John Calhoun Breckinridge commanded a division of three brigades at Chickamauga. (*Library of Congress*)

Fayette Road. He threatened the rear of Pap Thomas's salient in an open field on the Kelly farm. Breckinridge's attack eventually failed because of poor coordination and lack of support, but it did draw Union reinforcements northward. Early in the fighting, Brig. Gen. Benjamin H. Helm, leading the famed Kentucky "Orphan Brigade," fell mortally wounded with a gunshot to his chest. The 32-year-old Helm died the following day in a field hospital. The death of Abraham Lincoln's brother-in-law brought private grief and mourning to the Executive Mansion in Washington.[12]

Ector's Brigade

As Breckinridge's and then Cleburne's divisions struggled to crack the Union left, a yawning gap opened between them in D. H. Hill's line. To fill the void, Hill requested assistance from Maj. Gen. W. H. T. Walker and his Reserve Corps. Most of Brig. Gen. States Rights Gist's brigade had arrived on September 19 at Catoosa Platform after a short train ride from Rome, Georgia. The Georgians and South Carolinians had been in Rome on detached service. On paper, Gist commanded Walker's former division during the entire battle, but he had been absent the previous two days. Now on the scene, he assumed divisional command and assigned Col. Peyton H. Colquitt to head his former brigade. In addition to Colquitt, Gist now had the battle-depleted brigades of Brig. Gen. Matthew Ector and Col. Claudius Wilson under him.[13]

Colonel Colquitt led his brigade forward in the same general area where General Helm had received his mortal wound earlier in the morning. There, Brig. Gen. Absalom Baird's division of Thomas's XIV Corps manned the ridgetop line at the northern curve of the salient. To the south, the divisions of Brig. Gens. Richard W. Johnson, John M. Palmer, and Joseph J. Reynolds struggled all morning with Pat Cleburne's division. Kelly Field lay a short distance to Baird's right rear, and his division lined the thick woods about 150 yards beyond the northeastern corner of the field. Colonel Benjamin F. Scribner's and Brig. Gen. John M. Starkweather's brigades were in front of Wilson's and Ector's oncoming brigades,

12 Warner, *Generals in Gray*, 132-133; Powell, *The Maps of Chickamauga*, 148-151. Helm was married to Emilie Todd, a half-sister of Mary Todd Lincoln. Elisha Kelly rented the farm from his brother, Elijah.

13 *OR* 30, pt. 2, 244-245. Because of a shortage of railcars at Rome, the 16th South Carolina and Ferguson's Light Battery of Gist's brigade did not arrive until the morning of Sept. 23.

with Brig. Gen. John H. King's brigade of Regulars on the far left of the salient. All were in a double line. King's left flank was open and exposed, so he refused it (bent it back) to guard against an enemy attack from the north, such as Breckinridge's movement against this same position earlier that morning. On his right, Scribner positioned four guns of the 4th Indiana Battery on his right in a salient that allowed them to sweep the woods to the northeast, east, and southeast of the Union line.[14]

Colquitt, who erroneously believed that Breckinridge's division was directly ahead of him, advanced toward the La Fayette Road without the customary skirmishers out front. He wheeled to the left until his brigade roughly paralleled King's brigade at the left of Baird's divisional line. Sudden volleys of musketry and intense artillery fire indicated to Colquitt that he had stumbled onto the Yankee line in the thick woods. Half an hour later, Colquitt lay dead and his brigade was in shambles. More than a third of his 980 soldiers had fallen, and only two field officers remained unhurt. A galling fire pinned down the survivors.[15]

About 10:00 a.m., General Walker formed Wilson's and Ector's brigades to relieve Colquitt's shattered command. A youthful soldier in the 14th Texas Cavalry worried about going into action this day. Little Jimmie Arnold, a teenaged orphan from Carthage, was "the pet of his company and of his regiment," according to a 1923 newspaper article. "They were proud of his courage and fidelity, and he was fond of each and every one of his comrades." Arnold especially revered Col. John Camp. As Camp formed his regiment into line behind Wilson, Arnold experienced a strong premonition of death. He told Camp he was not a coward. He had always obeyed orders, but now he pleaded, "Don't let me go into this fight." He said he would be killed and asked to take Camp's horse to the rear. Camp gently refused and told the lad to do his duty as he always had. "All right, Colonel, I will," he manfully replied, "but I'll never come out of this fight alive."[16]

Ector's command, including the 9th Texas Infantry and the 10th, 14th, and 32nd Texas Cavalry, had remained relatively inactive since the Saturday morning fight. The Chubs were in reserve near Jay's Mill on Sunday morning until Walker ordered them to support Colquitt. The two brigades stepped off at the double-quick, with Wilson leading and Ector trailing in a second line. The veteran Confederates moved to the left (northeast) of the fortified Kelly Field salient. As

14 Ibid., pt. 1, 277.

15 Ibid. Colquitt's older brother Alfred, a Confederate general in the Eastern Theater, led a brigade at Sharpsburg, Fredericksburg, and Chancellorsville.

16 "Little Jimmie Arnold," *Marshall* (TX) *News Messenger*, Mar. 9, 1923.

they pushed through the heavy woods toward Alexander's Bridge Road, they encountered several disorganized throngs of Colquitt's Georgians and South Carolinians.[17]

One of Ector's men noticed a little hut in the woods into which at least 50 wounded men had crowded, without any surgeon among them. "They had no water, no food, no one to offer consolation," he lamented. "They were absolutely alone—awaiting death." After crossing Alexander's Bridge Road, the Southerners ran forward, loudly giving the Rebel yell. They received a raking fire from the left and direct fire to their front. Soon, dozens of dead and wounded men marked Wilson's and Ector's course. The casualties included youthful Jimmie Arnold; the Carthage orphan with the premonition of death died only 10 minutes after stepping off. "The very air seemed filled with bursting shells and minnie balls," another Texan recalled. The Union resistance was so stubborn that a Native American soldier in the brigade reportedly remarked, "Yankee fight good this time," as he aimed his musket and coolly picked off Federals.[18]

Wilson and Ector halted and directed their respective brigades to lay down a covering fire, which allowed Colquitt's remnants to reform in the woods. They all then engaged in a long-range, one-sided firefight with Baird's Federals. "At this time the three brigades were occupying the same line nearly, and this arrangement necessarily resulted in some confusion," General Gist reported. "After a very unsatisfactory fight, lasting probably forty-five minutes, and in which we lost some valuable officers and a few men, we were ordered to fall back and reform." Under orders from D. H. Hill, Gist withdrew his battered division a few hundred yards east to its starting point. "We lost in less than two hours over one-third of our Texas brigade," Capt. Ryland Todhunter, Ector's assistant adjutant general, reported, "which made our loss in the two days' fighting 60 percent of men and officers, and every horse killed. I was pulled from under my horse by members of the 14th Texas."[19]

17 *OR* 30, pt. 2, 249.

18 "Horrible War Memories"; "Ector's Brigade in the Battle of Chickamauga"; *Fairfield* (TX) *Recorder*, Oct. 1, 1897; CSR of James Arnold, 14th Texas Cavalry, NARA RG109, M323, Texas, roll 0081.

19 *OR* 30, pt. 2, 246; "Battle of Chickamauga," *Des Moines Register*, Powell, *The Maps of Chickamauga*, 165. During the war, Todhunter was wounded five times and had five horses shot from under him. He returned to Texas and became a significant breeder of champion thoroughbreds.

The 14th Texas Cavalry's Sgt. James C. Hudson lay dead near the Union lines. Severely wounded on Saturday, he had retired from the field to seek medical attention. Despite his painful injury, the Alabama native returned to the ranks early on Sunday morning to continue the battle; he had a reputation of always being near the front in past engagements. During Ector's advance, Hudson fell near several comrades in Company D. "By his companions in arms he was universally beloved," a friend later recounted. "Kind, affable, liberal—he won the esteem of all classes . . . he is gone; his friends feel his loss irreparable." Hudson left a wife and several children in Rusk County.[20]

Matthew Ector received four slight wounds and had two horses shot from under him. His talented assistant adjutant general, Capt. "Buck" Kilgore (who had skillfully guided the brigade out of the potential Union encirclement on Saturday morning), went down with a severe injury and was taken a prisoner. Ector's aide-de-camp, Lt. Henry M. Lane, also fell. Every member of Ector's staff, including the orderlies, lost at least one horse, and every mounted officer in the brigade had his horse killed or severely wounded. The 14th Texas's Col. John L. Camp, known to admirers as "the Christian warrior," went to the rear with a severe leg wound. His slave, King Beasley, reportedly saved Camp's life by using an iron heated over a fire to stanch the bleeding.[21]

Gist and Walker reformed their men into a battle line facing southwest, with Ector's brigade on the left, Wilson in the center, and Gist on the right. With Colonel Colquitt dead, Lt. Col. Leroy Napier of the 8th Georgia Battalion took command of Gist's brigade. The reserve division, reduced by then to perhaps 1,600 men, remained inactive throughout the afternoon.[22]

20 "Camp Near Meridian, Miss., October the 18th, 1863," *Henderson* (TX) *Times*, Nov. 21, 1863.

21 "Ector's Brigade in the Battle of Chickamauga"; *Fairfield Recorder*, Oct. 1, 1897; Kathy Arth family history of her great-great-grandfather, J. L. Camp. Kilgore was taken by rail to Pennsylvania and confined in Fort Delaware. He was exchanged in 1864, returned to his regiment, and served until the end of the war. He later became a U.S. congressman and federal judge. The Indiana-born H. M. Lane had attended Bastrop Military Academy and was a lieutenant in the Texas Rangers before the war.

22 For an excellent treatise on the final day of Chickamauga, see David A. Powell, *The Chickamauga Campaign: Glory or the Grave: The Breakthrough, the Union Collapse, and the Defense of Horseshoe Ridge, September 20, 1863* (El Dorado Hills, CA: 2015), 546.

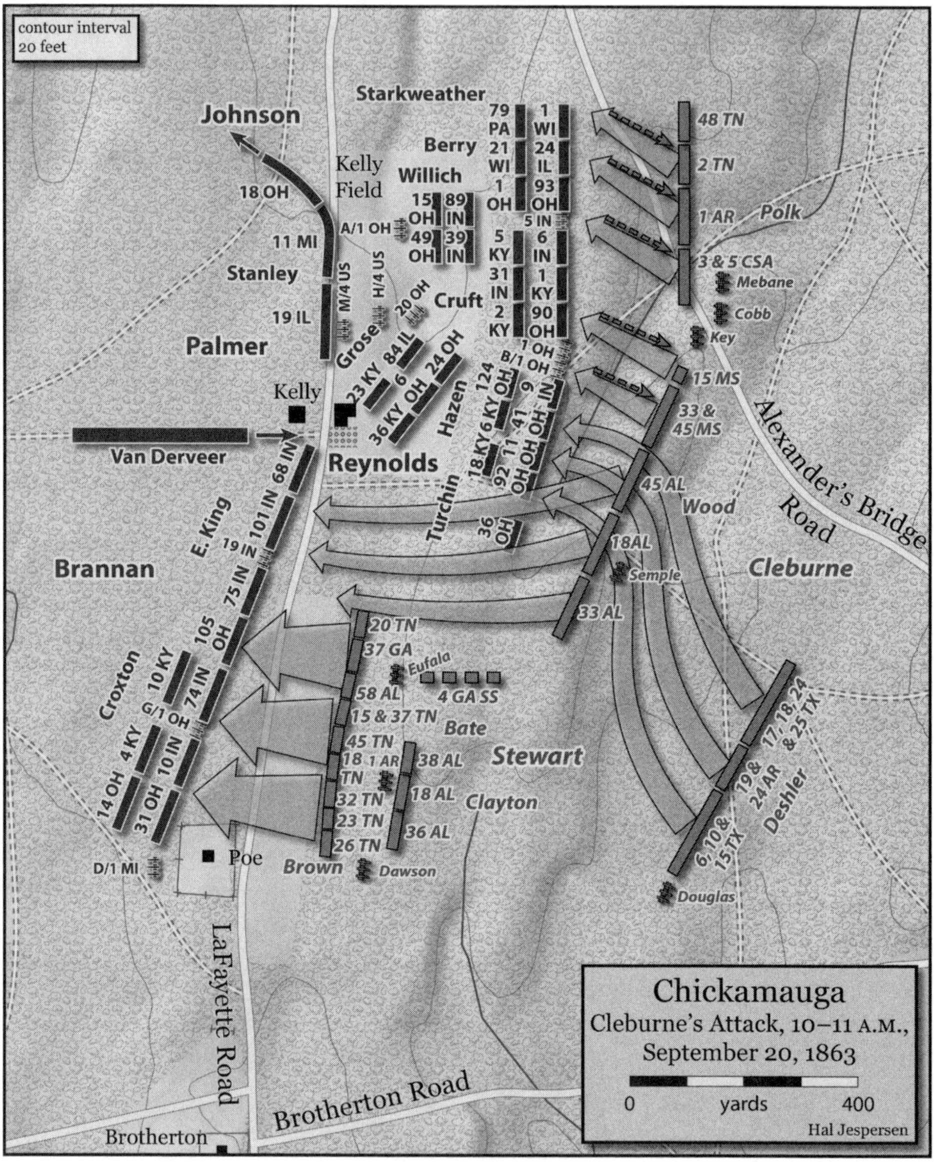

Deshler's Brigade

Just before Breckinridge began his belated advance, Patrick Cleburne ordered his quartermasters to quickly distribute additional rations to Deshler's, Wood's, and Polk's brigades (aligned left to right, or south to north). Cleburne's veteran division lay in the woods toward the center of a large, irregular triangle formed by the La Fayette, Alexander's Bridge, and Brotherton roads. His starting point was about 200 yards west of his final position of the previous night. The Irishman led his mile-wide line of battle west through the woods toward a bulge or salient in the Union breastworks on the Kelly farm east of the La Fayette Road. "We moved off a short distance by the left flank," he reported, "and then advanced to the front, passing through a portion of Major General Cheatham's division." He kept his staff officers busy delivering instructions as the line moved out.[23]

Deshler had positioned Mills's 6th-10th Texas–15th Texas Cavalry on the left of his line, with Hutchison's 19th-24th Arkansas in the center. The 17th-18th-24th-25th Texas Cavalry made up his right wing. Colonel Mills's calm demeanor impressed his men, one of whom later recalled, "There he sat on his horse, to the right of his leading regiment, a little advanced, firm and unchanged as though he and his horse were cast of iron." Captain Rhodes Fisher and Mills's Company G moved out in front of the brigade's center as a skirmish line. Many of the men in this company, including Sgt. Dick Harper, had enrolled in Denton County. The youthful Harper's booming voice carried back to the main line, where the men could hear him repeat Fisher's every command. Wood's brigade was to Deshler's right. The Mississippians had been among the troops repeatedly deriding the Arkansas Post parolees. As the two lines passed, the Texans would "salute strange soldiers as we passed them and crack jokes as if feeling relieved at the certainty of ending the campaign, one way or the other pretty soon."[24]

The 25th Texas Cavalry's Sergeant Grady described the terrain: "Just in our front was an old field in which a heavy growth of short-leaved pines had been cut down some months before. Beyond this field a wooded slope reached down to a small stream and on the rising slope beyond the stream was the enemy's line of battle entrenched behind a strong earthwork. Higher up the slope, beyond the defenses, batteries and single field pieces defied us." The Kelly Field, east of the La Fayette Road, was about three-fourths of a mile wide and a quarter mile deep. A smaller 20-acre open field was west of the road, directly opposite the Kelly house and outbuildings.[25]

23 *Wilmington Daily Journal*, Oct. 25, 1863; *OR* 30, pt. 2, 188; Heartsill, *Fourteen Hundred and 91 Days*, 153.

24 "Roger Q. Mills," *Navarro Scroll*, Navarro County Historical Society, Corsicana, TX, 1958; Collins, *Chapters*, 156.

25 *Wilmington Daily Journal*, Oct. 25, 1863; *OR* 30, pt. 1, 249. Reynolds, a future governor of Illinois, commanded the 4th Division of Thomas's XIV Corps.

Major General John M. Palmer's division of Crittenden's XXI Corps rested behind breastworks 800 yards west of Deshler on the Kelly property. To Palmer's left (north) lay Brig. Gens. Richard Johnson's and Absalom Baird's divisions; to his right front was Maj. Gen. Joseph J. Reynolds's division just north of the house of Larkin and Sarah Poe. Several brigades and batteries of unlimbered artillery were in reserve behind the tightly packed front line. The Union infantrymen crouched behind a broad concave line of sturdy breastworks of rocks, fence rails, and felled timber. Piles of brush provided some camouflage. Small redoubts at critical points along the defensive line offered exceptional firing platforms.[26]

Palmer's and Reynolds's skirmishers lay in the Poe field several dozen yards in front of their respective breastworks. The 17th Texas Cavalry's Pvt. Andrew J. Murphey claimed that at the first Rebel volley, the Federal pickets retreated to their fortifications. General Deshler provided overall guidance as his men slowly worked their way west through the many fallen pine trees choking the field. He had informed Capt. James Douglas about 9:00 a.m. that the division was going to attack the enemy and that he should follow the brigade as closely as was practicable. Douglas was to decide on the best positions to unlimber his guns. The downed trees, however, soon proved to be a significant issue for his limbers and guns. Douglas rode to the right of the brigade but discovered that the way forward was impassable. Quickly riding south, he found a usable route in a defile well off to the left of Deshler's advancing line. He ordered his four guns to swing behind the brigade and head south.[27]

According to the 15th Texas Cavalry's Lieutenant Collins, "All at once an artillery officer comes down the line, going at a speed as if shot from a cannon, giving the command as he passed: 'By the right flank, double quick, march!'" Captain Douglas soon reached the south end of the ragged infantry line, which was now running forward as fast as possible. Just then, a cannonball sliced off the top of a pine tree, striking it some 40 feet from the ground. The massive piece fell

26 Ruger, *Map of Chickamauga*, Plates 5 and 6; James Alfred Sartain, *History of Walker County, Georgia* (Dalton, GA: 1932), 99. Larkin H. Poe was a teamster in the 4th Georgia Cavalry in Wheeler's division. His wife Sarah was a daughter of the Brothertons, who owned a farm a third of a mile south of the Poe farm.

27 Yeary, *Reminiscences*, 553; *OR* 30, pt. 2, 196.

lengthwise on Captain Fisher's Company G but failed to hurt anyone seriously. Collins expressed surprise that the timber did not cripple anyone.[28]

"As the brigade emerged from the cover of the timber into an open field," a 6th Texan from Matagorda recorded, "it was saluted with a severe artillery fire, which tore up the earth, cutting off tree-tops and mutilated the men in a shocking manner. The field had many dead trees still standing, though sapless and leafless, and whenever a cannon ball or shell struck one of these, wood and iron scattered about in dreadful profusion." The unidentified soldier added, "The brigade was not accustomed to an 'open field fight' and the terrible noise of the missiles, more than their destructiveness, affected more or less the nerves of the whole command. When about half way across this open space, the brigade was halted for some reason, for a few minutes."

Deshler halted and dressed his lines after moving to the right several hundred yards. One of the 6th Texans "was seized with a violent chill," the Matagorda soldier noted. His captain ordered some nearby men to carry him to the rear. A German soldier in the same company, unnerved by the "diabolical discord of inharmonious sounds made by the bursting shells and hurtling balls," decided to try his luck. "Och, dunder and blitzen," he uttered to the captain, "I would give one thousand tollar for dat shill!" He stayed in the ranks, however.[29]

Deshler began advancing to the northwest. A good reason existed for his change in direction. Polk's and Wood's brigades had become entangled with A. P. Stewart's division off to Cleburne's left. That mix-up forced Deshler's brigade to move by the right flank and circle to the north. It also exposed his men to enemy artillery, most notably the 21st Indiana Battery and, farther to the west across the La Fayette Road, the 19th Indiana Battery. "We had to march and counter march across a field in easy range and in view of two Yankee batteries," Sergeant Grady complained. "Of course, they gave us no small share of their attention. Shells burst over us, under us, and in our midst. Balls of all sizes, grape, canister and 6 and 12 lb. balls, whizzed among us in copious profusion and fearful proximity." Grapeshot killed one man in Grady's company and tore the shoulder off another. "A 12 lb. ball went through Co. B, (next to us), took off one man's head and tore two others into

28 Collins, *Chapters*, 157. Collins later claimed that one of his men encountered General Longstreet during a brief halt. There is little supporting evidence that Longstreet ventured that far north during Cleburne's advance, but it is conceivable he was trying to straighten out Stewart's entanglement with Polk and Wood. Colonel Mills also reported meeting Longstreet, in his case near an unnamed house during an artillery barrage.

29 "The Haversack," *The Land We Love*, vol. 2, no. 3, Jan. 1867, 222.

ragged pieces," he continued. The men soon got a little relief as they moved out of sight of the 19th Indiana's guns.[30]

Casualties climbed as Deshler's brigade moved northward, where two Ohio batteries added their fire to that of the 21st Indiana. According to Sam Moore of the 17th Texas Cavalry, "The Yanks had two batteries a playing on us as well as the infantry pouring minnie balls at us as fast as they could load and shoot." The 6th Texas's Pvt. William J. Oliphant wrote that "[t]he enemy's fire was terrific. Besides the infantry's fire, eighteen Napoleon guns poured a deadly shower of grape and canister into our ranks as we advanced. Half of our Brigade went down before that terrible rain of missiles." Colonel Mills later reported that he lost 15 to 20 men as they crossed the obstacle-laden field. On the right, Colonel Wilkes's command was also under intense fire. In the 18th Texas Cavalry, a shell fragment knocked out two of Pvt. William M. Summers's teeth and then struck his shoulder, incapacitating him for two months. Private William E. Eckhardt of the 24th Texas Cavalry narrowly escaped death when grapeshot severely wounded him and tore the sole and heel off his shoe. The soldier to his immediate right, Sgt. Tom Moore, died instantly, and the man just ahead of Moore in the front rank fell gravely wounded. Wilkes lost about 10 men in the forward movement. "The Texas command advanced, bending low as though they were in a hailstorm," one soldier recalled. "And so it was, but it was a hail whose stroke meant death. Their lines were enfiladed by double-shotted batteries whose brass guns leaped from the ground like things of life when they were fired."[31]

In the 6th Texas, the German soldier who had offered a thousand dollars for a ride to the rear now got his wish in a way he had not anticipated. About 20 minutes after his brash pronouncement, a shell fragment sliced off one of his big toes. As litter-bearers carried him to the rear, his face shined as he exclaimed, "Danks to Himmel! Did is so better as a shill, ya, I gits mine furlough now." Smacking his lips with joy, he headed out of the fight.[32]

30 *Wilmington Daily Journal*, Oct. 25, 1863; Powell, *The Maps of Chickamauga*, 159.

31 McCaffrey, *Only a Private*, 46; John Henry Brown, *Indian Wars and Pioneers of Texas* (Austin, TX: 1890), 405-406; *OR* 30, pt. 2, 188, 194; *A Memorial and Biographical History of McLennan, Falls, Bell and Coryell Counties, Texas* (New York, NY: 1893), 790; *OR* 30, pt. 2, 193; "Roger Q. Mills," *Navarro Scroll*.

32 "The Haversack," 222. The soldier received his furlough and returned to the regiment after recuperating. He served through the rest of the war without incident. Several Germans served in Company D. Medical records are sparse, but none of those men is known to have lost a toe.

Meanwhile, according to Lt. John W. Stewart of the 15 Texas Cavalry, "the fight was becoming general all along the line" from the right all the way south to Cleburne's division. By now Deshler's men had traversed almost 600 yards from their starting point. They were still subject to a heavy fire of canister "which swept inroads as they went." The Yankees were "awaiting us," Pvt. Alexander Orr recalled; "We lit in on them." The Texans and Arkansans kept their heads down against the incoming fire and determinedly continued to push ahead.[33]

South of Deshler's hard-pressed infantry, Captain Douglas's Texas battery picked its way through the defile. Yankee artillery (likely the 21st Indiana Battery) spotted the column of limbered guns and opened fire on his flank. The Texans emerged in an open field several hundred yards wide only to find that two Federal batteries (Palmer's Batteries B and F, 1st Ohio) commanded the ground. After incoming fire killed a horse and destroyed a wheel on one of his pieces, Douglas quickly took shelter behind a hillock. When he came out to examine the terrain, the captain observed that Deshler's brigade was much farther to the right than he supposed it would be. He withdrew at a gallop back through the felled pine trees as best as he could, losing a second horse to enemy fire. His battery took cover behind another hill somewhat closer to Deshler's left flank. Douglas learned that the brigade was being held in reserve while Wood's and Polk's brigades advanced, and Cleburne ordered him to remain in position on the hill's reverse crest. Wood's and Polk's brigades soon joined him.[34]

The firing intensified off to Deshler's front as Cleburne's center and right engaged the well-fortified enemy. The attack stalled and then collapsed. The dismounted Texas cavalrymen soon spotted part of Wood's Mississippi brigade double-quicking to the rear in the woods off to their right. "This was the same outfit that had poked so much fun at us Texas fellows," Lt. Robert Collins of the 15th Texas Cavalry remembered, "and the boys seemed to enjoy it as a good joke on the mud-heads." On the right, the 17th-18th-24th-25th Texas Cavalry opened ranks to allow Wood's men egress from the field. Lucius Polk's brigade also fell back as Cleburne's fractured divisional attack fizzled in the Union firestorm. One account suggests that Cleburne rode up to Deshler and curtly said, "General, your brigade has not been engaged today." With flushed face, the young brigadier spiritedly replied, "It is not my fault, General." Cleburne then ordered Deshler to

33 Stewart, "Proceedings of Granbury's Regiment," 296; Anderson, *Campaigning with Parsons' Texas Cavalry Regiment*, 122.

34 *OR* 30, pt. 2, 196.

advance. "While we were going into the fight," Pvt. William W. Royall of the 18th Texas Cavalry recalled, "we were ordered to a place where our line had been broken twice. I was struck by a spent ball across the back of my left hand, disabling me for a short time. I remained in the fight all day."[35]

"Having crossed this old field in the midst of a storm of shot and shell," Sergeant Grady recalled years later, "we came to General Cleburne sitting on his horse near an oak and wincing as the shells flew by his head." Several of Wood's men, claiming their ammunition was exhausted, came rushing past on their way to the rear. "General Deshler," Cleburne said, "two of my best brigades have been driven out of that gap [between Cleburne and Breckinridge] yonder. Take yours into it, and hold it till further orders." Before Chickamauga, Deshler's men had never been in battle under Cleburne, Grady wrote, "and he did not know what stuff we were made of, and hence he ordered Douglas' battery to post itself in our rear as our substitute if we gave way to the terrible fire of the enemy." Lieutenant Collins reported, "Our loss in officers and men for the first few minutes was alarming in the extreme." The 6th Texas's Lt. Robert B. Harvey was trying to form Company H to fire a return volley when the Victoria resident was killed.[36]

"We were again ordered forward to regain and hold a place in the line from which three brigades had been driven in confusion," the 6th Texas's Jim Turner noted. "The enemy's fire was simply terrific." Turning to the right, the brigade moved steadily to the spot on a thinly timbered ridge that Cleburne wanted them to occupy. Sergeant Grady was the foremost man in his regiment, with Maj. William A. Taylor guiding the line, which marched 20 or 30 steps forward in a shower of missiles. One projectile whizzed past Grady's head and killed or maimed eight men in his company. As the veteran sergeant stepped down into a ditch, an artillery round dug a furrow in the ground three feet in front of him. The incident reminded him of Pat Cleburne's frequent admonition that "no two balls would hit in the same place." Once Deshler's brigade reached the designated position, the men found the situation worse than they could imagine. The Yankees had three batteries placed so well that they could easily rake the ridge with a deadly crossfire. "The fire of the infantry was terrible beyond description," Grady wrote. Just off to the right was a

35 Ibid., 195; Yeary, *Reminiscences*, 656; Willis Brewer, *Alabama, Her History, Resources, War Record, and Public Men: From 1540 to 1872* (Montgomery, AL: 1872), 192.

36 "Amid the Crash of Shells at Chickamauga"; Collins, *Chapters*, 158; Charles D. Spurlin, ed., *The Civil War Diary of Charles A. Leuschner* (Fort Worth, TX: 2000), 21.

knoll, "a sort of truncated cone," which hid the rest of the brigade from view; beyond it lay thick woods.[37]

This ridge, with its distinctive knoll, was east of two of Palmer's brigades, specifically those of Brig. Gens. Charles Cruft and William B. Hazen, with Russian-born Brig. Gen. John B. Turchin's brigade of Reynolds's division to the right of the concave portion of Rosecrans's left-center. "The ground was favorable for a line," Cruft reported. "It lay along a crest which fell off gradually to the front for a distance of about good musketry range, and then rose up to a corresponding ridge, lower, however, than that which we occupied." The 2nd Kentucky and 31st Indiana manned Cruft's front line, with the 90th Ohio and a four-company battalion of the 1st Kentucky in reserve behind them. Cruft positioned Battery B of the 1st Ohio Light Artillery on the right of his line. Hazen's brigade filled the line immediately south of the guns. The Ohioan commanded the 41st and 124th Ohio, 9th Indiana, 6th Kentucky, and Battery F, 1st Ohio Artillery. To the right of Hazen, Turchin arrayed the 36th and 92nd Ohio and a portion of the 11th Ohio in the front line, holding the rest of the 11th Ohio and the 18th Kentucky in reserve. The 21st Indiana Battery provided veteran artillery support.[38]

Across the shot-torn field from Palmer's division and Turchin's brigade, Capt. Henry Semple's Alabama battery had accompanied S. A. M. Wood's brigade in the initial advance. His 12-pounder Napoleons now sat idle on the eastern side of the ridge. Deshler's men and Brig. Gen. William B. Bate's Tennesseans of Stewart's division passed through the battery. "We advanced to the crest some 200 yards in front of the enemy's barricades and breastworks when he opened a destructive fire upon us," Colonel Mills reported. "We were ordered to lie down and commence firing. We now began the engagement in earnest, but at great disadvantage." The enemy had breastworks and two batteries of artillery; Deshler's men only had the ground and the thin woods for cover. Off to their right, Captain Semple maintained a "constant, although slow and deliberate" fire with his guns, along with several other batteries farther north along the Confederate line. They were of little immediate help to Deshler, however.[39]

37 Deanne Labenski, ed., "Jim Turner Co. G, 6th Texas Infantry, C. S. A. From 1861 to 1865," *Texana*, vol. 12, no. 1, Spring 1974, 164; "Amid the Crash of Shells at Chickamauga."

38 *OR* 30, pt. 1, 732; Powell, *The Maps of Chickamauga*, 162-163.

39 Heartsill, *Fourteen Hundred and 91 Days*, 153; "What Mills Saw"; *OR* 30, pt. 1, 472, 474-475, 761-763; pt. 2, 174-175, 188.

According to an unidentified Texan using the pen name "Adolphus," "We moved up in point-blank view of their lines, and were required to lay on our arms in front to prevent them from moving to the aid of their comrades who might need their presence on some other part of the field." In one of the Northerners' first volleys after Deshler halted, a minié ball struck Adolphus just as he started to kneel. He stayed on the field; it was then too dangerous to rise and head for the rear.[40]

Deshler's Texans and Arkansans had a strong motivation not to flee. "We had the defeat of Arkansas Post ringing in our ears," Sergeant Heartsill explained; "[W]e had four long months of suffering in Camp[s] Douglas and Butler fresh on our minds; while the long-cherished memory of over nine hundred of our brave comrades who sleep upon the shores of Michigan and Sangamon inspire us onward, and then the cool deliberate bravery of our commander Deshler." Private George Cagle of Mills's regiment had picked up four or five discarded muskets during the advance. As he lay prone on the ridge, he kept the weapons firing constantly. All the while, he called out imaginary commands to non-existent comrades, hoping to fool Hazen's distant Yankees. "Attention Cagle's Battery!" he shouted. "Make ready, load, take aim, fire." His efforts, though creative, fooled no one.[41]

Deshler and his men endured a trying forenoon as they lay on the military crest. Colonel Mills later stated that "[t]he enemy poured on our heads from 10:30 a.m. to 1:30 or 2 p.m. a constant and terrible fire of artillery and musketry, which we returned with our rifles with the same constancy and stubbornness." During that time, Brigadier General Polk reformed his broken regiments off to Mills's right, but left a wide gap between the brigades. S. A. M. Wood was rallying most of his men in a hollow behind the ridge to Mills's left rear. Bate's Tennessee brigade also pulled back. Two of Semple's artillery pieces fired a few last shots before withdrawing to Wood's position under canister fire. The other Confederate batteries along the hard-pressed line also retired.[42]

That left Deshler's brigade alone on the ridge facing Hazen and Turchin. The Federals concentrated their fire on his position, focusing on the truncated knoll. An artillery shell slammed into a large pine tree directly above the teenage Pvt. William J. Oliphant's company, the "Travis Rifles" of the 6th Texas. The entire top

40 "Letter from Adolphus," *Corsicana* (TX) *Daily Sun*, Sept. 29, 1911; *OR* 30, pt. 2, 194.

41 Heartsill, *Fourteen Hundred and 91 Days*, 153, 159.

42 *OR* 30, pt. 2, 175, 188.

Monument at the approximate location where Brig. Gen. James Deshler was killed. (*Scott Mingus*)

of the tree crashed down onto the Austin boys but, amazingly, did not seriously injure anyone. Oliphant's luck ran out not long afterward. "I was severely wounded at about eleven o'clock on Sunday morning September 20th," he related, "and lay on the field until sometime in the afternoon."[43]

Not everyone stayed prone throughout the long day. Colonel Mills noticed Pvt. William C. McCann standing upright, "cheerful and self-possessed in the very hell of deadly missiles." After McCann expended his allotted ammunition, he helped gather the cartridge boxes from the dead and wounded and passed out rounds to fellow soldiers. "He bore himself like a hero throughout the entire contest and fell mortally wounded by the last volleys of the enemy," Mills later stated. "I promised him during the engagement that I would mention his good conduct, he turned his boyish face upon me and, with a light and pleasant smile, reminded me of my promise."[44]

About noon, several companies of Mills's 6th-10th Texas–15th Texas Cavalry on Deshler's left began to run low on ammunition. Captain John A. Formwalt ordered Lieutenant Collins and another courier to report that fact to Mills, who then dispatched them north to General Deshler to inform him of the issue and ask where he could get more rounds. Under the galling fire, Deshler refused to ask them to deliver the reply, and he decided to check the reserve cartridge boxes personally. "I saw him coming toward my right some forty paces from me," Mills reported, "when he was struck by a shell in the chest and his heart literally torn from his bosom." The 30-year-old Deshler dropped lifeless in the center of his brigade near several fallen Arkansans.[45]

43 McCaffrey, *Only a Private*, 48-49.

44 "What Mills Saw."

45 Collins, *Chapters*, 158-159; *OR* 30, pt. 2, 188; "What Mills Saw"; "Letter from Adolphus." Collins and a soldier pen-named "Adolphus" said that Deshler was crawling on his hands and

News of the beloved general's death slowly spread among his men. "The almost-worshiped Deshler fell; torn to atoms by a shell," Sgt. William Heartsill mourned; "[I]t was over an hour before it was known down the lines that our beloved commander was slain, it sent a pang to every heart; while it nerved us on to renewed energies, and not was the duty ten times more determined felt; to hold the position to the memory of Deshler." Many soldiers later echoed Heartsill's sentiments about their general. To Mills, "He was brave, generous and kind even to a fault." According to brigade surgeon A. A. Lawrence, "This officer, after winning the love and confidence of the entire command, by his courteous bearing, his delicate consideration for the feelings of others, and his very evident military ability, fell, fighting bravely in the centre of his line of battle." Robert E. Lee later told President Jefferson Davis that "[t]here was no braver soldier in the Confederate army than Deshler."[46]

A courier from Wilkes's 17th-18th-24th-25th Texas Cavalry made his way south to Colonel Mills. He informed Mills of Deshler's death and mentioned that Colonel Wilkes was wounded and no longer with the regiment. Just after the brigade went prone, Wilkes had suffered a contusion to his right leg, and Maj. William Taylor of the 24th Texas Cavalry had assumed command. After Colonel Mills took command of the brigade, Lt. Col. T. Scott Anderson replaced him in charge of the 6th-10th Texas-15th Texas Cavalry on the left of the line. Mills later praised his three regimental leaders, Anderson, Hutchison, and Taylor, who "remained constantly in the line, handled their commands with ability, and conducted themselves gallantly through the entire action."[47]

In his first act as brigade commander, Mills ordered the soldiers to fix bayonets and gather cartridge boxes from the dead and wounded. Each man was to receive one round to load into his gun, but they were told to hold their fire until it was time to repel an assault. Lieutenant Colonel Anderson, on the left of Mills's former regiment, sent the 10th Texas's Lt. Matthew Graham to inform Mills that the four

---

knees when he was killed. Other soldiers claimed the general was walking along his lines. At least one postwar account says he was knocked from his saddle. The shell likely came from the 21st Indiana Battery to Deshler's left front.

46 Heartsill, *Fourteen Hundred and 91 Days*, 154; *OR* 30, pt. 2, 189; "Medical Records of Granbury's Brigade," *The Galveston Daily News*, July 22, 1866; Charles H. Mills, "General James Deshler," *CV*, vol. 22, no. 2, Feb. 1914, 67. Charles Mills was Colonel Mills's son.

47 *OR* 30, pt. 2, 189; Earnest Mac Seaholm, "The Angus McNeill Family, Thomas Scott Anderson," *Nesbitt* (TX) *Memorial Library Journal*, vol. 8, no. 2, May 1988, 68-69. Lieutenant Collins of the 15th Texas Cavalry also claimed to have delivered the news of Deshler's death to Colonel Mills.

left companies had not been firing and had plenty of ammunition left. They were the farthest from the enemy (Turchin's 36th Ohio) so Graham had wisely ordered them to hold their fire rather than waste it at long range. Pleased at this unexpected good news, Mills ordered those companies to move to the front of the knoll (opposite Turchin's 92nd and 11th Ohio), where the fighting was the hottest, and instructed Anderson to take charge of the companies and hold the position at every hazard until he could locate and distribute ammunition to the rest of the brigade. Graham volunteered to carry orders and messages up and down the line despite the enemy fire.[48]

Mills managed to procure enough ammunition for his men to refill their cartridge boxes. About that time, Cleburne dispatched a staff officer to Mills with orders to hold the ridge. "I was not permitted to advance," Mills later reported, "and must not retire if it were possible to hold my position." He immediately moved his command 30 yards east behind the ridge for cover and left several sharpshooters behind the trees on the crest to keep firing at the enemy. Nutt's 10th Texas company moved into the vacancy between Mills's left and Bate's Tennesseans. The firing intensified along Cleburne's and Stewart's lines. "All this time," Sgt. William Heartsill recalled, "it seemed that if ten thousand earthquakes had been turned loose in all their power, they could not have made so much racket."[49]

About 1:30 p.m., Turchin's and Hazen's fire slackened and the engagement turned into a sporadic contest between the opposing skirmishers. Half an hour later, General Palmer pulled Hazen's brigade from the line and sent it southward to reinforce Rosecrans's center. He replaced it with the remains of Col. William Grose's reserve brigade, which had been cut up earlier in the morning while fighting against Breckinridge. Palmer was pleased with the ease with which his soldiers had repulsed the Confederates. "A glance at the field along the front proved what these efforts were costing the enemy," the veteran general from Illinois reported. According to General Cruft, however, the Rebel sharpshooters "kept up a continuous and irregular fire," killing or wounding several of his

48 *OR* 30, pt. 2, 193. Graham's bravery that day attracted considerable praise. Not only did Mills praise him in his official report, but so did Lieutenant Colonel Anderson. He wrote that Graham was "active and daring to such an extent as to attract the attention of all his superior officers and companions. He deserves promotion."

49 Ibid.; Heartsill, *Fourteen Hundred and 91 Days*, 154.

officers. They also picked off a few adventurous Federals perched in trees along his line.[50]

With the lessening of the musketry, Mills finally evacuated his wounded. The 17th-18th-24th-25th Texas Cavalry had lost more than 175 men in the long fusillade, and the 6th-10th Texas-15th Texas Cavalry and the 19th-24th Arkansas also were in bad shape. In total, the brigade had lost more than 420 soldiers, including the lamented General Deshler, in a little more than three hours of one-sided fighting. The casualties amounted to almost a quarter of the men who had been in the ranks at sunrise. Two brothers in Company B of the 24th Texas, Daniel and John Chambers of Montgomery County, were killed. "Only a soldier can imagine the sight of so many dead comrades," the 10th Texas's Pvt. William O. Wynn wrote, "comrades that had fought right by my side, as bravely as I, but lost their precious lives in the great cause."[51]

The 6th Texas's Pvt. William Oliphant lay on the field until the afternoon, when litter-bearers carried him to Cleburne's divisional hospital in an old field well behind Mills's brigade. Stewards placed Oliphant on a pallet of straw near the operating tables and then washed and bandaged his wounds. The temporary field hospital consisted of "a few hastily constructed brush arbors and [a] large quantity of straw spread over the ground," he related. "Hundreds of blood-covered men were lying in the straw and the number constantly increased as the ambulances and litter-bearers arrived from the battlefield. Many of the wounded were groaning, a few were crying out in their agony, while others were quietly dying." Assistant surgeons and attendants moved rapidly among the stricken men, providing medical aid as fast as possible. "The head surgeons, with bared arms and wearing long blood stained aprons," Oliphaunt continued, "were busy with knives and saws amputating shattered limbs and coolly tossing them to a large pile of severed arms and legs which grew in size until [it] was so large that it would have more than filled the body of a large two-horse wagon."[52]

While surgeons worked to save the lives of mangled soldiers, the healthy Texans and Arkansans on the reverse side of the ridge could hear the battle

50 *OR* 30, pt. 1, 715, 732-733.

51 George W. Watson, "Our Trip to Chattanooga," *Jefferson* (TX) *Jimplecute*, June 12, 1913; "Ex-Confederate Tells of Pioneer Days," *Stamford* (TX) *American*, Feb. 7, 1930. Another of the four Chambers brothers in the Danville Mounted Riflemen had perished shortly after Arkansas Post. Wynn, the son of a Mexican War veteran, was a cowpuncher and Indian fighter before the war.

52 McCaffrey, *Only a Private*, 48-49.

escalating around them. "The cannon fire became very heavy all along the line, on both sides," Capt. Samuel Foster of the 24th Texas Cavalry stated. "The small arms then occasionally turned loose to the right and left of us. Then they really turned loose for about twenty or thirty minutes. It seemed as if the Yanks were trying to envelop us. The constant roar of the small arms mixed in with the artillery fire. Somebody is bound to be hurt where all that shooting was going on." Foster added, "We could hear a Confederate yell every now and then. We could always tell a Confederate from a Yank by the yell. When we heard a Confederate yell, we knew that a point or battery had been captured, or that a Yankee charge had been repulsed. We heard these yells all along the line, some closer than others, then to our left, then far off. Two or three of these yellings, and shootings, were often carried on at the same time."[53]

A significant breach had opened in the Union center, one that Hood's Texans, Bushrod Johnson's division, and other elements of Longstreet's left wing soon exploited.

53 Barron, "The Diary of Captain Samuel F. Foster," 50-51; Brown, *One of Cleburne's Command*, 55-56.

Chapter 9

September 20, Midday—Hood's Texans and Gregg's Brigade

Colonel Roger Q. Mills's Texans and Arkansans, in their isolated position east of Kelly Field, heard but did not understand the ongoing collapse of the Union center. General Thomas dispatched staff officers to seek reinforcements. Brigadier General John Brannan's division manned the center of the line west of Poe Field between Reynolds's and Wood's divisions. Brannan sent his reserve brigade north to help Thomas but received word at about 10:00 a.m. that Thomas desired additional aid. He realized that if he pulled the rest of his division out of line, he would expose the adjoining divisions' flanks. He consulted with Reynolds, who agreed with the proposed movement and sent word to Rosecrans. Brannan stayed put as he awaited headquarters' approval.

The messenger, however, was unaware that Brannan was waiting, and he told Rosecrans that Brannan's division had moved out of the line, exposing Reynolds's right flank. Rosecrans quickly sent word to Maj. Gen. Thomas J. Wood, commanding a division in Crittenden's XXI Corps, to "close up on Reynolds as fast as possible and support him." At the time, Wood was near the George Brotherton house in the center of the Federal line. Brannan's division, stationary between Wood's left and Reynolds's right, had to contend with A. P. Stewart's oncoming Confederates. Wood, obeying the order after corps commander General McCook sanctioned it, marched his division north behind Brannan to "close up on

Col. Van H. Manning commanded the 3rd Arkansas Infantry in Robertson's brigade of Hood's division. (*Texas Heritage Museum-Historical Research Center*)

Reynolds." That movement left a half-mile-wide gap in the Union line south of the Brotherton farm. Longstreet's left wing of the Army of Tennessee, including Hood's Texans and John Gregg's 7th Texas, would soon fill that void.[1]

It had already been a long day for these Texans. At daybreak, the survivors of Brig. Gen. Jerome Robertson's Texas Brigade still rested in a line of battle in the timber three-quarters of a mile east of the La Fayette Road, near the Alexander-Viniard Road. They lacked basic camp equipage, having left it in Virginia before boarding the southbound trains. "Nor did my men have a single wagon," Hood reported, "or even an ambulance in which to convey the wounded. They were destitute of almost everything, I might say, except pride, spirit, and forty rounds of ammunition to the man."[2]

About 7:00 that morning, Longstreet rode along his lines, receiving hearty cheers. He had positioned Hindman's division on the left with Law in the center and Bushrod Johnson to the right, near A. P. Stewart. He kept Kershaw's South Carolinians and Mississippians in reserve. Colonel Van Manning's 3rd Arkansas remained on the left of Robertson's brigade of Law's division, with the 1st, 4th, and 5th Texas successively to the right. Manning was the only remaining regimental commander of the original quartet who had taken the trains from Virginia. With Lt. Col. Philip Work fatigued and Lt. Col. John Bane wounded, Captains Richard J. Harding and Robert H. Bassett now led the 1st and 4th Texas, respectively. Major Jefferson C. Rogers of the 5th Texas had fallen; Capt. John S. Cleveland took charge of the regiment, with Capt. Tacitus T. Clay assisting him. These changes

1 "Complete, Authentic Story of the Battle of Chickamauga," *Chattanooga Daily Times*, May 29, 1913.

2 Hood, *Advance and Retreat*, 62.

trickled down through the command structure, with lieutenants or sergeants stepping up to command several companies.

Some of Hood's missing Texans had rejoined the ranks overnight, but many dead and immobile wounded men still lay in the Viniard fields. Private John C. West of the 4th Texas was "pretty sore" from his groin wound on Saturday afternoon, but he could walk. After rejoining his comrades in Company E along the battle line, his mind drifted to home: "I thought of Waco and its peaceful days and the sweet-faced, innocent children on their way to church," he wrote. This Sabbath day at Chickamauga would certainly not be peaceful or innocent.[3]

The men in the ranks knew this would be another day of bloodshed. When Braxton Bragg issued his peremptory orders to Leonidas Polk to attack in the early morning with his right wing, he also instructed Longstreet to advance after the assault stepped off to his right. Like Bragg, Longstreet fretted during the lengthy, unplanned delay. He decided to move those elements of his old corps from the Army of Northern Virginia into the front line. "Longstreet, I suppose, saw from the way the Army of Tennessee proper was fighting that nothing would be accomplished unless methods of attack were in some way changed," Cpl. Miles V. Smith opined. "So, he planned to mass Hood's division, and forming its brigades in lines of battle, the one behind the other, moved them forward and cut the Federal army in two. The Texas brigade was in the rear line."[4]

About 9:00 a.m. Longstreet moved Stewart's division north across Brotherton Road, intending to open a space for Law's division on the front line. Bushrod Johnson, however, followed Stewart rather than remain on Law's left. No one instructed him to stay put. Johnson thus inadvertently moved in front of the Texans. Hindman maneuvered through the woods off to Johnson's left, leaving no space for Law. Johnson formed his men in a double line of battle just south of the Brotherton Road, with Fulton's brigade in the center and McNair's brigade to the right. The 50th Tennessee, 1st Tennessee Battalion, and 7th Texas formed on Fulton's left. The rest of Gregg's brigade, under Col. Cyrus Sugg, constituted Johnson's second line. Johnson interspersed his three artillery batteries throughout the first line with orders to go in with the infantry.[5]

3 West, *A Texan in Search of a Fight*, 107.

4 *San Antonio Daily Express*, Dec. 5, 1909.

5 *OR* 30, pt. 2, 456; "Tennessee Confederate Regiments," *Nashville Banner*, June 27, 1914. The 50th and 1st Tennessee Battalions were consolidated under Maj. Christopher W. Robertson, who died in the attack.

Law, also arrayed in double echelon in the assault column, was forced to deploy in a second line on John Brock's farm behind Johnson. Law arranged Perry's Alabamians (formerly Sheffield's) in his first line, with Robertson's Texans and Arkansans on the left about 200 yards behind Perry. "Rock" Benning's Georgia brigade was to Robertson's right. Law's divisional line was 600 to 800 yards east of the La Fayette Road. Kershaw's two brigades (his own and Benjamin Humphreys's) formed behind Law. Longstreet placed Brig. Gen. William Preston's division of Buckner's Corps in reserve at the Park farm facing East Viniard Field. Stewart's sudden movement to the northwest tangled his right brigades with Cleburne's left (S. A. M. Wood's brigade), so a surprised Longstreet temporarily withheld the order for the planned assault. The attacking force was now five columns deep instead of the planned three. Miles Smith said the "Texas Brigade was in the rear column, and I thought the front brigades would fight until exhausted and we would go over them, but such was not the case."[6]

Captain Tacitus T. Clay of the 5th Texas recorded, "We were moved by the right flank about half a mile where we were held in line of battle until about 10 a.m. when we were ordered to lie down to allow Polk's corps to pass over us to the front, but they never appeared on that portion of the field." After Hood arranged his columns for the attack and awaited the signal to advance, Longstreet rode up and joined him. "I could see him and other officers riding up and down the line," Pvt. James M. Polk of the 4th Texas, noted, "and I knew from this that we would soon have another big killing." Longstreet asked Hood about the formation of his lines, the spirit of the troops, and the supposed impact that yesterday's assaults had made on the Yankees. Hood responded that the attitude of the officers and men had never been better. They had driven the enemy a mile on Saturday and "would rout him before sunset." Longstreet agreed that they would whip the Yankees and drive them from the field. Hood later reported, "I could but exclaim that I was rejoiced to hear him so express himself, as he was the first general I had met since my arrival who talked of victory."[7]

Robertson and Johnson Advance

In mid-morning, Longstreet and Hood finally heard Breckinridge's belated attack off to their right. The noise of battle drifted southward as Walker's and

6 National Park Service files, CCNMP; M. V. Smith, *Reminiscences*, 41.

7 *OR* 30, pt. 2, 516; Polk, *Memories of the Lost Cause*, 21; Hood, *Advance and Retreat*, 62-63.

Cleburne's divisions advanced. Longstreet was to pick up the attack as Polk drove the Union forces southward. After Polk's assault failed, however, Bragg sent orders for Longstreet to attack. Shortly after 11:00 a.m., Hood sent Bushrod Johnson's division up a low wooded rise in his front, where it pushed the aggressive 100th Illinois back to the fence-lined Brotherton farm. The Confederates surged out of the timber west across the La Fayette Road, not realizing they were heading directly at the gap in the Federal line. They captured many of the Illinoisans on the Brotherton farm, including the regiment's colonel, and routed the rest. According to Hood, "The firing on the right commenced; we immediately advanced and engaged the enemy, when followed a terrible roar of musketry from right to left."[8]

"Our lines now emerged from the forest into open ground on the border of long-open fields, over which the enemy were retreating," Johnson reported. "The resolute and impetuous charge, the rush of our heavy columns sweeping out from the shadow and gloom of the forest into the open fields flooded with sunlight, the glitter of arms, and onward dash of artillery and mounted men, the retreat of the foe, the shouts of the hosts of our army, the dust, the smoke, the noise of firearms—of whistling balls and grape-shot and of bursting shell—made up a battle scene of unsurpassed grandeur."[9]

Longstreet's desire to move his old corps in front of Bragg's men, along with Stewart's sudden movement, soon fouled the right wing's advance. As Robertson's line waited to move forward behind Johnson and Perry, officers gave last-minute instructions. Captain John Cleveland delivered "a few encouraging words" to the 5th Texas and then stood in front of the colors. Some of Hood's Texans teased one another to relieve the tension. At the command "Attention, forward, guide center, march," the 4th Texas's Pvt. Jack Massey grabbed his friend James M. Polk. "You get by the side of me," he said; "when you fall, I want that watch you have got on." Bob Crawford quickly added, "I want his boots." Robertson's line then surged through the woods.[10]

The Texas Brigade advanced in quick time across a wooded flat area east of the La Fayette Road. Behind it, one of Kershaw's South Carolinians noted, "Hood's Texans . . . gallantly moved forward, as they always did in battle, with their familiar Texas yell ringing clear above the din and roar of conflict." Distant Union artillery

8 Hood, *Advance and Retreat*, 63.

9 "Tennessee Confederate Regiments" *OR* 30, pt. 2, 457-458.

10 *OR* 30, pt. 2, 430; Polk, *Memories of the Lost Cause*, 22. Polk misspelled Massey's name as "Massie."

Sgt. John C. Cox, 5th Texas Infantry. (*Courtesy of Mickie Hill*)

began hurling shells and solid shot into the timber, but Robertson pressed onward. After crossing a small field on the Brock farm, the Texans entered another woodlot. Private Polk recalled that "when we reached the first line of breastworks, which was composed of trees and parts of houses, the Federals were on the retreat. Shot and shell were flying in every direction; minnie balls could be heard whizzing through the air, and the roar of artillery was deafening. About this time, I fell to the ground." Polk slipped into unconsciousness as the regiment swept past him. Private J. W. Pamplin of the 4th Texas dropped out of the advance when a shell fragment mangled his hand. Private John Calhoun Cox, the 5th Texas's color-bearer, was the first man in the regiment to pierce the Federal works. "Uncle John" had lost a finger at Sharpsburg and was wounded again at Gettysburg. He would fall later this day and would lie wounded under a hickory tree for a full week until two Confederate surgeons found him.[11]

Hood's Texans began encountering dead and wounded Yankees scattered in the woods. A soldier near Quartermaster Sgt. Joe Polley noticed an enemy corpse with a bulging knapsack that offered the promise of excellent plunder. "The balls were flying thick and fast and death was busy in our ranks," Polley recalled, "but the temptation was irresistible for all that. 'Here John,' said the fellow to the man at his side: 'Hold my gun, will you, until I administer on the estate of this blue-coated cuss.'" The unidentified Texan snatched up the haversack and found a roll of greenbacks in the dead Yankee's pocket.[12]

11 "Gettysburg to Chattanooga," *Yorkville* (SC) *Enquirer*, Apr. 12, 1883; Polk, *Memories of the Lost Cause*, 22; "Black Jack's Ball," *Atlanta Constitution*, Mar. 18, 1894; Simpson, *Gaines Mill to Appomattox*, 161. The physicians who found Cox were Drs. Crawford and Ware. Cox's cousin, E. C. Cox, traveled to the battlefield to take Uncle John home to recuperate. John later fashioned a cane from the hickory tree.

12 "Reminiscences of a Private."

North Dyer Field, based upon Powell, *Maps of Chickamauga,* 197, 199.

Out in front of Robertson, McNair's brigade struck the right flank of Brig. Gen. John M. Brannan's division. Suggs's 7th Texas and 1st and 10th Tennessee, along with Fulton's brigade, crossed the La Fayette Road near the Brotherton cabin. They moved north and struck Col. George P. Buell in the flank, driving his Federals back 200 yards until they formed a second line. The Texans fell flat on the ground until the men of the 13th Michigan emptied their rifle-muskets. Then, they rose with a Rebel yell and smashed through this second line, sending the Northerners scrambling for cover. "Just beyond the Brotherton House was an old orchard with a rail fence around it," the 7th Texas's Major Van Zandt reported. West of it was a narrow grove of trees. Martin's brigade (formerly Heg's) hid in this timber, although the Confederates knew they were in there. After one of Johnson's batteries shelled the woods, the 7th Texas and its supports climbed over a rail fence and pushed into the trees. They drove the 8th Kansas, 25th Illinois, and 15th Wisconsin into Dyer Field and then paused briefly to rest. About noon, General Hood rode up and instructed Johnson to "go ahead and keep ahead of everything." The 7th Texas stayed with Fulton's brigade in reserve. The Federals fled to the ridges to the northeast, so Johnson wheeled to the right to pursue them. Those

Tennessee regiments of Gregg's brigade that went with him soon seized nine Union guns.[13]

Now with a chance to reflect, the 7th Texans recounted the day's fight. "It was [a] hotly contested & bloody field much worse than any I have ever seen & such as I hope never to see again," Pvt. C. W. Trice remembered. "I had not been in the fight more than about two hours when I was struck on the cap of the knee which for three or four days struck me rather lame." Major K. M. Van Zandt now led the 7th Texas after Colonel Granbury's wounding on Saturday. "Our Regiment was in the front all the time, entirely ahead of our Brigade a portion of the time," he reported. "And when I tell you that our Brigade is acknowledged to have done the best fighting of any in the Army, you can imagine what our Regiment did. I am proud to have had command of it during most of the fight, and I am deeply thankful to Our Heavenly Father that through the whole of the engagement I was preserved unscathed, though I had several narrow escapes."[14]

North Dyer Field

Meanwhile, Colonel Perry's Alabamians had wheeled farther north and slammed into Brannan's right flank and the rear of Wood's retiring division. Yankee soldiers began breaking ranks and fleeing with howling Rebels in pursuit. The Alabama brigade attacked the left of a line of 26 Union artillery pieces hastily organized by Maj. John Mendenhall, the XXI Corps's chief of artillery. Law detached Benning's brigade and sent it off to the right toward the Larkin Poe farm to assist in Johnson's attack on Brannan and Buell. That left Jerome Robertson alone in the center with little opposition other than persistent artillery fire. "On looking to my right," the Texas brigadier reported, "I found that there was considerable space between our forces on the left and those on the right occupied by the enemy and I determined to engage them."[15]

Some 300 yards west of the first line of enemy breastworks, Robertson's four regiments crossed the La Fayette Road between the Brotherton and Poe houses

13 Goodrich, "Gregg's Brigade in the Battle of Chickamauga," 264; Sandra L. Myres, ed., *Force Without Fanfare: The Autobiography of K. M. Van Zandt* (Fort Worth: Texas Christian University Press, 1995), 101-102; Powell, *The Maps of Chickamauga*, 168-173.

14 C. W. Trice, "Seventh Texas Regiment in Gregg's Brigade," *CV*, vol. 23, no. 2, Feb. 1915, 77; K. M. Van Zandt to My Dear Wife, Sept. 28, 1863, Van Zandt Family Papers.

15 *OR* 30, pt. 2, 511.

and entered another thin strip of woods. "Thus it happened that the Texas brigade, being the rear of the division, moved fully a mile without encountering in its front a single line of Federals," Cpl. Miles V. Smith of the 4th Texas recalled, "but it was under fire all the time, and doing more or less firing itself from its flanks at enemies to its right and left. Bullets, round shot and shell came, or seemed to come, from all directions, and our comrades were falling wounded or dead."[16]

Robertson led the bulk of his brigade through the timber, across the Glenn-Kelly Road, and into an expansive sage- and stubble-filled field on Robert Dyer's 320-acre farm. "The regiment moved forward in line of battle about noon through a wood into a field," the 1st Texas's Captain Harding reported, "the enemy throwing both shells and grape upon us from a battery on an elevated position." The guns firing from a narrow, timbered ridge on the northwestern side of North Dyer Field were from Capt. Frederick Schultz's Battery M of the 1st Ohio Light Artillery of Negley's division, XIV Corps. A single gun from Church's Battery D, 1st Michigan, soon unlimbered on Schultz's right. Elements of the 17th and 31st Ohio of Connell's shattered brigade reformed near them, as did Colonel Buell and most of the 58th Indiana from his brigade. A motley assortment of small groups and individuals from other mauled regiments, including the 100th Illinois and 9th Kentucky, also arrived at the rallying point.[17]

Other Federals, including the 10th and 74th Indiana of Brig. Gen. John T. Croxton's brigade of Brannan's division, also turned their attention to the advancing Texans. Croxton had just driven off Benning's Georgians and was still in the timber east of Dyer Field. The 4th Texas's Captain Hunter reported, "On arriving at a field about 1 mile from where the advance commenced, the enemy appeared on our right flank. This made it essential that our direction should be changed. This was done on the move by making a wheel to the right." With Captain Cleveland's 5th Texas still lagging, Robertson quickly shifted his track to the north to counter this threat. "I moved my brigade by the right flank to the proper point and then changed my front forward on the first battalion," he later reported.

16 *San Antonio Daily Express*, Dec. 5, 1909.

17 *OR* 30, pt. 2, 513. Robert and Carrie Dyer lived on another of their properties in Hamblen County, Tennessee. Schultz's Knoll (known today as Harker's Knoll or South Carolina Knoll), an extension of Snodgrass Hill and Horseshoe Ridge, was between North Dyer Field and the Hiram Vittetoe cabin. Multiple spellings of the Vittetoe surname turn up in period accounts of the battle.

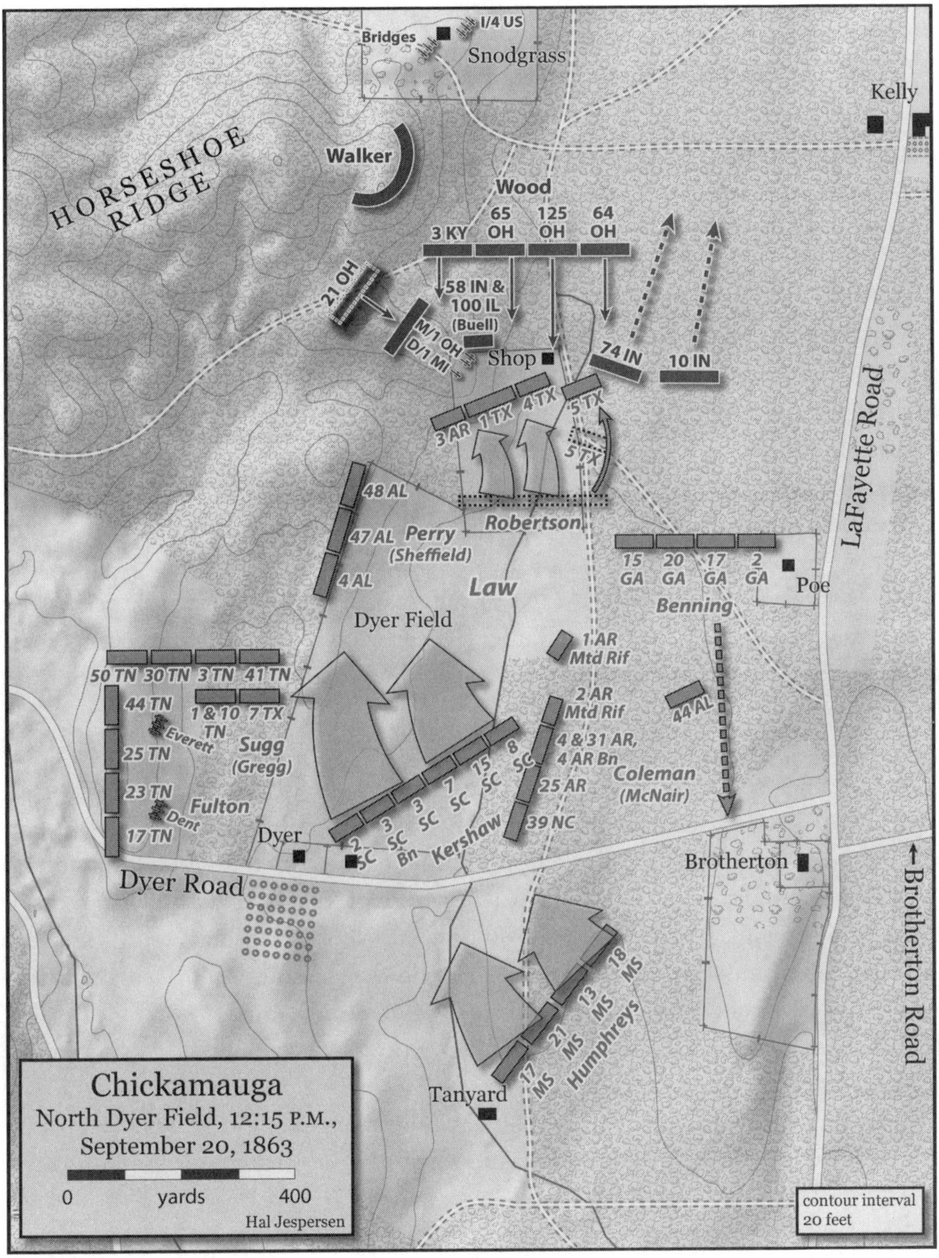

Robertson sent messengers to Johnson and Benning requesting assistance, but Benning was retreating toward the Brotherton farm.[18]

18 *OR* 30, pt. 2, 511; Powell, *The Maps of Chickamauga*, 177.

Some confusion necessarily arose as the Texas Brigade suddenly changed front. Hood, after his favorite warhorse, Jeff Davis, had been sidelined with a wound, was now riding his "valuable mare." He was on a slight ridge about 300 yards away from the Texans. He galloped up and "speedily corrected their alignment." At the same time, Kershaw's South Carolinians and Humphreys's Mississippians arrived in support and Maj. Gen. Thomas Hindman's division, on Longstreet's left, began its assault toward the Benjamin Brock and Widow Glenn farms. Seeing that Kershaw's line was at an angle to the Federals, Hood rushed back to them and "ordered a change of front forward on his right which was promptly executed under a galling fire."[19]

From the knoll, Captain Schultz's Ohio and Michigan guns on the knoll poured in canister as the Texas Brigade moved 700 yards toward them through the vortex in North Dyer Field. Private James H. Hendrick of the 1st Texas had a close call. A bullet nicked his arm, and his thick blanket roll stopped several more. Many others were not as fortunate. Union fire killed two 4th Texas soldiers from Waco, Tom Norwood and 18-year-old Charles Whitehead. Private Durham Holloway of Company E fell with a severe leg injury. The regiment's color-bearer, Sgt. Fred Makeig, received a nasty wound to his neck but carried the flag for the rest of the day.[20]

On the far right of Robertson's line, the 5th Texas entered a thicket of scrub oak and other vegetation on the Poe farm that temporarily hid the regiment from the rest of the brigade. An unnamed officer on the right sent word to Captain Cleveland for the 5th to fall back. Supposing it to be a general order and thinking that Benning must have fallen back, Cleveland obeyed. After withdrawing for 100 yards and leaving the thicket, Cleveland noticed that the brigade had not followed suit. He halted and reformed into a line of battle just as another courier arrived with Robertson's order for the regiment to press forward. By then, the 5th Texas was significantly behind the rest of the brigade, exposing the vulnerable right flank of the unsuspecting 4th Texas.[21]

During the rapid march across the field, the straggling 5th Texas began taking fire from the 10th and 74th Indiana, hidden in the woods off to the right near a

19 Hood, *Advance and Retreat*, 63-64.

20 Hugh E. Power, Jr., *Texan at War: The Letter of Private James Henry Hendrick, Army of Northern Virginia*, unpublished manuscript, THM, 32-33; Simpson, *Gaines Mill to Appomattox*, 163; West, *A Texan in Search of a Fight*, 107. Hendrick was killed in the Wilderness on May 5, 1864.

21 *OR* 30, pt. 2, 516-517; Powell, *The Maps of Chickamauga*, 179.

Kneeling Rifleman by Alfred R. Waud. (*Library of Congress*)

blacksmith shop. Captain Cleveland ordered a right half wheel and then a volley that temporarily silenced the two Hoosier regiments, which were already retreating northward. Cleveland then took the 5th Texas's color guard with a portion of the regiment and rejoined Robertson's main line. He left Captain Clay and 25 or 30 officers and men as a skirmish line to counter any further enemy appearances in the woods. Clay accomplished that task and then drove another Federal body from its breastworks, capturing several prisoners and three pieces of artillery. He would hold on to the prized guns until relieved by Kershaw's 8th South Carolina.[22]

The 4th Texas's Pvt. Jack Sutherland enjoyed a reputation as a marksman, a skill he had honed before the war as a hunter in Texas's wilds. His unerring aim and trusty rifle served him well as either a skirmisher or a scout. During the advance, he pressed far to the front "in search of the human game then being hunted." He noticed a solitary soldier, a stray from a Mississippi regiment, firing from behind a rock. Sutherland made his way to the boulder and joined in sending "some of those Yankees over yonder to kingdom come." Soon, more than a hundred of Benning's disordered Georgians joined them among the rocks and shrubs. They were busily loading and firing when Rock Benning rode up and thundered, "God d—n you, men, get from behind those trees and rocks, and give 'em hell!" Almost immediately, a Federal shell killed the general's horse. Unhurt, he sprang to his feet and shouted, "God d—n you, men, stay behind those trees and give 'em hell!"

Five minutes later, as Sutherland rose behind the sheltering rock to fire his gun, a shell fragment severed the straps of his canteen and haversack and plowed a furrow across his right shoulder. Blood spurted from the injury. Realizing he needed surgical attention, he decided to leave the rock and try to make his way to

22 "Gettysburg to Chattanooga"; *OR* 30, pt. 2, 517.

the rear. As he turned to go, his anonymous comrade from Mississippi cried, "Leave me your cartridge box, Texas, mine is empty, and I want to stay here as long as there is light enough to get a bead on a Yankee." He cut the box from Sutherland's belt and continued firing while Sutherland headed to the field hospital.[23]

While Robertson and Benning advanced, other elements of Longstreet's left wing exploited the growing void in the Union center. Tom Hindman's howling Confederates rushed across the La Fayette Road, scattering Carlin's and Martin's brigades. Wilder's 39th Indiana counterattacked and temporarily stabilized the position. Brigadier General William H. Lytle of Philip Sheridan's division of the XX Corps, a renowned poet, suffered a mortal wound while leading another counterattack east of the Dry Valley Road.[24]

Return to Dyer Woods

Robertson's brigade, meanwhile, continued to head northwest at quick time through North Dyer Field toward Colonel Buell and the motley Union line on the knoll. The Texas Brigade, still well out in front of its supports, took fire from the front and both flanks. Schultz's battery, despite the cover of strong breastworks, soon rolled away as the Texans and Arkansans ascended the long slope. The Confederates gleefully climbed over the breastworks and temporarily seized the position, giving a rousing cheer that General Hood could hear above the din.[25]

Disaster soon struck the Texas Brigade, however. According to Hood, "From a skirt of timber to our left, a body of Federals rushed down upon the immediate flank and rear of the Texas Brigade." The 500-plus men of the 21st Ohio of Col. William Sirwell's brigade, XIV Corps, poured musketry into the left of the 3rd Arkansas. "The distance and speed with which we were required to move before engaging the enemy, together with the annoyance and confusion consequent upon our moving so close in rear of other troops, threw us into battle under serious

23 Polley, *Hood's Texas Brigade*, 210-211.

24 "Complete, Authentic Story of the Battle of Chickamauga"; Powell, *The Maps of Chickamauga*, 180-189.

25 *OR* 30, pt. 2, 513, 515; Hood, *Advance and Retreat*, 64. General Negley ordered Schultz to limber up and leave. General Brannan later sent Schultz back to the knoll.

Capt. George T. Todd, 1st Texas Infantry. (*Texas Heritage Museum-Historical Research Center*)

disadvantages," Colonel Manning reported. He blamed "the fatigue of the men and the deranged condition of the line" for his predicament.[26]

Adding to the confusion was the uncertainty of who was causing the damage—friends or foes? "We received a very destructive fire from some regiment not known, but supposed to be friends, on our left and to the rear," the 1st Texas's Captain R. J. Harding reported. The new uniforms issued to the Texans back in Virginia may have played a role. According to Capt. George Todd, "Our regiment and the 4th Texas advanced so far in front of Bragg's lines that with our new uniforms, looking blue, we drew the line of fire of our own men in our rear, and caused some confusion. Here it was that I tried to get on both sides of a tree at the same time, as 'minnies' were zipping from both directions." Many Texans never forgave Bragg's soldiers for this tragic error. "Chickamauga was the most demoralizing fight of the war to me," Cpl. Miles V. Smith bemoaned. "At one time when we were fighting the enemy with all our might, we were fired into from the rear by some comrade command of the Tennessee army, and if then I had had as little reputation to sustain as the old Tennessean's cotton-tail rabbit, I would have run from the front as fast as that little animal did."[27]

General Robertson directly blamed his supports for the mistake. "After holding the hill a few moments, pouring a destructive fire into his fleeing columns in my front, a fire was opened on both my right and left flanks," he claimed. "This fire I believe came from our own men in the rear of my flanks—the same line I had asked to advance with me—but before I could stop it my line had been thrown

26 Hood, *Advance and Retreat*, 63; *OR* 30, pt. 2, 513.

27 *OR* 30, pt. 2, 514-515; Todd, *First Texas Regiment*, 18-19; *San Antonio Daily Express*, Dec. 5, 1909.

back into confusion." Having failed to obtain the cooperation of the only forces in reach, Robertson soon had a new problem.[28]

Complicating the matter was the arrival in Robertson's front of Col. Charles Harker's brigade of Wood's division. Harker's men had halted their retrograde on the Glenn-Kelly Road and were waiting for orders when they turned around and headed south to attack Robertson. General Brannan noticed Schultz's guns leaving the knoll; he rode forward and ordered them to head back to that position. Under fresh fire from multiple sides, the 3rd Arkansas and 1st Texas began withdrawing down the slope into North Dyer Field. This left the 4th Texas alone momentarily. "After holding the position a short time," Captain Hunter recalled, "the line on our left gave way, crying out they were flanked." About this time, Captain Cleveland and his flag-bearing, tardy battalion of the 5th Texas approached the knoll, but they also had to withdraw.[29]

Soon, all of Robertson's Texans were retreating east across the field toward the inviting tree line. "Our brigade retired, rather unexpectedly to me, from a warm spot in an open field which we had just entered," the 4th Texas's Pvt. John C. West recalled. "I had no notice of the reverse movement except that I heard two or three voices near me say: 'We will have to get out of here!' and by the time I could turn to look back, I saw the whole line in reverse order, making quick time towards the timber from which we had just emerged." West, already tired from the sleepless night and at least 50 steps behind the retreating line, ran as fast as he could. He had not gone more than 100 yards before he saw a Federal soldier lying in high weeds near a fence. West ran over to him and ordered the man to get up and go ahead of him. The Yankee complied and took off running.[30]

Harker's Northerners vigorously pursued Robertson's retreating Confederates. They fired a volley and then advanced for 15 to 20 seconds before firing again. This "Advance, Firing" technique yielded a wall of flame that accelerated the Texans' and Arkansans' retrograde movement. Robertson's four regiments disintegrated as many soldiers broke ranks and raced for the timber. Harker's 64th and 125th Ohio reached a fence bordering the southern edge of a thin copse of trees that projected into the stubble field. This position was about

28 *OR* 30, pt. 2, 512. Robertson claimed to have crested the hill. If so, it was not for long, as the 21st Ohio and Harker's brigade soon ejected them.

29 Ural, *Hood's Texas Brigade*, 190; *OR* 30, pt. 2, 514-515, 517; Powell, *The Maps of Chickamauga*, 198-199.

30 *Waco* (TX) *News-Tribune*, May 16, 1923.

halfway between the knoll and the south edge of North Dyer Field. Their fire added to the Confederates' confusion.[31]

George Branard, the 1st Texas's color sergeant, had predicted the previous evening that an enemy bullet would strike his elbow today. So far, he had escaped unharmed, and some of his companions called him a "false prophet." Branard typically kept his left arm behind him and held the flagpole with his right until fatigue forced him to lend his left to the effort. Halfway down the hill, a Union regiment rose from the bushes on an adjoining rise and fired a volley. Branard, true to his premonition, lost the use of his left arm when two minié balls slammed into it. One of them hit just above the elbow; the other broke the bone near his shoulder. "I was shot by a sharpshooter from behind a big pine stump," he complained; "if he had come out in the open my color guard would have had a chance to protect me." Nearby soldiers, including members of the color guard, hauled him to the rear.[32]

"In recrossing this field," Captain Hunter recorded, "the gallant and highly esteemed Capt. Joseph C. Billingsley fell. Several other gallant men fell in this fight, and a number of men and officers were wounded." Billingsley, a former deputy U.S. marshal, took a bullet to the head while trying to rally Company E, the "Lone Star Guards." Captain Cleveland of the 5th Texas received a severe wound in the fleshy part of his thigh. Corporal George Lock of the 1st Texas fell near the edge of Dyer's woods. By the time Sgt. D. H. Hamilton made it to his side, Lock was unconscious. "I poured all the water I had in my canteen on his face to revive him," Hamilton recalled, "and picked him up and carried him out." One of Manning's men remembered, "It was simply fearful, and amid all of this carnage and death there was J. H. Alexander, a member of my company, wearing a silk plug hat that he lifted from someone's head as we passed through Ringgold coming into the field of battle. It was real comical and looked so out of place amid all of this fighting. Looking down the line during the fighting, the first thing we saw was Joe's hat."[33]

31 Powell, *The Maps of Chickamauga*, 200-201. For an excellent discussion of the Union movements around North Dyer Field throughout the day, see Powell, *Glory or the Grave*, 354-381.

32 "George Branard as a Prophet," *San Antonio Daily Express*, Apr. 4, 1909; "How a Presentiment Came True."

33 *OR* 30, pt. 2, 514; Hamilton, *History of Company M*, 35; CSR of J. C. Billingsley, 4th Texas, NARA RG109, M323, Texas, roll 0283; Samuel Henry Emerson, *History of the War of the Confederacy* (Malvern, AR: 1918), 49.

Jerome Robertson inspired his men as he directed the retreat and tried to maintain order amid Harker's ongoing musketry. "Gen'l Robertson was to be seen on all occasions in front of his Brigade leading them on and exposing himself to every danger," Lt. Benjamin I. Franklin later informed his wife. "Man never acted more gallantly. He had two horses shot under him but escaped unhurt himself. [Captain] Clay & myself went through the fight without a scratch. Clay got a bullet through his coat sleeve my clothes were not even touched but we lost some of our bravest and best men."[34]

As Robertson approached the timber about 2:00 p.m., he spotted General Hood calmly riding along the edge of the tree line carrying the battle flag of his former regiment, the 4th Texas. He rode over to the acting corps commander to get orders. Just as he started to speak, Hood slumped in his saddle. A minié ball had pierced his right thigh, creating a five-inch fracture in the femur. Hood fell into the arms of some of his men, including his courier, Pvt. Albert S. Roberts of the 4th Texas. Roberts helped Hood down from his mare and then gathered a party to carry the stricken major general some 300 yards east, where hospital stewards took Hood to the rear for surgery.[35]

Dr. Tobias G. Richardson, medical inspector for the Army of Tennessee, and two other surgeons carefully examined the wound. He believed that Hood, already in a weakened condition due to his Gettysburg injury, likely would not live through an amputation. According to Richardson, Hood asked whether he had a chance, even one in a thousand, to survive the operation. If so, "then cut it off," he ordered; "I'll take that chance—I must fight this war through." Should he die, Hood said, he wanted his remains buried "in the soil of Texas, where my strongest affections and most glorious associations are centered." About 4:00 that afternoon, Dr. Richardson administered chloroform to the stricken general. He and his assistants then amputated Hood's right leg about four inches from the hip.[36]

By then, the Texans and Arkansans were already casting blame for Hood's wounding. "This scribe saw this and believes a bullet from our own men struck

34 B. I. Franklin to Mary Franklin, October 2, 1863, CCNMP.

35 *OR* 30, pt. 2, 512; Todd, *First Texas Regiment*, 19; Hood, *Advance and Retreat*, 64; "A Texan on Chickamauga Field," *Houston Post*, Feb. 22, 1909; "Texas History," *Bonham* (TX) *News*, Jan. 3, 1902.

36 "The Death of a Hero," *Savannah* (GA) *Morning News*, Sept. 3, 1879; Stephen M. Hood, ed., *The Lost Papers of Confederate General John Bell Hood* (El Dorado Hills, CA: 2013), 27-28. Acting Chief Surgeon William O. Hudson of Hood's division and acting Brigade Surgeon David C. Jones of Robertson's brigade assisted Richardson.

Hood Wounded at Chickamauga. (*Illustrated London Times, December 26, 1863*)

him," the 1st Texas's Captain Todd opined. "As it appeared that no other officer of the 1st was near, I took command for a while." Private Lawrence Daffan of the 4th Texas added, "It was believed by many Confederate soldiers that General Hood was accidentally shot by a Confederate soldier, probably of the Florida troops. The troops thought the brigade were federal soldiers, as Bragg's army had never seen a well-uniformed Confederate regiment. Couriers were hurried to tell the troops to stop firing and to explain the situation."[37]

Robertson's remaining men huddled in Robert Dyer's woods. "We were here exposed to a heavy fire from the enemy's artillery," Capt. J. T. Hunter wrote, "and here it was that Captain Bassett, who had ably and gallantly commanded the regiment since the wounding of Colonel Bane, received a severe wound by a fragment of shell, which deprived us of his services." An enemy shell struck the fork of a large red oak about 20 feet above the ground, splitting the tree in two. Half of it crashed down into several Texans sheltered under it. A massive limb mangled

37 Todd, *First Texas Regiment*, 19; *Waxahachie* (TX) *Daily Light*, Feb. 16, 1907.

Approximate location of where General Hood was wounded. (*Scott Mingus*)

Bassett's shoulder. Hunter, as the senior-most officer, assumed command of the 4th Texas; he was the regiment's third leader in less than 24 hours.[38]

Several soldiers realized just how close they had come to sharing a similar fate. Earlier in the war, Pvt. Jim Dickie of the 5th Texas appropriated a watch, overcoat,

38 *OR* 30, pt. 2, 514; "In Storm of Battle"; Laswell, *Rags and Hope*, 203-204; CSR of R. H. Bassett, 4th Texas, NARA RG109, M323, Texas, roll 0283.

and silver half-dollar from a dead Union major. He fashioned the coin into a star-shaped hat badge inscribed with the legend "5—J. A. Dickie—Hood's Texas Scouts." Now, when he took off his hat, he noticed that a bullet had clipped off the upper point of the star. Dickie had missed having his life snuffed out at Chickamauga by a fraction of an inch.[39]

While in the woods, the 4th Texas's Pvt. John C. West located his German-immigrant prisoner among his company. "I swapped canteens with him," West remembered; "his was new and in perfect condition, and mine was old and battered." He examined the captive's knapsack and found a Webster's blue-book spelling manual. The Yankee could not speak English, but he indicated that the Federals had three or four German regiments. West turned the Teuton over to the provost guards and never saw him again. He tucked the Webster's speller into his knapsack and kept it the rest of the war. Reflecting on Hood's injury, West noted, "As we were going into the fight General Hood rode down the line in our rear towards our right. He said: 'Move up men; those fellows are shooting in the tops of trees.' We thought then that he was a little too close in."[40]

Later, as West headed to the rear to have his injured wrist treated, he encountered General Benning, bareheaded and riding a horse, harness still attached, that he had cut from an artillery wagon. Munching on a biscuit, he demanded, "Where are you going?" When West showed the general his wound, Benning exclaimed, "Great God! Is everybody killed? I have lost my brigade." In some places, it looked as if the dead outnumbered the living. Benning soon passed by Pvt. Tom S. Haynie and several men of the 5th Texas. When one of the boys informed the general that his horse had been shot, Benning answered, "Yes, and I am shot up a little too, but fight on boys, and let us whip this fight. And that is what your old comrade says to you. Fight on boys and we are sure to win." The injured battery horse was Benning's third mount of the battle. Benning and Robertson soon reported to General Law, who had arrived on the scene after Hood's wounding. Kershaw's two unbloodied brigades pushed ahead and soon drove off Harker's Federals. Law ordered Robertson to reform on the left of the division and

39 "Jim Dickie," *Temple* (TX) *Daily Telegram*, June 28, 1913.

40 *Waco* (TX) *News-Tribune*, May 16, 1923; West, A Texan in Search of a Fight, 109. According to West, the Texans captured many of these spelling books after the battle.

throw up temporary works in his front. The fighting, at least for now, was over for Hood's Texas Brigade.[41]

Cavalry Actions at Glass's Mill and Lee and Gordon's Mills

Well to the south, Robertson's fellow Texans in the 8th and 11th Cavalry Regiments were recovering from a fight earlier in the day. Union troopers had arrived at the West Chickamauga Creek fords near Glass's Mill in midmorning with orders to hold that point at all hazards. Brigadier General George Crook's brigade occupied some rocky woods just west of the creek. About 11:00 a.m., most of Joe Wheeler's cavalry dismounted and attacked. Terry's Texas Rangers remained mounted on the left of the Confederate line. Wheeler drove the Federals back 200 yards before Crook received orders to withdraw, having lost more than 120 men. The Rangers spotted Lt. Col. Valentine Cupp of the 1st Ohio Cavalry lying wounded. "We passed back over the field, and saw the colonel still living and gasping for breath was sitting with his back against a tree," Pvt. J. K. P. Blackburn remembered. "Some of our boys approached him and said to him, 'Well, colonel, as you will not need your hat or boots any longer, we beg the privilege of exchanging with you,' and as the colonel could not reply, the boys concluded that silence gives consent, and proceeded to make the exchange." Cupp's injuries proved mortal. Around 3:00 that afternoon, Wheeler again attacked, this time closer to Lee and Gordon's Mills. After a brief engagement, the Rebel troopers drove off the Federals and seized hundreds of prisoners, 20 wagons, arms, and supplies. A few wounded Rangers and those of the 11th Texas made their way back to medical stations for treatment.[42]

In the respective field hospitals that dotted the rear behind the opposing armies, many wounded men, cut off from direct knowledge, tried to guess the status of the ongoing battle from the ebb and flow of the musketry and cannonade. Sergeant Bill Fletcher of the 5th Texas was still hobbling on one foot from his gunshot wound the previous day. At one point, he believed the left-center of the Confederate line must be breaking. If it did, he was going to start for Catoosa

41 West, *A Texan in Search of a Fight*, 109; *Mississippi Union Advocate and Farm and Home* (Jackson, MS), June 4, 1908; "Incidents of Chickamauga," *Richmond Daily Dispatch*, Oct. 1, 1863; Powell, *The Maps of Chickamauga*, 204-207.

42 Dennis W. Belcher, *The Cavalry of the Army of the Cumberland* (Jefferson, NC: 2016), 211-212; Blackburn, "Reminiscences of the Terry Rangers," 144; Graham Landrum, *An Illustrated History of Grayson County, Texas* (Sherman, TX: 1960), 55.

Pvt. J. K. P. Blackburn, 8th Texas Cavalry (Terry's Texas Rangers). (*Texas State Library and Archives Commission*)

Platform despite it being several miles away. A comrade from Company F said it was a foolish idea; Bill would drop by the wayside long before reaching the depot. Fletcher responded, "I can hop as fast as I can walk, and it does not tire me much more than walking." Finally, a perceptible decrease in the volume of the fighting gave him relief from his concern. He teased another company mate about his wounded nose that the man would have better luck courting the girls back home if he kept his back to them. His friend retorted that his injury was better because Fletcher "can't run away to hide your wooden leg." Watching a nearby amputation, Fletcher decided a wooden leg was not in his future. He refused to allow doctors to cut off his foot.[43]

Fletcher was listening to the shifting fortunes of the Army of Tennessee. Bushrod Johnson's division was struggling in South Dyer Field. Evander McNair's brigade fell back after unsuccessfully attacking the nine guns that Gregg's brigade later took. A shell fragment took General McNair out of action; Col. David Coleman of the 39th North Carolina assumed command. Most of Hindman's division to Johnson's left withdrew after several spirited Union counterattacks. Fulton's and Gregg's brigades fought from 2until 4 p.m. against Whitaker's and Mitchell's brigades of Granger's Reserve Corps and other Federals. Major Christopher W. Robertson, the new commander of the 50th Tennessee, suffered a mortal wound. Johnson frequently sent staff officers scurrying to the rear to plead for reinforcements but none came. During brief lulls, Johnson's men scrounged among the dead and wounded to replenish their cartridge boxes.[44]

Meanwhile, Col. Roger Q. Mills's Arkansans and Texans were still engaged against the stubborn Union line holding out in the now-isolated salient in Kelly

43 Fletcher, *Rebel Private*, 101-103.

44 Goodrich, "Gregg's Brigade at the Battle of Chickamauga," 265.

The George Brotherton house was located along the La Fayette Road in the center of the Union line. (*Library of Congress*)

Field. Their beloved General Deshler likely would have been pleased had he lived to see them in action on Sunday.[45]

45 *OR* 30, pt. 2, 512.

Chapter 10

September 20, Late Afternoon and Evening

Mills's Brigade

While Jerome Robertson's Texas Brigade reformed in the woods bordering North Dyer Field, and Bushrod Johnson's division battled it out with Federals lining South Dyer Field, Col. Roger Q. Mills's brigade was still on the reverse side of the unnamed ridge southeast of the Federal salient in Kelly Field. The men listened with keen interest as Longstreet's attack progressed.

"About 3 o'clock, we heard cheering on our right, a half mile distant, and soon learned Crittenden's right had given way," Sergeant Grady of the 25th Texas Cavalry remembered. "The firing then abated a half hour after our right [Polk's brigade] fell back, their ammunition being exhausted. Our brigade then expected to be flanked, and one company was thrown out on the exposed flank to watch the enemy." Company K manned Mills's line on the extreme right. In an isolated position on the north side of the ridge, Grady and his companions could not see the rest of the brigade because of the intervening knoll. Fearing that Federals could pour through the gap, Grady suggested to Lt. F. M. Bell that he deploy the company as a skirmish line in the woods in front of the opening. When Bell refused, Grady insisted that they send to General Deshler for permission. Bell sent a courier, who soon returned with word that Deshler was dead. By then, the entire

Iron marker commemorating the position of Deshler's brigade on September 20. (*Scott Mingus*)

company had joined Grady in demanding that Bell take responsibility. Under pressure, the lieutenant yielded. As Company K filed into position, the oncoming Federals spotted them and halted behind their skirmish line.[1]

Colonel Mills had received word that a line of enemy skirmishers was moving toward the vulnerable gap between his brigade and Polk's, and he sent orders for Major Taylor to send out a company of flankers to engage them. In less than 20 minutes, Mills learned they were retiring before the enemy. He immediately ordered Lieutenant Colonel Hutchison to reinforce them with one company from his 19th-24th Arkansas, which Hutchison promptly did. Reports kept coming in that the Union flanking movement was continuing, however. Mills ordered Capt. John R. Kennard to take Company A out to reinforce the two recently dispatched companies on the skirmish line. Kennard was to take personal command of all three companies, put the men under good cover, and hold the enemy in check at all hazards. He promptly took charge of the situation and repulsed the Yankees, holding his position without a significant struggle. For the next half hour, the opposing sides kept up a desultory fire, and sharpshooters plied their deadly trade. Colonel Edward A. King, commanding Reynolds's 2nd Brigade, was dismounting when a bullet struck him just above the right eye, killing him.[2]

About 4:00 p.m., "before you could say 'Jack Robinson' the ball opened again hot and heavy on our right," the 25th Texas's Sergeant Grady wrote. Sergeant Heartsill believed the firing "seemed to break out, if possible, with tenfold more fierceness than ever. On our right the very heavens and earth seemed to vibrate and quake, never was there louder or more prolonged volleys of musketry." At the same time, the Union line off to the south began to give way.[3]

The Final Attack on the Kelly Field Line

With the Federal line collapsed on the center and right, Lt. Gen. Leonidas Polk ordered his wing to resume the offensive. About 4:30 p.m., Breckinridge's and Cleburne's long line of infantry stepped off. Spearheading the attack on the salient, Brig. Gen. Lucius Polk's brigade aimed for the northwestern angle in the enemy breastworks. Colonel Mills's soldiers gave the Texas yell and surged forward.

1 "Amid the Crash of Shells at Chickamauga"; *Wilmington Daily Journal*, Oct. 25, 1863.

2 *OR* 30, pt. 2, 189-190, 193.

3 *Wilmington Daily Journal*, Oct. 25, 1863; Heartsill, *Fourteen Hundred and 91 Days*, 154.

Company K of the 17th-18th-24th-25th Texas Cavalry was still on the skirmish line off to the brigade's right. A sudden noise to the right rear brought the cheering news that Pat Cleburne was leading fresh troops forward to plug the gap. Grady and his companions hustled to take their place in Mills's advancing line. Cleburne, spotting Mills's advance, reportedly shouted, "By God, just look at that Texas colonel. He is rolling over them like the waves of the sea."[4]

Mills halted his brigade some 300 yards east of the Federal line in a small ravine that offered adequate protection. The three badly mauled regiments remained there until dusk. "The firing did not cease with the darkness," the 24th Texas Cavalry's Capt. Sam Foster explained. "Instead, the Yanks appear to be charging at our guards." Mills ordered a charge when the rest of Cleburne's line again advanced. "The entire line got up," Foster continued. "Contrary to anything that might be said, we yelled first. And such yells! I cannot blame the Yanks for running. They had every reason to believe that we had at least a million men just to the front of their works and charging at them. Not one of us held back. It seemed as if the entire army was ordered forward at the same time. There was such a noise and yelling that it made Arkansas Post seem but child's play. At best, fighting has been a terrible business. But when it comes to fighting at night, and so black that you cannot see anything, then it is awful. It is sublime."[5]

Cleburne ordered Capt. Henry Semple's Alabama battery and Key's Arkansans to support Jackson's attack, following Jackson's brigade, with Douglas's Texas battery posted on the division's far right. Semple was acting as Cleburne's chief of artillery since Maj. T. R. Hotchkiss's injury the previous night. He deployed his Alabamans, temporarily under the command of Lt. Richard W. Goldthwaite, and Key's guns on top of the ridge 200 yards from the Union line on the Kelly farm. Their fire was effective and on target, "and the artillerymen went wild," in Grady's words. According to Sergeant Heartsill, "Such deafening peals of thunder as those Napoleon guns are now sending forth, scattering death and destruction into the ranks of the Federals."[6]

Well to the left of Goldthwaite and Key, Capt. James Douglas and his artillerymen had hand-pulled the four guns of the Texas battery to a position 300

4 "Amid the Crash of Shells at Chickamauga"; "Soldiers of the Senate," *Savannah Morning News*, Feb. 4, 1894.

5 Barron, "The Diary of Captain Samuel F. Foster," 51; Brown, *One of Cleburne's Command*, 55-56.

6 Ibid.; Heartsill, *Fourteen Hundred and 91 Days*, 154.

yards from the Union breastworks. Douglas opened fire with shell to enfilade the 4th Indiana Battery, which had been instrumental in holding the Kelly Field line for much of the day. After Douglas fired for 15 or 20 minutes, the Federals began to yield. General Cleburne ordered him to cease firing and moved the battery to the right and front, where Polk's brigade was about to gain the works. At Polk's direction, Douglas unlimbered a two-gun section within 80 yards of the breastworks and fired a few rounds. They were in the general vicinity of where General Helm had been mortally wounded the previous day.[7]

After Semple's battalion fired several shots of double canister, the Federal guns finally stopped replying. Lieutenant Richard W. Goldthwaite realized he could now enfilade part of the enemy's infantry and began raking the Yankees from right to left with canister. Captain Semple then shifted the fire of Goldthwaite's and Key's batteries to the Union lines farther to the south. Together with Douglas, they pummeled the ground over which the Federals might send reinforcements to discourage that action. Under the intense bombardment, small groups of frightened Federals began to break and scatter.[8]

Seeing this, the eager Texans and Arkansans gave out the Rebel yell. Immediately to their front was a strongly fortified and well-supported redoubt. When they got to within 30 or 40 yards of it, the Union artillery fire became so heavy that the 17th-18th-24th-25th Texas Cavalry wavered for a moment and then halted. One of the last casualties in Deshler's/Mills's brigade was Lt. Samuel A. Cooke of the 17th Texas Cavalry. Late on Sunday afternoon, a shrapnel shot passed almost entirely through his right forearm. It sheared off parts of both bones and partially emerged out the backside. Cooke put his left thumb on the ball and pushed it back through the hole. He left the field and had his arm dressed at a field hospital.[9]

Captain Douglas lugged "Sallie," the Napoleon named for his sweetheart back in Texas, through an opening in the breastworks. By brute strength, he managed to get the cannon into the redoubt and aim it at the fleeing Yankees. "I fired the last

7 *OR* 30, pt. 2, 187, 196.

8 Ibid., 156, 175.

9 Charles Alonza Cooke, "The Civil War Memories of Samuel Alonza Cooke," *SHQ*, vol. 74, Jul. 1970–Apr. 1971, 540-541.

gun," Douglas later claimed. "'Sallie's' voice spoke out in tones of gladness amidst the deafening cheers of 60 thousand and the day, the glorious day, was ours."[10]

At 5:00 p.m., General Thomas, then forming a last-ditch defensive line on a prominent hill on the George W. Snodgrass farm, ordered General Palmer to retire with his division. Palmer had the impression that he was to reform in order to resist the attacks that then threatened both flanks. He sent orders to his brigade commanders (Cruft, Hazen, and Grose) and then rode off with his staff to the La Fayette Road to await the head of his retreating column. Looking back some 400 yards, he discovered that his men were halfway across but were taking tremendous fire from Confederate artillery and infantry. Rebel guns, including Henry Semple's three batteries, continued to sweep the road and Kelly Field from opposite directions. "It seemed impossible to bring men across the field in anything like good order," Palmer later reported. Grose's brigade was disorganized, but Cruft's men stayed in reasonably good order, serving as a nucleus around which to rally and reform the masses of stragglers that were pulling back from the breastworks.[11]

"In 10 minutes, a shout—a perfect tiger—was raised on the right and soon extended all along our lines. Those old woods joined us in exaltation," the 25th Texas Cavalry's Sergeant Grady penned. "The Yankees were running like frightened wolves." Captain Semple kept banging away with his field pieces, adding to the growing confusion among the enemy. Grady added, "The joy and their manifestations of it on the part of our artillerymen, at every fire, amused me very much. One little fellow went into ecstasies, jerked off his hat, threw it on the ground, jumped and shouted. You would have thought him crazy."[12]

Sensing victory, the Confederates pushed across Kelly Field toward the La Fayette Road. Off to Mills's right, Ector's and Wilson's brigades advanced through the timber northeast of the field with little to no opposition. General Dodge had withdrawn his brigade to the north when the Union line along the road began to collapse. As Matt Ector's Texans tramped through the same timber that they had earlier traversed, they noticed that fire had swept through the area, charring the trees and consuming some of the underbrush and vines. The "little hut" they had passed in the morning, which had contained at least 50 wounded men, had burned down. No one knew how many had perished, but the advancing Confederates

10 Douglas, *Douglas's Texas Battery*, 75.

11 *OR* 30, pt. 1, 715.

12 *Wilmington Daily Journal*, Oct. 25, 1863.

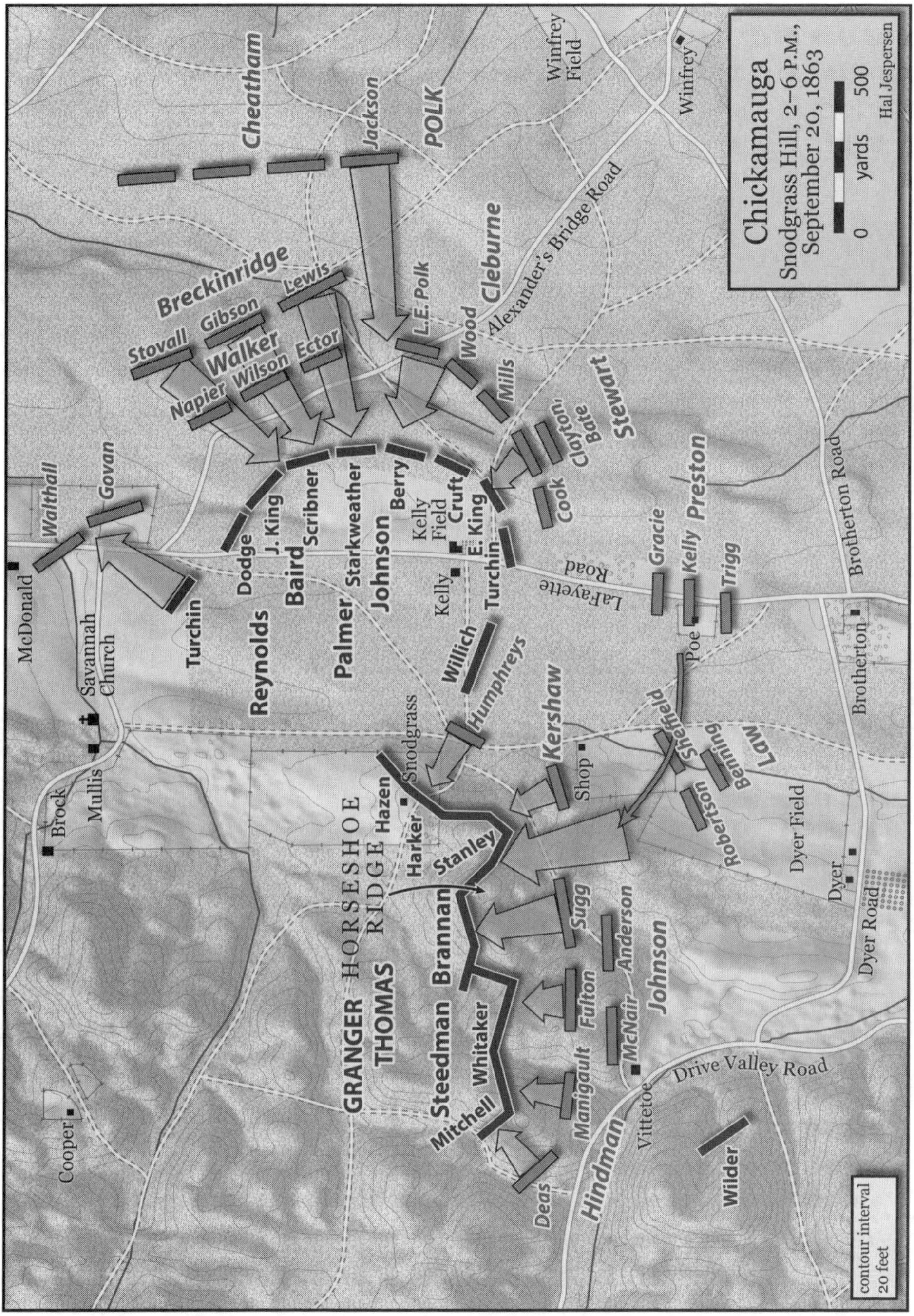

Chickamauga
Snodgrass Hill, 2–6 P.M., September 20, 1863
0 yards 500
Hal Jespersen
contour interval 20 feet
Cheatham
Jackson
POLK
Breckinridge
Lewis
Gibson
Stovall
Walker
Wilson
Ector
Napier
L.E. Polk
Wood
Cleburne
Mills
Alexander's Bridge Road
Winfrey Field
Winfrey
Clayton
Bate
Stewart
Cook
Preston
Gracie
Kelly
Trigg
Brotherton Road
Brotherton
Poe
LaFayette Road
Walthall
Govan
McDonald
Savannah Church
Turchin
Reynolds
Dodge
J. King
Baird
Scribner
Palmer
Starkweather
Johnson
Berry
Kelly Field
Cruft
E. King
Kelly
Willich
Humphreys
Snodgrass
Kershaw
Shop
Sheffield
Benning
Law
Robertson
Dyer Field
Dyer
Dyer Road
Brock
Mullis
HORSESHOE RIDGE
GRANGER
THOMAS
Hazen
Harker
Stanley
Brannan
Steedman
Whitaker
Mitchell
Sugg
Anderson
Johnson
Fulton
McNair
Manigault
Deas
Hindman
Vittetoe
Drive Valley Road
Wilder
Cooper

could see charred bodies and bones in the ashes. Putting the gruesome sight and concerns over missing comrades out of their minds, they pressed onward.[13]

Johnson and Baird finally withdrew from the Kelly Field line. Some Southerners claimed the Federals took to their heels. "They run to the four winds of the earth," Pvt. Ben Seaton noted in his diary, "and we captered [sic] a large number of them." Mills's Texans and Arkansans soon passed through the abandoned Federal camp. "The dead, wounded and dying were thick there," Foster wrote. "Still, we went. We passed artillery wagons, their baggage wagons and kept on going." Intermixed with the howling dismounted cavalrymen and infantrymen, Captain Douglas took one of his pieces as far as the La Fayette Road, where he received orders from Captain Semple to halt. He brought up his other three guns and went into bivouac.[14]

Snodgrass Hill

Union resistance on the southern end of the battlefield had evaporated. Many of the survivors of Sheridan's, Davis's, Van Cleve's, and Negley's divisions escaped to Missionary Ridge or McFarland's Gap and headed for Rossville. General Rosecrans, along with James Garfield and his other staff officers, joined Generals McCook and Crittenden in trying to rally the retiring men before leaving the field. Rosecrans dispatched Garfield to tell Pap Thomas to take command of all the forces remaining at Chickamauga and then retire north to Rossville. Groups of soldiers began gathering on the oak-timbered Horseshoe Ridge and an adjoining broad, cultivated eminence on the George W. Snodgrass farm, as well as on nearby ridges and hills. Thomas's men quickly felled trees and constructed breastworks. Artillery dotted the line. As more and more soldiers arrived, Thomas decided to fight it out so that the rest of the Army of the Cumberland could escape to Chattanooga.[15]

Meanwhile, Bushrod Johnson's division pushed onto the Vittetoe property along the Dry Valley Road, which was choked by retreating Union wagons, limbers, guns, and troops. As the 7th Texas passed a small windowless house in the center

13 *OR* 30, pt. 2, 249; "Horrible War Memories."

14 Barron, "The Diary of Captain Samuel F. Foster," 51-52; Brown, *One of Cleburne's Command*, 56; *OR* 30, pt. 2, 196; Simpson, *The Bugle Softly Blows*, 40-41.

15 For a comprehensive account of the Union actions in this sector, see Powell, *Glory or the Grave*, 382-474.

of the field, Elizabeth Vittetoe ran out of it shouting and clapping her hands for joy. Elizabeth and her three young daughters (Samantha, Laura, and Evada) had hidden in the potato cellar for three days without food while the Yankees occupied the farm. They had only one jug of water to share, while Hiram Vittetoe and their young son stayed upstairs and peered through chinks in the walls of the log cabin. According to Maj. K. M. Van Zandt, "The enemy had been all over the house—indeed, they had even placed a number of wounded there—but they had never discovered the occupants of the cellar." Johnson's men soon ascended a steep-sloped, elongated hill parallel to the Federal position on Horseshoe Ridge.[16]

Deas's and Manigault's brigades of Maj. Gen. Thomas Hindman's division formed to the left of Johnson, with Brig. Gen. Patton Anderson's brigade to the right. Kershaw's South Carolinians and Humphreys' Mississippians from the Army of Northern Virginia deployed to Anderson's right. Major Felix Robertson, Jerome's son, arrived with the reserve artillery and began firing at the distant Yankees. About 4:30 p.m., General Longstreet sent Brig. Gen. William Preston's division toward the Union position, starting a prolonged series of Confederate attempts to drive off Thomas and seize the various heights. The troops assisting Thomas included Brig. Gen. James Steedman's division of Granger's Reserve Corps. At one point, Sgt. Frank W. Gates and another man of the 115th Illinois decided to recover a wounded lieutenant who had fallen soon after their arrival. They could not locate the officer but instead captured "two of the enemy who were secreted where a large tree had been upturned, forming a hole in the ground. One of them belonged to a Mississippi and the other to a Texas regiment." [17]

About 8:00 p.m., Preston's men surrounded the ammunition-depleted 22nd Michigan, 21st Ohio, and 89th Ohio on what was later dubbed "Hill Three" and forced them to surrender. Many of Jerome Robertson's Texans on the edge of the thin timber on the Dyer farm heard the final Confederate assaults that cleared the

16 "Van Zandt Tells the Story," *Marshall* (TX) *News Messenger*, Oct. 29, 1921; Myres, *Force Without Fanfare*, 103-104; Sartain, *History of Walker County*, 108; Powell, *The Maps of Chickamauga*, 210-211. Van Zandt attended a Confederate reunion in Chattanooga in 1913. As he left the convention hall and walked into the lobby of the Hotel Patten, a woman asked him where she might find Major Van Zandt. "You are shaking hands with him," he replied. She then told him, "I am Mrs. Vittetoe's daughter. Mother has been dead three years, but she told me if I ever see you to thank you for driving the Yankees away."

17 Powell, *Glory or the Grave*, 475-650; Powell, *The Maps of Chickamauga*, 216-217. Rice was the editor of the *Chattanooga News*; F. W. Gates, "Chickamauga: The Important Service of the Reserve Corps on the Second Day," *National Tribune*, Apr. 14, 1887. The prisoners were likely from the 7th Texas and Humphreys's nearby Mississippi brigade.

remaining Yankees from Snodgrass Hill and Horseshoe Ridge. "Upon a general charge of the line," the 1st Texas's Sgt. D. H. Hamilton noted, "the enemy was driven back about a mile. It was in fact a regular stampede. By this time, it was nearly night."[18]

There was breathless anticipation among the Confederates all along Braxton Bragg's line that the long-contested field really was won. "There was a lull, as if both armies were tired of that terrible strife and carnage," a young Confederate officer on Longstreet's left recalled. "Suddenly, miles away from our extreme right, Hood's boys sent a shout—a shout of triumph, solid, invigorating, unmistakable. 'Twas peculiar to Southern troops, and all instantly knew what it meant. Quickly it was caught up by the next command, and the next, and thus, with increased volume, passed on to the left. Each command, in its turn, caught up the refrain and added to the chorus none dropping it, however, and soon those old woods and hills rang again with the spirit-stirring yell."[19]

Several Texans recalled the moment the victorious Rebel yell pierced the smoke-clouded air. "At sunset, there is a death-like stillness for a second," Sergeant William W. Heartsill recalled; "oh what the suspense of that short second; we knew that one side had given away, my God! Listen! Those shouts as they go up to the heavens, we have gained the victory, THANK GOD, the day is won and the Federals are in full retreat, the loud huzza is soon caught up by Longstreet's men on the left and it seemed that the shouts of victory are louder than the din of battle a few moments ago, all everyone engages in one loud, long shout." He opined, "Rosencrantz [sic] may thank his stars that night is so near at hand; for if Bragg had three hours of daylight there would not be an armed Federal in Rosencrantz's Army."[20]

The distinctive yell carried to the retreating Federals. "It was the ugliest sound that any mortal ever heard," Lt. Ambrose Bierce of Hazen's staff believed, "even a mortal exhausted and unnerved by two days of hard fighting, without sleep, without rest, without food and without hope. There was, however, a space somewhere at the back of us across which that horrible yell did not prolong itself;

18 Hamilton, *History of Company M*, 35.

19 *Houston Tri-Weekly Telegraph*, Dec. 22, 1863. The writer placed this incident late on Saturday afternoon, but from the narrative it appears he was referring to Sunday.

20 Heartsill, *Fourteen Hundred and 91 Days*, 154.

and through that we finally retired in profound silence and dejection, unmolested." The fighting at Chickamauga was finally over.[21]

Joe Wheeler's cavalrymen, fresh off their fight at Lee and Gordon's Mills, had pushed forward. Before darkness fell, they seized five Union field hospitals filled with medical supplies and equipment. About 100 Federal surgeons became prisoners. The 18th Kentucky's Dr. Joseph Fithian, one of many Union physicians who stayed behind to treat the wounded, claimed that General Wheeler and his staff confiscated their horses. The Rebels also denied them the use of Confederate ambulances to collect the Federal wounded from the field. Texas cavalrymen soon arrived and at gunpoint ordered the Yankee physicians and their patients to "shell their overcoats." The troopers also appropriated oilcloths, blankets, and hats and forced the nurses to go with them as prisoners, "thus leaving the surgeons to perform the duties of doctors, nurses, cooks, and grave-diggers."[22]

The 68th Indiana's Dr. John L. Wooden made a similar claim. Wheeler's provost guards arrived at the hospital of Reynolds's division of the XIV Corps and marched off all the cooks, nurses, and stewards. They reportedly stole blankets from the wounded lying under the trees. Wooden related that a major, a lieutenant, and a private of the 8th Texas Cavalry came in and told the surgeons to form a line. The Confederates then ordered all 10 to shed their overcoats. After speaking with some of the patients inside a nearby house, the Texans learned that these were Reynolds's men. "That damned old fox," the major uttered. He lined up the surgeons again and confiscated their hats in revenge. The doctors futilely appealed to Bragg's medical director, adjutant general, and provost marshal to obtain transportation and rations for their patients. Wooden later complained about the "fiendish barbarity of the rebels toward our wounded." Wooden, Fithian, and several other doctors were eventually transported by rail to Libby Prison in Richmond.[23]

The Texans Reflect

Still being held in reserve, Ector's troops began burying their dead. Three of Capt. James A. Howze's men had died near one another. Taking a few men of

21 Ambrose Bierce, "A Little of Chickamauga," *The Collected Works of Ambrose Bierce* (Princeton, NJ: 1909), 277-278.

22 "From Atlanta and Richmond," *Cincinnati Daily Commercial*, Dec. 3, 1863.

23 "The Federal Surgeons at Chickamauga," *Indianapolis Daily Journal*, Dec. 10, 1863.

Company D, Sgt. Zachariah W. Bailey of the 14th Texas Cavalry went back to the spot and interred them. Private J. M. Spinks of the 10th Texas Cavalry helped bury his friend "Jimps" Hudson on Sunday night. He carved an "H" on a post tree near Hudson's head to mark the grave. D. Willoughby Howard of Greenville had enlisted with his brother and some friends in the 32nd Texas Cavalry in February 1862. Federals killed Private Howard on September 19. Just 26 years old, he had left a young wife, a son, and a daughter to join the Confederate Army. A friend dug Howard's grave and buried him by himself. "It was hard to lose him and put him away in such a hurried way," the comrade lamented, "but it was the best we could do under the circumstances."[24]

The other Texans in the Army of Tennessee were also preparing for the evening. Most expected to resume the hostilities in the morning somewhere near their position. General Robertson received orders to move the Texas Brigade to the front left along Horseshoe Ridge, relieving Kershaw's two brigades and Col. Archibald Gracie's brigade of Preston's division. The Texans and 3rd Arkansans settled down to bivouac for the night and reflected on the long day. John C. Cox, the 5th Texas's last color-bearer on Sunday, had been shot about 5:00 p.m., but the wound was relatively minor. He would carry the minié ball inside his body for more than 30 years. The 4th Texas's Pvt. John C. West nursed a painful injury to his right wrist. "When we found that the Yankees were gone and the field was ours," West recalled, "I was much rejoiced." He planned to mail the Webster's blue-book speller taken from the German prisoner home to his children. He informed his wife, "I got a splendid gun and accouterments, plenty of paper, and a nice pair of woolen gloves." He added that "the old Texas brigade is fearfully cut up. There are not more than 150 in our regiment. The Fifth numbers about 100 and the First about the same. There is said to be a company in the First Texas with one officer and no men left; another has one man left. Our company has about twenty-five men. Of course, there is an exaggeration in these statements, but we are terribly thinned out."[25]

24 Spinks, "Thrilling and Varied War Experiences," 168; W. Bailey, "The Star Company of Ector's Texas Brigade," *CV*, vol. 22, no. 9, Sept. 1914, 404; Yeary, *Reminiscences*, 353-354. Bailey named the third soldier killed in Howze's company as Billy Hurst, but Hurst's CSR indicates that he was detailed to the provost guard in October 1863 by Ector's orders. Friddle had received a severe wound to his arm at Murfreesboro but had recovered and rejoined the regiment.

25 *OR* 30, pt. 2, 432, 517; *Semi-Weekly Courier Times* (Tyler, TX), Sept. 24, 1910; West, *A Texan in Search of a Fight*, 108-109; Watson Dugat Williams to Wife, Oct. 2, 1863, THM.

According to Capt. George Todd of the 1st Texas, several demoralized Union soldiers came into camp and surrendered. Some of the Yankees said that the Rebels could simply march into Chattanooga. Few in the ranks thought it could be so simple and expected to engage the Yankees again on the morrow. "We again slept on our arms on our extreme front," Todd remembered. "We suffered a heavy loss in killed and wounded. Out of 15 men rank and file of Col A (my Co.) which went into battle, only 5 were with us that night and 3 of them were commissioned officers. Co. A lost 17 killed and wounded." The 5th Texas's Pvt. Watson D. Williams noted, "Out of four that were members of Company F I am the only one left after the battle."[26]

Some Texans could not help but compare the soldiers of the Army of the Cumberland to their usual foes back east in the Army of the Potomac. "Brave fellows they were," Pvt. O. T. Hanks of the 1st Texas commented. "These troops were better fighters than the Virginia army; they came from the northwestern states, kinder frontiersmen. A part of the enemy battle line surrendered, grounding their arms in perfect order, the guns lying side by side, the muzzles all pointing in the same direction." Others believed the fighting at Chickamauga exceeded that at Gettysburg some 11 weeks earlier. "The old soldiers agree that they have never seen the like," Private West wrote in a letter to his wife; in his opinion, Chickamauga had been "far more dangerous" than any battle of the war.[27]

The 7th Texas of Sugg's brigade camped that brilliantly moonlit night on Snodgrass Hill, sleeping among the dead and dying. "We gained a victory but not one which was complete," Sgt. Leroy F. Moody opined. "The loss on both sides was very heavy indeed. Their loss more than ours judging from what I saw. . . . I had the opportunity of visiting a part of the field. Such as I saw can't be described wounds of every character, the dead & dying lying together both of friend & foe. It was not the dead that affected me so much as the pitiful & beseeching tones of the wounded. But from the way the wretches treat us we should not have any sympathy for them."[28]

26 Todd, *First Texas Regiment*, 19.

27 O. T. Hanks, *History of Captain B. F. Benton's Company, Hood's Texas Brigade, 1861–1865* (Austin, TX: 1984), 20; West, *A Texan in Search of a Fight*, 106.

28 "A Story of Terry's Texas Rangers," *Austin American*, Apr. 14, 1918; L. F. Moody to Haley Cole, Oct. 20, 1863, CCNMP; C. W. Trice, "Seventh Texas Regiment in Gregg's Brigade," *CV*, vol. 23, no. 2, Feb. 1915, 77.

"About nine o'clock that night," Maj. Khleber Van Zandt reported, "we made camp at a spot the Federals had been using for a field hospital. Their wounded and dead were all around us, and all night we could hear the groaning of the injured. Early next morning our men went foraging. Some went for water. Others went to see if there was any food to be found in the haversacks of the dead Yankees. Billy Rogers, one of my men, was in a mighty bad fix; but he found some coffee and made himself a cup of it. He was just putting it to his lips, when a wounded Ohio captain dragged himself up to our fire. Without a word, Billy handed the coffee to the Yankee, saying, 'You are worse off than I.' I think this instance, and many others, show that men who did the fighting did not have any animosity toward each other. What we hated were men we called 'wagon dogs,' who did not take any risk but followed along after the troops getting what gain they could."[29]

Later that night, around their campfires, Roger Mills's surviving Arkansas Post parolees were justifiably proud of their performance that day. "Our old soldiers may relate their experiences of that war and the many tests of physical and moral courage," a Texan recalled, "but I feel sure none of them will deny the fact that lying in close range of an enemy's guns for many hours will come about as near trying the souls of men as any other, and there is but little doubt that Hardee's corps would have much preferred charging the enemies lines on that occasion." The soldier from the Lone Star State closed with a personal admonition: "May none of you ever have any of those horrible experiences."[30]

29 Myres, *Force Without Fanfare*, 104.

30 "Letter from Adolphus," *Corsicana* (TX) *Daily Sun*, Sept. 29, 1911.

Chapter 11

Return to Chattanooga

At dawn on Monday, September 21, the rising sun cast its first rays over the war-torn fields and forests between West Chickamauga Creek and Snodgrass Hill. Many Confederates rose and cooked their breakfasts, expecting they would soon resume the attack. But rumors spread that the Federals had departed the area, and they were soon confirmed. "On Monday morning the Yanks were gone," Pvt. John C. West of the 4th Texas wrote. "I could hear artillery, which I presume was hurrying up their retreat." The men expected to pursue Rosecrans's Yankees to Chattanooga and recapture the strategically important city and its railroad network. Most of them believed they should have undertaken that movement the previous night after Pap Thomas withdrew. Little did they know that Braxton Bragg had not yet decided what to do next.[1]

Years later, a few veterans of the 1st Texas claimed they had witnessed an extraordinary meeting of the army's high command. "Gen. Bragg seemed to have gathered all the big Generals in our immediate front, in council," Capt. George Todd recalled. "Bragg, Longstreet, Breckenridge, Buckner, Forrest and Wheeler were all there present with us. The question seemed to be whether we should continue our advance, or wait and throw out scouts and feelers." Todd continued, "Our men in the ranks called to them to let us go on at once. But Gen. Bragg, never

1 West, *A Texan in Search of a Fight*, 115.

having gained a complete victory before, seemed to fear ambuscades and reserves, and we remained all day doing nothing." Private O. T. Hanks noted, "Just before we left the battlefield there were several generals were assembled, I suppose discussing. About 40 feet above their head was a six-pound cannonball half buried in a large pine tree."[2]

Youthful Pvt. John M. Pinckney of the 4th Texas also said he witnessed the meeting. "On this morning we arose early, and just at the head of our brigade we noticed a crowd of men collected, some of whom were on horseback. Among them we could plainly distinguish the tall form of John C. Breckinridge and our bull-dog leader, General James Longstreet, Lee's famous war-horse." Pinckney and his company mate, Tom Wallingford, walked close to the generals. Braxton Bragg was on foot. Longstreet spoke in a loud and distinct, "yet very angry," voice, according to Pinckney. Bragg was quiet and calm, speaking in such low tones that the two Texans could not hear him. They certainly could hear Longstreet, who argued, "General, this army should have been in motion at dawn of day." Bragg's reply was inaudible, but Longstreet responded, "Yes, sir; but all great captains follow up a victory." Pinckney could not hear Bragg, but he later claimed that Longstreet retorted, "Yes sir, you rank me, but you cannot cashier me." The two privates returned to the ranks and began talking the matter over with their comrades, with some asking, "Why don't we follow our victory?"[3]

To determine the enemy's whereabouts, Forrest rode toward Rossville, where his saddle soldiers briefly skirmished with Federals. The probing actions and scouting patrols revealed that the Yankees blocked the road north to Chattanooga. Bragg realized he could not afford a frontal assault against the Rossville line, considering his Chickamauga losses. He dispatched Joe Wheeler's 3,000-man mounted division, including the 8th and 11th Texas Cavalry Regiments, to scout the area around Lookout Mountain. The cavalry crossed West Chickamauga Creek at Lee and Gordon's Mills and rode toward Lookout Mountain through "a perfectly desolate country," Chaplain Robert F. Bunting recalled. Reaching Lookout Valley along the foot of the imposing mountain, they turned right onto the Chattanooga Road with orders to hold the Union cavalry in check until

2 Todd, *First Texas Regiment*, 17-18; Hanks, *History of Captain B. F. Benton's Company*, 24. Longstreet is known to have met with Bragg in Dyer Field but not with the other generals Todd mentioned. The Texans' remembrances may have been a decades-later faulty composite of various meetings they saw during the day.

3 James M. Goggin, "Chickamauga—A Reply to Major Sykes," *SHSP*, vol. 12, no. 4, Apr. 1884, 222-223.

relieved. During the afternoon, the two Texas regiments occasionally skirmished with the enemy south and southeast of Rossville. "Although the Yankee cavalry was in view, yet they did not press us," the Presbyterian minister commented.[4]

After spotting a telltale dust cloud, Wheeler's troopers engaged the retreating Federals in Cooper's Gap near Lookout Mountain and captured more than 200 enemy cavalrymen. The Confederates struck while the 4th, 5th, and 6th Kentucky Cavalry ascended the pass to escape to Chattanooga. The 5th Kentucky swiftly rode over the mountain, leaving the 4th and 6th to fend for themselves. A few prisoners later complained that the Rangers of the 8th Texas Cavalry mistreated them. "The first act of Confederate kindness that I received was at the hands of a Captain who threatened to blow my brains out for refusing to inform him of the direction taken by our retreating column," Assistant Surgeon William Forrester of the 5th Kentucky claimed. "He also kindly relieved me of my sash, which I had refused to deliver to him." Little did the 8th and 11th Texas cavalrymen realize that they would be in the saddle for almost three weeks.[5]

During the cavalry movements near Lookout Valley, Capt. George W. Littlefield received orders to take six companies of the 8th Texas Cavalry and backtrack some 12 miles to West Chickamauga Creek. His orders were to guard a ford near

Crawfish Springs that a brigade of Federals reportedly was threatening to cross. On the way, the Texans traversed the La Fayette Road through the battlefield. "It was the most distressing ordeal of my career as a soldier to ride through that two miles of country where the guns of both the north and south had shot the trees into splinters and mown the undergrowth like a giant reaper," Littlefield wrote years later. "Everywhere lay the wounded and dying and the slain of both armies. The screams of the mangled artillery horses made the night hideous with their heart-rending appeal for relief, and the pitiful moans of those brave fellows who had fought so gallantly, through that dreadful carnage made the tears flow from my eyes, and even to this day I cannot talk of it without great emotion."[6]

4 "Forrest at Chickamauga," *The Southern Mercury* (Dallas), Mar. 30, 1905; "Letter from the Rangers."

5 "Thrilling Narrative of Libby Prison," *Louisville Daily Journal*, Dec. 14, 1863. For an overview of the fighting at Cooper's Gap, see Belcher, *The Cavalry of the Army of the Cumberland*, 157-160, and Powell, *Barren Victory*.

6 "A Story of Terry's Texas Rangers"; *Lamb County* (Littlefield, TX) *Leader*, Aug. 18, 1938. Littlefield returned to the battlefield again at the end of Wheeler's three-week ride: "We had completely circled Rosecrans's army and our way again led over the battlefield of Chickamauga

Capt. George Littlefield, 8th Texas Cavalry (Terry's Texas Rangers). (*Dolph Briscoe Center for American History-University of Texas at Austin*)

The Burial of the Dead

Meanwhile, those in the Army of Tennessee who had survived Chickamauga were largely inactive throughout September 21. With unexpected idle time on their hands, several Texans took the opportunity to tour the shell-scarred battleground. "We got up in the morning and beheld the horrible effects of the fight," the 24th Texas Cavalry's Capt. Sam Foster remembered. "One man, by himself, could not cover the entire battleground. Still, each man saw enough to satisfy any human being." He and his comrades had heard wounded enemy soldiers calling out all night long, but they were not permitted to leave the ranks to assist them. Now, in the morning light, he was exploring the woods at former Union positions. He found telegraph wire strung between the trees, and assumed the Yankees had used the line for communications from Rosecrans's headquarters to his various generals. Details from his brigade and other nearby units collected the wounded and buried the dead. Other men assisted the ordnance department in gathering the serviceable arms left on the battlefield.[7]

Lieutenant Isaac C. Madding of the 16th Alabama had died the previous day with a bullet in his brain. His slave Josh and a soldier in his Company B walked to a sawmill to obtain planking to make a coffin. They retrieved the body and prepared it for burial. Extracting nails from a nearby fence, they fashioned a rude coffin and buried the 25-year-old Madding in a yard under a tree. Next to that they interred the remains of General Deshler, Madding's prewar friend and neighbor. The soldier

where the dead still lay unburied. The river was so polluted from dead animals and men that we were compelled to boil the water and skim the maggots off before we drank."

7 Brown, *One of Cleburne's Command*, 50. Rosecrans's headquarters maintained telegraphic connections with Washington through much of the battle.

A dead soldier by Alfred R. Waud. (*Library of Congress*)

inscribed the two men's names on a board and placed it at the head of the fresh graves. After the war, Madding's brother and Deshler's father accompanied Josh to Chickamauga. They exhumed the bodies and took them back to Alabama, reburying Deshler in Oakwood Cemetery in Tuscumbia and Lieutenant Madding at the family cemetery near Leighton.[8]

"That day was set aside for burying the killed on the battlefield," the 18th Texas Cavalry's Pvt. Alexander Orr recalled. "I went over a good deal of the battle ground and the ded were strewed for miles; such a sight I never saw before nor never want to see a gain. Our beloved General Deshler was killed; he was shot by a cannon, and his hole brest was shot off. There was men shot all to pieces, some with there heads busted open; some shot in too and armes and legs shot off, and evry where that they could bee." Soldiers of Jerome Robertson's 4th Texas buried 22 of their men in a mass grave near the Viniard House. Captain J. T. Hunter

8 "Isaac Croom Madding," *CV*, vol. 26, no. 12, Dec. 1918, 529-530; Eleanor Finley Holder, "The Deshlers and Tuscumbia's Schools," *John Deshler, July 19, 1806–January 14, 1869* (East Lansing, MI: 1960). The Pennsylvania-born David Deshler, James's father, was a prominent civil engineer and railroader in Tuscumbia. Upon his death, he bequeathed money to establish a college, the Deshler Female Institute, in his late son's honor. His other two children had preceded James in death, including a son who drowned in the Hudson River while attending West Point.

reported, "The enemy's killed on that field, some two hundred, were never buried."[9]

Hunter permitted Lt. Wash Masterson and Sgt. Val Giles to return to the battlefield. "We really had no business back there, and were prompted by curiosity alone," Giles remembered. "We wanted to see the ground over which our Brigade had fought." Coming to the old road, they noticed it was filled with dead men lying thick in every direction. Giles's gaze turned to the nearby shot-riddled pine trees, some of which had bullet holes as high as 10 feet up. After crossing the field, Giles and Masterson climbed the nearby hill. "Caissons and gun carriages lay in splinters, covered with fallen trees and limbs," Giles noted, "and all around the demolished batteries, along the crest of the ridge and fifty yards out in the field, the ground was covered with blue uniforms." He counted 32 dead and wounded artillery horses where two enemy batteries had been deployed. "The sight of those poor, pitiful dumb brutes affected me more than all the gruesome sights I had witnessed on the battlefield," he continued. "Innocent of any wrong, and ignorant of the cause of their suffering, the poor wounded creatures lay there moaning and dying from thirst and ghastly wounds. There was no helping hands for them, no surgeon to dress their broken and mangled limbs, no hand to pass them a bucket of cold water. . . . Eight or ten fine animals lay there desperately wounded, all famishing for water." Later, Giles learned that a detail had been sent around the battlefield to shoot the stricken steeds.[10]

Private Orlando T. Hanks of Company K was among the men of various companies of Robertson's 1st Texas detailed as a burial party. They dug trenches six to eight feet long by about 20 inches deep, collected their dead comrades, and lined them up by the graves. The group then spread articles of clothing and blankets on the floor of the trenches, picked up the dead soldiers, and "lay them tenderly side by side." Nearby, the men noticed a corpse burnt beyond recognition behind a decayed and charred oak tree. One of the gravediggers from Company F believed he knew the fallen soldier; he had last seen him behind that same tree. If the body were that of his friend, he would have had six half-dollars in his pocket. He suggested they scratch through the ashes and find the coins to prove the man's identity. Seconds later, they began finding them. The men then turned their attention to the dead Texan. "We bore him tenderly to the grave on two ramrods

9 Anderson, *War Journal*, 123; Hunter, "Hard Fighting Fourth Texas," 22.

10 "In Storm of Battle"; Laswell, *Rags and Hope*, 208-209.

Pvt. William Oliphant, 6th Texas Cavalry.
(*DeGolyer Library, Southern Methodist University, Lawrence T. Jones III, Texas Photographs*)

which were plentiful, and laid him beside the others, spread clothing, blankets, etc. over them, then covered them with soil, that being their last resting place."

As the gravediggers searched the area again for any men they may have missed, Hanks noticed a piece of paper folded into a square. It proved to be a $25 Confederate note. After the soldiers returned to their respective companies, they wondered who had lost the money. Some thought the burned man had tossed it aside to save it. Although Hanks wanted to keep the banknote for himself, "Captain [Samuel F.] Wilson informed me the man had a wife and a large family of small children and poor. He advised that I send it to them. I could not stand it any longer. I sent it to them. I do not know whether they ever received it or not, neither do I remember the name. I feel glad in my heart to this day that I sent it to them."[11]

"Oh! What horrors are to be seen and felt in this war!" an anonymous member of the 25th Texas Cavalry lamented. He was in Colonel Mills's provost guard, with the duty of keeping watch over the dead and wounded to prevent pilfering. In a rush to depart the field, Rosecrans had abandoned most of the Union fallen to the mercy of the Confederates. "Some of his dead are yet lying where they were shot down," the guard informed his father in Galveston. "We could not bury them all, and had to leave them as we found them. I saw some with their brains all scattered around them, still alive; others with holes through them, so that it seemed impossible for them to live, though they lived for days." He added, "It was a terrible fight, indeed, and I don't ever wish to see another.[12]

11 Hanks, *History of Captain B. F. Benton's Company*, 24. Private Emmanuel H. Crier and Cpl. Charles H. Hicks of Company F, the Woodville Rifles, were reported killed.

12 *Houston Tri-Weekly Telegraph*, Nov. 27, 1863.

The Plight of the Wounded Texans

That same day, more than 2,000 wounded men lay in temporary hospitals in Ringgold, including in the county courthouse, the Baptist church, private homes, and the nearby resorts at Catoosa Springs and Cherokee Springs. Thousands more remained at aid stations or temporary facilities surrounding the battlefield. Another 900 or so injured Confederates lingered at Catoosa Platform awaiting rail transportation to hospitals throughout Georgia, while others were being taken south to Tunnel Hill or Dalton. Soldiers loaded hundreds of other wounded onto supply wagons and hauled them over rough roads to the network of commissary depots south of the battlefield. Little provision was made to take this latter group to the railheads.[13]

Exposed to the weather, several soldiers suffered at Catoosa Platform when no trains arrived. The medical director of the Department of Tennessee, Dr. Samuel H. Stout, learned of the issue even as army engineers worked to rebuild the burned railroad bridges at Ringgold (a job they would complete on September 28). Based in Marietta, Stout managed to get 10 trains rolling north to Greenwood, a facility at the Western and Atlantic Railroad's woodyard a mile south of Catoosa Platform. The invalids waiting for transportation included William Oliphant of the 6th Texas. Four days after the battle, he arrived at a hospital at Newnan, Georgia, "where I was carefully nursed and dragged back from the verge of the grave," he recounted. "The kind ladies of Georgia hovered like ministering angels around my bed and gave me every possible attention, winning my undying admiration and everlasting gratitude."[14]

The wounded Confederates being evacuated on September 21 included Maj. Gen. John Bell Hood, nauseated by the chloroform administered before the amputation of his right leg. Newspapers across the South reported that Hood's wound was mortal; some, including the *Richmond Examiner*, published his obituary. The tough Texan was still alive, though in tremendous pain. About 3:00 p.m., stewards placed him on a litter. A group of men, reportedly including at least one slave, Jack Reed, carried Hood five miles south of the battlefield, where he spent a

13 For a detailed examination of the subject, see Maj. David A. Rubenstein, *A Study of the Medical Support to the Union and Confederate Armies During the Battle of Chickamauga* (Auckland, NZ: 2014).

14 "A Confederate Artillerist Comes to Chattanooga," *Chattanooga Free Press*, Sept. 17, 2017; McCaffrey, *Only a Private*, 50. Oliphant recovered from his wound in time to rejoin his regiment in mid-November just before the battle of Missionary Ridge.

quiet evening. The plan was to take him the following day to the residence of Col. Francis H. Little of the 11th Georgia, some 30 miles from Chickamauga. Little's property was southeast of La Fayette, in West Armuchee Valley in Walker County.[15]

The field hospitals near the battlefield resembled charnel houses. Surgeons and stewards worked amid piles of amputated limbs, blood-soaked rags, and other detritus. Eighteen-year-old Pvt. J. P. Alford of Granbury's 7th Texas grimly endured the amputation of his leg without anesthesia. Private George G. Gardenhire of the 10th Texas suffered from seven wounds, including one that blinded his left eye. He also permanently lost hearing in his left ear. Doctors patched him up and sent him to Ringgold. At the hospital there, surgeons examined the damage to Col. William H. Young of the 9th Texas of Ector's brigade. A minié ball had entered his chest above the left nipple and exited through his shoulder blade. Fortunately, all the major blood vessels and bones were intact. The doctors believed Young's wound would heal well.[16]

Some grievously injured soldiers took their fates into their own hands. Sergeant Bill Fletcher of the 5th Texas had suffered a gunshot wound to his left foot at the Viniard farm. Robertson's surgeons contemplated amputating it, but young Fletcher refused to allow the risky operation. He managed to get medical care from a group of Catholic Sisters of Charity and kept his foot. He did not, however, regain full movement in it and was declared unfit for further service. Still determined to be a soldier, he transferred to Terry's Texas Rangers so he could ride rather than march to fight Yankees.[17]

Private Robert E. Grantland was one of the youngest members of the 25th Texas Cavalry, running away from home at age 13 to join the army in 1861. At Chickamauga, he suffered a severe wound to one of his arms. When doctors said they would have to amputate it, he ran away from the hospital. Grantland spent the night holding the fevered arm in a cold stream. It worked, and he saved his limb. Private W. Augustus "Gus" Tompkins of the same regiment was also undergoing treatment for an injury. He had an unusual background, having reportedly escaped

15 *Richmond Examiner*, Sept. 23, 1863; *Honey Grove* (TX) *Signal*, May 8, 1925.

16 Andrew F. Lang, "The Bass Grays: An Economic, Social, and Demographic Profile of Company D, Seventh Texas Infantry," *ETHJ*, vol. 48, no. 1, article 11, 2010; Yeary, *Reminiscences*, 251; *Memphis Daily Appeal*, Sept. 29, 1863.

17 *Port Arthur* (TX) *News*, Feb. 22, 1999. Fletcher was captured in 1864 while on a scouting mission in Georgia. He escaped captivity by leaping from a moving train that was taking him to a Northern prison.

from a New York City prison before making his way through Union lines. He traveled to Houston and joined the 25th Cavalry.[18]

Several other severely injured Texans were beyond all hope, including 17-year-old Pvt. John Short of the 5th Texas, who died on September 21. In Short's company, Cpl. Junius W. Graves and Pvt. William Crabtree each had a leg amputated, but they slowly weakened. They had survived Gettysburg only to perish at Chickamauga. On September 19, Yankees had shot Lt. Allen G. Killingsworth of the 4th Texas as he led Company E across the La Fayette Road near the Viniard House. Comrades carried him four miles to a division hospital in Ringgold. They sat with the Waco soldier until he died on the morning of September 21, then buried him near the hospital.[19]

Private Thomas A. Elliott of the 24th Texas Cavalry had suffered a severe wound in the left thigh and a lesser injury to his right lower leg in Deshler's fight on Sunday. His friends found him lying in front of the skirmish line. They carried him on a litter to the field hospital, where he eventually expired. Elliott was "a favorite of the company; expressed himself perfectly willing to die; was a sincere Christian, patriot," a comrade related. "Peace to his ashes!" The 24th's Pvt. Leander "Lee" E. Adair also faced death. The Georgia native had recently visited his parents, whom he had not seen for several years, before rejoining his regiment before Chickamauga. A slight head wound proved mortal, and he "died from congestion of the brain." His grieving father soon came and retrieved Lee's body and brought him home to rural Morgan County for burial.[20]

After being wounded on Sunday, the 4th Texas's Pvt. James M. Polk lay unconscious in a hospital tent for several days. When he finally woke up on Wednesday, wounded men were all around him. He turned over and saw that his friend Jack Massey was right beside him. "Is that you, Jack?" he asked. "Yes," Massey answered. "My leg's cut off; Tobe Riggs died a few minutes ago." Surgeons

18 *Abilene* (TX) *Report News*, July 16, 1937; Houston Tri-Weekly Telegraph, Nov. 16, 1863. After Grantland's arm healed, he returned to duty in Galveston and helped build the first causeway across Galveston Bay.

19 B. I. Franklin to Mary Franklin, Oct. 2, 1863, CCNMP; "In Memory of Lieut. Allen Gay Killingsworth," *Galveston Daily News*, Oct. 10, 1867; CSR of A. G. Killingsworth, 4th Texas, NARA RG109, M323, Texas, roll 0288. Short's older brother William had been wounded and captured at Gettysburg in July.

20 "Letter from Tennessee," *Houston Tri-Weekly Telegraph*, Dec. 7, 1863; James Barnett Adair, ed., *Adair History and Genealogy* (Los Angeles, CA: 1924), 223. Lee's father, Jones B. Adair, had strongly opposed secession and "never ceased to blame the Confederate leaders for the horrors of the war between the States."

had administered chloroform to Private Riggs while amputating his leg; he never woke up. Polk had no idea about his own injury. Blood clouded his vision, he was sick and nearly dead from thirst, and his head pounded. He soon learned that a minié ball had struck his temple and lodged in the back of his head. Polk nevertheless recovered quickly and was able to walk in a few days. "I could see muskets lying on the ground in every direction, and a pile of arms and legs, which had been cut off men," he recalled. "I suppose it would have taken a wagon, and perhaps two, to have carried the arms and legs cut off of men on the battlefield of Chickamauga."[21]

Private William Schadt of the 1st Texas was also a patient in a field hospital. A minié ball had glanced off his knee bone, leaving a painful wound. He lay near Zeke Crawford, the member of the regiment's color guard who had begged Sgt. George Branard to get him a replacement hat from a dead Yankee. Grievously wounded by a shell fragment, Crawford lingered until September 24. His brother and Schadt were with him when he died. "His loss will be a severe one to his parents," Schadt informed his sister. "He was one of my messmates ever since we left Galveston and I regret his loss deeply."[22]

For days, scores of overlooked soldiers lay on the vast battlefield. Lieutenant Oliver P. Bowser of Deshler's brigade had been left in the woods on September 19 with a group of other invalids when the fighting moved elsewhere. He spent more than a week lying helpless and waiting for aid that did not come. He struck up a friendship with an injured Yankee. The enemy soldier said he was from the 13th Ohio of Dick's brigade in Van Cleve's division and he had been a locomotive engineer before the war. His mother was a widow and lived near Dayton. The unlikely pair of wounded men subsided on some corn left over from a hasty feeding of mules during the battle. Finally, on September 30, they managed to get word of their plight to the Confederate field hospital at Crawfish Springs. They were taken there for initial treatment and then moved to Ringgold, where Bowser shared some of his food and clothing with the prisoner and they separated. For decades after the war, he searched unsuccessfully for his Buckeye companion.[23]

21 Polk, *Memories of the Lost Cause*, 22. Riggs's personal effects were later given to his family in Corsicana. In 1896, his mother donated his pistol holster to the new Confederate Museum in Richmond (*Galveston Daily News*, May 18, 1896).

22 Stuart E. Schadt, ed., *Letters Home 1861–1865: Charles and William Schadt* (Falls Church, VA: 2015), 40-41; CSR of Ezekiel C. Crawford, 1st Texas, NARA RG 109, M323, Texas, roll 0248.

23 "Texas Abroad."

Nurse Kate Cumming had worked in the military hospitals at Catoosa Springs and Cherokee Springs since mid-summer. She later went to Atlanta to tend the wounded from Chickamauga. "We have numbers of Texas soldiers, members of Hood's division," she noted. "They are a fine-looking lot of men, and seem brave enough to face any danger. I have had not a little quarreling with them. They will have it that this army is not to be compared with the one in Virginia for bravery." The Scottish-born nurse disagreed with her opinionated patients, arguing that the Army of Tennessee had to contend with "the flower of the North" in the Army of the Cumberland. "But these things do for something to talk about," she reasoned.

Over time, several patients developed gangrene, a dangerous condition that often resulted in tissue death. "We have some dreadful cases of that awful disease," Cumming noted. Her patients included a "fine-looking" Texan named Deal. When he first arrived after being wounded three times at Chickamauga, he was carefree and full of laughter. As gangrene began killing tissue in his back, Kate noted, "he is grave enough." Doctors feared that they could not stop the gangrene before it reached a vital organ and that Deal was likely to lose a leg. Another gangrenous soldier, Pvt. George Hempfling of the 25th Texas Cavalry, lingered between life and death. Several men, rotating in 20-minute sessions, had to maintain continuous pressure on one of his arteries to prevent instant death. At times, the nurses and doctors could not save their patients. Eighteen-year-old Cpl. Thomas Watson of the 4th Texas came down with double pneumonia and a sore throat. As the "handsome lad" lay dying, he asked Cumming to collect the money the army owed him and send it to his mother. He died that night.[24]

The Belated Pursuit to Missionary Ridge

While a large cadre of dedicated Confederate surgeons and volunteers worked feverishly to save the lives of maimed men, the healthy soldiers still in the ranks began preparing to depart Chickamauga in the late afternoon of September 21. Braxton Bragg's Army of Tennessee was finally about to move. On Monday afternoon, contrary to orders to "be ready to march at a moment's warning," several soldiers strolled around the battlefield. "It is enough to make the stoutest heart sicken, and I cannot but feel emotions of sorrow, pity and sympathy for our

24 Kate Cumming, *A Journal of Hospital Life in the Confederate Army of Tennessee* (New Orleans, LA: 1866), 112, 116; *Houston Tri-Weekly Telegraph*, Nov. 16, 1863. Hempfling survived and returned to Texas, where he performed detached recruiting duty. The other soldier was likely Pvt. John W. Deal of the 4th Texas.

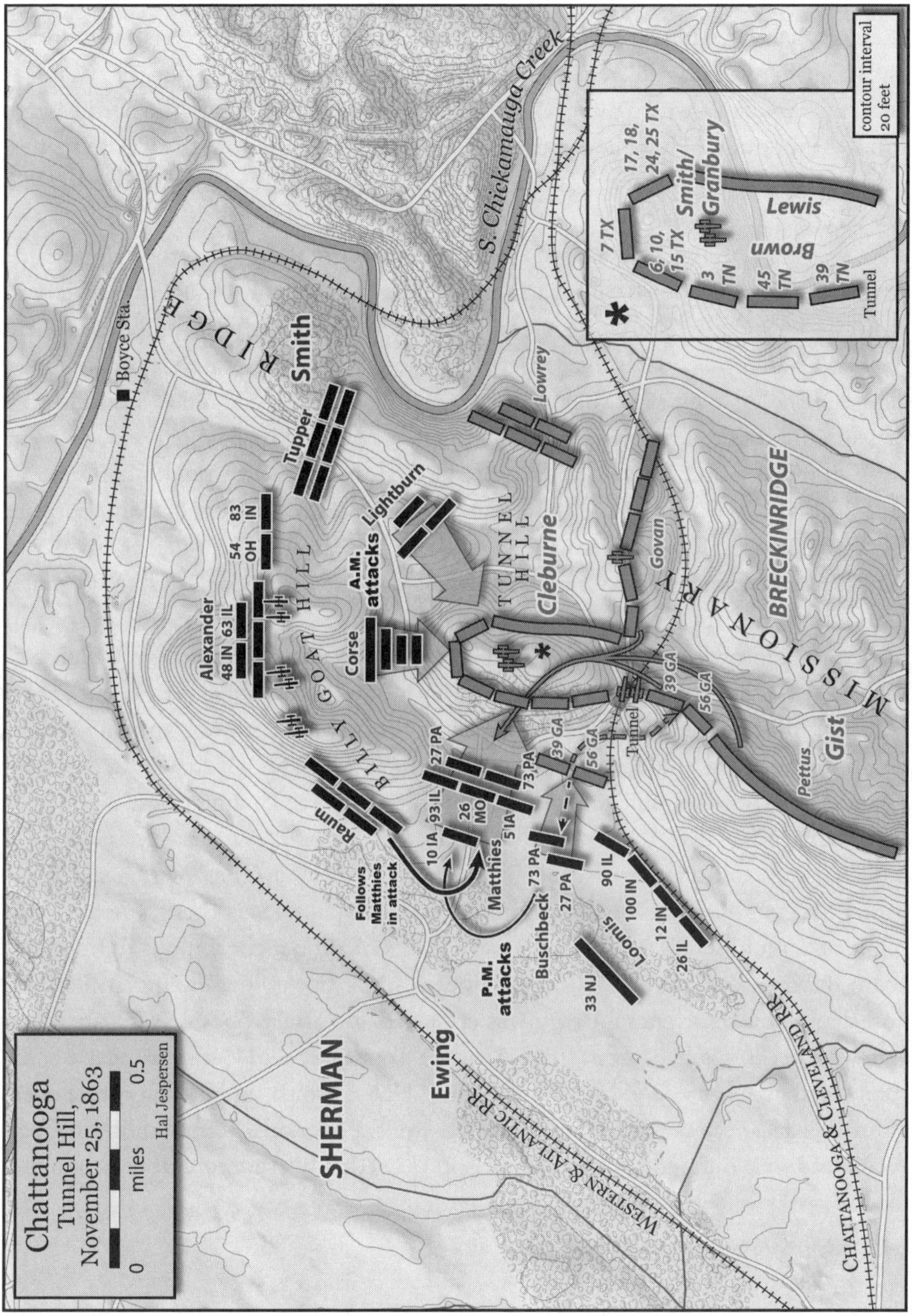
Chattanooga
Tunnel Hill,
November 25, 1863
0
miles
0.5
Hal Jespersen
SHERMAN
Ewing
Western & Atlantic RR
Chattanooga & Cleveland RR
P.M. attacks
A.M. attacks
Loomis
Buschbeck
Matthies
Follows Matthies in attack
Raum
Corse
Alexander
Lightburn
Tupper
Smith
Billy Goat Hill
Tunnel Hill
Cleburne
Lowrey
Govan
Breckinridge
Gist
Pettus
Missionary Ridge
Boyce Sta.
S. Chickamauga Creek
Tunnel
contour interval 20 feet
Lewis
Brown
Smith/ Granbury

enemy, when I see him cold and stiff in death, or suffering from ghastly wounds," Sgt. William W. Heartsill remembered. "But oh, how it makes our most inmost heart bleed, when we turn our eyes upon our own dear loved ones, the heroic brave sons of the south." He believed the Federal dead outnumbered the Confederates. Most heart-rendering were the hundreds of charred corpses in the areas that had burned.[25]

According to the 10th Texas's Pvt. Ben Seaton, "At dark, we took up the line of march and went som 10 miles and camped fer the night. The calvery [had a] hard fight on the rode to Chattanooga and took a good many prisners and drove them back to Chattanooga wher thay are fortifying as hard as they can." It proved to be an agonizingly slow pace. Mills's brigade marched only three miles the following day and then six miles on September 23 before reaching its destination.[26]

Grumbles about the slow pace of the pursuit spread throughout the army. Even the newcomers in Hood's division joined in the growing disillusionment with Braxton Bragg, although many soldiers in the Army of Tennessee remained supportive of him. "We lay on the battlefield all day Monday," Pvt. William A. Nabours of the 5th Texas lamented, "and thus for the want of energy on the part of our commander we lost nearly all of the fruits of an important victory, which cost many lives. On Tuesday we moved slowly on to Chattanooga, giving the enemy plenty of time to get into the fortifications and prepare for our coming." Ryland Todhunter, the assistant adjutant general of Ector's brigade, believed the Yankees "would have been annihilated had they been pursued to Chattanooga."[27]

Many men disagreed. "Why did not Bragg follow up his victory at Chickamauga and capture Rosecrans's Army?" Sgt. Val Giles of the 4th Texas asked. "If ever there was an army completely fagged out it was Bragg's army on the night of September 20, 1863. Forty-eight hours of almost continuous fighting had worn the men out and they dropped down on the firing line, hungry and thirsty, and slept like logs. General Bragg was criticized and abused because his army was human and not made of iron." The Army of Tennessee had lost more than 18,000 men killed, wounded, and missing. Generals Helm, Smith, and Deshler were dead, John Bell Hood was down, and hundreds of experienced field and line officers were dead or wounded. Thousands of sorely needed horses were dead or injured,

25 Heartsill, *Fourteen Hundred and 91 Days*, 160.

26 Simpson, *The Bugle Softly Blows*, 41.

27 W. A. Nabours, "Active Service of a Texas Command," *CV*, vol. 24, no. 2, Feb. 1916, 70; "Battle of Chickamauga," *Des Moines Register.*

straining the capabilities to move wagons, artillery, staff, and the flotsam of an army.[28]

To replace lost weapons and supplies, many Confederates foraged for useful items abandoned along the route northward. According to Sgt. D. H. Hamilton of Hood's 1st Texas, the Yankees had "left batteries, wagons, horses, guns and all kinds of baggage and equipment scattered from the battlefield to Chattanooga. We gathered up all this plunder." Several men claimed the Federals also left a wide path of destruction during the retreat. "I tell you what I saw & heard & which is the truth," the 7th Texas's Sgt. Leroy F. Moody informed a friend. "As far as they went from here towards Ga., they destroyed everything. All the fencing burned many houses destroyed all the cows, hogs, sheep, vegetables, wheat, corn, fowls, wagons, carts, plows, axes, hoes, looms, spinning wheels, cotton, cards & all else, literally leaving all to perish."[29]

Throughout the South, news of the victory came in slowly and often inaccurately, including false initial information that Union General Thomas was dead and Cheatham's division had his body. Braxton Bragg had previously ordered the Press Association of the Confederate States of America to depart from the front. That "unwise course," in the opinion of the Atlanta Daily Intelligencer, delayed full and accurate coverage of the battle. Reporters resorted to interviewing wounded officers stepping off the trains in Marietta and Atlanta, who stated that Walker's reserve division was pursuing Rosecrans and that Longstreet would attack the Yankees on Tuesday morning, September 22. The editor believed, "The military flame of Gen. Bragg has begun to burn with a lustre which we trust may increase until the independence of our country is secured." Like so many others, he expected news shortly of another crushing victory to secure Chattanooga.[30]

By dawn on September 22, the vanguard of Bragg's army approached Missionary Ridge, a long, steep, wooded ridge on the southern outskirts of Chattanooga. Ector's brigade was not with them, however. General Ector had received orders to move that afternoon to Chickamauga Station and take a train back to Mississippi in order to counter a threatened Yankee raid. It would take five days to complete the roundabout journey through Mobile, Alabama. "The reins of discipline hung very loose upon the necks of the Texans," according to one of

28 "In Storm of Battle"; Laswell, *Rags and Hope*, 200. Rosecrans lost about 16,000 men at Chickamauga.

29 Hamilton, *History of Company M*, 35; L. F. Moody to Haley Cole, Oct. 20, 1863, CCNMP.

30 "The Victory of Chickamauga," *Atlanta Daily Intelligencer*, Sept. 24, 1863.

Stone's Alabama sharpshooters. "As we passed along at different points on our way, two, three, and sometimes half a dozen men would step off the train and salute General Ector, and say, 'General, we will come on in a few days,' and away they would go. In a few days, the wayward Texans returned to the ranks." Once in Jackson, Mississippi, Ector's brigade joined the division of Maj. Gen. Samuel G. French.[31]

During the morning, while Ector's men packed for their train trip, General Wheeler took part of his cavalry division to Crawfish Springs. There, the men captured 50 loaded Union supply wagons coming from McLemore's Cove. The Rangers of the 8th Texas Cavalry passed through the Chickamauga battlefield later that day on their way north to Rossville. "Here is the ground over which Hood's Texas Brigade fought so gallantly," Chaplain Robert F. Bunting recalled. "The scarred and riven trees, the dead Yankees, and newly-made graves bearing the inscription, 1st Texas, 4th Texas, 5th Texas, all told eloquently the fearful struggle in which our gallant brothers had fallen. We could not refrain from dropping a tear of sorrow to think that after all their miraculous escapes and perils on the bloody fields of the Old Dominion; they had come here to die."[32]

Beyond Rossville lay the Confederate lines, which extended from the Tennessee River along the side of Lookout Mountain east along the crest of Missionary Ridge, where Bragg had established his headquarters. The breastworks ranged one to two miles from the Union lines. "The enemy are well fortified," a Texas sergeant reported, "having an inner line of strong fortifications and an outer one of rifle pits for sharpshooters." The Federal defenses included some small forts, one of which had been built by the Confederates when Bragg occupied the town after the Tullahoma campaign. From west to east, Bragg aligned his corps as follows: Longstreet (far left), Hill, Buckner, and Polk (far right). The opposing sharpshooters and pickets frequently exchanged fire.[33]

Like many of Bragg's soldiers, the quartermaster sergeant of the 4th Texas, J. B. Polley, thought the Army of Tennessee should immediately assault the Union fortifications protecting Chattanooga. The entrenchments were only "fairly

31 "Sumter in the Civil War." For more on the Texans' movements, see David V. Stroud, *Ector's Texas Brigade and the Army of Tennessee 1862–1865* (Longview, TX: 2004), 141, and Chuck Carlock and V. M. Owens, *History of the Tenth Texas Cavalry (Dismounted) Regiment 1861–1865* (North Richland Hills, TX, 2001), 109-110.

32 "Letter from the Rangers."

33 *Charleston* (SC) *Daily Courier*, Oct. 1, 1863. The author of the article, written in Marietta on Sept. 28, was likely Joe Polley of the 4th Texas.

Pvt. Sam R. Burroughs, 1st Texas Infantry.
(*Texas Heritage Museum-Historical Research Center*)

tenable," in Polley's opinion. To his dismay, Bragg "could not see it that way. Bragg was given to make such blunders and was doubtless encouraged to them by the favor in which he was held by President Davis." Several senior Confederate generals openly argued with Bragg that he should take the offensive.[34]

Many of Bragg's soldiers believed an attack was imminent. "I know that we are now in line of battle at the foot of Lookout Mountain and expect an attack in the morning," the 4th Texas's Pvt. John C. West informed his wife on September 24. "Our pickets had some skirmishing this afternoon, but the main body did not advance. I trust that God will spare my life, and have prayed Him to watch over you and the little ones if I am taken. You must not hope to get my body if I am killed, as it will be impossible to do otherwise than leave me on the field in a soldier's careless grave."[35]

Instead of attacking, Bragg planned to besiege Chattanooga. This decision dismayed or angered many, including several of his generals, who believed Bragg was seemingly focused on the mundane rather than formulating plans to dislodge the Yankees. His headquarters staff had collected several Union flags captured at Chickamauga. On Friday, September 25, orders came to transfer the trophies to Gen. Seth Cooper, the Confederate Army's adjutant general in Richmond. Three staff officers had charge of the special mission and, the orders directed, "Privates J. D. Smith, Company H, 10th Texas, and William H. Barnett, 21st Mississippi, on account of gallant service, are hereby detailed to accompany them. The

34 "Reminiscences of a Private," *San Antonio Daily Express*, Apr. 22, 1906.

35 West, *A Texan in Search of a Fight*, 108.

Quartermaster will furnish transportation both going and returning to Privates Smith and Barnett."[36]

The same day that Smith learned of his impending journey to Virginia, some fellow Texans were busy capturing unsuspecting Yankees near Chattanooga. Four scouts from Ector's brigade fired on a flatboat filled with Federals hauling provisions across the Tennessee River. According to a reporter, the frightened Yankees jumped into the river, and fifteen of them drowned. Another 22 soldiers and a black man accompanying them made it to the south riverbank, where they surrendered. Three others escaped by swimming back to the north bank. On September 26, the same quartet of Confederate scouts captured five hungry Federals who were busy killing hogs some eight miles south of Chattanooga. The captives claimed they were from Crittenden's corps but had not participated in the recent fighting.[37]

Some of Bragg's men, including a few Texans, also became prisoners. Private Samuel R. Burroughs of the 1st Texas was only 15 minutes into his picket duty when Kentucky cavalrymen from Maj. Gen. Alexander McCook's headquarters guard captured him. The Northerners took Burroughs and another man to McCook to be interrogated. According to Burroughs, McCook exchanged haversacks with him after the interview; the general apparently wanted his biscuits and fresh bacon. Another prisoner, Steve, the slave of the 1st Texas's quartermaster, was soon brought in. Steve wore his owner's new uniform coat and possessed his money, pocket watch, and jewelry. The quartermaster had given the items to Steve for safekeeping in case he died. Two Federals repeatedly asked the old black man whether he was a Confederate officer but received no answer. Burroughs explained that Steve was just a servant, but the Yankees persisted in their questioning. Finally, Steve rose in a dignified manner and intoned, "Can't you tell an officer by his uniform?"[38]

While skirmishers sparred along the front lines, Texans who had not been engaged at Chickamauga began hearing about the battle. The Reverend John

36 J. D. Smith, "Inquiries for and About Veterans," *CV*, vol. 15, no. 5, May 1905, 239.

37 *Charleston* (SC) *Mercury*, Oct. 1, 1863. Some captive officers said Rosecrans's army had been badly whipped and morale was low.

38 Frank W. Johnson, *A History of Texas and Texans* (Chicago, IL: 1914), vol. 2, 2442-2443. A comrade later told Burroughs's family in Palestine, TX, that he had died at Chickamauga. Much later, after being freed, Burroughs went home but found them gone. After learning they were in Raymond, he visited them. His mother initially did not recognize him because he had changed so much during his captivity.

Capt. Charles M. Winkler, 4th Texas Infantry.
(*Texas Heritage Museum-Historical Research Center*)

Kennedy Street, chaplain of the 9th Texas in Ector's brigade, was ministering to patients in a Confederate hospital. He learned on September 23 that Rosecrans had recrossed the Tennessee River and "we now occupied Chattanooga." The latter soon proved erroneous, as was the report that General Hood had suffered a mortal wound. Chaplain Street was anxious to hear from his regiment. Two days later, he penned in his diary, "It is now ascertained on orthority deemd reliable that we have driven the enemy beyond the Tenn and occupy Chattanooga. The loss of the enemy is variously estimated at 25,000 to 30,000—it is represented as 'immence, unprecedented in the history of war.'" The preacher from Lamar County added, "We have every reason to thank God for such a glorious and complete victory." Street did not learn until September 28 that Rosecrans still held Chattanooga.[39]

News of the unexpected victory at Chickamauga temporarily buoyed the morale of many people throughout the South. Early reports filtering into Austin, however, were only partially accurate. Thomas H. DuVal had been the judge of the U.S. district court for West Texas before the war. Refusing to resign, the staunch Unionist remained in Austin for two years. He recorded in his diary on September 23, "Rumored that Lee had defeated Meade & killed him and that Rosencranz was whipped by Bragg." Major General George G. Meade, the commander of the Army of the Potomac, was very much alive, rumors notwithstanding. Judge DuVal departed Austin on October 10 and started a five-week journey to Washington. He did not return to Texas until after the war.[40]

39 Julie Williams Coley, ed., *J. K. Street Civil War Letters: 9th Texas Infantry from Paris, Lamar County, Texas* (Wichita Falls, TX: 2010), 176-178.

40 James Marten, ed., "The Diary of Thomas H. Duval: The Civil War in Austin, Texas, February 26 to October 9, 1863," *SHQ*, vol. 94, no. 3, Jan. 1991, 454-455.

With so much free time and no prospects of an imminent end to the siege of Chattanooga, several Texans went sightseeing. Captain Charles M. Winkler of the 4th Texas sent his wife a compelling description of the panorama from the summit of Lookout Mountain:

> On Friday last a party, of which I was one, obtained permission to visit Lookout Mountain, and about noon, the day being beautiful, set out, and in the course of an hour, had ascended as far as our horses could carry us, and dismounting, were climbing up its steep and rugged sides, when I disengaged myself from the balance of the party, and sat down upon a shelving rock, to contemplate the grandest scene my eyes ever beheld. Looking away to the northward, the Tennessee river could be seen winding its way through the mountain range southward, until it seemed to empty itself into the foot of the mountain where I sat, it being so high and steep as seemingly, to overhang and exclude from the view the river sweeping its base. The town of Chattanooga, situated on the east side, some half a mile from the river is plainly seen, together with the large depot, and railroad creeping down the valley, while across a large horseshoe bend of the river, in which the town is located, may be traced the line of fortifications some time since evacuated by General Bragg, and within which Rosecrans has taken shelter since his defeat at Chickamauga.
>
> The enemy's encampment, along and within the heavy works, are plainly visible to the naked eye, and viewed through a glass, presented a scene of life and bustle, interesting to contemplate, especially when we consider them our mortal enemies. Their batteries are planted and frowning down upon us, their long lines of bayonets glistening in the sun, their rows of tents, the cloud of dust that is constantly ascending as they move to and fro, as officers dash along the lines, of their trains of wagons passing down to the pontoon bridge, and crossing the river, lose themselves among the mountains to the right, the whole surrounded and surmounted by mountains grand and gloomy, and as I gazed in amusement at the scene, I thought of the exclamation of Bascomb at the falls of Niagara: 'God of grandeur, what a sight!'—almost bewildered by the beauty spread out before me.[41]

Disillusionment Grows

On September 26, Lt. Gen. Leonidas Polk joined the chorus complaining that Bragg should have pursued Rosecrans more aggressively instead of allowing the Army of the Cumberland to escape so easily. Polk claimed that Generals Hill and Buckner agreed with him. The next day, he reiterated his concerns in a letter to President Jefferson Davis. Bragg retaliated by arresting Polk and Maj. Gen.

41 Winkler, *The Confederate Capital and Hood's Texas Brigade*, 145-146. Winkler penned his letter on Sept. 27.

Thomas Hindman. Events quickly spiraled out of control. Longstreet demanded that Bragg be relieved and sent a note to Hill and Buckner asking them to submit similar letters. Several of Longstreet's Texans commented on the affair. According to the 4th Texas's Pvt. John C. West, "It is said among the men here that General Bragg has put Generals Polk, Hindman and Forrest under arrest, for what cause I do not know, but my impression is, that with either Hood or Longstreet or Lee in command, half of Rosecrans's army would have been captured." West added, "I do not admire Bragg. . . . Longstreet is a bulldog soldier and cares nothing about flank movements. He makes a dead set at the center, and can whip any army on earth if he has men enough to fight with until he is tired of it."[42]

In addition to disillusionment with the senior leadership of the Army of Tennessee, many soldiers lacked variety in their diets. Food supplies proved insufficient. "Appetite comes with eating," Sgt. Joe Polley believed, "but to the Texans in Bragg's army it comes with fasting. Blue beef and musty corn meal have not only become monotonous but, as the boys say, 'We have soured on 'em.'" He and Jim Somerville slipped away from camp, walked five miles, and killed a pig. Upon their return to camp, however, they ran afoul of the provost guards, who believed they had stolen the animal. The provost marshal allowed them to keep the carcass with the caveat that they had to provide proof the next day that they had legitimately paid for it. That night at the much-appreciated pig roast, their mates in Company F heartily thanked Polley and Somerville for satisfying their hunger, and collected $100 for them to give to the farmer.[43]

Many hungry and tired soldiers in Bragg's army mourned the deaths of comrades. They debated the fate of the hundreds of men missing since Chickamauga, as did loved ones. News on the soldiers' fates was agonizingly slow. In Marietta, Mrs. Julia Morgan "scarcely ate or slept, and the suspense was maddening." Irby, her husband, served under his brother Col. John T. Morgan, who commanded a brigade in Wheeler's Cavalry Corps. A southbound train steamed into Marietta's Western and Atlantic depot one morning in late September. Its passengers included the seriously wounded Brig. Gen. John Gregg. The gritty Texan, still suffering from the gunshot wound to his neck and face at Chickamauga, planned to recuperate at a friend's house in the vicinity. Julia saw Gregg "in a bad condition," with his face and head bandaged and seemingly in great

42 West, *A Texan in Search of a Fight*, 115.

43 Polley, *Letters to Charming Nellie*, 100.

pain. His wife, Mary, soon arrived to help care for him. Julia was relieved to learn that Irby Morgan was fine, although some family friends were dead or injured.[44]

Throughout the South, hundreds of families awaited word of missing relatives. On October 4, Sgt. Allen Templeton and Pvt. Moses Walters of Ector's 10th Texas Cavalry were among a large group of Confederates that was sent to Chicago's Camp Douglas prison. Comrades informed Templeton's father that he was a prisoner, but the teenaged soldier would not get out a letter to home until August 5, 1864.[45]

In Cleburne's division, the survivors of Deshler's brigade also had to adjust to changes in the command structure. Half the brigade was now gone. With Colonel Wilkes convalescing and Lt. Col. John Coit ill, Maj. William Taylor of the 24th Texas took command of the 17th-18th-24th-25th Texas Cavalry. With the popular Deshler lying in a soldier's grave, the men got a new brigade leader. On October 8, Lt. Henry T. Curl of the 17th Texas Cavalry wrote of the lamented general, "You can imagine the gloom that has been cast on this brigade, for there was not a man who did not love him, and they are satisfied they will never get another Brigadier who will treat them so kindly." By then, Col. Roger Q. Mills had relinquished temporary command of the brigade and returned to his 6th-10th Texas–15th Texas Cavalry. Bragg brought in an outsider, newly promoted Brig. Gen. James A. Smith, to lead Deshler's men. Smith, who had graduated from West Point with Deshler in 1853, assumed the role on October 6.

Morale continued to falter as the boredom of the siege wore on and illness struck the ranks. "Several have deserted from our Regt since the fight," 2nd Lt. Henry V. Smith of the 17th-18th-24th-25th Texas informed his loved ones in a letter home. "Look out for Tom Richards he is among them." Those leaving without permission included Pvt. Jacob Clark, who had spent most of the summer in the field hospital at Tunnel Hill with chronic diarrhea. Despite his weakened condition, Clark and his friend Pvt. Jehu H. Moore disappeared on the night of October 7 and headed for Texas.[46]

44 "Casualties of the Battle," *The Weekly Advertiser* (Montgomery, AL), Sept. 30, 1863; Julia Morgan, *How It Was: Four Years Among the Rebels* (Nashville, TN: 1892), 59. Gregg returned to duty in January 1864 to take command of Robertson's brigade, only to be killed by another shot to the neck in Virginia in October 1864.

45 J. A. Templeton, "A Chickamauga Prisoner," *CV*, vol. 31, no. 6, June 1923, 238.

46 H. T. Curl to his parents, Oct. 8, 1863, as cited in John R. Lundberg, *Granbury's Texas Brigade: Diehard Western Confederates* (Baton Rouge, LA: 2011), 158; CSRs of Jacob Clark and Jehu H. Moore, 24th Texas Cavalry, NARA RG109, M323, Texas, rolls 0119 and 0122. Moore returned

Confederate prisoners in Chattanooga awaiting transportation to northern prisons. (*Library of Congress*)

A Houston newspaper reported on October 6, "Those who have been blue because Gen. Bragg evacuated Chattanooga and fell back slowly into Georgia, to use a Yankee expression, will now feel green as they read the following: When Bragg had fallen slowly back in the direction of Rome, and have got just between Rome and Dalton, and while Rosecrans was in full and close pursuit, suddenly Gen. Ewell, with thirty thousand troops, pounced in Rosecrans's rear. A sharp engagement took place. . . . Rosecrans has been outgeneraled for once, and was forced to retreat." Richard Ewell was still in Virginia, and it had been Longstreet, of course, with fewer troops, but the early reports at least indicated that Eastern Theater troops had reinforced Bragg and contributed to a rare victory for the Army of Tennessee. Other "cheering intelligence" soon filtered in that Rosecrans indeed had retired to Chattanooga after losing to Bragg at Chickamauga.[47]

As additional and more accurate reports circulated throughout Texas over the following week, however, nagging doubts about the war's outcome returned.

to the ranks and later transferred to the 25th Texas Cavalry. Clark, still absent without leave, was captured in February 1865.

47 "By Pony Express," *Houston Weekly Telegraph*, Oct. 6, 1863.

Lt. Jesse P. Bates, 9th Texas Infantry. (*Courtesy of Nathan Eddy*)

Bragg's failure to recapture Chattanooga negated much of the early euphoria. It became clear the war would drag on with no easily foreseeable path to a short-term strategic victory for the Confederacy. On October 13, while away from the 9th Texas on detached duty in Meridian, Mississippi, Lt. Jesse P. Bates penned a letter home to his wife, Susan, in Tarrant. He tried to encourage her. "My love, I want you to manage the best you can and be contented. I hear that the people in Texas are very much discouraged and I think it is without a cause for I think that the prospect is britening [sic] and ought to cheer every true heart. I am not discouraged in the least."[48]

Bates may have been masking his true feelings to avoid worrying his spouse. Most Texans in the Army of Tennessee, frustrated with Bragg's persistent failures as a commander, were openly discouraged about the conflict's outcome. "If the war is protracted a few years longer the Confederacy will not be worth a farthing," Pvt. Isaiah Harlan of the 10th Texas predicted; "I am afraid it will. I can see no prospect of an early close. To tell the truth, I am afraid the contest will go against us. There is such a lack of confidence and determination amongst the people and army here. A great many are despondent both in and out of the army and they have cause to be so. Bad generalship and short-sighted legislation have brought us to the very brink of destruction, and negligence and corruption in officials and greed in the masses are working to the same end. God only knows what the result will be."[49]

Harlan informed another friend, "Although we have gained a great and complete victory, I am afraid we will not realize as much from it as might have been

48 Jesse Bates to Dear companion, Meridian, Mississippi, Oct. 13, 1863, Tennessee State Library and Archives, Confederate Collection, Box C28, Folder 11, Jesse P. Bates 1861–1864; Henry V. Smith to his father and mother, Oct. 12, 1863, Harold B. Simpson Confederate Research Center, Hill College, Hillsboro, Texas.

49 Isaiah Harlan to Elizabeth Harlan, Jan. 13, 1864, THM.

expected, no, nor as much we could have realized had we followed up our successes with the vigor and promptness that we should." Harlan continued: "Who is to blame is another question. Bragg has arrested Gens. Polk, Hindman & Forrest all for disobedience of orders and I suppose saddles upon each a share of the responsibility in his failure to bag old Rosey. It is a pity that as much blood should be spilt and so little gained. Another great and bloody battle must be fought before we can recover Tennessee or reach Kentucky."[50]

Many Confederates still believed Bragg would attack the Federal lines at some point. "The opinion prevails that when our artillery opens up the place, Chattanooga will become too warm for the cold blood of the North," the 4th Texas's Capt. Charles M. Winkler wrote, "but I have no confidence in shelling them out. I believe, unless we interrupt their communication, so as to compel them to withdraw, we will be compelled to storm their works to get at them. There is little likelihood that General Rosecrans will attack now that we are fortified." Winkler had missed Chickamauga, but still he complained, "I fear we have been too tardy in our movements; we should have followed up the victory of the 20th, before the enemy had time to recover from the shock of defeat."[51]

Growing disillusionment led several other Texans to desert and head back to the Lone Star State. One evening, the 4th Texas's Sgt. Uriah Gould, described as "a rough-mannered old fellow," was sitting along the riverfront on a large boulder that had tumbled down from a cliff on Lookout Mountain. A comrade saw him doubled over, holding his face in his hand and weeping. A letter lay at his feet. In it, his wife had informed him that the prolonged drought had destroyed their crops, the well had gone dry, a horse had strayed off or been stolen, and there was no more cornmeal in the barrel. More importantly, their 10-year-old daughter had just died, and had been buried in a coffin neighbors built from planking they tore off the old corn crib. Mrs. Gould appealed to her husband: "For God's sake, come home." Several weeks later, he slipped away on a foggy day and deserted.[52]

A wounded officer in the 4th Texas refused to violate his commission and desert, but he was equally determined to find a way to go home. From the Medical College Hospital in Atlanta, Capt. Robert H. Bassett sent a letter to the Confederacy's postmaster general, fellow Texan John H. Reagan, "soliciting [his]

50 Isaiah Harlan to Mother, Oct. 11, 1863, THM.

51 Winkler, *The Confederate Capital and Hood's Texas Brigade*, 146.

52 *Austin-American Standard*, June 18, 1899. Gould disappeared into the mountain mists of East Tennessee after Longstreet's Corps had moved there to confront Ambrose Burnside.

kind intervention." Bassett was convalescing from a badly shattered shoulder courtesy of a shell fragment on Chickamauga's second day. The surgeons told him that it would be at least four months before he was fit to return to duty and that when he was well enough to travel, he would receive a furlough. That was far too long to wait, in Bassett's opinion. "Owing to the disgraceful straggling of the troops of this Department," he explained to Reagan, "they will not permit anyone to go on the other side of the river—This rule is first no doubt, but it falls heavy when applied to the three Texas Regiments that served in Va. who never shrank from duty at no time. Were Genl Hood not so severely wounded I would apply to him and get the evil remanded as far as I am individually concerned."

Surrounded by strangers at the hospital, without access even to Atlanta's daily newspapers for comfort, Bassett informed the postmaster general, "You can imagine the unpleasantness of my situation." He asked Reagan to "get me some dispatches to carry on the other side of the river; if that can't be done try and get me a passport from Richmond to Anderson Texas. . . . It's true I could get over the River anyway by doing as many have done 'go on anyhow' but I don't care to travel in that kind of style—and I don't think the Government should force me to do it after rendering me the services as I have." If Reagan could obtain the necessary papers, he was to give them to Bassett's brother in Richmond for forwarding to Atlanta. "My shoulder pains me that I can't sit up to write but very few hours at a time," Bassett added. The desired leave was not granted.[53]

Rumors circulated that Hood's Texans soon would be transferred permanently to the Western Theater. "Longstreet's Corp[s] may possibly return again to enjoy those pleasures we all so much deplore, but I am apprehensive that our Brig. will be transferred to a corps composed entirely of Texas troops," Pvt. John P. Maloney of the 1st Texas reported. "If this be done, we will have bidden a final adieu to the pleasant hills and valleys of Va. where often we have reveled in joyous mirth, or wrested victory from the hands of our country's foe. This is yet not certain, merely a camp rumor, not however without some foundation I fear." Other Lone Star soldiers focused on home, eagerly awaiting mail from loved ones and friends. For many, that little bit of relief was not forthcoming. One of Ector's men explained, "A large portion of this brigade is composed of Texans—cut off entirely from home, and all the association, and benefits to be derived from kindred, and friends.

53 R. H. Bassett to John H. Reagan, Sept. 26, 1863, CCNMP. Bassett, a Louisiana-born bookkeeper, resigned his commission on Apr. 6, 1864, and returned to Grimes County, Texas. He died Apr. 5, 1870, at the age of 34 from the lingering effects of his wound. Bassett is buried in Anderson.

Even the poor privilege of mail communication is denied them. But their conduct will speak for them—they need no higher eulogy."[54]

Sergeant Major John Marquis "Mark" Smither of the 5th Texas suffered a serious wrist wound at Chickamauga. In mid-October, he was convalescing at an estate five miles from Marietta. "A letter from home these times give me a touch of homesickness for a week," he wrote to his mother in Walker County, "but lately I've got to remembering home among the things that were. I never talk or think about going home for it seems to be an impossibility to get there." The good news was that he was having a "splendid time," especially considering the three friendly young women who helped care for him and his host's two wounded nephews.[55]

Other Texans also mentioned the personable Georgia nurses. "Poor Green Morgan was wounded in the head in this last fight," Pvt. Henry W. Berryman of the 1st Texas mentioned in a letter to his mother; "he was getting along fine the last time I heard from him. He had gone down to Georgia where he can receive the tender treatment of those kind Georgia girls who are ever ready to serve a wounded soldier." Berryman went on to complain about the regiment's shirkers. "Mite Caster is getting along finely, he is a splendid soldier, always ready for duty, not like those dandy fellows about home, who come here to serve their country by living in the hospital and running out of every fight. We have such men; they are an expense to the government."[56]

Georgians were not the only ladies to make a positive impression on Lone Star soldiers. Sergeant William A. Hart of the 7th Texas, an expert rifleman, was severely wounded and taken prisoner during the fighting. He was sent to a military prison in Chicago, where his health declined precipitously. A kind-hearted local woman, Miss Ella Bailey, convinced authorities to release him into her care. She eventually nursed him back to health.[57]

Private Charles S. Worsham of Hood's 4th Texas informed his mother that he had not received a letter since spring. "Texas has been as a land of dreams for the last five months, for during that time no news has reached me from its shores." The

54 John Percy Maloney to "Little Friend," Oct. 19, 1863, THM; "Ector's Brigade in the Battle of Chickamauga."

55 Eddy R. Parker, ed., *Touched by Fire: Letters from Company D, 5th Texas Infantry, Hood's Brigade, Army of Northern Virginia 1862–1865* (Hillsboro, TX: 2000), 77-78. Smither recuperated in the country home of Joshua Welch, a prosperous merchant and the former mayor of Marietta.

56 Henry Waters Berryman to My Dear Ma, Oct. 12, 1863, THM.

57 *Galveston Weekly News*, Nov. 9, 1864; *The Gilmer* (TX) *News*, Aug. 15, 1968.

Pvt. Henry W. Berryman, 1st Texas Infantry.
(*Wilson County, Texas, History Commission*)

losses of friends and comrades since the start of the war weighed heavily on his mind, and he subscribed to camp rumors that the regiment would soon head back to the Lone Star State. "Our little Regt. that came out numbering 900 men now only musters 137 muskets—a sad reduction indeed. If they can entirely rout Rosy and Grant and establish communication once more, they intend furloughing the Texas Brigade."[58]

Sam Worsham and his companions in John Bell Hood's division eagerly awaited the return of their stricken leader. "General Hood is getting well, that is he sent word to tell us that he would soon be with us again," the 1st Texas's Private Berryman told his mother on October 12; "he said he would fight Yankees as long as he lived. We miss the old General very much." A couple of weeks later, Sgt. James H. Kennedy of the same regiment wrote to his sister, "Our Brigade has thrown in money to buy Genl. Hood an artificial leg when he takes the field. His men will follow him or go where he orders them." Little did they know that Chickamauga was the last time Hood and his beloved Texans would be on the same battlefield.[59]

Hood remained popular with the men; Braxton Bragg was an entirely different matter. Since the slow pursuit after the battle of Chickamauga, the rank and file's overall dissatisfaction with Bragg had continued to fester. He did have his supporters, however. The 4th Texas's Sgt. Val Giles opined, "Poor old Bragg, the boys never admired him much. He always reminded me of a bronzed statue of some martinet, but he was a fine soldier, brave and true." In early October, President Davis traveled to Tennessee to inspect Bragg's army and confer with the commander. "Well, Mary, the other morning Uncle Jeff and Old Corporal Bragg gave us a visit," Pvt. Alexander L. Orr informed his wife. "They came riding down

58 C. S. Worsham to Dear Mother, Sept. 24, 1863, THM.

59 Berryman to My Dear Ma; James H. Kennedy to Mary E. Kennedy, Oct. 25, 1863, THM.

our lines; Old Jeff is a fine-looking ole chap; he looks more like a farmer than a president. He is a spare made man, gray hair and dark eyes. General Bragg is a fine-looking old man."[60]

The 1st Texas's Pvt. John P. Maloney complained that Bragg "should have acted some time ago." He told his girlfriend in a letter dated October 19 that the enemy had not yet received reinforcements and should still be vulnerable to an attack. "Their situation is one of peril and suffering," he believed, as they were "[c]rowded in a small space immediately in and around Chattanooga, deprived of many necessaries and but scantily supplied with fuel." Their fortifications, however, were strong. Bragg had wasted time and allowed the Yankees to dig in. Maloney noted that Bragg had become even more unpopular through his recent arrest of several generals and Forrest's subsequent resignation in protest. "I greatly fear These despicable prejudices and his tardiness in action will secure adversity to our arms here unless he is superseded," he opined. He then *sarcastically told his "Little Friend,"* "I Think you are a better Genl Than [Bragg]." Many veterans in the Army of Tennessee agreed with the young Texan's dire assessment. General Bragg remained in command, and the stalemate at Chattanooga stretched on, with no end in sight.[61]

60 "In Storm of Battle"; Anderson, *War Journal*, 122-123.

61 John Percy Maloney to "Little Friend," Oct. 19, 1863, THM.

Chapter 12

The Gateway to the South Opens

As Braxton Bragg's performance came under question, so did William Rosecrans's. On October 18, President Lincoln and the war department assigned Gen. Ulysses S. Grant to take command of the new Military Division of Mississippi, which included Rosecrans's army at Chattanooga. Grant, enjoying the limelight of his July victory at Vicksburg, arrived on the 23rd and immediately relieved Rosecrans. Morale on the Union side started to improve as Grant began executing ambitious plans to resupply the army. His "Cracker Line," a Rosecrans idea that Grant implemented on the afternoon of October 28 by seizing Brown's Ferry over the Tennessee River, brought much-needed food and supplies into Chattanooga. In a move reminiscent of Longstreet's transfer from the East to the West, Washington had also sent Maj. Gen. Joseph Hooker and the veteran XI and XII Corps from the Army of the Potomac to Tennessee before appointing Grant as department commander.

James Longstreet was determined to sever Grant's new supply line. He sent Brig. Gen. Micah Jenkins's (formerly Hood's) division to the vicinity of Wauhatchie, a crossroads village just southwest of the river near the foot of Lookout Mountain. The road to Brown's Ferry ran nearby. Late on the night of October 28, the Confederates arrived in the area and deployed. "Our soldiers were rantingly opposed to night fighting," the 4th Texas's Cpl. Miles V. "Pony" Smith complained, "especially when the locality was entirely unknown to them."

The Rebels Firing on Our Supply Train. (*Harper's Weekly*, January 9, 1864)

Benning's Georgia brigade engaged Brig. Gen. John W. Geary's Federals, who were guarding the crossroads and the nearby Nashville and Chattanooga Railroad. Along with Col. James Sheffield's Alabama brigade, Jerome Robertson's Texas brigade occupied a steep wooded hill between the Brown's Ferry Road and the Tennessee River that overlooked the critical Union supply route. Brigadier General Evander Law, commanding both Sheffield and Robertson, placed the 3rd Arkansas and 1st Texas to the left of the Alabamians, with the 4th Texas on the far right. Law kept the 5th Texas in reserve to guard a vital bridge.[1]

After midnight, Col. Orland Smith's 700-man brigade of Ohio, Massachusetts, and New York troops (veterans of Gettysburg, like Robertson's and Law's men) brushed aside cursory fire from Law and began climbing the slope. "A gunshot away off to the left aroused an alarming feeling," the 4th Texas's Cpl. Miles V. Smith later recalled. "Soon the rattle of musketry, borne upon the night air, forced us to believe that a desperate battle was on hand. At the same time the beating of the long roll and the shouts of the men in the quiet depths below, the knowledge being brought to us by scouts, that our right to the river, a half a mile away, was wholly unprotected by a single Confederate guard, with our ears now wide open, we believed we heard the Yanks crawling up the opposite slope just in front."[2]

The initial Union assault failed but Smith sent his soldiers forward several more times. Law, having heard erroneous reports to retreat, withdrew his entire force. Colonel Frederick S. Bass, an accomplished woodsman now commanding the 1st Texas, managed to withdraw his regiment without losing a man. The 5th Texas and 3rd Arkansas also retired without incident. For some reason, however,

1 M. V. Smith, *Reminiscences*, 42-43.

2 Ibid., 43.

Law's orders did not reach the 4th Texas, and the regiment was inadvertently abandoned in the darkness. With Yankees converging from multiple sides, the men of the 4th Texas panicked and broke ranks for the first time in the war. Chaos ensued, and individuals and small groups streamed for the rear. "A loneliness had taken possession of them," "Pony" Smith mentioned, "and it seemed with a unanimity they believed, if they were going to serve their country in the future they also had better right about face, and make a speedy march to the rear. Speedy does not express the velocity with which they went."[3]

"Then and there—deeming it braver to live than to die, and moved by thoughts of home and its loved ones," Sgt. J. B. Polley wrote, "the officers and privates of the heretofore invincible Fourth Texas stood not upon the order of their going, but with a celerity stampeded and plunged recklessly into the shadowy depths behind them." Several terrified Texans stumbled into trees and suffered injuries; others slipped and painfully plunged down the steep slope. Sulfurous oaths filled the air. Lieutenant Colonel Bane of the 4th Texas struck a three-inch-diameter sapling with such force that he bent it over and had to scramble through the rest of the trees some 15 to 20 feet before extricating himself. Joe Polley, worried about the "haunting apprehension of being gobbled up by a pursuing blue-coat," made good time escaping. It was an inglorious and confusing end to the night fight at Wauhatchie and to Bragg's and Longstreet's last best chance to disrupt Grant's Cracker Line. Officers finally restored order. The men of the 4th Texas, many nursing scrapes and bruises, finally got some much-needed rest.[4]

A humorous event occurred during the retrograde down the slope. The 4th Texans nicknamed Pvt. A. R. Rice "Old Pontoon." Among the oldest men in Company A (the "Tom Green Rifles"), Rice was one of the first soldiers to leave when the order came to pull out. While trying the cross a ditch, he fell on his hands and knees. According to Sgt. Val Giles, "the whole regiment made a pontoon out of him." Giles himself was taken prisoner, along with 20 men. He was taken before Union General Hooker and interrogated, but revealed nothing of military value. A

3 Ibid.

4 "Col. F. S. Bass," *The Marshall* (TX) *Messenger*, July 16, 1897; M. V. Smith, *Reminiscences*, 43; J. B. Polley, "A Battle Above the Clouds," *CV*, Mar. 1897, vol. 5 no. 3, 105. Captain J. T. McLaurin later certified "that during the mo. of Oct. in an engagement with the enemy at Racoon Mt. & on picket duty, etc., in front of Chattanooga the 4th Texas Regt. expended the ammount [sic] of ammunition set forth below, to wit: 9,525 cartridges cal. 57 or 58" (CSR of J. T. McLaurin, NARA RG109, M323, Texas, roll 0289).

Chattanooga, Tennessee, circa 1864. (*Library of Congress*)

frustrated Hooker finally uttered, "Take him away, he is the biggest know-nothing I ever saw."[5]

As the siege of Chattanooga dragged on, more organizational changes affected the Texans. In early November, Bragg rid himself of the feuding Longstreet by dispatching the Army of Northern Virginia veterans to East Tennessee to deal with Union Maj. Gen. Ambrose Burnside's occupying army. "We felt like orphans, and had been treated like orphans," griped "Pony" Smith. Some men were shoeless; none had sufficient clothing to deal with the wintry weather they would encounter. Robertson's brigade departed Georgia for good, leaving behind the graves of their dead and their wounded still convalescing in various military hospitals. The memories of Chickamauga stayed with Hood's Texans as they turned their attention to new dangers. A homesick Pvt. John C. West of the 4th Texas informed his wife, "I am satisfied there are few or no occasions which are sufficient causes

5 "The Old Tom Green Rifles," *Austin American-Statesman*, June 6, 1897; "Taps Sounded for Capt. Val C. Giles," *Fort Smith* (AR) *Daily Herald*, Feb. 18, 1915.

for war; its horrors will never be dreamed of except by soldiers actually engaged in it."[6]

On November 12, Pat Cleburne transferred the 19th and 24th Arkansas from Brig. Gen. James Smith's brigade to Govan's Arkansas brigade in his division. To replace them, he moved Col. Hiram Granbury's 7th Texas to Smith, forming an all-Texas unit with the 6th-10th Texas–15th Texas Cavalry under Colonel Mills and the 17th-18th-24th-25th Texas Cavalry under Major Taylor. The addition of the highly regarded 7th pleased most of the Arkansas Post parolees. Some Texans, however, remained disillusioned, despite the organizational restructuring. The 10th Texas's Sgt. Aaron D. Estes informed his wife, Elizabeth, that he was "sick and tired of this nonendable ware [sic] and I am going to git out of it as soon as I can."[7]

The morale-sapping stalemate around Chattanooga continued, but General Grant finally found an opportunity to seize the initiative. On November 22, Bragg weakened his lines by sending Cleburne to take his and Buckner's divisions southeast to Chickamauga Station. From there, he planned to send these 11,000 men to reinforce Longstreet in East Tennessee. Smith's Texas Brigade and the rest of the Confederates withdrew from their lines and tramped back into Georgia. Correctly discerning Bragg's plan, Grant decided to disrupt the movement. On November 23, his Federals seized Orchard Knob, forcing Bragg to adjust his strategy. He recalled Cleburne, whose men had started boarding the trains for Knoxville. The following day, Hooker's XI and XII Corps drove the Confederates from Lookout Mountain, and Bragg moved them eastward to join his right wing on Missionary Ridge. Cleburne's men defended Tunnel Hill, the northern part of the steep, wooded ridge beyond the Nashville and Chattanooga Railroad. James Smith's brigade (6th-10th Texas–15th Texas Cavalry on the left, 7th Texas in the center, and then the 17th-18th-24th-25th Texas Cavalry) formed on the right of the line. They erected rude barricades of logs along the crest. Little did they know that their old nemesis from Arkansas Post, Maj. Gen. William T. Sherman, was readying his 16,600 men for an assault. Sherman later informed his brother, "The whole philosophy of the battle was that I should get, by a dash, a position on the extremity of the Missionary Ridge from which the enemy would be forced to drive me, or

6 Polley, *Hood's Texas Brigade*, 221; West, *A Texan in Search of a Fight*, 129; M. V. Smith, *Reminiscences*, 44.

7 Lundberg, *Granbury's Texas Brigade*, 162; Aaron Estes to Mrs. E. L. Estes, Nov. 15, 1863, Estes Collection, Baylor University, Waco, Texas. Sergeant Estes was killed in August 1864 during the Atlanta campaign.

Cleburne's Repulse of Sherman at Missionary Ridge, November 25, 1863.
(*Library of Congress*)

allow his depot at Chickamauga Station to be in danger. I expected Bragg to attack me at daylight, but he did not, and to bring matters to a crisis quickly, for the sake of Burnside in East Tennessee, Grant ordered me to assume the offensive."[8]

On the crystal-clear mid-morning of November 25, Federals under Thomas and Sherman attacked Missionary Ridge and Tunnel Hill, respectively. From atop the hill, General Smith's Texans spotted the enemy's dark lines emerging from the distant woods. The Yankees advanced "in splendid order" across the level, cultivated ground north of the heights. "The men mount the breastworks and gaze in breathless silence at the advancing columns of the enemy," the 10th Texas's Lt. Harvey F. Prendergast reported. Confederate artillery soon opened, creating large gaps in Sherman's assault waves. "For about an hour, this artillery continued," a Texan using the penname "Horatics" later recounted, "and I must say the enemy

8 "Back from Chickamauga," *Galveston Daily News*, Aug. 4, 1893; B. H. Liddell Hart, *Sherman: Soldier, Realist, American* (New York, NY: 1993), 220.

did splendid shooting, and the very trees were shivered, rocks splintered and scattered, and men and horses placed *hors du combat* was exciting if not interesting." Soon, the Yankees surged forward. "With a wild huzzah, they dashed at us, never heeding the fire of our artillery and skirmishers," Horatics continued. "With banners waving and bugles blowing the charge, they came on in splendid style, and our hearts began to beat fast, for it seemed as though nothing could stem the tide of that human torrent." The Northerners entered the woods at the foot of the ridge.[9]

About 10:00 a.m., Mills and Smith shouted, "Texans, charge!" The Confederates leaped over their breastworks, marched at the double-quick down the slope, and drove off the forward most Federals. During the charge, General Smith fell wounded in both legs. Colonel Mills went down with a severe arm injury; he would languished in the woods for 11 days before being taken to a hospital. Union artillery finally forced the depleted 6th-10th Texas–15th Texas Cavalry, now under Maj. Valerius P. Sanders, to withdraw up the slope. For the next few hours, the Texas Brigade, currently under Col. Hiram Granbury of the 7th Texas, held its breastworks under sporadic Union pressure, and made another charge about 4:00 p.m. as part of a general advance by Cleburne's reinforced line. Major Sanders and Sgt. Maj. Thomas J. Sheffield each lost an arm as the day progressed. Capt. John R. Kennard assumed command of the regiment. The 7th suffered several casualties in the center of the line, while Major Taylor's 17th-18th-24th-25th on the right saw comparatively little action. Kennard reported 79 men lost. As the rest of Bragg's men withdrew from Missionary Ridge, the Texans held their ground. They were among the last Confederates to abandon the defenses, marching off well after dark in profound silence. The siege of Chattanooga was over, and the door to Atlanta was now open. The "Gateway to the Lower South" was firmly in Union hands.[10]

As Granbury's Texans waded South Chickamauga Creek and withdrew into the chilly night, many sensed that this unexpected retrograde from the seemingly impregnable position doomed their cause. "This, Captain, is the death-knell of the Confederacy," Lt. Robert Collins told Capt. Jackson Leonard, "for if we cannot cope with those fellows over the way with the advantages we have on this line, there is not a line between here and the Atlantic ocean where we can stop them."

9 "Letters from Georgia," *Houston Weekly Telegraph*, Feb. 2, 1864; "Letters from Georgia," *Houston Tri-Weekly Telegraph*, Jan. 30, 1864.

10 "Letters from Georgia," *Houston Weekly Telegraph*, Feb. 2, 1864; Bowser, "History of Granbury's Brigade," 744. Mills recovered and fought in the 1864 Atlanta campaign as colonel of the 10th Texas.

Rebel wounded coming in as prisoners on the field of battle by Alfred R. Waud.
(*Library of Congress*)

Leonard quietly admonished his subordinate, "Hush, Lieutenant, that is treason you are talking." They marched on in silence, lost in their thoughts.[11]

11 Collins, *Chapters*, 186.

Statue of Confederate Maj. Gen. Patrick R. Cleburne at Ringgold. (*Phil Spaugy*)

At 4:00 a.m. on November 26, Bragg ordered his beaten army to retreat from the Chickamauga-Ringgold area. The 10th Texas helped burn some of the bridges over West Chickamauga Creek to delay the Yankees' pursuit. Those were not the only conflagrations in the area. "At Chickamauga station we witnessed sights that caused us to deplore anew the loss of the day at Missionary ridge," Pvt. August F. Leuschner of the 6th Texas recalled. "Immense commissary stores were being burned, to prevent their falling into the enemy's hands. Our boys filled their haversacks with crackers and bacon."[12]

At the field hospitals in Ringgold, Catoosa Springs, and elsewhere, surgeons announced that the army was falling back, abandoning the wounded to the oncoming Federals. Stunned, the 1st Texas's Color Sgt. George Branard rose from his sickbed. With assistance from other ambulatory patients, he managed to get dressed despite his injured arm. Not knowing where Robertson's brigade had gone, he and a comrade struck out for Virginia. They walked all the way—a difficult accomplishment given the distance, the terrain, and their weakened condition—but they finally rejoined Lee's Army of Northern Virginia.[13]

On November 27, Cleburne's division waded the ice-cold Chickamauga Creek, "which proved to be an unpleasant bath on so cold and frosty a morning," Lt. Oliver P. Bowser vividly recalled. Later that morning, Bragg ordered Cleburne to hold Ringgold Gap until noon to allow the bulk of the army time to escape southward and save as much of its commissary and quartermaster's wagon trains as possible. Cleburne replied that he could save every wagon and team in the army and that Bragg would not lose a canteen or frying pan to the Yankees. He formed his men on Taylor's Ridge astride the road through the narrow, "V"-shaped gap, with

12 "Incidents of the Past," *Victoria* (TX) *Advocate*, Dec. 18, 1880.

13 *OR* 31, pt. 2, 778; "George Branard as a Prophet," *San Antonio Daily Express*, Apr. 4, 1909.

Douglas's Texas Battery concealed by felled pine tree tops at the apex. "The Federals came rushing on in four lines marching in flank," without skirmishers out front, Bowser recalled. When the enemy got within 70 to 80 yards of the masked guns, the cannoneers quickly removed the pine tops and opened fire. At the same time, the Confederate infantry line erupted with musketry. "The astonished and panic-stricken men fled in the utmost confusion," Bowser bragged. "The rout was complete and the Federal loss fearful, while the Confederate loss was light." The army later tendered a vote of thanks to the Texas Brigade for its gallantry in the fight. "Right well did they earn it," Bowser opined, "for they enabled Pat Cleburne to keep his promise to Bragg, and not a canteen or frying-pan was lost. It won for Colonel Granbury, their heroic commander, a brigadier's commission."[14]

After the successful delaying action, Cleburne retired southward. Granbury's Texas Brigade had suffered 62 casualties at Ringgold, mostly in Major Taylor's consolidated regiment. "It was to the check here given to the enemy that the country is indebted for the safety of the immense transportation of the army," the 10th Texas's Lieutenant Prendergast boasted. A correspondent informed a newspaper in Houston, "We saved all the railroad stock at Chickamauga and destroyed such stores as could not be removed. The people all along the road retire with the army. Nearly everybody had left Ringgold. The wagon roads are in horrible condition."[15]

Bragg retreated south on those same horrible roads, made worse by heavy rain and bitter cold, ending the Chickamauga and Chattanooga campaign. He claimed General Breckinridge was drunk during the disaster at Missionary Ridge and dismissed him. In turn, Bragg's days as the commander of the Army of Tennessee finally ran out. He sent his letter of resignation to President Davis on November 29, and Maj. Gen. William J. Hardee temporarily replaced him on December 2.

Three weeks later, news circulated that Gen. Joseph E. Johnston would take over the army. The appointment gratified a Houston newspaper editor, despite his having "never joined in the condemnation of Gen. Bragg." He believed the Confederate government had placed Bragg in a situation more difficult than any other army commander. "He has had to encounter the best army of the enemy,

14 Bowser, "History of Granbury's Brigade," 745; *OR* 31, pt. 2, 753-757.

15 "Incidents of the Past"; "Dispatches from Bragg's Army," *Houston Weekly Telegraph*, Dec. 15, 1863. According to Prendergast, in the battles of Chickamauga, Missionary Ridge, and Ringgold, Deshler's/Mills's/Smith's/Granbury's brigade captured nine stands of colors and 700 prisoners while losing 650 men.

Gen. Joseph E. Johnston took command of the Army of Tennessee, replacing Maj. Gen. William J. Hardee. (*Library of Congress*)

with inadequate means, both in the number of his troops and the equipments of an army," the newsman opined. "Gen. Bragg has been faithful, stubborn and valiant. He has marched straight forward with resolution, he has fought successive battles well and desperately, he has retreated back, holding his army well and in hand, and preventing a superior force from reaping advantage from victory, and at all seasons and under all circumstances he has exercised the most unremitting care for the comfort of his soldiers. But we do not think he has exhibited genius."[16]

His last statement resonated with many of Bragg's former soldiers, but not all. "I have always admired many points in Bragg's character," Lt. Harvey Prendergast opined, "and I still believe him to be an able commander. He has of late labored under difficulties which, independent of all military skill, would have weighed down almost any military commander. He had not had the cordial confidence of his officers and his army, and without these the battle is half lost before it commences." Prendergast continued, "From Shiloh, where he won his honors, down to Chickamauga, he has had no bed of roses."[17]

Meanwhile, news of soldiers killed at Chickamauga, Missionary Ridge, and Ringgold continued to trickle home to Texas. "I noticed my dear mother in tears," 8-year-old Allen H. Lewis recalled years later, "and I will never forget how she looked when she told me my father was dead." Corporal John J. "Jack" Lewis of the 1st Texas left a wife and four children, including an infant. The bereaved family eventually moved from its home in Beaumont to West Texas to be with relatives.[18]

"The present year is about to close, and will close leaving many a widow and orphan to moan the loss of the brave hoo have falen on the battlefields to rise no more," Benjamin Seaton of the 6th-10th Texas–15th Texas Cavalry noted in December. "O[h] that this war wold end and let peace raign again." His comrades who had finished the previous year at Murfreesboro, Tennessee, and now shivered in their winter camp far to the south at Tunnel Hill, Georgia, would have surely agreed.[19]

Chickamauga and Missionary Ridge were behind them. Ahead lay more battles and the loss of several long-time comrades. Jerome Robertson performed poorly in the campaign against Burnside in East Tennessee, in James Longstreet's opinion. Robertson appeared before a court-martial, received a reprimand, and accepted a transfer to Texas to command the state's reserve forces. Brigadier General James Gregg took command of the Texas Brigade after Robertson departed. He was killed in October 1864 during the siege of Petersburg, Virginia. Despite a mangled arm and missing leg, John Bell Hood became a corps commander in the Army of

16 "Gen Johnston and Gen Bragg," *Houston Tri-Weekly Telegraph*, Dec. 22, 1863.

17 "By Pony Express."

18 John J. Lewis correspondence, CCNMP. Mrs. Lewis died in 1869 of a "broken heart."

19 Simpson, *The Bugle Softly Blows*, 46.

Tennessee. In July 1864, he replaced General Johnston in command of the army. A few days later, Matthew Ector lost his left leg in fighting near Atlanta, ending his military career. Colonel Roger Q. Mills survived a severe injury at Atlanta. Later in the year, Hood led his forces back into Tennessee, where he launched a series of ill-fated assaults at the battle of Franklin on November 30. Hiram Granbury of the 7th Texas, by then a brigadier general, joined Pat Cleburne and four other Confederate generals in death at Franklin.

Chapter 13

Legacy

As the years passed, many Texans reflected on Chickamauga and their war experiences. "What gallant times were those," Capt. D. H. Ridley of the 9th Texas recalled. "What excitement. What uneasy brooding before the battle, but once in it what exhilaration, what madness. The boom of cannon, the rattle of musketry, the shriek of the bomb, the angry hiss of the minie ball, the charge and the counter charge, the advance and the retreat—all pass through memory and we live all over again the days of the past, and I think of the time intervening between the close of the war and this good hour."[1]

Eventually, some men were willing to bury the hatchet regarding their former enemies. After doctors removed a minié ball from Chickamauga that John Calhoun Cox had carried in his body for more than 30 years, the former 5th Texas color sergeant remarked, "Now, more than ever, I am ready to make peace with the Yankees."[2]

1 "Memory of War After 30 Years," *The Paris* (TX) *News*, Jan. 20, 1955. Ridley survived a severe thigh wound at Chickamauga.

2 *Nolan County* (TX) *Record*, Feb. 15, 1894. Cox kept the ball in a little velvet bag in his pocket the rest of his life. The wife of a former officer in the brigade presented him with a small piece of red alpaca cloth from the battle flag he had carried at Chickamauga. Cox, much beloved in his community, lived until 1917.

Yet other Confederates remained far from ready to forgive even their own commanders. Oliver P. Bowser, a lieutenant in Granbury's brigade, remained upset with Bragg's (and later Johnston's) leadership for the rest of his life. "It can be asserted without boasting that the men of this brigade, as well as of Cleburne's division, were never satisfied with the policy of their commanders from Nashville to Atlanta, and would have rather met the enemy in sanguinary conflict every day than to have yielded one foot of territory. The men who knew the troubles had to be fought out in the end never could understand why it could be done as well one place as another." He continued, "They could never understand why Rosecrans and Sherman could flank us all the time and we not flank them. Of course, the men were not West Point graduates, and, therefore, not up on the science of warfare; but they always believed, and some still think, that if there had been less sparring and more real fighting over the territory mentioned fewer Federal soldiers would have lived to draw pensions."[3]

"We had a hard time in the States of Georgia and Tennessee," the 17th Texas Cavalry's Pvt. Bryan W. Bailey admitted. "We gained the battle, but paid very dearly for it." His comrade Cpl. James P. Mims bragged, "I will say that if our brigade was ever whipped, we never knew it." Several veterans considered Chickamauga to have been a soldier's battle in the absence of senior leadership. According to the 4th Texas's Sgt. Joe Polley, "There was little maneuvering, little strategy—it was simply a test of the fighting qualities of the Western men largely composing the Union Army and the men of the South, and in result, never went a step beyond." Former artillery captain James P. Douglas remained proud of Chickamauga for the rest of his life: "It was a great battle and a great victory. The Confederacy, through all time, should celebrate the 20th of September as a great event in our history."[4]

In the late summer of 1893, a delegation of U.S. Senator Roger Q. Mills, Texas State Senator Oliver P. Bowser, and James Douglas went to the Chickamauga battlefield to select a location for the proposed Texas State Monument. The group located the positions of all the Lone Star troops except for Ector's brigade.

3 Bowser, "History of Granbury's Brigade," 745.

4 Yeary, *Reminiscences*, 30-31; "Reminiscences of the Boys in Gray," *Finders Keepers*, Johnson County Genealogical Society, vol. 12, no. 4, Winter 1995, 118; *San Antonio Daily Express*, Jun. 2, 1907; Douglas, *Douglas's Texas Battery*, 73.

Members of that command would need to visit the park to mark their former battle lines. The delegation also recommended erecting a memorial to General Deshler.[5]

Through the early 1900s, the Texas veterans of Chickamauga slowly died out, leaving their reminiscences of the battle as lasting legacies. One of the last old Rebels to leave this world was Wiley Wood Foster of the 18th Texas Cavalry. The Jasper County native had enlisted at age 16 and survived two wounds, including one at Chickamauga when a bullet passed through him and nipped a lock of hair off a friend who was lying on the ground next to him. Twice captured, Foster finished the war at the Camp Chase prison near Columbus, Ohio. Though almost deaf, he attended the 75th-anniversary commemoration of Chickamauga in 1938. When Foster passed away in October 1946 at the age of 101, he was likely the last remaining Texan who had fought at Chickamauga.[6]

Wiley Foster and the thousands of Confederate Texans who preceded him in death since September 18–20, 1863, had personally experienced the "unceasing fury" of Chickamauga. Their legacy, and that of their equally valiant blue-clad opponents, lives on.

Trees on a Battlefield

There were not many old trees left
After the dreary days of battle.
But had their bodies badly cleft,
And lying still as slaughtered cattle.

Trees are not as good as they are wise:
Not one of them believes in war,
And yet they seem to sympathize
With him who wears a battle scar.

5 "Back from Chickamauga," *Galveston Daily News*, Aug. 4, 1893. The state of Texas finally erected a granite memorial stone along Battle Line Road in 1964 to commemorate the Lone Star soldiers who fought at Chickamauga. The site is between Deshler's and Turchin's lines near the Deshler mortuary marker.

6 *Abilene* (TX) *Reporter-News*, Dec. 30, 1945. Foster is buried in Putnam in Callahan County, Texas.

Trees die in battles fought by men,
The cannon and the musket balls,
Are just as fierce and fatal when
They strike a soldier and he falls.

Trees are not cowards, well we know.
They sense not such a thing as fear.
But follow men in war, although
Death and destruction hover near.

If trees could speak their thoughts of us,
I wonder what their words would be?
Is man a warring blunderbuss,
And just because he can't agree.

To settle quarrels and disputes
In peace, as peaceful persons feel.
He chooses power and its fruits
To make heart-wounds that never heal.

See that rough knot upon yon tree?
It holds an iron cannonball:
Its bark-slit scars today decree
That warring folks one day shall fall.[7]

7 "Death of Deshler Commemorated," *Chattanooga Daily Times*, Aug. 23, 1936.

State of Texas Monument dedicated in 1964. (*Scott Mingus*)

Appendix A

Overall Casualties at Chickamauga in Texas Commands

Deshler's Brigade—Brig. Gen. James Deshler (killed)

6th-10th Texas–15th Texas Cavalry, dismounted (700 men): 20 killed, 95 wounded, 28 missing; *17th-18th-24th-25th Texas Cavalry, dismounted* (767 men): 24 killed, 174 wounded; *Douglas's Texas battery* (about 60 men): 1 wounded

Ector's Brigade—Brig. Gen. Matthew D. Ector (wounded)

9th Texas (145 men): 6 killed, 36 wounded, 18 missing; *10th Texas Cavalry, dismounted* (272 men): 11 killed, 84 wounded, 24 missing; *14th Texas Cavalry, dismounted* (197 men): 10 killed, 47 wounded, 29 missing; *32nd Texas Cavalry, dismounted* (217 men): 13 killed, 65 wounded, 40 missing

Gregg's Brigade—Brig. Gen. John Gregg (wounded)

7th Texas (177 men): 10 killed, 82 wounded

Harrison's Brigade—Col. Thomas Harrison
8th Texas Cavalry (412 men): 1 killed, 14 wounded; *11th Texas Cavalry* (about 398 men): losses unknown

Robertson's Brigade—Brig. Gen. Jerome B. Robertson
1st Texas (409 men): 19 killed, 124 wounded, 12 missing; *4th Texas* (322 men): 26 killed, 102 wounded, 5 missing; *5th Texas* (247 men): 13 killed, 87 wounded, 12 missing

Total (4,323 men present): 153 killed, 911 wounded, 168 missing (28.5% casualty rate)[1]

1 Powell, *The Maps of Chickamauga*, 274-279. The 8th Texas Cavalry figures are from the *Houston Weekly Telegraph*, Dec. 1, 1863. One of the wounded men, W. M. Dromgoute, died shortly after the battle. No similar listing for the 11th Texas Cavalry has been found. The 5th Texas's death total rose to 17 after four wounded men died.

Appendix B

Individual Texas Casualties at Chickamauga by Regiment

Robertson's Brigade—
Brig. Gen. Jerome B. Robertson, commanding.

1st Texas—Capt. Richard J. Harding, commanding; Capt. David K. Rice (acting major), taken prisoner.

Co. A, "Marion Rifles"—Capt. George T. Todd, commanding. Killed: Pvt. Hugh Daugherty. Wounded: Lt. Wesley W. Laney, leg; Lt. Harry H. Robinson, arm; Sgt. Argyle "Gulie" Campbell, leg; Sgt. Edward D. Smith, shoulder and mouth; Cpl. T. E. "Dick" Brewer, severe; Pvts. T. Benjamin

Allen, leg; Frank E. Blackburn, leg amputated, mortal; John C. Veal, thigh, disabled. Missing: Cpl. John Calhoun Hawkins.

Co. B, "Livingston Guards"—Capt. Richard J. Harding, later Lt. William F. Walker, commanding. Killed: Sgt. Adolph D. Sanderson; Pvts. Rufus R. Choate, Richard Ellis. Wounded: Pvts. M. E. "Pat" Donnelly; Jordan M. Canterberry, head, slight; James P. Stevens, mortal. Missing: Pvt. George H. Johnson.

Co. C, "Palmer Guards"—Capt. David King Rice, commanding. Killed: Pvt. Alfred B. Harris. Wounded: Sgt. Edwin B. Searle, Pvts. A. J. W. Armstrong, Solomon Lassiter, John H. McGinnis, J. P. Neil, James Rainey, William T. Stamper.

Co. D, "Star Rifles"—Capt. Henry E. Moss, commanding. Killed: none. Wounded: Lt. Jack M. Thomas, face, mortal; Lt. Absalom C. Oliver, arm, slight; Sgt. E. C. Powell, multiple chest wounds, severe; Sgt. A. J. "Jack" Wood, arm, severe; Pvts. Reuben W. Blalock, illness; John P. Cook, side, slight; William L. Durrum (Durham), head, severe; Jacob J. Durrum (Durham), breast, mortal; James S. Easley, slight; Aquilla Miles, ankle, slight; William O. Moss, mortal, awarded gold medal for bravery; William H. Oliver, mortal; John C. Robinson, mouth, disabled; James P. Snellgrove, foot, severe; William M. Snow, thigh, severe. Missing: Pvt. James P. Dunklin.

Co. E, "Marshall Guards"—Capt. Berry W. Webb, commanding. Killed: none. Wounded: Sgt. James O. Bradfield, finger; Sgt. James A. Lindsey; Cpl. W. D. Prescott, side; Cpl. Thomas W. Willingham; Pvts. Robert J. Marshall, mortal; J. N. Kirksey, hip; Rhodes B. Stephens, leg amputated; Eugene O. Perry, hip.

Co. F, "Woodville Rifles"—Lt. Allen J. Rigsby, commanding. Killed: Pvt. Emmanuel H. Crier, Cpl. Charles H. Hicks. Wounded: Sgt. James F. "Maje" Perryman, shoulder; Sgt William Virginius Smith, head, slight; Cpl. Henry C. Jones, leg amputated; Pvts. Benjamin Bradham, foot; Josh W. Poole, hip, slight; James T. Tiner, face, slight; Uriah M. Gilder, forearm, disabled.

Co. G, "Reagan Guards" or *"Anderson County Guards"*—Lt. A. W. Buckner, commanding. Killed: none. Wounded: Lt. W. Park Mynatt, mortal; Lt. John James Quarles; Sgt. George W. Kyle, mortal; Cpl. Edwin Dagg; Cpl. W. T. Hazelwood, mortal; Cpl. John R. Keeling; Cpl. Ira Parker, mortal; Pvts. Henry F. "Hy" Bradley; Sam Raymond Burroughs; Haywood Darnell; Green B. Davis; Lewis Grooms, mortal; Marshall G. Hamby; Thomas F. Main; James W. Mathews; Elias Newsom; A. T. Ratcliff; N. D. Reed; Thomas J. Reed; Jasper M. Stallcup; John C. Stinson; Albert Thompson; Alex J. Watts; Willis J. Watts, three wounds. Missing: Sgt. William C. Wren; Pvt. John T. Woodhouse (wounded and captured).

Co. H, "Texas Guards"—Capt. Bedford Parks, commanding. Killed: none. Wounded: Capt. Bedford Parks, foot, slight; Lt. Sam P. Torbett, bowels, slight; Sgt. George W. Small, knee, mortal; Sgt. Jasper E. Hickman, back, slight; Cpl. Miles A. Berry, ankle, slight; Cpl. James E. Evans, shoulder, severe; Pvts. James Briggs, shot above right knee, slight; Robert R. Birdwell, ankle, slight; J. A. Graham, ankle, slight; Alonzo F. Erwin, hip, slight; George W. Lumpkin; N. A. Mendenhall, breast, mortal; Seatt L. Scott, back, disabled; Jarrett P. Smith; Joseph P. Smith.

Co. I, "Crockett Southrons"—Lt. John H. Wooters, commanding. Killed: Sgt. Jonathan H. Foster, Sgt. Christopher C. Morris, Pvts. William Y. Salter, W. B. Mason, Joseph Rudicil. Wounded: Lt. Albert A. Aldrich, thigh; Sgt. David B. Bush, hand; Sgt. Rufus F. Emmons, ankle; Cpl. Samuel J. Bradston, slight; Cpl. James M. Drawhorn, hip; Pvts. James M. Corley, foot amputated; Samuel O. Foster, thigh, severe; John Harris, slight; Green P. Mann, thigh; John A. Morris, head; James W. F. Norford, severe; Wilfred Oliphant, slight. Missing: Pvts. George M. Wetherred (mortally wounded), Thomas A. Boone.

Co. K, "Texas Invincibles"—Capt. John H. Massey, commanding. Killed: Pvt. Lafayette M. Mason. Wounded: Lt. John N. Wilson; Sgt. Isaac N. Ruddell, severe; Cpl. William J. Cureton, slight; Cpl. F. H. Tucker; Pvts. John Brandon, slight; J. O. "Ike" Noble, slight; Samuel M. Peterson, slight; James W. Stallings, severe; William H. Watson, slight. Missing: Sgt. Henry S. Bennett.

Co. L, "Lone Star Rifles"—Capt. William A. Bedell, commanding. Killed: Cpl. John J. "Jack" Lewis. Wounded: Lt. Robert R. Armstrong, arm; Sgt. Charles H. Kingsley, arm; Sgt. William B. Robinson, shoulder; Cpl. James C. Pratt, leg; Pvts. Augusto Brandt, face; Ezekiel C. Crawford, hit by shell fragment, mortal; David Elmendorf, foot; John Fralish, arm; P. S. Gibbs, finger; John P. Gillis; Aaron Kelso, both legs; Salem S. Lazarus, leg; William Leach, right leg, severe; James W. Murphy, foot; James E. Nagle, face; William Schadt, leg; Frank S. Schmidt, arm; William G. Shepherd, foot; F. Leslie Thompson; Albert W. Wood, leg. Missing: Lt. Whitaker P. Randall, Pvt. John Coffey.

Co. M, "Sumter Light Infantry"—Lt. William Cecil, commanding. Killed: Lt. William Cecil, Pvts. A. Jack Adams, George W. Oglesby, Joseph Ratcliffe, John D. Stevens. Wounded: Sgt. William A. "Shady" Roach, arm and shoulder; Sgt. Frank M. Slater, neck; Cpl. J. George Lock, arm; Pvts. John F. Bellamy, broken arm; Crockett Dunlap, leg amputated; Ephraim Dial, chest; William E. Forsythe, leg; James A. Jones, thigh; Green "Mutt" Morgan, head, slight; Daniel M. Morrow, foot; Harvey H. Pinson, head, slight; Edmund Pope, leg, severe; George Smith, leg; John R. Stewart, slight shell injury to the side; Samuel Stubblefield, thigh; James A. White, both legs; Thomas White, neck. Missing: Sgt. George B. Lundy.

4th Texas—Lt. Col. John P. Bane, Capt. Robert H. Bassett, commanding.

Field and staff. Wounded: Lt. Col. John P. Bane, arm; Capt. Robert H. Bassett (acting field officer), shoulder, slight; Lt. T. W. Masterson (acting adjutant), leg, severe.

Co. A, "Hardeman Rifles"—Capt. Richard M. Bomar, commanding. Killed: Color Sgt. Edward M. Francis, Pvt. Daniel McDonald. Wounded: Lt. John H. Grundy, hip, severe; Pvts. William C. Cavitt, leg amputated; John Clark, jaw broken, disabled; John W. Deal, disabled; Green R. Derrington, shoulder, slight; Sherrod A. Drennan, leg amputated, mortal; George W. Fletcher, head; Wesley C. Francis, leg; John Futch, arms, disabled; Riley

N. Hammond, finger shot off; James M. Hopkins, breast, severe; Robert W. Lockridge, head, slight; William B. Walker, head, slight. Missing: Cpl. Napoleon A. Strong; Pvt. Benjamin F. Freestone (wounded and captured).

Co. B, "Tom Green Rifles"—2d Lt. John T. Price, commanding. Killed: Cpl. George W. W. Nichols, Pvts. J. K. P. Jones, John Schuler. Wounded: 2nd Lt. John T. Price, slight; 2nd Lt. T. L. Masterson, disabled; Sgt. Garland "Snooks" Colvin, slight; Pvts. Franklin M. Burnham; A. A. Durfee, severe; Alfred M. George, severe; Thomas A. Glasscock; Uriah Gould, slight; John Griffith; J. B. W. Henderson; A. Jeff Howard, slight; Archibald R. Masterson, slight; Campbell M. McPhall (litter-bearer), slight; Samuel T. C. "Dock" Stone. Missing: Pvts. Robert A. Davidge, Charles H. Rushton, Frank Strohmer, A. G. Wagoner (wounded).

Co. C, "Robertson Five Shooters"—1st Lt. M. L. Livingston, commanding. Killed: Sgt. Egbert O. Wood, Sgt. J. A. Simmons, Cpl. Winthrop Norton, Pvts. J. H. Griffin, John J. Jones, Daniel Kinsey. Wounded: Lt. M. L. Livingston, arm; Sgt. William C. Steel, leg amputated; Pvts. Frank Barton, leg, severe; Philip I. Barziza, breast, slight; William B. Hill, right arm amputated; S. J. Mitchell, arm, mortal; John A. Smith, breast, mortal.

Co. D, "Guadalupe Rangers"—1st Lt. William H. McClaugherty, commanding. Killed: Sgt. William R. Smith; Pvts. James Campbell, E. J. Cody, R. Thomas Jefferson. Wounded: Lt. William H. McClaugherty, severe; Lt. R. Nathaniel "Nat" Franks, finger shot off; Cpl. Miles Vance "Pony" Smith, slight; Pvts. H. D. Flores, slight; Julius H. Glazer, bayonet, severe; S. Augustin Jones, slight; John Rogers, slight; William M. Shumate, slight. Missing: Cpl. Adam G. Green.

Co. E, "Lone Star Guards"—Capt. Joseph C. Billingsley, commanding. Killed: Capt. Joseph C. Billingsley, 1st Lt. Allen G. Killingsworth, Pvts. W. M. Hicks, John D. Miller, Thomas L. Norwood, Charles M. Whitehead. Wounded: Sgt. Jim H. Manahan, shoulder and breast, slight; Sgt. Edmund Tilly, leg, slight; Cpl. Thomas Macon Mullens, leg, slight; Cpl. Frederick Miller Makeig (color-bearer), neck, severe; Pvts. William H. P. "Billy" Burton, arm, severe; Samuel H. Chambers, thigh, leg amputated;

J. Boze Chapman, thigh, severe; L. Durham Holloway, neck and face, severe; J. T. Pamplin, hand, severe; John C. West, groin, slight.

Co. F, "Mustang Greys"—1st Lt. Haywood W. Brahan, commanding (acting regimental adjutant). Killed: none. Wounded: Sgt. Edward R. Crockett, thigh, slight; Sgt. James C. Murray, foot, slight; Sgt. Jacob Quick, breast and arm, disabled; Cpl. Joseph R. Currie, leg amputated; Pvts. James Alford, arm, slight; Cincinnati H. Brooks, right breast, severe; Harrison Dansby, arm, slight; William M. Givens, disabled; Thomas J. McCann, thigh, severe; Marshall M. Pengra, arm, slight; Abraham C. Penn, hip, disabled; Michael Pickett, left arm, severe; Jack Sutherland, shoulder, slight.

Co. G, "Grimes County Greys"—Capt. Robert H. Bassett, commanding. Killed: Lt. J. M. "Bob" Bookman, Cpl. Joseph McGowan, Pvts. John D. Barry, Thomas Churchwell, David Silverbaugh. Wounded: Capt. Robert H. Bassett, shoulder, severe; Lt. John J. Atkinson; Pvts. Josiah G. Duke, mortal; J. W. Thomas, hand.

Co. H, "Porter Guards"—2nd Lt. R. J. Tedford, commanding. Killed: Pvts. James A. Kirby, William Peacock. Wounded: Lt. R. J. Tedford, slight in the hand first day, severe in the leg second day, disabled; Sgt. James G. W. Cartwright, arm, severe; Cpl. R. H. Stuart, leg, severe; Pvts. Burrell Anders, leg, disabled; William S. Fisher, foot, disabled; Green Griggs, side, slight; James H. Hall, shell, slight; Willis J. Landrum, shoulder, slight; John Long, leg, slight; Marion F. Myers, ankle, slight; John I. Smith, knee, mortal; Ephraim H. Stanfield, leg, slight; John H. Taliaferro, shoulder, severe; Alex Taylor, head, slight; Henry Travis, arm, slight; D. J. Tucker (courier for General Robertson), foot, slight.

Co. I, "Navarro Rifles"—1st Lt. James R. Loughridge, commanding (Capt. Clinton M. Winkler arrived after the battle). Killed: Sgt. Stephen M. "Tobe" Riggs, Cpl. Benjamin F. "Dock" Childress, Pvts. William E. "Billie" Carroll, J. Chisum Walker. Wounded: Lt. Matthew S. Beasley, hip, slight; Sgt. Frank Smith, arm, severe; Cpl. A. J. Brewster, foot, slight; Pvts. James H. Austin, thigh, disabled; John W. Halderman, side, slight; J. B. Lanham, head, slight; James H. "Jack" Massey, left leg amputated; James

M. Polk, head, severe; Leonard W. Rice, thigh, slight; John L. Utzman, side, severe; H. E. Walker, hip, slight. Missing: Pvts. Ambrose Barry, John F. Green.

Co. K, "Sandy Point Mounted Rifles"—1st Lt. Matthew O. Clanahan, commanding (Capt. William H. Martin arrived after the battle). Killed: Pvt. James M. Allen. Wounded: 1st Lt. Matthew O. Clanahan, mortal; Sgt. A. H. Rogers, foot, disabled; Cpl. Milton Autle, shoulder, severe; Cpl. Andrew J. Larue, back, severe; Pvts. William R. Clanahan, leg, slight; David N. Green, mortal; James J. Pickering, thigh, slight.

5th Texas—Maj. Jefferson C. Rogers, commanding.

Field and staff. Wounded: Maj. Jefferson C. Rogers, hip, severe; Capt. John S. Cleveland (acting lieutenant colonel), thigh, severe; Sgt. Maj. J. M. Smither, wrist, severe.

Co. A, "Bayou City Guards"—Lt. B. Pugh Fuller, commanding. Killed: none. Wounded: Pvts. Robert Campbell, arm, severe; William Hobson Clark (color-bearer), leg, severe; C. B. Gardner, arm, slight; John Morris, hand, severe; Owen O'Malley, arm, severe; F. W. Plummer, back, slight; George H. Robbins, arm, severe. Missing: Pvt. Matthew L. Steele.

Co. B, "Echo Company"—Lt. Edward Collier, commanding. Killed: none. Wounded: Lt. Edward Collier, toe amputated; Lt. Benjamin M. Baker, thigh, severe; Sgt. J. S. Obenshain, thigh, severe; Cpl. Webb Sheppard, hip and ankle, severe; Pvts. W. L. Burton, arm, slight; Wesley Cherry, slight; August Enke, wrist, severe; George Andrew Gegenworth, face, severe; W. S. Hart, foot, mortal; John B. Harvey, arm, severe; Dominick Hurley, leg, slight; John Lake, abdomen, slight. Missing: Pvt. John Morrissey.

Co. C, "Leon Hunters"—Capt. J. J. McBride, commanding. Killed: Pvt. Benjamin R. Perry. Wounded: Lt. George F. Border, neck, slight; Lt. Zachary Lewis "Lew" Logan, thigh, severe; Sgt. John Calhoun Cox (color-bearer) side, disabled; Pvts. John J. Gough, head, slight; T. M. Robinson, thigh, severe; H. H. Rowe, mortal; John S. Skinner, thigh, severe; J. D. Stephens, arm; Richard Turner, thigh, slight; Eli Yow, thigh. Missing: Pvt. Thomas M. Lee.

Co. D, "Waverly Confederates"—3rd Lt. Oliver H. P. Caldwell, commanding. Killed: Cpl. T. L. Watson, Pvts. M. C. Brown, John Tomlinson. Wounded: Lt. Oliver H. P. Caldwell, slight; Sgt. John M. Robinson, leg amputated; Pvts. James A. Dickie, arm, slight; James E. Gilbert, leg, slight; Martin L. Gilbert, foot, severe, disabled; Thomas J. Lewis, arm, slight; Isaac N. Parker, thigh, slight; W. B. Rome, head; Alexander H. Traylor, arm.

Co. E, "Dixie Blues"—Capt. Thomas A. Baber, commanding. Killed: none. Wounded: Sgt. W. B. W. George, thigh, slight; Sgt. Frank A. Eldridge, leg, severe; Cpl. William C. LeGrand, head, slight; Pvts. Samuel T. Coffield, leg, slight; M. A. J. Evans, shoulder, severe; James B. Gee, breast; Thomas E. Maddox, bowels, mortal; Thomas H. Mullins, thigh, severe; J. T. Sedgely, arm, severe; James W. Spann, thigh, mortal; Joseph W. Wallace, leg, severe.

Co. F, "Company Invincibles"—Lt. R. J. McKinnon, commanding. Killed: Sgt. William S. Evans (with colors); Pvt. Pinkney C. Buxton. Wounded: Acting Adjutant Charles McCally, neck, slight; Sgt. Henry V. Angell, severe; Sgt. William A. Fletcher, foot, severe; Pvts. Thomas Coogan, thigh, leg amputated; Julius Beckman, shoulder; Thomas William Bryan, shoulder, slight; John M. Dillon, side and head, severe; W. L. McCary, lungs, severe; William McVey, knee, leg amputated; H. L. Taylor, head and hip, slight; Demosthenes Toups, mortal; Frank J. Whittington, face, severe.

Co. G, "Milam County Greys"—Lt. Samuel S. Streetman, commanding. Killed: Lt. Samuel H. Streetman; Pvts. C. L. Bagwell, Robert Griffin. Wounded: Pvts. John T. Austin, hip, severe; M. D. Garrett, knee, severe; A. G. Jones, leg, severe; H. H. Rowe (assigned to division engineering staff), hip, mortal; John B. Small, leg, slight. Missing: Pvts. Robert B. Mayes, John H. Odum, James L. Stewart.

Co. H, "Texas Polk Rifles"—Lt. William Robinson, commanding. Wounded: Lt. T. B. Sprott, ankle, slight; Sgt. J. A. Jemings, head, mortal; Pvts. Jonathan Barber, thigh, slight; R. E. Lee, arm amputated; Harvey

Rose, slight; Thomas J. Simmons, head, mortal; Robert T. Wilson, head, slight.

Co. I, "Texas Aides"—Lt. Benjamin I. Franklin, commanding. Killed: Pvt. John W. Kilby. Wounded: Cpl. Junius W. Graves, leg, amputated, mortal; Cpl. W. H. Holmes, leg, slight; Pvts. Benjamin J. Baldwin, head, slight; William Crabtree, leg amputated, mortal; John Davis, thigh, slight; Joseph D. Holmes, shell fragment smashed knee, disabled; A. W. Holt, shoulder contusion, slight; John Short, mortal; R. H. Spence, abdomen, slight; John W. Tooley, thigh, slight. Missing: Pvt. Stephen S. Driscoll (later reported killed).

Co. K, "Polk County Flying Artillery"—Lt. Joseph Turner, commanding. Killed: Sgt. John C. Beard, Sgt. Nathan Oats (with colors). Wounded: Lt. Joseph Turner, arm, severe; Cpl. L. B. Dortch, head, both eyes, severe; Pvts. Frederick Butler, arm and side; Abraham J. Fairchilds, shoulder; T. W. McCrory, abdomen, slight; William M. McDonald, back, severe; W. D. S. Nettles, foot, slight. Missing: Pvt. James W. McCoy.[2]

Deshler's Brigade

Field and staff. Killed: Brig. Gen. James Deshler, commanding brigade.

6th–10th Texas–15th Texas Cavalry, dismounted—Col. Roger Q. Mills, commanding.

(Company designations are from the original 6th Texas.)

2 *Memphis Daily Appeal*, Sept. 29, 1863, and Oct. 10, 1863; *Galveston Weekly News*, Oct. 28, 1863; Polley, *Hood's Texas Brigade*, 304-347; Seaborn Dorminy to Caroline Dorminy, Oct. 11, 1863; B. I. Franklin to Mary Franklin, Oct. 2, 1863, CCNMP; Stuart E. Schadt, ed., *Letters Home 1861-1865: Charles and William Schadt* (Falls Church, VA, 2015), 40-41; CSR, RG19, NARA, M323, Texas; West, *A Texan in Search of a Fight*, 107; *Seguin* (TX) *Gazette-Enterprise*, Sept. 5, 1990. Note that these casualty lists are based on multiple sources but may be incomplete. A few reported names do not match known company rosters.

Co. A, "La Vaca Guards"—Capt. John R. Kennard, commanding. Killed: Sgt. Charles Steel, Pvts. Joseph M. Debranch, Benjamin F. Montgomery. Wounded: Pvts. Charles W. Campbell, left shoulder, severe; William J. Cantwell, foot, slight; John W. Hogan, left hip, slight; Frances E. Blossman, breast, slight; John J. Knopp, right shoulder, slight; John W. Marsh, left leg, amputated; Robert Martin, groin, severe; William C. McCann, thigh, mortal; Patrick C. McKee, side, slight; John L. Ruddell, left foot, slight; Peter Seery, left hip, slight; Gustavus A. Schneider, shoulder, slight; Simpson L. Sherrell, groin, severe; William F. Shott, head, slight; William E. Stanton, left knee, severe. Missing: Pvt. George Kell.

Co. B, "Lone Star Rifles"—Lt. William C. Burrus, commanding. Killed: Pvt. Benjamin Reiger. Wounded: Cpl. Victor Pela, foot, slight; Pvts. George G. Gardenhire, seven wounds, blinded in the left eye; Alexander M. McDonald, hip, slight; Alvarado Steele, right shoulder, severe; William M. Wilder, illness.

Co. C—Capt. William R. Shannon, commanding. Killed: Cpl. John M. Norfleet. Wounded: Pvts. John B. Landry, hand and body, severe; John H. McPherson, hip, slight; Henry B. Batling, thigh, severe.

Co. D, "Matagorda Coast Guards"—Capt. James Selkirk, commanding. Killed: none. Wounded: 1st Lt. Greenberry Stewart, hip, slight; Sgt. Charles W. Waldeman, leg, slight; Pvt. Thomas C. Nye, hand, slight.

Co. E—Capt. Jackson L. Leonard, commanding. Killed: Pvts. Dandridge Anderson, Sylvester R. Cochran, Alexander Ochiltree, Jephthah N. White. Wounded: Sgt. William R. Vickers, left arm, slight; Cpl. Lemuel T. Newton, head, slight; Cpl. Thomas J. Norrell, left shoulder, slight; Cpl. Adam Sanders, right hip, severe; Pvts. James W. Burrow, right, severe; Thomas M. Caldwell, left shoulder, severe; William J. Clarke, left shoulder; Hardy D. Cox, right thigh, severe; John R. Donnegan, back, severe; James T. Echols, left thigh, severe; Rodom A. Ensey, side, slight; William H. Ensey, left thigh, slight; Francis Followell, right shoulder, severe; James A. Hargas, face and hand; John W. Hayfield, chest, slight; Burlin A. Hoke, right hand, slight; Levi Maddox, face, slight; John C. McKnight, slight; William H. Owens, face, severe; Edward G. Rea, side and head, slight; Edward Thompson, severe; William O. Vannoy, face, severe. Missing: Pvts. Samuel G. Criner, Benjamin F. Stewart.

Co. F, "Bell County Invincibles"—Lt. Samuel H. Atkins, commanding. Killed: Pvt. Cyrus A. Harper. Wounded: Lt. James S. Perry, leg, slight; Sgt. Christopher H. F. Wood, arm, slight; Pvts. Nathan T. Holt, arm, slight; Perry A. Hurley, arm, slight; Joseph Pace, foot, slight; William J. Walker, mortal; Edward D. Wheeler, leg, slight. Missing: Sgt. Abner Steele, Cpl. Cornelius M. Atwood, Pvts. Elson G. Bennett, Henry D. Greer, P. R. Robinson, James Valentine, Thomas M. Vivian.

Co. G, "Travis Rifles"—Capt. Rhodes Fisher, commanding. Killed: Pvt. Benoni C. Robertson. Wounded: Pvts. Benjamin M. Cotton, leg, slight; James W. F. Hamilton, hand, slight; Hendrix P. Harris, leg, slight; Jacob Kelly; Hugh M. McClure, hand, slight; William J. Oliphant, slight. Missing: Pvts. Charles W. Bradford, Robert R. Crozier, Fredrick Espine, Thomas B. Guthrie, J. C. Smith, George W. Williams, A. Jephta Wilson.

Co. H—Lt. Robert B. Harvey, commanding. Killed: Lt. Robert B. Harvey, Cpl. William R. Deane, Pvts. Frank Collier, James P. S. Fine, George W. Simmons. Wounded: Sgt. George Johnson, arm, slight; Sgt. John Powers, arm, severe; Cpl. John W. Kay, arm, slight; Cpl. John W. Scott, arm, slight; Cpl. Robert S. Scott, head and knee, serious; Pvts. William Brewer, arm, severe; John Burns, leg, slight; S. F. Cocke, face, slight; Alexander G. Cromwell, finger, slight; Jasper L. Draper, head, slight; J. L. Jones, face, slight; Martin A. Jones, shoulder, severe; Marion Sanchez, shoulder, severe; Patterson S. Lenihen, thigh, severe; William P. Linkenhoker, side, slight; Thomas L. Napier, head and hand, slight; Solomon H. Robinson, head, slight; James D. Smith, leg, slight; Joseph Prowse, head and thigh, slight; Henri M. Sessions, head, slight; Allen Turley, head, slight; George W. Turley, thigh, slight; Asa Williamson, neck, slight; George W. Wilson, knee, slight. Missing: Cpl. John Cox, Pvts. John Bishop, Joseph Fulfer, Albert Lindsay.

Co. I—John A. Formwalt, commanding. Killed: none. Wounded: Pvts. Asa Chambers, face, slight; J. W. Taylor, arm, slight; Samuel Vanover, arm, slight; Henry Preston Vickers, right arm, amputated; Spencer Wright, face, slight. Missing: Sgt. William M. Evans, Pvts. John Adams, Wiley P. Alexander, William M. Hamby.

Co. K, "The Alamo Rifles"—Capt. Mathew M. Houston, commanding. Killed: Pvts. Anderson W. Bell, Noah Snider. Wounded: Pvts. Adam Braden; Morgan J. Milton; James M. N. Roberson, severe; Dedlef Schlunz, slight. Missing: Sgt. William R. McCutchen, Sgt. Thomas Copeland, Cpl. Uriah Coots, Pvts. Thomas L. Doyle, Alexander Duby, Henry W. Embry, William E. Morris.

Nutt's company—Capt. Leroy M. Nutt, commanding. Killed: none. Wounded: Pvts. R. P. Benge of the Rangers, Dave Hein of Nutt's company, G. W. Herring and M. J. Dupree of Denson's company. Missing: Pvts. Frank Cain, John Beard, A. H. Anderson, J. A. Willingham (adjutant).[3]

17th-18th-24th-25th Texas Cavalry, dismounted—Col. Frederick C. Wilkes, commanding.

Field and staff—Wounded: Col. Frederick C. Wilkes, leg, slight; Lt. Col. John T. Coit, slight.

Co. A—Lt. William W. Chorn, commanding. Killed: none. Wounded: Lt. Samuel A. Cook (17th); Cpl. James P. Mims (17th); Pvts. James R. Boisseau (17th); Howell Lewis (17th); Larkin W. Longshore (17th); Pinckney Elliott (17th); William Wells (17th); William C. Boatright (18th); Samuel T. Benge (18th); Francis M. Huffman (18th); J. W. Brownlow (24th); Henry Dean (24th); G. B. Kenney (24th); James M. Markley (25th), disabled; Phillip Thews (25th).

Co. B—Capt. Joshua P. Spears, commanding. Killed: Sgt. John H. Chambers (24th), Pvts. J. C. Smith (17th), John H. Chambers (18th),

3 *Galveston Weekly News*, Nov. 11, 1863; *Corpus Christi Caller-Times*, June 26, 1936.

Charles A. Fowler (24th), Daniel L. Chambers (24th). Wounded: Sgt. Charles Vorin (18th); Cpl. Michael M. McMahan (18th), slight; Pvts. Leonard Black (18th), slight; R. M. Castleman (18th), side, serious; Alfred M. Fore (18th), slight; John Jackson (18th), slight; P. Marehern (18th), thigh, severe; Nathan J. Moore (18th), slight; Gobe L. Page (18th), thigh, leg amputated; William M. Summers (18th), teeth and shoulder, slight; Lt. John M. Lewis (24th), breast, slight; Sgt. John D. G. Whitten (24th), hand, slight; Pvt. Adam M. King (24th), slight; Sgt. F. R. Hillyer (25th); Cpl. W. N. B. Lewis (25th), arm amputated; Pvts. J. K. Jones (25th), groin, slight; M. W. Jordan (25th), arm amputated; J. M. Kerr (25th), slight (mortally wounded at Ringgold Nov. 27). Missing: Pvt. John T. Westmoreland (24th).

Co. C—Capt. Charles Cupples, commanding. Killed: Capt. Charles Cupples (24th); Sgt. Thomas F. Moore (24th); Pvt. Mordecai A. Bryan (24th). Wounded: Lt. Rice W. Durrett (18th); Cpl. Henry Burkett (18th), slight; Pvts. Lafayette Davis (18th), slight; Jesse Jones (18th); Thomas B. Lanham (18th); Riley T. Little (18th), mortal; Jesse Moon (18th), slight; William Myers (18th), mortal; John M. Sheppard (18th), slight; John M. Summers (18th), severe; Sgt. Christopher T. Hill (24th); Pvts. Samuel L. Chambliss (24th); Ferdinand A. Arnim (Arman) (24th), severe; William E. Eckhardt (24th), foot, severe; William Elson (24th); William S. Friar (24th); C. Lanzeria (24th); William Lawhorn (24th); R. L. McCauley (24th); Jerry D. McFarland (24th); John F. Powell (24th), slight; James B. Rankin (24th); Bugler Ferdinand Zedler (24th).

Co. D—Capt. John F. Matthews, commanding. Killed: Sgt. Newton Allen (24th); Pvts. Leander D. Adair (24th); Thomas J. Short (24th); Thomas A. Elliott (24th). Wounded: Pvts. Joel D. Blair (18th); Wiley W. Foster (18th), slight; Samuel D. Wheat (18th), head, slight; Harvey G. Caruth (24th), shoulder, slight; William H. Cole (25th); James R. Deggs (24th), arm; Frederick A. Grote (24th), leg, slight; A. Rocher (24th), arm, slight; Greenberry B. Springer (24th), hand amputated; Cpl. Jesse W. Barfield (25th); Pvts. Robert E. Grantland (25th); William B. Sessions (25th), leg amputated, mortal; August A. Shultz (25th).

Co. E—Capt. William M. Allison, commanding. Killed: Sgt. F. Y. Hodge (25th); 2nd Sgt. Joseph Delay (25th). Wounded: Capt. William M. Allison, face and right shoulder, severe; Lt. William F. T. Barnett (18th), leg, slight; 1st Sgt. William H. Drake (18th), shoulder, slight; Cpl. Wyatt Harmon (18th), arm, slight; Pvts. Oliver P. Bowser (18th), right knee, severe; Jasper Byrd (18th), right arm amputated; James Collins (18th), arm amputated; Bayley B. Fowler (18th), thigh, severe; J. Johnson (18th), head, slight; Isaac Sparks (18th), leg, slight; William H. Pettitt (18th), arm, slight; Simon Williams (24th), hand shot off; James E. Wooldridge (24th), face, severe; 2nd Lt. Wesley J. Millican (25th), slight; Sgt. Willis L. Hunter (25th), arm, slight; Pvts. George Hempfling (25th), leg, slight; Marvey D. D. Wilson (25th), hand, slight. Deserted: Pvts. Jacob Clark (24th), Jehu H. Moore (24th).

Co. F—Capt. William H. Perry, commanding. Killed: Cpl. Ward Murray (18th); Pvts. W. Latterner (Latimer) (24th); Thomas McGee (24th). Wounded: 1st Sgt. William Clifton (18th), slight; Sgt. John Boyd (18th), severe; Pvts. Albert J. Boyce (18th), slight; William Boyce (18th), severe; William W. Gibson (18th), slight; Cpl. Thomas Brewer (18th), slight; David L. Hall (18th), slight; Green B. Lackey (18th), severe; John A. McCrocklin (18th), slight; Cpl. William W. Pentecost (24th), slight; Pvts. Hendry T. Compton (24th), slight; A. H. Foster (24th), slight; Dudley Gibson (24th), slight; Henry McConnell (24th), slight; Thomas H. B. Morris (24th), severe; Thomas Phillips (24th), slight; Cpl. Thomas J. Britton (25th), severe; Cpl. John Richardson (25th), slight; Louis Ulrich (25th), arm amputated.

Co. G—Lt. William B. Brown, commanding. Killed: Pvts. Addison Gibbs (18th); Jacob L. Sigler (18th); E. L. M. Jennings (24th); John C. Beaty (24th); William Caddell (24th); Irby Lewis (24th); Christian Furr (25th); J. R. Tanner (25th). Wounded: Lt. William A. Harrison (17th); Pvts. Frank South (17th); Thomas J. Craft (18th), slight; Boone Daugherty (18th); James Gibbs (18th), mortal; Edward A. Long (18th); William P. Loving (18th); J. J. W. Mahan (18th); John Martin (18th); John W. McCaslin (18th), mortal; Orderly Sgt. Hiram Bane (24th), slight; Pvts. James Snelling (24th), slight; Lt. J. R. Hardison (25th); Pvt. Richard Williams (25th).

Co. H—Capt. John R. Proudfoot, commanding. Killed: Pvt. Samuel T. M. Hutchison (24th); Pvt. Everett N. Adams (25th); Pvt. Albert L. Brown (25th). Wounded: Cpl. Gustavus A. Treadwell (17th), slight; Pvt. Benjamin Coleman (17th), slight; John C. Bates (24th), thigh, slight; Pvts. John Henry Bringhurst (24th), shoulder, severe; Edward Chipman Cullen (24th), foot, slight; Daniel Thomas Jones (24th), hand, slight; John Asbury Poe (24th), head, slight; Hiram Runnels Rogers (24th), head, slight; John Templeton (24th), hip, severe; Capt. John R. Proudfoot (25th), grapeshot to foot, slight; W. Augustus "Gus" Tompkins (25th), left arm, flesh wound; Sgt. Oscar DeBlanc (25th), arm, slight; Pvts. Henry S. Byerly (25th), hand, slight; Holmes S. Cowart (25th), slight; L. Ernest Lacour (25th), head, severe; Sgt. Jule J. Lacour (25th), thigh, slight; Pvts. Louis R. Longtoff (25th), back, slight; Alfred Richard (25th), slight; Robert P. Shelby (25th), slight; William Simpson (25th), slight.

Co. I—1st Sgt. Harrison Eberhart, commanding. Killed: 1st Sgt. Harrison Eberhart (17th), Cpl. Joseph E. Phipps (18th). Wounded: Pvt. Oliver H. P. Thomas (17th); Pvt. Joel H. Myers (17th); Pvt. William F. Lawrence (17th); Pvt. James N. Orr (18th); Sgt. Thomas J. Lovitt (18th); Pvt. Franklin Lovett (18th); Sgt. F. E. Martin (24th); Pvt. Charles D. Maynard (25th), leg, severe.

Co. K—Lt. F. M. Bell, commanding. Killed: none. Wounded: Pvts. Matthew F. Graham (17th), arm and leg, slight; James Blakely (18th), right elbow; William W. Clay (18th), thigh, slight; George S. Collins (18th), calf, severe; Nathan Howard (18th), head and arm, the latter amputated, mortal; Erastus M. Moorehead (18th), head, slight; John M. Pate (18th), shoulder, severe; William Simms (18th), leg, slight; Bernard Buschen (25th), calf, severe; Thomas Y. Childress (25th), leg, slight; F. M. Raley (25th), leg, severe; D. W. Wyche (25th), thigh, slight.

Ector's Brigade

General staff. Wounded: Brig. Gen. Matthew D. Ector, three times, including in his arm, slight; Capt. Constantine B. "Buck" Kilmore (assistant adjutant general), thigh, severe; Lt. Henry Milton Lane (aide-de-camp), wrist, slight; Sgt. Maj. J. W. Kelly, slight.

9th Texas—Col. William H. Young, commanding.

Field and staff. Wounded: Col. William Hugh Young, left breast, severe; Sgt. Maj. Charles W. Moore, left foot, severe.

Co. A—Capt. William H. H. Long, commanding. Killed: none. Wounded: Capt. William H. H. Long, groin, slight; Pvts. Thomas J. Calloway, thigh, slight; Frank G. Evans, thigh, slight. Missing: Pvts. Harrison Thurmond, Joseph Penall.

Co. B—Lt. George W. Thompson, commanding. Killed: none. Wounded: Lt. George W. Thompson, hand, severe; 1st Sgt. John M. Wallace, hip, slight; Sgt. Charles E. Dale; Cpl. Redding Bass, foot, slight, captured, died at Camp Douglas July 1864; Pvt. Newton Liles, shoulder, severe. Missing: Pvts. William R. Harris, Leander K. Masters, Martin Van Buren Gentry.

Co. C—Capt. Leander F. Ely, commanding. Killed: Lt. Samuel C. Fitch. Wounded: Pvts. Moses J. Chapin, arm, slight; Daniel Fallis, leg, severe; James T. Garrison, leg, severe; John C. McLean, leg and hips, severe; David R. Reynolds, leg, slight.

Co. D—Capt. James H. McReynolds, commanding. Killed: none. Wounded: Sgt. W. B. Willis, foot, slight; Pvts. William F. Fowler, hand and thigh, slight; Hugh F. Freeman, breast, slight; Jesse M. Hays, both legs, severe; Thomas J. Justice, thigh, slight; Andrew J. Moulton, thigh, slight; J. L. Penley, head, slight; Arthur C. Reynolds, shoulder, slight; C. H. Smith, arm, slight. Missing: Pvts. J. W. M. Jones, John E. Williams.

Co. E—Lt. Thomas H. Ligon, commanding. Killed: Pvt. William R. Bruce. Wounded: Pvt. John N. Harris, foot, severe. Missing: 1st Sgt. John R. Miller.

Co. F—Lt. John E. Agee, commanding. Killed: none. Wounded: Lt. John E. Agee, breast and thigh, slight; Pvts. Warren Clayton, shoulder, severe; Moses W. Houston, head, severe; Thomas J. Vansickle, finger, slight.

Co. G—Lt. A. L. Hamilton, commanding. Killed: Lt. A. L. Hamilton. Wounded: Lt. James B. Ferrell, foot, slight. Missing: Pvts. Peter W. Conner, Nebo Grizzle.

Co. H—Capt. George W. Daniels, commanding. Killed: none. Wounded: Cpl. Moses P. Davis, arm, severe. Wounded: Pvts. J. R. Bush, grapeshot wound to thigh, disabled; John Mitchell, hand, slight. Missing: Pvts. John S. Beaty, William M. Yates.

Co. I—Capt. Robert M. Board, commanding. Killed: Pvts. J. M. Burns, J. M. Harris. Wounded: Pvts. Solomon Dobson, finger, slight; John W. H. Whisenant, neck, slight. Missing: Pvts. Jefferson Day, John F. Odell.

Co. K—Capt. D. H. Ridley, commanding. Killed: Pvt. B. R. Worthingham. Wounded: Capt. D. H. Ridley, thigh, severe; Sgt. James H. Harmon, thigh; Pvt. Benjamin S. Roland, ankle. Missing: Lt. George W. Bedford; Cpl. William H. Owens; Pvt. George I. Terrell.

10th Texas Cavalry, dismounted, Lt. Col. Cullen Redwine Earp, commanding.

Field and staff. Killed: Assistant Surgeon Marshall C. Hillyard. Wounded: Adjutant W. J. Sparks, arm, slight; Sgt. Maj. J. W. Kelly, mouth, severe.

Co. A—Capt. J. J. T. Wright, commanding. Killed: Pvt. Thomas W. Greene, Cpl. James W. McMillan. Wounded: Capt. J. J. T. Wright, slight; Cpl. A. J. Waldrip, arm, mortal; Bugler R. H. Noyes, leg; Pvts. Z. R. Finley; A. A. McBride; J. M. Shipp, arm, disabled. Missing: Pvts. J. R. Butler, William L. Essary, S. C. White.

Co. B, "Wood County Rebels"—Capt. Joseph W. Cannon, commanding. Killed: none. Wounded: Capt. Joseph W. Cannon, mortal; Lt. John W. Huggins, breast, mortal; Sgt. John W. Brown, slight; Sgt. J. L. Shamburger, slight; Cpl. John D. Garrett, thigh; Pvts. J. David Attaway, foot, slight; J. S. Brown, arm, slight; William F. Hanson, slight; Robert A. Lindley, severe; F. M. Rogers, mortal. Missing: Pvts. Franklin L. King, taken prisoner, died in Chattanooga; C. J. Millsaps.

Co. C—Capt. William G. McGee, commanding. Killed: Pvts. Archibald Hamilton, John D. Neal (32nd Texas Cavalry temporary color-bearer), Cullen C. Weir. Wounded: Capt. William G. McGee, knee, slight; Sgt. E. S. Phillips, leg, slight; Pvts. John B. Hilliard, leg, slight; John B. Wright, hand, severe. Missing: Pvts. John W. Hicks, John J. Spratt.

Co. D—Capt. Richard W. Smith, commanding. Killed: none. Wounded: Capt. Richard W. Smith, face, severe; Sgt. William C. Calvert, loins, severe; Pvts. W. L. Goss, leg, slight; H. Morris, thigh, slight; Richard William Smith, severe; Samuel T. Wilson, face, severe. Missing: Pvt. Elisha Schrum.

Co. E, "Bully Rocks"—Lt. W. Frank Young, commanding. Killed: none. Wounded: Lt. W. Frank Young, slight; Sgt. Wade B. Turner, right leg amputated; Cpl. Joel Eaton, slight; Pvts. John Wesley Davis, thigh, severe, captured but returned through the lines; William Harvey, head, slight; Anderson Kelly, leg, severe; Lewis Hanack; William J. Matthews, mortal; William D. Melton, knee, disabled; Elijah H. Oliver, ankle, disabled; Ira John Spence, slight. Missing: Pvts. David T. Melton, James Terry.

Co. F—Capt. Augustus James Booty, commanding. Killed: Pvts. Jabel W. Shivers, J. R. Roland. Wounded: Capt. A. J. Booty, thigh, disabled; Sgt. James N. Gray, slight, transferred Nov. 10, 1863, to 3rd Texas Cavalry; Sgt. Alexander C. Hilliard, hip, slight; Pvts. Smith L. Fite, leg, severe; W. H. Hill; William A. McClanahan; J. C. Thompson; Conrad H. Wall, mortal. Missing: Pvts. W. V. Cogswell, prisoner, died at Camp Douglas in Chicago, November 1863; J. M. Murphy.

Co. G, "Texas Troopers"—Lt. George W. Trammell Jr., commanding. Killed: Sgt. Baylis W. Lay. Wounded: Lt. Elijah "Liege" Phillips; Lt. George W. Trammell Jr., slight; Sgt. Joseph F. Becton, leg, slight; Sgt. Charles A. Birdwell, leg, severe; Cpl. James H. Gatlin, slight; Ensign Reuben Goforth, leg; Pvts. James Anderson, arm amputated; Edward

Barthold, slight; Stokely D. Hutchins, arm, slight; Robert B. Irwin, knee; John A. Lee, hip, severe; Columbus H. Monk; William H. Smith; James M. Watson, severe. Missing: Sgt. William Butler, Pvt. James H. Wade.

Co. H, "Warriors"—Lt. Richard S. Lyles, commanding. Killed: none. Wounded: Lt. Richard S. Lyles, slight; Cpl. James T. Hatton, heel, slight; Cpl. A. J. Odom, slight; Pvts. Thomas H. Benton, hand, slight; W. G. Harper, leg broken, mortal; D. M. McBride, slight; E. H. Smith, slight. Missing: Pvts. William A. Allen, Peyton Smith.

Co. I, "Cherokee Cavalry"—Capt. J. F. M. Hall, commanding. Killed: Cpl. James A. Holmes. Wounded: Capt. J. F. M. Hall, arm, slight; Lt. James A. Spaulding, slight; Cpl. Joseph M. Francis, hip, severe; Pvts. Tandy Ball, foot, severe; James S. Loden, leg, severe; James W. Scurlock, back, severe; F. W. Welch, slight. Missing: Sgt. John Allen Templeton, Pvts. John H. Burks, George T. Egbert, Cornelius G. Odom, Moses Walters.

Co. K—Capt. Quentin K. Gibson, commanding. Killed: none. Wounded: Capt. Quentin K. Gibson, slight; Cpl. J. D. W. Spear, slight; Cpl. L. L. Speer, slight; Pvt. William T. Coker. Missing: Pvts. William Riley Glenn (wounded), John N. Slimmer, Edward Wooten.

14th Texas Cavalry, dismounted—Col. John L. Camp, commanding.

Field and staff. Wounded: Col. John L. Camp, leg, severe; Maj. J. H. Garrison, slight; Lt. J. T. Wells (acting adjutant), slight.

Co. A—Capt. S. V. Lusk, commanding. Killed: Cpl. James H. McCarty. Wounded: Sgt. William Burchfield, slight; Pvt. E. H. Egan, slight. Missing: Cpl. William Donahue, Pvts. William S. Fulton, James A. Hopkins (died at Camp Douglas, Oct. 21, 1864), Charles R. Huff, Charles T. Rathbone.

Co. B—Lt. Josiah T. Tunnell, commanding. Killed: none. Wounded: Lt. Josiah T. Tunnell, slight; Pvts. Hewlett S. Calhoun; G. G. Cole, slight;

Anderson Leadford, severe; Solomon T. Lanham; Absalom Stephenson, slight; William B. Tunnell, severe.

Co. C—Lt. Daniel Haynes, commanding. Killed: Pvt. William Gregg. Wounded: Cpl. James A. Hart, severe; Pvts. James R. Boatman, severe; James Grigsby, severe; Thomas A. Latimore, severe; John E. Myrick, severe; Crue S. Russell, severe; William W. Youngblood, severe. Missing: Pvts. John Hale, John J. Patterson.

Co. D—Capt. James A. Howze, commanding. Killed: Sgt. James C. Hudson, Pvt. William Friddle. Wounded: Lt. C. C. Doyle, slight; Sgt. J. L. Hall, slight; Pvt. C. H. Bailey, slight; Pvts. R. H. Gary, severe; W. O. Nicholson, slight; J. R. Russell, slight; H. H. Shadden, slight; Jones Williams. Missing: Pvts. Henry Clay Horton (wounded), Zachariah W. Robinson.

Co. E—Capt. Robert H. Harkey, commanding. Killed: Sgt. Joel S. Irvin, Pvt. Rufus Ashberry. Wounded: Pvt. Othello D. Richardson, severe. Missing: Pvt. James Cooper (wounded).

Co. F—Capt. Lem Purdy, commanding. Killed: Pvt. James F. Campbell. Wounded: Cpl. James Sheegog, severe; Pvts. George W. Box, slight; William Spencer, leg, severe; Nathaniel Greenberry Lackey, severe. Missing: Pvts. Caleb S. Fuller (died at Camp Douglas May 31, 1864), William M. Groves, Martin M. Harkins (died at Camp Douglas, December 17, 1863), Daniel McKay.

Co. G—Capt. Alexander M. Sanford, commanding. Killed: Pvts. James "Jimmie" Arnold, Brice M. Lynch. Wounded: Sgt. Shelton W. Gorum, severe (taken prisoner and paroled); Sgt. Paul Potts, mortal. Missing: Capt. Alexander M. Sanford; Sgt. John A. P. Hill; Cpl. John L. Pierce; Pvts. Sterling M. Price, William L. Taylor (wounded and captured).

Co. H—Capt. Claiborne W. Merchant, commanding. Killed: none. Wounded: Sgt. George W. Thompkins, slight; Sgt. Marion V. Wisdom, severe; Pvts. Beverly Case, slight; Daniel Crites, slight; Uriah C. Harless, slight; James L. McLain, slight; William E. O'Hair, mortal; William Welch, slight. Missing: Sgt. Charles T. Clayton, Sgt. William Wills.

Co. I—Capt. Stephen C. Ragan, commanding. Killed: none. Wounded: Lt. W. L. Russell, severe; Cpl. A. P. Grimsley, slight; Pvts. W. L. Bearden, slight; O. D. Bell, slight; James W. Linn, slight; D. Morris, slight; Silas Poe, slight; Jefferson Rolland, severe; A. Shelton, slight. Missing: Cpl. Peter H. Hopson, Pvts. George W. Burke (died at Camp Douglas, Oct. 19, 1863), Ludwick Holt, John Polvado.

Co. K—Killed: Pvt. William W. Gaston.

32nd Texas Cavalry, dismounted—Col. Julius A. Andrews, commanding.

Field and staff. Killed: none. Wounded: Col. Julius A. Andrews, thigh, severe; Adjutant George M. Lindsay, hip, severe.

Co. A—Killed: Pvts. D. Willoughby Howard, Solomon Simpson. Wounded: Lt. Robert H. Hays, head, slight; Pvts. E. T. Anderson, leg, slight; George W. Crabtree, arm, slight; Andrew J. Fanning, leg, slight; Henry C. Hamilton, both thighs, slight; W. F. Jolly, leg, slight; George A. Watson, head, slight. Missing: Lewis W. Traylor.

Co. B—Killed: Lt. Luther A. Williams, Cpl. D. R. D'Spain, Sgt. E. D. Posey. Wounded: Lt. H. H. Garrison, back, slight; Lt. William H. Vaden, foot and knee, slight; Pvts. J. M. Ashcroft, thigh, slight; L. S. Midget, severe; L. A. Johnston, hip, slight; S. F. Rowe, leg, slight; M. L. Wolf, knee, slight. Missing: John C. Hill, Ephraim Marion Patrick.

Co. C—Killed: none. Wounded: Capt. Elijah D. Gayden, arm, slight; Sgt. T. R. Friddle, thigh, slight; Pvts. John Smith, knee, slight; N. C. Williams, knee, slight. Missing: John C. Cook, Nathaniel R. Hillin, J. Thomas Merchant, John Sanders.

Co. D—Killed: Sgt. Robert H. Huling, Pvt. William C. Lyster. Wounded: Capt. H. E. E. Lyon, leg, severe; Lt. H. W. Crawford, leg, severe; J. H. Mathews, shoulder, severe; J. R. Paul, ankle, severe; J. A. Williams, arm and side, severe; Pvts. E. L. Anderson, hip, slight; James R. Mounce, abdomen and hip, slight; J. R. Taylor, side, slight; J. C. Wylie, shoulder and hip, slight. Missing: Pvts. Amos Beam, Thomas J. Elder (died Nov. 17, 1863, at Camp Douglas), James M. Harmon, Columbus C. Payne, Samuel B. McGill, Thomas B. McGill.

Co. E—Killed: Cpl. W. D. Oldfield. Wounded: Lt. E. A. Estes, severe; Sgt. George T. Johnson, finger off, slight; Pvt. Philip N. Mabes, foot, slight. Missing: Pvts. John W. Godsby, Robert H. Tisdale.

Co. G—Killed: none. Wounded: Lt. H. H. Hayes, arm and breast, severe; Cpl. Nehemiah Williams, leg, severe; Pvts. Coleman E. Burns, shoulder, slight; George W. James, leg, slight; John W. Jones, Jr., neck, severe; Napoleon B. Littlejohn, ankle, severe; James W. McClure, leg, mortal; W. T. Nixon, side, slight; Robert P. Roland, breast, severe; Samuel E. Smart, leg, slight; George W. Wells, breast, slight; Henry Wells, left arm, slight. Missing: Pvts. Edward C. Cavin, Dennis C. Crosby, Thomas M. Griffie, William W. Johnson, William R. Long.

Co. H—Killed: none. Wounded: Lt. Norfleet Smith, knee, slight; Sgt. James A. Moore, hip, slight; Cpl. Marshall Smith, thigh, mortal; Pvts. John Burns, thigh, slight; James Riley Tidwell, thigh, slight; William H. Walker, leg, slight; R. Wilburn, arm, slight. Missing: Cpl. Jerome B. Barkman, Pvts. Gillespie, Solomon D. Power, Benjamin W. Walker.

Co. I—Killed: Sgt. James M. Skelton, Pvts. R. T. Barnes, J. R. Brown, A. G. Gary. Wounded: J. M. Fitzgerald, hand, slight; L. W. Garrett, arm and side, severe; Robert C. Graves, elbow, arm amputated; Francis M. Lee, thigh, slight. Missing: Eli Patton.

Co. K—Killed: none. Wounded: Lt. James C. Todd, thigh, slight; Sgt. William M. Dunn, foot; Sgt. J. A. Ferguson, breast; Cpl. J. G. McCown, elbow; Pvts. J. A. J. Goode, hip and arm; William Wingo, thigh. Missing: Pvts. Austin Bush, William A. J. Chesser, Thomas S. Ellington, William B. Gholston, Samuel Gray, George Hughes, Thomas P. Hurt, Thomas W. Kearney, William Lorance, Hiram C. McPherson.

Gregg's Brigade

7th Texas—Col. Hiram B. Granbury, Maj. Khleber M. Van Zandt, commanding.

Field and staff. Killed: none. Wounded: Col. Hiram B. Granbury, Sgt. Maj. Dixon B. Hall.

Co. A—Killed: none. Wounded: Lt. J. Sam Norvell, Sgt. Martin V. Abernathy, Sgt. N. L. Roberts, Cpl. William A. Gill, Cpl. J. F. Woods, Pvts. Allen H. Bryan; Franklin M. Caldwell, severe; John L. Cantrell; Thomas J. Harrison; M. M. Leonard.

Co. B—Killed: Sgt. David Arden, Sgt. John T. Gillespie, Pvts. Frank Ford, Peter W. Lansdale. Wounded: Lt. Adam H. Appleton, Sgt. H. H. "Tipp" Johnson, Cpl. William H. Gillespie, Pvts. William B. Derrick, John W. Duffey, R. M. Earp, James A. George, George W. Henry, Alfred H. Howard, William B. Lewis, Elias M. Stone.

Co. C—Killed: Sgt. William P. Sanders. Wounded: Lt. William C. Bush; Sgt. James F. Henderson; Sgt. James K. Fisher; Pvts. W. A. Atkins; A. J. Davidson; Edward J. Guthrie; Downey H. Rose; Daniel Donell, severe.

Co. D, "Bass Grays"—Killed: Sgt. William P. Saunders. Wounded: William Surry Thompson; Joseph P. Alford, left leg amputated; James M. Duncan; Jesse Hall; Felix H. Johnson, severe; William Mattox, severe; Henry Y. Mills; Marcus D. Peaks; Henry C. Rain, leg amputated; Lee Sanders; Howell Tervis, slight.

Co. E—Killed: Pvts. James R. Leadbetter, W. J. Garner. Wounded: Lt. P. F. Moody; Sgt. Thomas J. Alvis; Sgt. James M. Williams; Pvts. A. Y. B. Atwood, slight; John Burleson; G. Jackson; Benjamin F. Mims; Charles J. Purtell; Robert E. Steele, slight.

Co. F, "Lone Star Greys"—Company disbanded in May 1863. Most of the men transferred to Company A.

Co. G, "Freestone Freemen"—Wounded: Sgt. Leroy F. Moody; John T. Balch, severe; S. C. Crenshaw, Robert Holt, W. H. Hollingsworth.

Co. H, "Texas Invincibles"—Killed: John Frazier. Wounded: Sgt. Julian S. Foscue; Sgt. James K. Rush, slight; Cpl. William T. Clark, severe; Pvts. James H. Clark; Charles J. Brazeale; Preston Henderson; Charles W. Powell, severe; H. J. C. Rogers; Valentine Russell; C. W. Wells, slight.

Co. I, "Sabine Greys"—Killed: none. Wounded: Sgt. L. Montgomery Keener; Pvts. Robert F. Land; T. Riley Mathews; James E. McDavid, severe; R. Scott Montgomery; Williams H. Williamson.

Co. K—Killed: Pvt. J. L. Smith. Wounded: Capt. William L. Coppedge; Pvts. Richard H. Clauswell, slight; John C. Colley, severe; J. M. Hastings, severe; William T. Hooks, severe; George W. Hoot, slight; P. Jarrett, severe; Jefferson Mosely, severe; William H. Reid, severe; George W. Robinson, slight.

Harrison's Brigade

8th Texas Cavalry (Terry's Texas Rangers)—Lt. Col. Gustave Cook, commanding.

Co. A—Killed: none. Wounded: none.

Co. B—Killed: none. Wounded: Pvt. W. W. Echols, groin, severe.

Co. C—Killed: Pvt. M. Van Wright. Wounded: Sgt. A. D. Walker, shot through the ear; Pvt. William H. Drumgoole, both thighs, mortal; Pvts. James C. Kirkner, arm, slight; J. C. Latimer, thigh, severe.

Co. D—Killed: none. Wounded: Capt. Ferguson Kyle, elbow, slight; Pvt. Aaron J. Burleson, leg, slight.

Co. E—Killed: none. Wounded: Pvt. J. P. Caldwell, wrist, slight.

Co. F—Killed: none. Wounded: Pvts. Benjamin F. Burr, neck, severe; J. H. McCreary, bottom, slight.

Co. H—Killed: none. Wounded: Sgt. Addison Moore, nose, slight; Sgt. William P. A. Murray, knee, severe; Cpl. David S. Terry, chest, severe.

Co. I—Killed: none. Wounded: Pvt. W. H. Sadler, knee, severe; Pvt. A. G. Wood, foot, severe.

Douglas's Texas Battery—Capt. James P. Douglas, commanding: Killed: none. Wounded: one unidentified man disabled per Douglas's official report.

Chickamauga Wounded Who Died in Atlanta Hospitals September 23 to October 12, 1863

Thomas Churchwell, *Co. G, 4th Texas*; William E. O'Hair, *Co. H, 4th Texas*; Michael Pickett, *Co. F, 4th Texas*; H. H. Rowe, *Co. C, 5th Texas*; Alfred H. Howard, *Co. B, 7th Texas*; Henry C. Rain, *Co. A, 7th Texas*; A. L. Hamilton, *Co. C, 10th Texas*; J. A. Lee, *Co. G, 10th Texas*; James P. Stevens, *Co. B, 14th Texas Cavalry*; James Gibbs, *Co. G 17th–18th–24th–25th Texas Cavalry* (18th); James W. McClure, *Co. G, 32nd Texas Cavalry*.[4]

Texans Cited in the Confederate Congress 'Roll of Honor' for Chickamauga

6th–10th Texas–15th Texas Cavalry: Pvts. Henry E. Cox, James D. Smith, Robert Cosby.

4 *Houston Tri-Weekly Telegraph*, Nov. 16 and Oct. 21, 1863, and Dec. 1 and 22, 1863; *Memphis Appeal*, Oct. 10, 1863; *Atlanta Daily Intelligencer*, Sept. 27 and Oct. 1, 1863; *Galveston Weekly News*, Apr. 19, 1865, citing the *Chicago Journal; Paris* (TX) *News*, May 25, 1976; The *Democrat* (McKinney, TX), Nov. 21, 1901; *Dallas Morning News*, Sept. 30, 1901; and the CSRs for the respective regiments.

17th–18th–24th–25th Texas Cavalry: Sgt. W. R. Burleson, Sgt. Julian J. Lacoure, Pvt. David L. Hall.[5]

5 "The Civil War Centennial," *Belton* (TX) *Journal*, Feb. 6, 1964.

Bibliography

Primary Sources

Unpublished

Manuscript Collections

Baylor University, Waco, TX

Estes, Aaron Douglas. Family Papers

Chickamauga and Chattanooga National Military Park, Fort Oglethorpe, GA

Bassett, Robert H. Letters

Denson, N. C. Reminiscences

Dodd, Ephraim S. Diary

Franklin, B. I. Letters

Harlan, Isaiah. Letters

Lewis, John J. Correspondence

MacMurphey, G. I. Diary

Moody, L. F. Letters

Rice University, Houston, TX

Heartsill, William Williston. Journal

Sam Houston State University, Huntsville, TX

Smither, J. Mark. Letters

Texas Heritage Museum, Historical Research Center, Hill College, Hillsboro, TX

Bates, Jesse P. Letters

Berryman, Henry Waters. Letters

Fogle, Andrew J. Letters

Harlan, Isaiah. Letters

Hendrick, James Henry. Manuscript

Maloney, John Percy. Letters

Sims, Alfred C. Account
Smith, Miles Vance. Reminiscences
Tunnell, William B. Recollections
Watson, Henry. Letters
Williams, Watson Dugat. Letters
Worsham, Charles Samuel. Letters
Young, William G. Letters
Texas State Library and Archives Commission, Austin, TX
Oliphant, William J. Memoirs
Thomas Holder Collection, Weatherford, TX
Van Zandt, K. M. Letters
United States Army Heritage and Education Center, Carlisle, PA
Daffan, L. A. Autobiography
Giles, Val C. Papers
Foster, Samuel F. Diary
Sims, A. C. Recollections
University of North Carolina, Chapel Hill, NC
Stout, Samuel Hollingsworth. Papers
University of Texas, Dolph Briscoe Center for American History, Austin, TX
Giles, Annie B. Papers
Hanks, O. T. Reminiscences
Mills, Roger Q. Papers
Templeton, John A. Papers
University of Texas–San Antonio, C. Stanley Banks Collection, San Antonio, TX
Francis, II, Sidney J., "Dublin Plantation: History of a Texas Family," Typescript
Joskins, Joe (pen name of Robert Campbell), "A Sketch of Hood's Texas Brigade of the Virginia Army," Typescript

Published

Books

Anderson, Archer, *The Campaign and Battle of Chickamauga.* Richmond: William Ellis Jones, 1881.

Anderson, John Q., ed., *Campaigning with Parsons' Texas Cavalry Brigade, C.S.A.: The War Journal and Letters of the Four Orr Brothers, 12th Texas Cavalry*. Hillsboro, TX: Hill Junior College Press, 1967.

Blegen, Theodore C., ed., *The Civil War Letters of Hans Heg*. Northfield, MN: Norwegian-American Historical Association, 1936.

Bowser, O. P., "Notes on Granbury's Brigade," in *A Comprehensive History of Texas 1685 to 1897*, 2 vols. Dallas: William G. Scarff, 1898, vol. 2.

Coley, Julie Williams, ed., *J. K. Street Civil War Letters: 9th Texas Infantry from Paris, Lamar County, Texas*. Wichita Falls, TX: Amazon CreateSpace, 2010.

Collins, Robert M., *Chapters from the Unwritten History of the War Between the States: Or, The Incidents in the Life of a Confederate Soldier in Camp, on the March, in the Great Battles, and in Prison*. St. Louis, MO: Nixon-Jones Printing Company, 1893; reprinted Dayton, OH: Morningside Press, 1988.

Cutrer, Thomas W., ed., *Our Trust is in the God of Battles: The Civil War Letters of Robert Franklin Bunting, Chaplain, Terry's Texas Rangers*. Knoxville: University of Tennessee Press, 2006.

Douglas, James P., and Lucia Thompson Rutherford, ed., *Douglas's Texas Battery, CSA*. Tyler, TX: Smith County Historical Association, 1966.

Fletcher, William A., *Rebel Private: Front and Rear: Experiences and Observations from the Early Fifties through the Civil War*. Beaumont, TX: Press of the Greer Print, 1908.

Foster, Samuel T., and Norman B. Brown, ed., *One of Cleburne's Command: The Civil War Reminiscences and Diary of Capt. Samuel T. Foster, Granbury's Texas Brigade, C.S.A.* Austin: University of Texas Press, 1980.

Gallagher, Gary W., ed., *Fighting for the Confederacy: The Personal Recollections of General Edward Porter Alexander*. Chapel Hill: University of North Carolina Press, 1989.

Giles, Leonidis B., *Terry's Texas Rangers: The 8th Texas Cavalry in the Civil War*. Austin: Von Boeckmann-Jones, 1911.

Graber, Henry W., *The Life Record of H. W. Graber, A Terry Texas Ranger, 1861–1865*. Self-published, 1916; republished as *A Terry Texas Ranger*. Austin: State House Press, 1987.

Gracie, Archibald, *The Truth About Chickamauga*. Boston and New York: The Riverside Press Cambridge, 1911.

Hamilton, D. H. and W. H. Morrison, ed., *History of Company M First Texas Volunteer Infantry. Hood's Brigade, Longstreet's Corps, Army of the Confederate States of America*. Waco: W. M. Morrison, s. n., 1962.

Hanks, O. T., *History of Captain B. F. Benton's Company, Hood's Texas Brigade, 1861–1865*. Austin: W. M. Morrison, 1984.

Heartsill, William W., and Bell Irvin Wiley, ed., *Fourteen Hundred and 91 Days in the Confederate Army: A Journal Kept by W. W. Heartsill For Four Years, One Month and One Day.* Jackson, TN: McCowat-Mercer Press, 1953.

Hood, John Bell, *Advance and Retreat: Personal Experiences in the United States and Confederate States Armies.* New Orleans: Hood Orphan Memorial Fund, G. T. Beauregard, 1880.

Lasswell, Mary, ed., *Rags and Hope: The Recollections of Val C. Giles, Four Years with Hood's Brigade, Fourth Texas Infantry, 1861–1865.* New York: Coward-McCann, 1961.

McCaffrey, James M., ed., *Only a Private: A Texan Remembers the Civil War. The Memoirs of William J. Oliphant.* Houston: Halcyon Press, 2004.

McClure, Judy Watson, ed., *Confederate from East Texas: The Civil War Letters of James Monroe Watson.* Quanah, TX: Nortex Press, 1976.

Myres, Sandra L., ed., *Force Without Fanfare: The Autobiography of K. M. Van Zandt.* Fort Worth: Texas Christian University Press, 1995.

Parker, Eddy R., ed., *Touched by Fire: Letters from Company D, 5th Texas Infantry, Hood's Brigade, Army of Northern Virginia 1862–1865.* Hillsboro, TX: Hill College Press, 2000.

Polk, J. M., *Memories of the Lost Cause; and Ten Years in South America.* Austin, TX: s. n., 1905.

Polley, J. B., *Hood's Texas Brigade, Its Marches, Its Battles, and Its Achievements.* New York and Washington: The Neale Publishing Company, 1910.

———, *A Soldier's Letters to Charming Nellie.* New York and Washington: The Neale Publishing Company, 1908.

Power, Jr., Hugh E., *Texan at War: The Letter of Private James Henry Hendrick, Army of Northern Virginia.* Unpublished typescript, Texas Heritage Museum, Hill College, Hillsboro, TX, 1964.

Schadt, Stuart E., ed., *Letters Home 1861–1865: Charles and William Schadt.* Falls Church, VA: Bradley Stuart Books, 2015.

Skoch, George, and Mark W. Perkins, *Lone Star Confederate: A Gallant and Good Soldier of the Fifth Texas Infantry.* College Station: Texas A&M University Press, 2003.

Simpson, Harold B., *The Bugle Softly Blows: The Confederate Diary of Benjamin M. Seaton.* Waco: Texian Press, 1965.

Sorrel, G. Moxley, *Reflections of a Confederate Staff Officer.* New York and Washington: The Neale Publishing Co., 1905.

Spurlin, Charles D., *The Civil War Diary of Charles A. Leuschner.* Madison, WI: Eakin Press, 1992.

Stewart, J. W., "Proceedings of Granbury's Brigade," *Report of the Proceedings of the Various Associations of Ex-Confederates held at Dallas County, Texas August 6th, 7th, 8th and 9th, 1884*. Dallas: Dallas Herald Printing, 1884.

Tanner Stephen J., and E. Russell Tanner, compiler, *The Stephen Jennings Tanner Autobiography and Tanner Family Genealogy*. Boulder, CO: E. Russell Tanner, 1970.

Todd, George T., and Harold B. Simpson, ed., *First Texas Regiment*. Waco: Texian Press, 1963.

The War of the Rebellion: A Compilation of the Official Records of the Union and Confederate Armies, 70 volumes in 4 series. Washington, DC: United States Government Printing Office, 1880-1901.

West, John C., *A Texan in Search of a Fight: Civil War Diary and Letters of a Soldier in Hood's Texas Brigade*. Waco: J. S. Hill and Co., 1901.

Winkler, Mrs. A. V., *The Confederate Capital and Hood's Texas Brigade*. Austin: Eugene Von Boeckmann, 1894.

Yeary, Mamie, compiler, *Reminiscences of the Boys in Gray 1861–1865*. Dallas: Smith and Lamar, 1912.

Periodical Collections

Bailey, W., "The Star Company of Ector's Texas Brigade," *Confederate Veteran*, vol. 22, no. 9, September 1914.

Blackburn, J. K. P., "Reminiscences of the Terry Rangers," *The Southwestern Historical Quarterly*, vol. 22, July 1918.

Brooks, Tam, "In and Out of Prison," *Confederate Veteran,* November-December 1921, vol. 29. nos. 11-12.

Cutrer, Thomas W., ed., "'We Are Stern and Resolved': The Civil War Letters of John Wesley Rabb, Terry's Texas Rangers," *The Southwestern Historical Quarterly*, No. 91, October 1987.

Chicoine, Stephen, ed., "'?. . . Willing Never to Go in Another Fight': The Civil War Correspondence of Rufus King Felder of Chappell Hill," *The Southwestern Historical Quarterly*, vol. 106, July 2002-April 2003.

Cooke, Charles Alonza, "The Civil War Memories of Samuel Alonza Cooke," *The Southwestern Historical Quarterly*, vol. 74, July 1970 – April 1971.

Dodson, W. C., "Errors Concerning Ector's Brigade," *Confederate Veteran,* vol. 13, no. 10, October 1905.

Goodrich, John T., "Gregg's Brigade in the Battle of Chickamauga," *Confederate Veteran*, vol. 22, no. 6, June 1914.

Goggin, James M., "Chickamauga—A Reply to Major Sykes," *Southern Historical Society Papers*, vol. 12, no. 4, April 1884.

Hunter, J. T., "Hard Fighting Fourth Texas," *Confederate Veteran*, vol. 14, no. 1, January 1906.

Ikard, Robert W., "Lieutenant Thompson Reports on Chickamauga: A Comparison of Immediate and Historical Perspectives of the Battle," *Tennessee Historical Quarterly*, vol. 44, no. 4, Winter 1985.

Jonas, S. A., "As to Gen. Gregg," *National Tribune*, June 30, 1892.

Jones, Joseph, "The Medical History of the Confederate States Army and Navy," *Southern Historical Society Papers*, vol. 20, January-December 1892.

Labenski, Deanne, ed., "Jim Turner Co. G, 6th Texas Infantry, C. S. A. From 1861 to 1865," *Texana*, vol. 12, no. 1, Spring 1974.

Marsh, Bryan, "The Confederate Letters of Bryan Marsh," *Chronicles of Smith County*, vol. 14, issue 2, Winter 1975.

Mills, Charles H., "General James Deshler," *Confederate Veteran*, vol. 22, no. 2, February 1914.

Nabours, W. A., "Active Service of a Texas Command," *Confederate Veteran*, vol. 24, no. 2, February 1916.

"Reminiscences of the Boys in Gray," *Finders Keepers*, Johnson County Genealogical Society, vol. 12, no. 4, Winter 1995.

Spinks, J. M., "Thrilling and Varied War Experiences," *Confederate Veteran*, vol. 15, no. 4, April 1907.

Stradley, J. H., "Ector's Brigade at Chickamauga," *Confederate Veteran*, vol. 13, no. 7, July 1905.

Templeton, J. A., "A Chickamauga Prisoner," *Confederate Veteran*, vol. 31, no. 6, June 1923.

Trice, C. W., "Seventh Texas Regiment in Gregg's Brigade," *Confederate Veteran*, vol. 23, no. 2, February 1915.

Van Zandt, Khleber M., "The City Builder," *The Junior Historian*, vol. 10, no. 3, December 1949.

Williams, Jr., Robert W., & Ralph Wooster, eds., "With Terry's Texas Rangers: The Letters of Dunbar Affleck," *Civil War History*, vol. 9, no. 3, September 1963.

Maps

Alabama Department of History and Archives, Montgomery, AL

Betts, Edward, and C. E. Park, *Map of the Battlefield of Chickamauga* (1896)
Kellogg, S. C., *Map of the Battlefield of Chickamauga* (1889)
McElroy, J. C., *Chickamauga Battlefield* (1895)

Library of Congress, Washington, DC
Boyd, Charles H., *Battle-field of Chickamauga* (1864)
Morris, Walter J., *Battle of Chickamauga, Ga. Sept 19 and 20, 1863* (1863)
Ruger, Edward, *Map of the Battlefield of Chickamauga* (1892)
Sneden, Robert K., *Plan of the Battle of Chickamauga, Tenn. [sic]* (1863)
———, *The Battlefield of Chickamauga Fought the 19th and 20th of Septr 1863*
Wells, Jacob, *Battle-Field of Chickamauga* (1887)
Western and Atlantic Railroad, *Map of Chattanooga and Vicinity (1863-64)*

Newspapers

*Atchison (*KS*) Champion*
Atlanta Daily Intelligencer
*Austin (*TX*) American-Statesman*
*Bonham (*TX*) News*
*Bryan (*TX*) Daily Eagle*
*Charleston (*SC*) Mercury*
*Chattanooga (*TN*) Daily Times*
(Clarksville, TX*) The News*
(Clarksville, TX*) The Standard*
Dallas Daily Herald
*Denton (*TX*) Record-Chronicle*
*Des Moines (*IA*) Register*
*Fairfield (*TX*) Recorder*
Galveston Daily News
Galveston Weekly News
*Graham (*TX*) Leader*
*Henderson (*TX*) Times*
Houston Post
Houston Tri-Weekly Telegraph
*Huntsville (*AL*) Daily Confederate*

*Indiana (*PA*) Weekly Messenger*
*Jefferson (*TX*) Jimplecute*
*Knoxville (*TN*) Daily Journal*
*Lamb County (*Littlefield, TX*) Leader*
(McKinney, TX*) The Democrat*
Memphis Daily Appeal
*Meridian (*MS*) Daily Clarion*
*(*Jackson*) Mississippi Union Advocate and Farm and Home*
*Montgomery (*AL*) Weekly Advertiser*
*Nashville (*TN*) Banner*
*Nashville (*TN*) Daily American*
New Orleans Times-Democrat
*Nocona (*TX*) News*
*Nolan County (*TX*) News*
*Our Southern Home (*Livingston, AL*)*
*Paris (*TX*) News*
*Port Arthur (*TX*) News*
*Pulaski (*TN*) Citizen*
San Antonio Daily Express
San Antonio Light
*Seguin (*TX*) Gazette-Enterprise*
*Sherman (*TX*) Courier*
*The Southern Mercury (*Dallas, TX*)*
*Stamford (*TX*) American*
*The Tennessean (*Nashville*)*
*Tyler (*TX*) Semi-Weekly Courier Times*
*Victoria (*TX*) Advocate*
*Waco (*TX*) News-Tribune*
*Waxahachie (*TX*) Daily Light*
*Wilmington (*NC*) Daily Express*
*Wilmington (*NC*) Daily Journal*
*Yorkville (*SC*) Enquirer*

Secondary Sources

Books

Arnold, James, *Chickamauga 1863: The River of Death*. London and New York: Bloomsbury Publishing, 2012.

Bailey, Anne J., *Texans in the Confederate Cavalry*. Abilene, TX: McWhiney Foundation Press, 1995.

Baumgartner, Richard A., *Blue Lightning: Wilder's Mounted Infantry Brigade in the Battle of Chickamauga*. Huntington, WV: Blue Acorn Press, 1997.

Belcher, Dennis W., *The Union Cavalry and the Chickamauga Campaign*. Jefferson, NC: McFarland and Company, 2018.

Bush, Bryan S., *Terry's Texas Rangers: History of the 8th Texas Cavalry*. Nashville, TN: Turner Publishing Company, 2002.

Carlock, Chuck and V. M. Owens, *History of the Tenth Texas Cavalry Dismounted Regiment, 1861–1865: "If We Ever Got Whipped, I Don't Recollect It."* North Richland Hills, TX: Smithfield Press, 2001.

Carter, Robert L., *The Fight for Snodgrass Hill and the Rock of Chickamauga*. Carrollton, GA: Bev Bruemmer Books, 2012.

———, *Longstreet's Breakthrough at Chickamauga: Accidental Victory*. Amazon CreateSpace, 2014.

Chicoine, Stephen, *The Confederates of Chappell Hill, Texas: Prosperity, Civil War and Decline*. Jefferson, NC: McFarland, 2011.

Collier, Calvin, *"They'll Do to Tie to!" The Story of the Third Regiment, Arkansas Infantry C. S. A.* Little Rock, AR: Pioneer Press, 1961.

Collins, Darrell L., *The Army of Tennessee: Organization, Strength, Casualties, 1862–1865*. Jefferson, NC: McFarland, 2017.

Connelly, Thomas L., *Autumn of Glory: The Army of Tennessee, 1862–1865*. Baton Rouge: Louisiana State University Press, 2001.

Cozzens, Peter, *This Terrible Sound: The Battle of Chickamauga*. Urbana: University of Illinois Press, 1992.

Cutrer, Thomas W., *The Terry Texas Ranger Trilogy*. Abilene, TX: State House Press, 1996.

Daniel, Larry J., *Conquered: Why the Army of Tennessee Failed*. Chapel Hill: University of North Carolina Press, 2019.

Disbrow, Albert, *Glimpses of Chickamauga: A Complete Guide to All Points of Interest on This Historic Battle-Field*. Chicago: Donohue & Henneberry, 1895.

Drake, Edwin L., *Annals of the Army of Tennessee and Early Western History.* Nashville: A. D. Haynes, 1878.

Eresman, Maj. Raymond Scott, *Union and Confederate Infantry Doctrine in the Battle of Chickamauga.* Auckland, NZ: Pickle Partners Publishing, 2015.

Fischer, LeRoy H., *Yankee Quaker Confederate General: The Curious Case of Bushrod Rust Johnson.* Kent, OH: Kent State University Press, 1971.

Goldman, Pauline, compiler, and Michelle M. Haas, ed., *Letters from the Carnival of Death: Correspondence of Three of Terry's Texas Rangers.* Corpus Christi, TX: Copano Bay Press, 2014.

Grear, Charles David, *Why Texans Fought in the Civil War.* Texas A&M University, 2012.

Hallock, Judith Lee, *Braxton Bragg and Confederate Defeat*, vol. 2. Tuscaloosa and London: University of Alabama Press, 1991.

Jones, Evan C., and Wiley Sword, *Gateway to the Confederacy: New Perspectives on the Chickamauga and Chattanooga Campaigns, 1862–1863.* Baton Rouge: Louisiana State University Press, 2014.

Lance, III, Maj. Joseph M., *Patrick R. Cleburne and the Tactical Employment of His Division at the Battle of Chickamauga.* Cleveland: Pickle Partners Publishing, 2015.

Lindsley, John Berrien, *The Military Annals of Tennessee. Confederate, First Series.* Nashville: J. M. Lindsley & Co., 1886.

Linton, Roger C., *Chickamauga: A Battlefield History in Images.* Athens: University of Georgia Press, 2004.

Lowe, Richard G., *Walker's Texas Division, C.S.A.: Greyhounds of the Trans-Mississippi.* Baton Rouge: Louisiana State University Press, 2004.

Lundberg, John R., *Granbury's Texas Brigade: Diehard Western Confederates.* Baton Rouge: Louisiana State University Press, 2011.

Mendoza, Alexander, *Chickamauga 1863: Rebel Breakthrough.* Santa Barbara, CA, Denver, and Oxford, UK: Praeger, 2013.

Moore, Frank, ed., *The Rebellion Record: A Diary of American Events, with Documents, Narratives, Illustrative Incidents, Poetry, Etc.*, 7 volumes. New York: G. P. Putnam, 1861-8.

Murrah, Jeffrey D., *None but Texians: A History of Terry's Texas Rangers.* Fort Worth, TX: Eakin Press, 2001.

Office of the Quartermaster General, War Department, *The Battle of Chickamauga, September 19–20, 1863: Organization of the Army of the Cumberland and of the Army of Tennessee.* Washington, DC: United States Government Printing Office, 1932.

Powell, David A., *The Chickamauga Campaign: A Mad Irregular Battle: From the Crossing of the Tennessee River Through the Second Day, August 22–September 19, 1863*. El Dorado Hills, CA: Savas Beatie, 2014.

———, *The Chickamauga Campaign: Barren Victory: The Retreat into Chattanooga, the Confederate Pursuit, and the Aftermath of the Battle, September 21 to October 20, 1863*. El Dorado Hills, CA: Savas Beatie, 2016.

———, *The Chickamauga Campaign: Glory or the Grave: The Breakthrough, the Union Collapse, and the Defense of Horseshoe Ridge, September 20, 1863*. El Dorado Hills, CA: Savas Beatie, 2015.

Purdue, Howell and Elizabeth Purdue, *Pat Cleburne, Confederate General: A Definitive Biography*. Hillsboro, TX: Hill Junior College Press, 1973.

Rigdon, John C., *Historical Sketch and Roster of the Texas 18th Cavalry Regiment*. Amazon CreateSpace, 2018.

———, *Historical Sketch and Roster of the Texas 32nd Cavalry Regiment*. Amazon CreateSpace, 2020.

Robertson, William Glenn, *River of Death: the Chickamauga Campaign*. Chapel Hill: University of North Carolina Press, 2018.

Robertson, William Glenn, Lt. Col. Edward P. Shanahan, Lt. Col. John I. Boxberger, and Maj. George E. Knapp, *Staff Ride Handbook for the Battle of Chickamauga, 18–20 September, 1863*. Fort Leavenworth, KS: U. S. Army Command and General Staff College, 1992.

Rogers, J. Littleton, *The Civil War Battles of Chickamauga and Chattanooga*. Chattanooga: Andrews Printing Co., 1942.

Rubenstein, Maj. David A., *A Study of the Medical Support to the Union and Confederate Armies During the Battle of Chickamauga*. Auckland, NZ: Pickle Partners Publishing, 2014.

Sartain, James Alfred, *History of Walker County, Georgia*, vol. 1. Dalton, GA: The A. J. Showalter Company, 1932.

Scaife, William Robert, *Atlas of Chickamauga and Chattanooga Area Civil War Battles*. Madison, WI: University of Wisconsin-Madison, 1983.

Schmutz, John, *"The Bloody Fifth": The Fifth Texas Infantry Brigade, Hood's Texas Brigade, Army of Northern Virginia, Vol. 2: Gettysburg to Appomattox*. El Dorado Hills, CA: Savas Beatie, 2017.

Sessums, Danny, *A Force to be Reckoned With: A History of Granbury's Texas Infantry Brigade 1861–1865*, 2 volumes. Cactus Rose Press, 2017 and 2019.

Sifakis, Stewart, *Compendium of the Confederate Armies: Texas*. New York: Facts on File, 1995.

Simpson, Harold B., *Gaines Mill to Appomattox: Waco & McLennan County in Hood's Texas Brigade*. Waco, TX: Texian Press, 1963.

———, *Hood's Texas Brigade: A Compendium.* Hillsboro, TX: Hill Junior College Press, 1977.

———, *Hood's Texas Brigade: Lee's Grenadier Guard.* Waco: Texian Press, 1970.

———, *Hood's Texas Brigade in Reunion and Memory.* Hillsboro, TX: Hill Junior College Press, 1974.

———, *Touched with Valor: The Civil War Papers of General Jerome B. Robertson.* Hillsboro, TX, Hill Junior College Press, 1964.

Spencer, John W., *From Corsicana to Appomattox: The Story of the Corsicana Invincibles and the Navarro Guards.* Corsicana, TX: The Texas Press, 1984.

Spruill, Matt, *Guide to the Battle of Chickamauga,* The U.S. Army War College Guides to Civil War Battles. Lawrence: University Press of Kansas, 1993.

Stroud, David V., *Ector's Brigade and the Army of Tennessee: 1862–1865.* Longview, TX: Ranger Publishing, 2004.

Sullivan, James R., *Chickamauga and Chattanooga Battlefields: Chickamauga and Chattanooga National Military Park, Georgia–Tennessee.* Washington, DC: National Park Service Historical Handbook Series, no. 25, 1956.

Symonds, Craig L., *Stonewall of the West: Patrick Cleburne and the Civil War.* Lawrence: University of Kansas Press, 1997.

Tucker, Glenn, *Chickamauga: Bloody Battle in the West.* Dayton, OH: Morningside House, 1972.

Ural, Susannah J., *Hood's Texas Brigade: The Soldiers and Families of the Confederacy's Most Celebrated Unit.* Baton Rouge: Louisiana State University Press, 2017.

Walter, John F., *Histories of Texas Units in the Civil War,* Mss., Historical Research Center, Texas Heritage Museum, Hill College, Hillsboro, TX, 1981.

Warner, Ezra J., *Generals in Gray: Lives of the Confederate Commanders.* Baton Rouge: Louisiana State University Press, 1959.

White, William Lee, *Bushwhacking on a Grand Scale: The Battle of Chickamauga, September 18–20, 1863.* El Dorado Hills, CA: Savas Beatie, 2013.

Williams, Edward B., *Hood's Texas Brigade in the Civil War.* Jefferson, NC: McFarland & Company, 2012.

Wittenberg, Eric J., *Holding the Line on the River of Death: Union Mounted Forces at Chickamauga, September 18, 1863.* El Dorado Hills, CA: Savas Beatie, 2018.

Woodworth, Steven E., ed., *The Chickamauga Campaign.* Carbondale: Southern Illinois University Press, 2010.

Wooster, Ralph A., *Lone Star Regiments in Gray.* Austin: Eakin Press, 2002.

Periodical Articles

Barr, C. Alwyn, "The Making of a Secessionist: The Antebellum Career of Roger Q. Mills," Southwestern History Quarterly, no. 79, October 1975.

Bishop, Judson W., "Van Der Veer's Brigade at Chickamauga," in *Glimpses of the Nation's Struggle* (MOLLUS, Minnesota, vol. 6). Minneapolis: A. Davis, 1909.

Daniels, Larry J., "Jay's Mill: The Opening Action at Chickamauga," *North & South,* June 2006.

Harrison, Jon P., "The Tenth Texas Cavalry, C. S. A.," *Military History of Texas and the Southwest*, vo. 12, no. 3, 1974.

Lang, Andrew F., "The Bass Grays: An Economic, Social, and Demographic Profile of Company D, Seventh Texas Infantry," *East Texas Historical Journal*, vol. 48, issue 1, article 11, 2010.

———, "Lone Star Pride: The Good-Douglas Texas Battery, CSA 1861-1865," *East Texas Historical Journal*, vol. 45, issue 2, article 8, October 2007.

Oates, Stephen B., "Texas Under the Secessionists," *The Southwestern Historical Quarterly*, vol. 67, no. 2, October 1963.

Robertson, William Glenn, "The Chickamauga Campaign: The Armies Collide: Bragg Forces His Way Across Chickamauga Creek," *Blue & Gray*, vol. 24, no. 3, 2007.

———, "The Chickamauga Campaign: The Battle of Chickamauga, Day 1," *Blue & Gray*, vol. 24, no. 6, 2007.

———, "The Chickamauga Campaign: The Battle of Chickamauga, Day 2," *Blue & Gray*, vol. 25, no. 2, 2008.

———, "Rails to the River of Death: Railroads in the Chickamauga Campaign," *Civil War*, vol. 9, no. 6, November/December 1991.

Skoch, George F., "Miracle of the Rails," *Civil War Times Illustrated*, September/October 1992.

Tucker, Glenn, "The Battle of Chickamauga," *Civil War Times Illustrated*, vol. 8, no. 2, May 1969.

Wooster, Ralph A., and Robert Wooster, "'Rarin' for a Fight': Texans in the Confederate Army," *The Southwestern Historical Quarterly*, no. 84, April 1981.

Maps

American Battlefield Trust, Chickamauga Animated Map website, Washington, DC: https://www.battlefields.org/learn/maps/chickamauga-animated-map

National Park Service, *Chickamauga Battlefield Map*. Washington, DC: U.S. Government Printing Office.

Powell, David A., and David A. Friedrichs, *The Maps of Chickamauga: An Atlas of the Chickamauga Campaign, Including the Tullahoma Operations, June 22–September 23, 1863*. New York: Savas Beatie, 2009.

Online Sites

Bell, Tim, with Ron Brothers and Gary Wisler, "History of the 9th Texas Infantry," http://gen.1starnet.com/civilwar/9thmain.htm.

Compiled Service Records, NARA Record Group 109, M323, Texas, Fold3 by Ancestry, https://www.fold3.com/title/41/texas

Golden, Randy, and Col. Samuel Taylor, "Chickamauga–An Introduction," *Our Georgia History*, http://www.ourgeorgiahistory.com/wars/Civil_War/Chickamauga/chickamauga_01.html

Randy's Texas, "Tenth Texas Cavalry," http://www.angelfire.com/tx3/RandysTexas/TenthTexasCavalry.htm

Powell, David A., "Failure in the Saddle," American Battlefield Trust, https://www.battlefields.org/learn/articles/fight-reeds-bridge

Texas State Historical Association, *Handbook of Texas*, https://tshaonline.org/handbook

"William E. Whitsett, Private, Company H, 9th Texas Infantry, 3 Nov 1837–15 Apr 1901," *Lamar County Texas Genealogy*, http://www.lamarcountytx.org/civilwar/whitsett.shtm

Dissertations and Theses

Eiserman, Frederick A., *Longstreet's Corps at Chickamauga: Lessons in Inter-Theater Deployment.* Master's thesis, U.S. Army Command and General Staff College, Fort Leavenworth, KS, 1985.

Foley, Maj. Kyle J., *Hood's Texas Division in the Battle of Chickamauga: A Historical Analysis.* Master's thesis, U.S. Army Command and General Staff College, Fort Leavenworth, KS, 2003.

Maki, Jr., Maj. Terrence W., *Daniel Harvey Hill and His Contribution to the Battle of Chickamauga.* Master's thesis, U.S. Army Command and General Staff College, Fort Leavenworth, KS, 2001.

Newsom, James L., *Intrepid Gray Warriors: The 7th Texas Infantry, 1861–1865.* Ph.D. dissertation, Texas Christian University, Fort Worth, TX, 1995.

Reed, Brian, *"We never met a foe in open field we did not drive, nor did we ever meet a foe who could drive us": The 9th Texas Infantry*. Master's thesis, Baylor University, Waco, TX, 2009.

West, Billy Kurtz, Jr., *Ector's Brigade in the Civil War.* Master's thesis, Texas Tech University, Lubbock, TX, 1987.

Acknowledgments

The authors are grateful to so many people, especially our families, for their steady support and encouragement during this project. Joe and I have not attempted to write a definitive account of the battle of Chickamauga or a tactical study covering both armies. David A. Powell, Dr. William G. Robertson, Peter Cozzens, Glenn Tucker, William Lee White, and several other authors have already produced outstanding works on this, the second bloodiest battle of the American Civil War. Nor are we trying to write a complete history of Hood's Texans in the campaign (Maj. Kyle Foley and others have tackled that subject previously), or of Deshler's brigade, Ector's brigade, Gregg's brigade, or other Texans at Chickamauga. We *are* also not giving a scholarly interpretive tome with a historiography of what past writers have said. What we are trying to do is look at the human side of the Texans' involvement in the Chickamauga campaign, interweaving first-person accounts of scores of participants with Lone Star roots.

We were not there at Chickamauga; they were.

A 19th-century reporter wrote, "The battle of Chickamauga was altogether the most horrible tragedy in the most tragic strife of modern times. The real history of that fight cannot be told in the marble sculpture of some magnificent memorial of history. It was written once, and best written, upon the hearts of thousands who saw the death struggle, in the shrieks of wounded men, dying in deserted heaps between the lines of battle, or perishing hopelessly or miserably in the flames kindled for the torch or by fiery shot."[1]

Far from home, army experiences became indelibly etched into the soldiers' minds and many Texans wrote about their experiences. We respectfully dedicate this narrative to these men's collective memory. Our goal is to give a broad overview of the general movements and tactics, provide some background context, and then let the Texans describe what happened in their small sphere of cognition.

1 "Horrible War Memories," *Indiana* (PA) *Weekly Messenger*, July 31, 1889.

Some of their quotations, particularly period newspaper accounts, have not been seen in print since the late 19th century, and then often only locally.

It is by design, therefore, that we have made liberal use of the Texans' words while striving to maintain a general sense of the tactical situations they faced. "In timber as thick as that in which the battle raged that afternoon, it was impossible for one in the ranks to see what was happening to the right or left," Sgt. Joseph B. Polley of the 4th Texas commented. "To do his share of the work on hand, he could only look straight before him, and tackle the foe immediately facing him." Few Texans knew the identities of their opponents, the names of roads or farms through which they traversed, or even the time frame. *Many confounded multiple events or confused details of the fighting in which they took part in their post-war memories and reminiscences.* Placing these oft-overlapping accounts in the proper chronology or context proved to be challenging. We apologize for any errors that have resulted from this necessity.[2]

We deeply thank Dave Powell for his time, counsel, and suggestions, which were a major contribution to the final work. Dave is one of the leading contemporary scholars on the actions in the Chickamauga and Chattanooga campaigns. He and Eric J. Wittenberg (the co-author of Scott's book on the Second Battle of Winchester) have written a new book on the Tullahoma campaign that promises to be the definitive account.

We also are grateful for the support of Robert Carter, a volunteer at Chattanooga and Chickamauga National Military Park. The author of two fine books on the battle, Robert helped with fact-checking, corrections, and historical accuracy. We appreciate it. Jerry Holsworth, a Texan transplanted to the Shenandoah Valley of Virginia where he has become an expert on the famed Stonewall Brigade, graciously shared his voluminous files on Hood's Texas Brigade.

John Versluis and the staff of the Texas Heritage Museum permitted the use of their extensive archives and graciously allowed us to use certain photographs of Texas soldiers and Brig. Gen. Evander Law of Alabama. Other images are courtesy of the Prints and Photographic Division of the Library of Congress and the National Archives and Records Administration. Terre Heydari, operations manager at the DeGolyer Library at Southern Methodist University, provided two

2 J. B. Polley, *Hood's Texas Brigade: Its Marches, Its Battles, Its Achievements* (New York and Washington, 1910), 210. Polley was a native of the Texas Republic, having been born in 1840 in Brazoria County. He lived in Farmersville at the time of his enlistment in 1861.

images of Texas soldiers. We also thank Patty Branard-Gambino, the great-granddaughter of Color Sgt. George A. Branard of the 1st Texas, for providing us with two photographs of her ancestor, and Michelle Lambing of the State Preservation Board of Texas for her great support and assistance of obtaining several photographs.

We thank each of the following for their gracious support: Lisa Marine of the Wisconsin Historical Society; Kenny Dee for the photograph of his ancestor, Sgt. David H. Hamilton; the office of the Clerk of the U.S. House of Representatives for the photograph of 1st Sgt. Benjamin F. Grady of the 25th Texas Cavalry; Nathan Eddy for the photograph of Lt. Jesse P. Bates of the 9th Texas; Kathy Arth for the photograph of her great-great-grandfather, Col. John Camp; Mickie Hill for the photograph of her great-great-grandfather, Sgt. John C. Cox of the 5th Texas; the Texas Archives and Library Commission; the Dolph Briscoe Center for American History at the University of Texas; and the Wilson County (TX) Historical Society for allowing us to use the photograph of Pvt. Henry Waters Berryman of the 1st Texas.

We also appreciate and thank long-time National Park Service Ranger and author Lee White for sending us several letters of soldiers who fought in the battle. Thomas Holder graciously provided copies of two letters that a direct descendant of Maj. K. M. Van Zandt of the 6th Texas gave him years ago. Cody Marshall, son of the late Texas artist Bruce Marshall, kindly gave us permission to use his father's excellent painting, "Hood's Texas Brigade in Action, Viniard Farm, Chickamauga, Sept. 19, 1863." Kirk Lyons introduced Joe to Cody Marshall and provided helpful advice on where to find some of the photographs and reminiscences. Duane Miller, Tom Buffenbarger, and Steve Bye of the library and archives of the U.S. Army Heritage and Education Center in Carlisle, Pennsylvania, were quite helpful in searching through their extensive records for specific material related to the battle of Chickamauga, Texans in the Civil War, and Confederate soldier accounts.

Our talented team of reviewers included several noted experts on the Tullahoma campaign and the battle of Chickamauga. They were Eric J. Wittenberg (the prolific author of many books on the Civil War with a strong focus on cavalry actions); Chickamauga park ranger Lee White; authors Dave Powell, Robert Carter, John Schmutz, Brad Butkovich, and Dr. Danny Sessums; Marc Grad; Phil Spaugy; Michael Rinehart; and Philip McBride, whose great-great-uncle was Capt. J. J. McBride of the 5th Texas in Robertson's brigade. NPS Ranger Jim Ogden also provided input. Charles Downs did the final proofreading before we submitted the manuscript to the publisher. Charlie, we thank you. Any spelling or punctuation errors or, more importantly, any omissions or factual mistakes in interpretation of this oft-confusing battle and the soldiers' accounts, are solely the fault of the authors, not our peer reviewers or publisher.

Finally, we acknowledge the constant support and guidance of Ted Savas and his entire fine staff at Savas Beatie, LLC. You are simply the best. From early advice to final editing, from concept to production, from marketing to author liaison, the capable SB experts have helped us all along the journey from the manuscript phase to commercialization and post-production support. We deeply appreciate everything you do, Ted and the SB team, as always. Onward.

Scott L. Mingus Sr., York, Pennsylvania

Joseph L. Owen, Blanco, Texas

Index

Adair, Pvt. Leander E. (24th TX Cav.), 220, 273
Affleck, Pvt. Dunbar (8th TX Cav.), 23
Alabama, 10, 12, 13, 14, 18, 19, 34, 41, 42, 77, 121n45, 159, 215
Alamo, battle of the, 1, 57
Alexander, Col. E. Porter, (CSA), 6-7, 40n33, 42-43
Alexander, Pvt. J. H. (3rd AR), 189
Alexander's Bridge, 50-52, 63, 64n20, 66, 71-73, 135, 154, 160
Alford, Pvt. J. P. (7th TX), 219, 283
Allegheny Mountain, battle of, 7
Allentown, PA, 7n7
Alpine, GA, 38-39
Anderson, TX, 236
Anderson, Brig. Gen. Patton (CSA), 205
Anderson, Lt. Col. T. Scott (6th-10th TX-15th TX Cav.), 170-71
Andrews, Col. Julius A. (32nd TX Cav.), 12-13, 82, 281
Arkansas, 6, 7n7, 8, 12, 48
Arkansas Post, battle of, 6-9, 23-24, 26n10, 32, 37, 68, 135, 145, 154, 161, 168, 172n51, 200, 210, 244
Army of the Cumberland (USA), 21, 28, 30, 47, 49, 53, 91, 125, 204, 209, 222, 230
XIV Corps, 51, 53, 70, 73, 96, 139, 152, 154, 156, 161n25, 182, 186, 207
XX Corps, 31, 51, 70, 89, 126, 152, 186
XXI Corps, 49, 70, 86, 97, 114, 152, 162, 174, 181
Reserve Corps, 49, 66, 70, 152, 195, 205
Army of Mississippi (CSA), 13, 14, 34, 38
Army of Northern Virginia (CSA), 5, 14, 15, 24, 39, 46, 54, 56, 67, 69, 148, 176, 205, 243, 248
Army of the Potomac (USA), 209, 229, 240
Army of Tennessee (CSA), Chickamauga Sept. 18, 71-72; Chickamauga Sept. 19, 85, 88, 175; Chickamauga Sept. 20, 195, 208; comparison to the Army of Northern Virginia, 67, 69, 176, 222, 232; leadership issues, 154, 224; 230-31, 249; morale; 3, 32, 37, 234, 239; organization, 2, 4-5, 7, 11, 13, 15, 21, 31, 34, 49, 56, 147, 190, 250; post-Chickamauga, 214, 222, 226; Tullahoma campaign, 12-39
Army of the West (CSA), 11
Arnold, Pvt. James (14th TX Cav.), 157-58, 280
Atlanta, GA, 21n1, 34, 36, 38-39, 43, 46, 99, 110n22, 222, 225, 236, 246, 252, 254, 285
Austin, TX, 1, 13, 169, 229
Bailey, Pvt. Bryan W. (17th TX Cav.), 254
Bailey, Ella (nurse), 237
Bailey, Sgt. Zachariah W. (14th TX Cav.), 208
Baird, Brig. Gen. Absalom (USA), 73, 81, 82, 139, 157-58, 162, 204
Baldwin, Col. Philemon P. (USA), 139, 140, 143
Bane, Lt. Col. John P. (4th TX), 16-17, 113, 175, 191, 242, 264
Barber, Pvt. P. B. (10th TX Cav.), 82
Barnes, Col. Sidney M. (USA), 114
Barnett, Pvt. William H. (11th MS), 227-28
Bass, Col. Frederick S. (1st TX), 241
Bassett, Capt. Robert H. (4th TX), 113, 175, 191-92, 236, 264, 266
Bate, Brig. Gen. William B. (CSA), 167-68, 171
Bates, Lt. Jesse P. and Susan (9th TX), 234, 303
Beal, Pvt. Thomas J. (7th TX), 67
Berryman, Pvt. Henry W. (1st TX), 237-38
Beaumont, TX, 104, 251
Beaumont, Lt. Col. Thomas W. (50th TN), 90
Bell, Lt. F. M. (25th TX Cav.), 197, 275
Belton, TX, 8
Benning, Brig. Gen. Henry L. (CSA), 41-42, 54, 60, 67, 100, 105, 110, 127-28, 177, 181-82, 184-86, 193, 241
Bentonville, AR, 19
Bierce, Lt. Ambrose (USA), 206
Billingsley, Capt. Joseph C. (4th TX), 118, 189, 265
Bingham, Lt. John H. (TX Battery), 141
Bishop, Capt. Judson W. (2nd MN), 76-78, 80

Blackburn, Lt. James K. P. (8th TX Cav.), 33, 194-95
Blalock, Pvt. R. W. (1st TX), 46-47, 262
Bostick, Pvt. Sion R. (5th TX), 17
Bookman, Lt. J. M. "Bob" (4th TX), 130, 266
Bowser, Lt. Oliver P. (18th TX Cav.), 150-51, 221, 248-49, 254, 274
Bradham, Pvt. Benjamin (1st TX), 114, 262
Bradley, Col. Luther (USA), 126
Bragg,Gen. Braxton (CSA): organization of the army 3-6, 34; Tullahoma campaign 21-24, 26-27, 30-35; maneuvers before Chickamauga, 36-39, 42-43, 46-47; Sept. 18 at Chickamauga, 48-52, 54, 58, 60, 67-68; Sept. 19 at Chickamauga, 71-73, 75-76, 79, 86, 88, 99, 102, 134; criticism of, 88, 211-12, 224, 227, 230-31, 234-35, 238-39, 250-51; meets with Longstreet, 146-47; Sept. 20 at Chickamauga, 152, 154, 176, 178, 187, 191, 206-207; post-Chickamauga maneuvers, 211-12, 222, 224-35, 238-240; Chattanooga, 242-46, 248-251, 254
Branard, Sgt. George A. (1st TX), 103-104, 108, 128-29, 132, 189, 221, 248, 303
Branchville and Columbia Railroad, 46
Brannan, Brig. Gen. John M. (USA), 73, 76, 174-75, 180-82, 186n25, 188
Brazoria County, TX, 18, 302n2
Breckinridge, Maj. Gen. John C. (CSA), 37, 88, 134, 152, 154-57, 160, 166, 171, 177, 199, 212, 249
Bridgeport, AL, 39n30, 108n19
Brock, Benjamin (farmer), 97-98, 184
Brock, John (farmer), 86, 141-42, 148, 177
Brown, John (abolitionist), 16
Brown's Ferry, 240-41
Brotherton, George and Mary (farmers), 86, 96, 162n26, 174, 175, 178, 180, 181, 184, 196
Buckner, Maj. Gen. Simon B. (CSA), 5, 34, 49, 50 64n20, 71, 86, 100, 148, 177, 211, 226, 230-31, 244
Buell, Col. George P. (USA), 114, 118-21, 126, 180-82, 186
Bunting, Chaplain Robert F. (8th TX Cav.), 26, 31-32, 38-39, 88, 212, 226
Burnside, Maj. Gen. Ambrose E. (USA), 27, 30, 34, 39, 235n52, 243, 245, 251
Burroughs, Pvt. Samuel R. (1st TX), 227-28, 263
Burton, Pvt. William P. (4th TX), 124, 265
Byram's Ford, 66, 75n9
Cagle, Pvt. George (6th-10th TX-15th TX Cav.), 168
Calhoun, Pvt. William (4th TX), 102
California, 10
Camp, Col. John L. (14th TX Cav.), 12, 157, 159, 279, 303
Camp Butler (Springfield, IL), 23
Camp Chase (Columbus, OH), 255
Camp Douglas (Chicago, IL), 232, 276, 278-82
Camp Henry C. McCullough (Victoria, TX), 7
Camp Reeves (Grayson County, TX), 19
Campbell, Pvt. Robert (5th TX), 44-45, 47, 64, 66, 101, 106, 115, 119-20, 267
Carlin, Brig. Gen. William P. (USA), 89-90, 94, 97, 105, 108, 113-16, 119-20, 126, 186
Carlton, Pvt. C. B. (10th TX Cav.), 83
Caroline County, VA, 40
Carroll, Pvt. William (4th TX), 111, 266
Carter, A. R. (AL), 153
Carter, Lt. Col. Benjamin F. (4th TX), 16
Carthage, TX, 157, 158
Caster, Pvt, Mite (1st TX), 237
Cater, Pvt. Douglas J. (3rd TX Cav.), 19
Cater, Lt. Rufus (19th LA), 19
Catholic Sisters of Charity, 219
Catlett's Gap, 39, 68
Catoosa County, GA, 72
Catoosa Platform (GA), 38, 43n39, 46, 47m48, 49n2, 54, 60, 104, 146, 148, 156, 194-95, 218
Catoosa Springs, GA, 47n48, 218, 222, 248
Chambers, Pvt. Daniel L. (24th TX Cav.), 172, 273
Chambers, Pvt. John H. (24th TX Cav.), 172, 272
Chambers, Pvt. Samuel H. (4th TX), 124, 265
Chappell Hill, TX, 46
Charleston, SC, 8, 33, 43, 45
Chattanooga, TN, 3, 21, 27, 30-34, 36, 37n27, 39n30, 49-50, 70, 81, 130n63, 133, 151n2, 204, 205n16, 209, 211-13, 224-29
Chattanooga, siege of, 227-30, 233-39, 240-49

Chattanooga Academy, 35n25
Chattooga County, GA, 38
Cheatham, Brig. Gen. Benjamin F. (CSA), 71, 86, 94, 96, 102, 103, 136, 140, 152, 161, 225
Cherokee County, TX, 8
Cherokee Nation, 5, 68n32, 71
Cherokee Springs, GA, 218, 222
Chesnut, Mary, 45-46
Chickamauga and Chattanooga National Military Park, 5n4, 302
Chickamauga Station, 225, 244-45, 248
Chickasawhay River, 38
Childress, Pvt. Benjamin F. "Dock" (4th TX), 111, 266
Churchill, Brig. Gen. Thomas J. (CSA), 6-7, 24-25, 30-33
Chustenahlah, battle of, 15, 18
Clark, Lt. Gov. Edward (TX), 2, 11
Clark, Pvt. Jacob (24th TX Cav.), 232, 274
Clark, Pvt. William H. (5th TX), 130
Clay, Capt. Tacitus T. (5th TX), 115, 119-21, 175, 177, 185, 190
Cleburne, Maj. Gen. Patrick R. (CSA), 6, 24-25, 27, 32, 37, 39, 68, 88; night attack at Chickamauga, 133-49; 156, 160, 163; September 20 fighting, 165-73, 177-78, 199-201; post-Chickamauga, 232, 244-46, 254; at Ringgold, 248-49; death, 252
Clements, Pvt. Robert H. (4th TX), 17
Cleveland, Capt. John S. (5th TX), 119-20, 175, 178, 182, 184-85, 188-89, 267
Coit, Lt. Col. John T. (18th TX Cav.), 142, 143m21, 232, 272
Coleman, Col. David (39th NC), 97, 195
Collins, Lt. Robert M. (15th TX Cav.), 32, 37, 58, 134-35, 148, 153-54, 162-63, 165-66, 169, 246
Colorado, 7
Colquitt, Brig. Gen. Alfred (CSA), 157n15
Colquitt, Col. Peyton H. (CSA), 156-59
Columbia, SC 43n39, 45, 54
Columbus, OH, 7, 255
Confederate military units:
Alabama: 10th Infantry, 63n; 18th Infantry Battalion, 136; 33rd Infantry, 136; Semple's Battery, 136, 141, 167-68, 200-202; Stone's Sharpshooters, 10, 77-78, 226
Arkansas: 3rd Infantry, 14, 40, 41, 54, 98-99, 106-108, 113-14, 116, 130-31, 175, 186, 188, 241; 19th-24th Infantry, 6, 136, 161, 172, 199; 25th Infantry, 96-97; Calvert's Battery 136
Confederate States: 10th Cavalry, 73
Georgia: 2nd Infantry, 60, 127; 4th Cavalry, 162n; Everett's 9th Georgia Battery, 54, 63, 88, 94
Kentucky: "Orphan Brigade," 156
Louisiana: 19th Infantry, 19
Mississippi: Pound's Sharpshooters, 10
Missouri: Bledsoe's 1st Missouri Battery, 13, 54n, 57, 88, 94
North Carolina: 29th Infantry, 10, 39; 39th Infantry, 96-97, 195
South Carolina: 8th Infantry, 185; 16th Infantry, 156n; Culpeper's Battery, 54n, 88
Tennessee: 1st Infantry Battalion, 13, 38, 88, 96, 176, 176n; 3rd Infantry, 57, 62-63, 88-89, 96; 10th Infantry, 72, 88, 91, 96, 180; 17th Infantry, 61, 94, 96; 23rd Infantry, 57; 30th Infantry, 90, 96-97; 41st Infantry, 88, 96; 44th Infantry, 65; 50th Infantry, 88, 90, 97; Huwald's Battery, 73
Texas: 1st Infantry, 14, 16, 41, 41n, 44, 46, 47n, 55, 63, 67, 68n, 98, 102-108, 113-14, 116, 126, 130,132, 182, 184, 187-89, 191, 206, 209, 211, 216, 221, 225-28, 236-39, 241, 248, 251, 260, 303; 3rd Cavalry, 9-10, 18-19, 67n, 278; 4th Infantry, 16-17, 33, 41-46, 54, 56, 59, 61, 64-65, 101, 103-104, 106, 108, 110-13, 115-19, 121-22, 124-26, 130-31, 175, 177-79, 182, 184-85, 187-88, 190-93, 208, 211-12, 215, 220, 222, 224, 226-27, 229-31, 235, 238, 240-43, 254, 259-60, 264, 285, 302; 5th Infantry, 14, 16-17, 40n, 44, 63, 64, 66, 99, 101-104, 106, 110, 114-15, 119-20, 130-31, 175, 177-79, 182, 184-85, 188-89, 192-94, 208, 219-20, 224, 226, 237, 241, 253, 260, 267, 269, 290, 303; 6th-10th Infantry; 6-8, 12, 26n, 30, 32, 34, 36n, 47, 68, 138, 142, 149, 164, 166, 168, 171, 218-19, 224, 227, 234, 259, 285, 292, 303; 7th Infantry; 7, 11n, 13-14, 38, 48, 63, 65, 67, 88-89, 96, 97, 135, 151, 175, 176, 180-81,

204, 205n, 209, 219, 225, 237, 244, 246, 252, 259, 283, 285, 300; 8th (Terry's) Cavalry, 18-19, 23, 26, 32-33, 38-39, 56, 57n, 194-95, 207, 213-14, 219, 284, 289; 9th Cavalry, 10-11, 34, 50, 75-77, 159, 219, 229, 234, 253, 259,289, 300, 301; 10th Cavalry, 6, 11-12, 25, 68, 81-84, 134, 137-38, 146, 161, 169-70, 172, 208, 232, 244, 246, 251, 259, 269, 277, 285; 11th Cavalry, 5, 17-18, 31, 34, 39, 50, 68, 71, 88, 194, 212-13, 260; 14th Cavalry, 10, 12, 84, 157-59, 208, 259, 279, 285; 15th Cavalry, 6, 8, 25, 32, 37, 68, 133-34, 136, 138, 146, 148, 154, 161-62, 165, 169-70, 172, 232, 244, 246, 251, 259, 269-70, 285; 17th-18th-24th-25th Cavalry, 6, 8-9, 23-25, 32, 37, 46n, 61, 134,136, 138-39, 141, 143, 145-46, 148, 151, 153-54, 161-62, 164-66, 170, 172-73, 184, 199, 200-202, 217, 219, 222, 233, 244, 246, 251, 255, 259, 269, 285-86; 32nd Cavalry, 10, 12, 34, 50, 66-67, 75, 77, 81-82, 84, 157, 208, 259, 278, 281, 285; Douglas's (Good's Dallas) Battery, 9, 10, 299

Connell, Col. John M. (USA), 76, 81, 182

Conner, Sgt. Festus O. (9th TX), 77

Cook, Lt. Col. Gustave (8th TX Cav.), 18-19, 56, 284

Cook, Pvt. Miles P. (20th OH Art.), 153

Cooke, Lt. Samuel A. (17th TX Cav.), 201, 272

Cooper, Gen. Seth, 227

Cooper, Pvt. Albert (5th TX), 17

Cooper, Pvt. William (5th TX), 17

Cooper's Gap, 213

Corinth, MS, 12

Corinth campaign of 1862, 8

Corsicana, TX, 8, 111, 131, 221n21

Cox, Pvt. John C. (5th TX), 179, 208, 253, 267, 303

Crabtree, Pvt. William (5th TX), 220, 269

Cracker Line, 240, 242

Crawfish Springs, GA, 49, 52, 68, 71, 73, 89, 213, 221, 226

Crawford, Pvt. Ezekiel C. (1st TX), 129, 221, 264

Crawford, Pvt. Robert (4th TX), 178

Crier, Pvt. Emmanuel H., 217n11, 262

Crittenden, Maj. Gen. Thomas L. (USA), 49, 51, 70, 97, 114, 152, 162, 174, 197, 204, 228

Crombie, Dr. Andrew C. (1st TX), 44

Crook, Brig. Gen. George (USA), 194

Crounsee, Lorenzo L., 42-43

Croxton, Brig. Gen. John T. (USA), 73, 77, 82, 182

Cruft, Brig. Gen. Charles (USA), 167, 171, 202

Crump, Maj. Richard P. (Crump's Texas Cav. Battalion), 12

Cupp, Col. Valentine (1st OH Cav.), 194

Curl, Lt. Henry T. (17th TX Cav.), 232

Cumming, Kate (nurse), 222

Daffan, Pvt. Lawrence A. (4th TX), 41-42, 111, 125, 191

Dallas, TX, 8, 19, 143n21

Dallas County, TX, 9

Dalton, GA, 40n33, 218, 233

Dalton's Ford, 50, 71

Dana, Asst. Sec. of War Charles A. (USA), 49

Daugherty, Pvt. Boone (18th TX Cav.), 145, 274

Davidson, Brig. Gen. Henry B. (CSA), 72-73, 76

Davis, President Jefferson (CSA), 39, 45, 170, 227, 230, 239, 249

Davis, Brig. Gen. Jefferson C. (USA), 89-91, 204

Davis's Crossroads, engagement at, 37

Dayton, OH, 221

Deal, Pvt. John W. (4th TX), 222, 264

Decatur, TX, 32

Denson, Cpl. N. C. (3rd AR), 131

Denton, TX, 8

Denton County, TX, 84, 161

Deshler, David (civil engineer), 6-7

Deshler, Brig. Gen. James (CSA): organization of brigade, 6-9, 30, 33, 259, 269-70; Davis's Crossroads/Dug Gap, 37, 39, 47, 61; arrival at Chickamauga, 68; Sept. 19 at Chickamauga, 86, 133-42, 144-46, 148; Sept. 20 at Chickamauga, 150-54, 160-70, 172; death and burial, 169-70, 214-15; mentioned postmortem, 196-98, 201, 220-21, 224, 232, 249n15; memorial 169, 255

Dibrell, Col. George G. (CSA), 84

Dick, Col. George (USA), 65, 221
Dickie, Pvt. James A. (5th TX), 192-93, 268
Dixon, Capt. James S. (32nd TX Cav.), 82
Dodge, Col. Joseph B. (USA), 138n10, 139, 141n18, 143-45, 202
Donahue, Pvt. William (14th TX Cav.), 84-85, 279
Dortch, Cpl. L. B. (5th TX), 120, 130, 269
Douglas, Capt. James P. (CSA), 9-10, 22-23, 136, 140-41, 151, 162, 165-66, 168, 200-202, 204, 249, 254, 285
DuVal, Judge Thomas H., 229
Dyer, Robert and Carrie (farmers), 180-182, 184, 191, 205
Dyer's Ford, 58, 62
Duck River, 21, 30, 31
Dug Gap, 39, 68
Earp, Lt. Col. Cullen R. (10th TX Cav.), 12, 277
Eckhardt, Pvt. William E. (24th TX Cav.), 164, 273
Ector, Brig. Gen. Matthew D. (CSA): pre-Chickamauga, 10-11; organization of brigade, 11-12, 34, 36n24, 50, 259, 275-76; Sept. 18 at Chickamauga, 66-67; Sept. 19 at Chickamauga, 70, 75-78, 80-85; Sept. 20 at Chickamauga, 134, 151-52, 156-59, 202, 207; post-Chickamauga, 219, 224-26, 228, 229, 232, 236-37, 252, 254
Elk River, 312
Elliott, Pvt. Thomas A. (24th TX Cav.), 46n47, 220, 273
Emerson, GA, 38
Enterprise, MS, 38
Estep, Capt. George (8th IN Art.), 118-19, 121
Estes, Sgt. Aaron D. (10th TX), 244,
Estes, Col. William N. (3rd Confederate Cav.), 39
Ewell, Lt. Gen. Richard S. (CSA), 233
Fairfield, TX, 13, 14,
Faulkner, Lt. William (86th IL), 72
Felder, Pvt. Rufus K. (5th TX), 46
Ferris, TX, 1
Fisher, Capt. Rhodes (6th TX), 138n10, 161, 163, 271
Fitch, Lt. Samuel C. (9th TX), 33, 276
Fithian, Dr. Joseph (18th KY), 207
Fletcher, Sgt. William A. (5th TX), 104, 116-18, 131-32, 194-95, 219, 268
Flo, TX, 1
Florence, SC, 43n39
Floyd County, GA, 33
Formwalt, Capt. John A. (10th TX), 169, 271
Forrest, Brig. Gen. Nathan B. (CSA), 5, 50, 54, 57-58, 61, 63-64, 67, 72-77, 79, 81, 83-84, 86, 135, 211-12, 231, 235, 239
Forrester, Dr. William (5th KY Cav.), 213
Fort Bend County, TX, 18
Fort Delaware, DE, 159n21
Fort Donelson, TN, 13-14
Fort Hindman, AK, 6, 7
Fort Sumter, SC, 7
Fort Warren (Boston, MA), 13
Fort Worth, TX, 8
Foster, Capt. Samuel T. (24th TX Cav.), 61, 133, 141-43, 173, 200, 204, 214
Foster, Pvt. Wiley W. (18th TX Cav.), 255, 273
Francis, Pvt. Wesley C. (4th TX), 103, 130n62, 264
Francis, Sgt. Edward M. (4th TX), 103, 121-24, 134, 264
Franklin, battle of, 135n5, 252
Franklin, Lt. Benjamin I. (4th TX), 102, 190, 220, 269
Fredericksburg, VA, 40, 42, 43
Freestone County, TX, 8, 13, 265, 284
French, Maj. Gen. Samuel G. (CSA), 226
Fuller, Lt. B. Pugh (5th TX), 121, 267
Fuller, Pvt. William S. (14th TX Cav.), 85
Fulton, Col. John S. (CSA), 48, 52-53, 57-58, 61-63, 65, 88, 94, 96, 176, 180, 195
Galveston, TX, 217, 220n18, 221
Gardenhire, Pvt. George G. (10th TX), 219, 270
Garfield, Brig. Gen. James A. (USA), 49, 204
Gates, Sgt. Frank W. (115th IL), 205
Geary, Brig. Gen. John W. (USA), 241
Gettysburg, battle of, 2, 14, 16, 31, 33, 41, 62, 103, 130n63, 148n31, 179, 190, 209, 220, 241
Gettysburg, PA, 21n1

Georgia, 3, 4, 10, 12, 13, 16, 34, 36, 37, 39, 40, 42, 44, 52, 56, 71, 72, 79, 100, 128, 135, 218, 219n17, 220, 233, 237, 243, 244, 254

Georgia Military Institute, 38n29

Gholston, Pvt. William B. (32nd TX Cav.), 77, 282

Giles, Sgt. Valerius C. (4th TX), 106-107, 118, 121-23, 216, 224, 238, 242

Gillespie, Col. Clayton C. (25th TX Cav.), 6, 8-9, 23-24

Gilmer, TX, 12

Gist, Brig. Gen. States Rights (CSA), 75n8, 156, 158-59

Glass's Mill, 68, 71, 88, 194

Glazer, Pvt. Julius H. (4th TX), 125-26, 265

Glenn, Eliza (farmer), 89, 90, 130, 184

Goldthwaite, Lt. Richard W. (Semple's AL Battery), 200-201

Gonzalez, TX, 8

Goodrich, Sgt. John T. (3rd TN), 89, 96

Gordon, James (miller), 49n2, 64n23, 68n32

Gould, Sgt. Uriah (4th TX), 235, 265

Gracie, Col. Archibald (CSA), 208

Grady, Sgt. Benjamin F. (25th TX Cav.), 23, 139-40, 142, 144, 151, 154, 161, 163, 166, 197, 199-200, 202, 303

Graham, Lt. Matthew F. (10th TX), 170-71, 275

Graham, Pvt. William H. (18th TX Cav.), 145-46

Granbury, Col. Hiram B. (7th TX), 14, 38, 65, 96-97, 181, 219, 244, 246, 249, 252, 254, 283

Granger, Maj. Gen. Gordon (USA), 51, 70, 152, 195, 205

Grant, Maj. Gen. Ulysses S. (USA), 27, 238, 240, 242, 244-45

Grantland, Pvt. Robert E. (25th TX Cav.), 219-20, 273

Graves, Cpl. Junius W. (5th TX), 220

Graves, Pvt. Robert C. (32nd TX Cav.), 66, 75, 81, 282

Grayson County, TX, 11, 19

Greenville, TX, 208

Gregg, Brig. Gen. John (CSA): organization of brigade, 13-14, 48, 259, 283; trip to Chickamauga, 38, 46; Sept. 18 at Chickamauga, 61, 64-65, 67; Sept. 19 at Chickamauga, 72, 86, 88-94, 104, 135; wounding and recovery, 96-98, 110, 231-32; brigade on Sept. 20 at Chickamauga, 175-76, 181, 195; death, 251

Gregg, Mary, 232

Griffin, Sgt. J. H. (17th-18th-24th-25th TX Cav.), 143, 265

Grimes County, TX, 8, 256n53, 266

Grose, Col. William (USA), 171, 202

Grosskopf, Capt. John (20th OH Battery), 141n18

Guadalupe County, TX, 103, 265

Gulf Coast, 1, 7, 20

Halleck, General-in-chief Henry W. (USA), 27, 30

Hanks, Cpl. Orlando T. (1st TX), 41-42, 209, 212, 216-17

Hamilton, Sgt. David H. (1st TX), 14, 102, 105-106, 113, 189, 206, 225

Hardee, Maj. Gen. William J. (CSA), 32, 34, 210, 249, 250

Harding, Capt. Richard J. (1st TX), 16, 56, 108, 113, 126, 175, 182, 187, 261, 262

Hargis, Pvt. Samuel H. (2nd AR Mtd. Rifles), 19

Harker, Col. Charles G. (USA), 97, 188, 190, 193

Harlan, Pvt. Isaiah (10th TX), 234-35

Harper, Sgt. Richard (6th-10th TX-15th TX Cav.), 161

Harpers Ferry, VA, 6n6, 16

Harrison, Col. Thomas (CSA), 17-18, 31, 38, 39, 260, 284

Hart, Pvt. Gus (8th TX Cav.), 39

Hart, Pvt. William A. (7th TX), 237

Harvey, Lt. Robert B. (6th TX), 166, 271

Haynie, Pvt. Tom S. (5th TX), 193

Hazen, Brig. Gen. William B. (USA), 167-68, 171, 202, 206

Heartsill, Sgt. William W. (10th TX), 25-26, 30-32, 33n19, 47, 68-69, 133-35, 142, 144, 148, 150-51, 153, 168, 170-71, 199-200, 206, 224

Heg, Brig. Gen. Hans C. (USA), 89-92, 94, 97, 105, 114-16, 119n42, 125-26, 180

Helm, Brig. Gen. Benjamin H. (CSA), 156, 201, 224

Hempfling, Pvt. George (25th TX Cav.), 222, 274
Hempstead, TX, 9
Henderson, TX, 10
Henderson farm, 68
Hendrick, Pvt. James H. (1st TX), 184
Hicks, Cpl. Charles H., 217n11, 262
Hicks, Pvt. W. M. (4th TX), 124, 265
Hill, Lt. Gen. Daniel H. (CSA), 5, 6, 31, 34, 37, 50, 71, 133, 138, 152, 154, 156, 158
Hill, Cpl. John (3rd AR), 131
Hill, Pvt. Robert E. (8th TX Cav.), 33
Hindman, Maj. Gen. Thomas (CSA), 37, 100, 148, 152, 175-76, 184, 186, 195, 205, 231, 235
Holloway, Pvt. L. Durham (4th TX), 184, 266
Hood, Maj. Gen. John B. (CSA), elevation to command, 5, 14, 16-17; movement of troops to Georgia, 39-46; Sept. 18 at Chickamauga, 54, 56, 58, 60-68; Sept. 19 at Chickamauga, 72, 79, 94, 96, 98-108, 124, 127, 129, 131, 146-47, 152; Sept. 20 at Chickamauga, 173, 175-80, 184, 186-87, 194, 206; wounding and recovery, 190-93, 218-19, 224, 229, 236, 238, 251-52; Hood's division post-Chickamauga, 222, 224-26, 231, 236, 238, 240, 243
Hooker, Maj. Gen. Joseph (USA), 240, 242-44
Hoover's Gap, battle of, 30
Hotchkiss, Maj. Thomas R. (CSA), 136, 140-41, 200
Houghton, Pvt. William R. (2nd GA), 127-28
Houston, TX, 1, 8
Houston, Governor Sam (TX), 2
Howard, Pvt. D. Willoughby (32nd TX Cav.), 208, 281
Howze, Capt. James A. (14th TX Cav.), 207-208, 280
Hudson, Sgt. James C. "Jimps" (14th TX Cav.), 159, 208, 280
Hudson, Dr. William O. (CSA), 190n36
Hufstedler, Lt. Col. Eli (25th AR), 97
Humphreys, Brig. Gen. Benjamin (CSA), 148, 177, 184, 205
Hunter, Capt. James T. (4th TX), 111-13, 121-25, 182, 188-89, 191-92, 215-16,
Huntsville, TX, 111n24
Hutchins, Pvt. Stokely D. (10th TX Cav.), 82, 279
Hutchison, Lt. Col. Augustus S. (19th AR), 6, 136, 140, 146n29, 161, 170, 199
Hyatt, Sgt.-Maj. Benjamin (3rd AR), 131
Illinois, 30, 90, 138, 145, 161n25, 171
Indiana, 20, 47, 68, 76, 77, 131, 159n21
Jackson, battle of, 13, 14
Jackson, President Andrew, 71
Jackson, Brig. Gen. John K. (CSA), 140, 152, 200
Jackson, Lt. Gen. Thomas J. "Stonewall" (CSA) 6n6, 24, 88
Jackson, MS, 226
Jasper County, TX, 255
Jay, William, 64
Jay's Mill, 64-65, 73, 75-76, 79, 86, 135, 157
Jefferson, TX, 67
Jenkins, Brig. Gen. Micah (CSA), 40n31, 240
Johnson, Brig. Gen. Bushrod R. (CSA), attack on Reed's Bridge, 48-54, 57-67; Sept. 19 actions, 71, 88, 91-92, 94-97, 99, 101, 105; Sept. 20 actions, 173, 175-178, 180-81, 184, 195, 197, 204-205
Johnson, Col. Middleton T. (14th TX Cav.), 12
Johnson, Col. Ole (15th WI), 91-92
Johnson, Brig. Gen. Richard W. (USA), 139, 156
Johnson's Island (Ohio), 135n5
Johnston, Gen. Joseph E. (CSA), 11, 34, 38, 249-52, 254
Jones, Pvt. Ans (4th TX), 123
Jones, Dr. David C. (CSA), 190n36
Jones, Pvt. J. K. P. (4th TX), 123, 265
Kansas, 7
Kennard, Capt. John R. (10th TX), 199, 246, 270
Kennedy, Sgt. James H. (1st TX), 238
Kentucky, 8, 10, 12, 16, 17, 18, 20, 57, 74n7, 90n6, 156, 235
Key, Col. John C. G. (4th TX), 16-17
Key, Lt. Thomas J. (Calvert's Battery), 136, 200-201
Kershaw, Brig. Gen. Joseph B. (CSA), 42n35, 148, 175, 177-78, 184, 185, 193, 205, 208

Kilgore, Capt. Constantine B. "Buck" (Ector's staff), 76, 79, 83-84, 159
Kilgore, TX, 76n10
Killingsworth, Lt. Allen G. (4th TX), 118, 220, 265
King, Col. Edward A. (USA), 96, 199
King, Pvt. John C. (16th US), 83n25
King, Brig. Gen. John H. (USA), 82-84, 157
King Beasley (enslaved servant), 159
Kingsville, SC, 43n39, 45
Knoxville, TN, 21n1, 34, 39, 244
La Fayette, GA, 36-38, 48-49, 58, 219
Lamar County, TX, 229
Lane, Lt. Henry M. (Ector's staff), 159, 276
Lavaca County, TX, 9
Law, Brig. Gen. Evander M. (CSA), 41, 42, 54, 67, 71, 88, 96, 100, 105, 110, 148, 152, 175-77, 181, 193, 241-42
Lawrence, Dr. Adolphus A. (24th TX Cav.), 23-24, 179
Lawton, QMGen. Alexander R. (CSA), 39
Leach, Pvt. James M. (1st TX), 113, 264
Lee, Maj. Pollock B. (CSA), 152
Lee, Gen. Robert E. (CSA), 14, 170
Lee and Gordon's Mills, 48-52, 63, 68, 70-72, 194, 207, 212
Leet's Tanyard (GA), 49, 52
Lehigh County, PA, 7n7
Leighton, AL, 215
Leuschner, Pvt. August F. (6th TX), 248
Lewis, Allen H., 251
Lewis, Pvt. John J. (1st TX), 251, 264
Libby Prison (Richmond), 207
Liddell, Brig. Gen. St. John (CSA), 79-81, 135, 137-38
Lilly, Capt. Eli (18th IN Battery), 98, 116, 128
Lindsay, Lt. George M. (32nd TX Cav.), 82, 281
Lincoln, President Abraham (USA), 22, 27, 156, 240
Little, Col. Francis H. (11th GA), 219
Little Rock, AR, 12
Littlefield, Capt. George W. (8th TX Cav.), 213-14
Livingston, TX, 130, 262
Lock, Pvt. George (1st TX), 189, 264
Locke, Col. Matthew F. (10th TX Cav.), 12
Longstreet, Lt. Gen. James (CSA), 5, 39, 40n31, 40n33; rail transport of corps to Georgia, 41-48, 54, 67, 72, 130, 134; arrival at Chickamauga, 146-48; Sept. 20 actions, 152-54, 163n28, 173, 175-78, 184, 186, 197, 206; post-Chickamauga, 211-12, 225-26, 231, 233, 235n52, 236; attack on Cracker Line, 240, 242-44, 251
Lookout Mountain 21, 31, 36-37, 47, 49, 150, 153, 212-13, 226-27, 230, 235, 240, 244
Loughridge, Capt. James R. (4th TX), 111, 266
Louisville, KY, 90n6
Lubbock, Gov. Francis R. (TX), 2-3
Lumsden, Capt. Charles L. (artillery reserve), 58
Lytle, Brig. Gen. William H. (USA), 186
Madding, Lt. Isaac C. (16th AL), 214-15
Makeig, Cpl. Fredrick M. (4th TX), 124, 184, 265
Maloney, Pvt. John P. (1st TX) 236, 239
Manassas (Bull Run), battle of, 18
Manning, Col. Van H. (3rd AR), 99, 108, 175, 187, 189
Marietta, GA, 36, 38, 123n51, 218, 225, 226n33, 231
Marsh, Capt. Bryan (17th TX Cav.), 24-25,
Marshall, TX, 19, 149, 262
Martin, Sgt. C. C. (17th-18th-24th-25th TX Cav.), 144n25
Martin, Col. John A. (8th KS), 90-94, 116, 126, 180, 186
Martin, Nancy (widow), 38n29
Martin, Capt. William H. "Howdy" (4th TX), 44, 267
Massey, Pvt. Jack (4th TX), 178, 220, 263
Masterson, Lt. T. Walsh (4th TX), 123, 216, 264, 265
Matagorda Bay, 8, 163, 270
McBride, Capt. J. J. (5th TX), 40n32, 267, 303
McCann, Pvt. William C. (6th-10th TX-14th TX Cav.), 166, 270
McCook, Maj. Gen. Alexander M. (USA), 31, 51, 66, 70, 125, 126, 152, 174, 204, 228
McCook, Col. Daniel Jr. (USA), 66-67, 70, 72-73
McCown, Pvt. J. G. (32nd TX Cav.), 77, 282
McDonald, John (farmer), 154

McKinney, TX, 8
McLaurin, Capt. J. T. (4th TX), 242n4
McLaws, Maj. Gen. Lafayette M. (CSA), 39, 42, 148
McLemore's Cove, 37-38, 47, 49, 51, 68, 88, 226
McLennan County, TX, 14
McNair, Brig. Gen. Evander (CSA), 34, 38, 46, 48, 61, 62, 65-66, 73, 75n8, 88, 96-98, 176, 180, 195
Meade, Maj. Gen. George G. (USA), 33, 229
Medical College Hospital (Atlanta), 235-36
Memphis, TN, 21n1
Mendenhall, Maj. John (USA), 181
Mexican War, 12, 17, 18, 34, 172n51
Milam County, TX, 17, 130, 268
Mills, Col. Roger Q. (10th TX Cav.): organization of brigade, 6, 8, 24, 269-70; Sept. 19 at Chickamauga, 134, 136, 138, 140-41, 145-46 Sept. 20 at Chickamauga, 161, 163n28, 164, 167-72, 174, 195, 197, 199-201, 204, 210, 217; post-Chickamauga, 224, 232, 244, 246, 249n15, 252; monument commission, 254-55
Mims, Cpl. James P. (17th TX Cav.) 254, 272
Minty, Col. Robert H. G. (USA) 51, 57-58, 60-66, 70
Missionary Ridge, 37n27, 50, 150, 153, 204, 222, 225-26
Missionary Ridge, attack o,n 218n14, 244-49, 251
Mississippi, 10, 14, 34, 77, 186, 205, 225
Mississippi River, 27
Missouri, 11, 20, 76n10
Mitchell, Col. John G. (USA), 70, 195,
Mobile, AL, 14, 33, 38, 225
Montgomery, Pvt. Lewis (17th-18th-24th-25th TX Cav.), 114n25
Montgomery County, TX, 172
Moody, Sgt. Leroy F. (7th TX), 209, 225, 284
Moore, Pvt. Jehu H. (24th TX Cav.), 232, 233n46, 274
Moore, Pvt. Samuel (17th TX Cav.), 164
Moore, Sgt. Thomas F. (24th TX Cav.), 164, 273
Morgan, Pvt. Green (1st TX), 237, 264
Morgan, Irby and Julia (CSA), 231-32
Morgan, Brig Gen. John H. (CSA), 57, 74n
Morgan, Col. John T. (CSA), 231
Morgan, Dr. Nathaniel A. (1st GA Volunteers), 19, 149
Morgan County, TX, 220
Murfreesboro, TN, 3, 26
Murfreesboro (Stones River), battle of, 10-13, 18, 21-23, 34, 47, 208n24, 251
Murphey, Pvt. Andrew J. (17th TX Cav.), 162
Nabours, Pvt. William A. (5th TX), 224, 292
Nacogdoches County, TX, 1, 8, 19
Napier, Lt. Col. Leroy (8th GA Battalion), 159
Nashville, TN, 21n1, 36, 254, 294
Nashville, Chattanooga, and St. Louis Railroad, 33, 241, 244
Neal, Pvt. John D. (10th TX Cav.), 82, 278
Nebraska, 7
Negley, Maj. Gen. James S. (USA), 37, 182, 186n25, 204
Nelson, Brig. Gen. William (USA), 90n6
Neuhaus, Lt. Frederick W. "Fritz" (24th TX Cav.), 9
New York, NY, 220, 289, 290, 295, 296, 297, 300
Nichols, Pvt. George W. (4th TX), 123, 265
North Carolina, 43, 48, 139
Norwood, Pvt. Thomas (4th TX), 184, 265
Nutt, Capt. Leroy F. (assigned to 10th TX), 26n10, 154, 171, 272
Oates, Col. William C. (15th AL), 148n31
Oats, Sgt. Nathan (5th TX), 120, 121n45, 269
Ohio, 7, 49, 52, 57, 70n1, 135n5, 255
Oklahoma (Indian Territory), 13, 71
Oliphant, Pvt. William J. (6th TX), 68, 138, 142, 149, 164, 168-69, 172, 217-18, 263, 271, 288
Opdycke, Col. Emerson (USA), 97
Orangeburg, SC, 47
Orchard Knob, 244
Orr, Pvt. Alexander L. (18th TX Cav.), 244, 143,165, 215, 239
Orr, Pvt. James (18th TX Cav.), 24, 275, 289
Palmer, Brig. Gen. John M. (USA), 156, 162, 165, 167, 171, 202
Pamplin, Pvt. J. W. (4th TX), 179, 206
Pea Ridge, battle, of 13, 18

Pea Vine Bridge, 52, 57-58, 61
Peak, Pvt. Junius (7th KY Cav.), 73, 74n, 81
Pemberton, Lt. Gen. John C. (CSA), 10n12
Pennsylvania, 3, 7n7, 20, 26, 56, 159n21, 303, 304
Perry, Pvt. Clinton (1st TX), 68n31
Perry, Pvt. Edward (1st TX), 68n31
Perry, Pvt. Eugene Osceola (1st TX), 68n31
Perry, Pvt. Howard (1st TX), 68n31
Perry, Col. William F. (44th AL), 148n31, 177-78, 181
Perryville, battle of, 11
Petersburg, VA, 40n, 41-43, 251
Pickett, Maj. Gen. George (CSA), 40n31
Pigeon Mountain, 37-39, 58, 133
Pinckney, Pvt. John M. (4th TX), 212
Pippen, Sgt. Benjamin G. (17th-18th-24th-25th TX Cav.), 144n25
Pleasant Grove Church, 52
Poe, Larkin H. and Sarah (farmers), 162, 181
Polk, Pvt. James M. (4th TX), 33, 43, 63, 103, 111, 131, 177, 178-79, 220-21, 267, 290
Polk, Lt. Gen. Leonidas (CSA), 5, 50, 71, 73, 86, 100, 152, 154, 176-78, 199, 226, 230, 235
Polk, Brig. Gen. Lucius E. (CSA), 37, 134, 136, 140, 143, 165, 168, 183, 199, 201
Polley, QM Sgt. Joseph B. (4th TX), 33, 42-44, 56-57, 101-102, 104-105, 111-13, 125, 179, 226-227, 231, 242, 254, 290, 302
Pound, Cap. Merriman, (Pound's Battalion, MS), 10
Prendergast, Lt. Harvey F. (10th TX), 245, 249, 251
Preston, Brig. Gen. William (CSA), 86, 100, 129, 148, 152, 177, 205, 208
Quitman, TX, 1, 11
Raccoon Mountain, 32, 242n4
Ramsay, Pvt. James (6th TX), 8
Randolph, Pvt. John (79th IL), 138n10, 145
Rappahannock River, 40
Raymond, battle of, 11n13, 14, 89, 228n38
Reagan, Postmaster General John H. (CSA), 44n42, 236
Red River County, TX, 8
Reed, Jack (enslaved), 218
Reedy, Maj. John W. (3rd AR), 127
Resaca, GA, 42
Reed, Jacob and Sallie, 63
Reed's Bridge, 3, 50-52, 54, 57-58, 60-63, 66, 70, 72, 75-77, 99n1, 100n2, 138
Reeves, Col. George R. (11th TX Cav.), 19
Reynolds, Brig. Gen. Joseph J. (USA), 96, 156, 161n25, 167, 174, 175, 199, 207
Rice, Pvt. A. R. (4th TX), 242
Rice, Capt. David K. (1st TX), 16n22, 56n8, 130, 261, 262
Richardson, Dr. Tobias G. (CSA), 190
Richmond, VA, 8, 16, 27, 33, 39, 40-43, 100, 111, 207, 227, 236
Richmond, battle of, 11
Richmond, Fredericksburg, and Potomac Railroad, 40
Ridley, Capt. D. H. (9th TX), 253, 277
Riggs, Pvt. Stephen M. "Tobe" (4th TX), 111, 220, 221n21, 266
Ringgold, GA, 38, 43n39, 46, 48, 50n3, 52, 54, 55, 57n9, 60, 67, 104, 118-19, 218-21, 248-49
Ringgold, battle of, 248-49, 251, 273
Rio Grande, 1, 20
Roberts, Pvt. Albert S. (4th TX), 190
Robertson, Maj. Christopher W. (50th TN), 90, 176n5, 195
Robertson, Col. Felix H. (CSA), 58, 60, 63
Robertson, Brig. Gen. Jerome T. (CSA), 14-17, 40-41, 44, 46, 54-58, 62-65, 86, 96, 98-100, 102, 104-106, 108, 110, 113-14, 119, 124-29, 132, 148, 175, 177-88, 190-91, 193-94, 205, 208, 215-16, 219, 232n44, 241, 243, 248, 258, 260-61, 266, 298, 303
Rogers, Maj. Jefferson C. (5th TX), 17, 115, 119-20, 175, 267
Rogers, Pvt. William (7th TX), 210
Rome, GA, 33n, 34, 75n, 156, 233
Rosecrans, Maj. Gen. William S. (USA), 21-22, 26, 28, 30-32, 34, 36-37, 47-51, 70, 72-73, 89, 130, 139, 148, 152, 167, 171, 174, 204, 211, 213n7, 214, 217, 224-25, 228n37, 229-31, 233, 235, 240, 254
Rossville, GA, 49, 70, 71, 204, 212-13, 226
Royall, Pvt. William W. (18th TX Cav.), 166
Rusk County, TX, 19

San Antonio, TX, 1
San Augustine County, TX, 8
Sanders, Lt. Col. Valerius P. (15th TX Cav.), 246
Sanders, Sgt. William P. (7th TX), 65, 283
Santa Anna, Gen. Antonio Lopez de (MEX), 1-2, 17
Schadt, Pvt. William (1st TX), 221, 264, 290
Schultz, Capt. Frederick (Battery M, 1st OH), 182, 186, 188
Scott, Dr. A. J. (4th TX), 44
Scribner, Col. Benjamín F. (USA), 156-57
Seaton, Pvt. Benjamin (10th TX), 68, 204, 224, 251, 290
Seddon, James (CSA), 39
Selma, AL, 56
Semple, Capt. Henry C. (AL Battery), 136, 141, 167-68, 200-202, 204
Sheridan, Brig. Gen. Philip (USA), 126, 186, 204
Sherman, Maj. Gen. William T. (USA), 6, 7, 9, 204, 244-45, 254
Sharpsburg (Antietam), battle of, 16, 17, 44, 132, 157n15, 179
Sheffield, Col. James (CSA), 54, 100, 105, 106, 110, 148
Sheffield, Sgt.-Maj. Thomas J. (15th TX Cav.), 246
Shelbyville, TN, 22, 33
Shiloh, battle of, 11, 17, 251
Short, Pvt. John (5th TX), 220, 269
Sims, Pvt. Alfred C. (1st TX), 41, 55-56, 114, 288
Sims, Maj. Frederick W. (CSA Railroad Bureau), 39
Simonson, Capt. Peter (5th IN Battery), 139, 141n18, 143
Sirwell, Col. William (USA), 186
Smith, Frank, 76, 82
Smith, Pvt. Henry V. (17th-18th-24th-25th TX Cav.), 232, 234n48
Smith, Pvt. J. D. "Jack" (4th TX), 227
Smith, Brig. Gen. James A. (CSA), 232
Smith, Cpl. Miles V. "Pony" (4th TX), 41, 112, 176, 182, 187, 240-43, 265
Smith, Col. Orland (USA), 241
Smith, Brig. Gen. Preston (CSA), 138, 140, 145
Smith, Capt. William H. (Ector's staff, CSA), 11
Smith County, TX, 9, 289, 292
Smither, Sgt.-Maj. John M. (5th TX), 237, 267, 287
Snodgrass, George W. (farmer), 202, 204
Sorrel, Lt. Col. G. Moxley (Longstreet's staff, CSA), 41, 148
South Carolina, 8, 9, 42n35, 43n39; 45, 46, 61n5, 143n16, 182
South Chickamauga Creek, 4n3, 46, 246
Spinks, Pvt. J. M. (10th TX Cav.), 82, 208, 292
Sprott, Capt. Samuel H. (Stone's AL Battalion), 10, 77, 79, 83
Stanton, Secretary of War Edwin M. (USA), 27, 49
Starkweather, Brig. Gen. John (USA), 139, 143, 146
Steedman, Brig. Gen. James (USA), 205
Stewart, Brig. Gen. Alexander P. (CSA), 86, 96, 102, 136, 148, 152, 163
Stewart, Pvt. John "Muley" (1st TX), 105, 106n15, 264
Stewart, Lt. John W. (15th TX Cav.), 165
Stone, Maj. Thomas O. (Stone's AL Battalion), 10, 77-78, 226
Stout, Dr. Samuel H.(CSA), 218
Street, Rev. John K. (9th TX), 229
Streetman, Lt. Samuel S. (5th TX), 130, 268
Sugg, Col. Cyrus A. (50th TN), 110, 176, 180, 209
Sulphur Springs, TX, 1
Summers, Pvt. William M. (18th TX Cav.), 164, 273
Summerville, TN, 38
Sumter, SC, 7, 45
Sutherland, Pvt. Jack (4th TX), 104-105, 185-86, 266
Swallow, Capt. George R. (7th IN Battery),
Talley, Capt. Charles E. (7th TX), 135
Tanner, Lt. Stephen J. (9th TX), 77, 78n14
Tarrant County, TX, 12, 234
Taylor, Pvt. J. William (15th TX Cav.), 138
Taylor, Maj. William A. (24th TX Cav.), 166, 170, 199, 232, 244, 247-49
Thedford, Deborah, 72n3

Thedford's Ford, 50, 65, 72, 133-34
Telegraphs, 49, 214
Templeton, Sgt. J. Allen (10th TX Cav.), 83, 232, 279
Tennessee, 3, 4, 11, 14, 22-24, 26-27, 33-34, 59, 70, 233, 235n52, 239-40, 243, 245, 251-52, 254
Tennessee campaign, 82n23
Tennessee River, 4n3, 22, 31, 32, 34, 36, 39n30, 47, 130n63, 226, 228-29, 230, 240-41
Terry, Col. Benjamin F. (8th TX Cav.), 18
Texas, 2, 13, 16, 17, 19, 26n, 103, 172
Texas Rangers, 18-19, 26, 33, 39, 56, 88, 159n21, 194-95, 213-14, 219, 226, 272, 284, 289, 291-92, 296
Thomas, Maj. Gen. George H. (USA), 53, 70, 72-73, 78, 139, 152, 156, 159, 161n25, 174, 202, 204-205, 211, 225, 245
Thompson, Capt. Heber S. (USA), 57, 89n4
Thompson, Lt. Col. Samuel (10th TN), 97
Todd, Capt. George (1st TX), 63, 67, 187, 191, 209, 211-12, 261, 291
Todd, Pvt. James (32nd TX Cav.), 67, 282
Todhunter, Capt. Ryland (Ector's staff), 75n9, 78, 80-81, 83, 151, 158, 224
Tompkins, Pvt. W. Augustus (25th TX Cav.), 219, 275
Trice, Pvt. C. W. (7th TX), 181, 292
Trigg, Col. Robert C. (CSA), 114, 129
Tullahoma, TN, 21, 23-24, 26, 30-31, 33
Tullahoma campaign of 1863, 30-31, 226, 300, 302-303
Tullos, Pvt. Willoughby (1st TX), 106
Tunnel Hill, GA, 55, 114, 218, 232, 244-45, 251
Turchin, Brig. Gen. John B. (USA), 167-68, 171, 255n5
Turner, Lt. Col. James J. (30th TN), 90
Turner, Lt. Joseph (5th TX), 220, 269
Turner, Pvt. Jim (6th TX), 34, 36n24, 166, 167n37, 292
Tuscumbia, AL, 215
Tyler County, TX, 9
Tyner's Station, TN, 32
Union military units:
Indiana: 5th Battery, 139, 143; 6th Infantry, 139, 143; 7th Battery, 118; 8th Battery, 118; 10th Infantry, 182, 185; 18th Battery, 98, 116, 128; 19th Battery, 163-64; 21st Battery, 163-65, 167, 170n45; 29th Infantry, 144; 30th Infantry, 144; 31st Infantry, 167; 32nd Infantry, 143; 38th Infantry, 110; 58th Infantry, 114-15, 182; 68th Infantry, 207; 72nd Infantry, 58, 116; 74th Infantry, 182; 81st Infantry, 113, 119n42; 87th Infantry, 76
Illinois: Chicago Board of Trade Battery, 57, 61, 63; 86th Infantry, 72; 25th Infantry, 94, 180; 35th Infantry, 89, 94, 97; 79th Infantry, 138n10, 144-45; 98th Infantry, 97; 100th Infantry, 114; 115th Infantry, 203; 123rd Infantry, 58
Kansas: 8th Infantry, 89-90, 92, 116, 180
Kentucky: 1st Infantry, 167; 2nd Infantry, 167; 5th Cavalry, 213; 5th Infantry, 140; 6th Cavalry, 213; 6th Infantry, 167; 9th Infantry, 182; 18th Infantry, 167, 207
Michigan: Battery D, 1st Artillery, 82, 182; 4th Cavalry, 57, 61; 13th Infantry 114, 180; 22nd Infantry, 205
Minnesota: 2nd Infantry, 76
Ohio: 1st Cavalry, 194; 1st Infantry, 108, 139, 143, 186; 11th Infantry, 167; 13th Infantry, 221; 20th Battery, 139, 142n18, 153; 21st Infantry, 186, 188, 205; 26th Infantry, 114, 119, 121n; 31st Infantry, 182; 35th Infantry, 76, 81; 36th Infantry, 171; 41st Infantry, 167; 64th Infantry, 98, 188; 69th Infantry, 66, 72; 89th Infantry, 205; 90th Infantry, 167; 92nd Infantry, 167, 171; 93rd Infantry, 140; 101st Infantry, 109, 119n42; 124th Infantry, 167; 125th Infantry, 188; Battery A, 1st Art., 139; Battery B, 1st Art., 167; Battery F, 1st Art., 167; Battery M, 1st Art., 182
Pennsylvania: 7th Cavalry, 57, 61; 77th Infantry, 143-45
United States: 4th Cavalry, 57, 82; 6th Infantry, 85; 16th Infantry, 83-84; Battery I, 4th US Light Artillery, 76
Wisconsin: 3rd Artillery, 113; 15th Infantry, 89, 90-92, 94, 126, 180
United States Military Academy at West Point, NY, 6, 17, 215n8, 232, 254
Upshur County, TX, 12

Utah (Mormon) War, 7
Van Derveer, Col. Ferdinand (USA), 76, 77, 299
Van Zandt, Maj. Khleber M. (7th TX), 89, 97, 180-81, 205, 210, 283, 288, 290, 292, 303
Vaughan, Col. Alfred J. Jr. (13th TN), 139, 144
Vicksburg, MS, 2, 10n, 11, 29, 31, 33, 34, 38
Victoria, TX, 7, 166
Viniard, Tabler C. and Ann (farmers), 65-66, 69, 99-100, 106-10, 112-19, 121, 123-29, 131, 135, 173, 176-77, 215, 219-20
Virginia, 7, 8, 16, 18, 39, 40, 42, 43, 51, 54, 56, 102, 107, 112, 125, 175, 187, 222, 228, 233
Virginia, University of, 11
Virginia Military Institute 16, 187
Vittetoe, Hiram and Elizabeth (farmers), 182n17, 204-205
Waco, TX, 14, 18, 124, 176, 184, 220
Waco Female College, 9
Wade, Pvt. James H. (10th TX Cav.), 14, 81, 279
Walker, Pvt. Chisum (4th TX), 11
Walker, Maj. Gen. William H. T. (CSA), 5, 10, 14, 34, 49, 50, 63n20, 64, 66, 71, 73, 75, 79, 81, 86, 152, 156-57, 159, 177, 225
Walker County, GA, 68, 219, 237, 297
Walters, Pvt. Moses (10th TX Cav.), 83, 232, 279
Wallingford, Pvt. Thomas (4th TX), 212
Wartrace, TN, 24-27
Washington, DC, 26, 27, 42, 49, 156, 214n, 229, 240
Washington County, TX, 8
Watson, Pvt. J. M. (10th TX Cav.), 82, 279, 290
Watson, Cpl. Thomas (4th TX), 222
Wauhatchie, battle of, 240, 242
Welch, Joshua (mayor), 237n55
Weldon, NC, 43
West, Pvt. John C. (4th TX), 45, 54, 64, 101, 108-109, 124, 176, 188, 193, 208, 211, 227, 231, 243
West Chickamauga Creek, 3, 4, 5, 21, 37n27, 38, 48-50, 52, 58, 66-68, 71, 134, 194, 212, 238
Western and Atlantic Railroad, 38, 46, 146, 218, 231, 293
Wharton, Brig. Gen. John A. (CSA), 17-18, 38
Wheeler, Brig. Gen. Joseph (CSA), 5, 17-18, 38, 50, 71, 87-88, 162n26, 174, 207, 211-13, 226, 231
White, Pvt. John C. (16th US), 84
White, Sallie, 10
Whitehead, Pvt. Charles (4th TX), 184, 265
Whitsett, Pvt. William E. (9th TX), 75, 76, 84, 300
Wilder, Col. John T. (USA), 30, 51, 58, 63-66, 69, 97, 116, 126
Wilkes, Lt. Col. Franklin C. (24th TX Cav.), 6, 9, 136, 139-40, 142-43
Wilkes, Dr. James H. (CSA), 135
Willard, Col. George (USA), 6n6
Williams, Sgt. James V. (3rd AR), 131
Williams, Lt. Luther A. (32nd TX Cav.), 82, 282
Williams, Pvt. Watson D. (5th TX), 209, 288
Willich, Brig. Gen. August (USA), 139-41, 143
Wills Valley, 38
Wilmington, NC, 43-44, 214
Wilmington and Weldon Railroad, 43
Wilson, Brig. Gen. Claudius (CSA), 73, 75, 77, 79, 81, 83, 156-59
Wilson, Capt. Samuel F. (1st TX), 217
Winfrey, George (farmer), 138, 140-41, 153
Winkler, Capt. Clinton M. (4th TX), 138, 140-41, 153
Wood, Brig. Gen. Sterling A. M. (CSA), 37, 134
Wood, Brig. Gen. Thomas J. (USA), 114, 174
Wooden, Dr. John L. (69th IN), 207
Wooters, Lt. John H. (1st TX), 108, 263
Work, Lt. Col. Philip A. (1st TX), 16, 55, 175
Worsham, Pvt. Charles A. (4th TX), 238, 288
Worthington, Lt. Warren W. (3rd AR), 130
Wynn, Pvt. William O. (10th TX), 172
Young, Col. William C. (11th TX Cav.), 18
Young, Col. William H. (9th TX), 11, 83, 219, 276

About the Authors

Ohio native Scott L. Mingus Sr. is a scientist and consultant in the global pulp and paper industry. Scott is the author of nearly two dozen books and numerous articles. His biography *Confederate General William "Extra Billy" Smith* won multiple awards, including the 2013 Dr. James I. Robertson, Jr. Literary Award for Confederate history. Scott is also the author of many articles for a wide variety of publications, including *Gettysburg Magazine.*

Joseph L. Owen is a National Park ranger at Lyndon B. Johnson National Historical Park in Johnson City, Texas. He served 15 years in the U.S. Navy, attended college at East Central University in Ada, Oklahoma, and received a bachelor's degree in history and a master's degree in secondary education. Joe is the co-author of two books on Hood's Texas Brigade, *Texans at Gettysburg* (2016) and *Texans at Antietam* (2017), and is the author of *Lone Star Valor: Texans of the Blue & Gray at Gettysburg* (2019). Joe received the 2019 Jefferson Davis Gold Medal from the United Daughters of the Confederacy for outstanding research and writing. He lives with his wife Cathy in Blanco, Texas.